THE DEVIL'S OWN PURGATORY

CONFLICTING WORLDS:
NEW DIMENSIONS OF THE AMERICAN CIVIL WAR

T. Michael Parrish, Series Editor

THE DEVIL'S OWN PURGATORY

THE UNITED STATES MISSISSIPPI RIVER SQUADRON IN THE CIVIL WAR

Robert Gudmestad

LOUISIANA STATE UNIVERSITY PRESS
BATON ROUGE

Published with the assistance of the V. Ray Cardozier Fund

Published by Louisiana State University Press
lsupress.org

Manufactured in the United States of America
First printing

DESIGNER: Michelle A. Neustrom
TYPEFACE: Garamond Premier Pro
PRINTER AND BINDER: Sheridan Books, Inc.

All maps created by Lucas Roy and Conner Siegfried, Geospatial Centroid, Colorado State University.

JACKET ILLUSTRATION: Detail of *The Bombardment and Capture of Island "Number Ten" on the Mississippi River,* 1862, by Currier & Ives. Reference 575305i, Wellcome Collection.

Cataloging-in-Publication Data are available from the Library of Congress.

ISBN 978-0-8071-8491-2 (cloth: alk. paper) — ISBN 978-0-8071-8546-9 (pdf) — ISBN 978-0-8071-8545-2 (epub) for Sam and Sadie

CONTENTS

ILLUSTRATIONS

FIGURES

following page 94

MAPS

TABLES

CHARTS

ACKNOWLEDGMENTS

I began this project about twelve years ago thinking that I would write a conventional military history of the Mississippi Squadron. The research and writing, I figured, would take three or four years. But once I began reading sailors' letters and the Union navy's records, I became convinced that most historians had missed the essential story of the fleet: the experience of the sailors. Only Michael Bennett had attempted to understand life aboard Civil War boats, and his book covered the entire Union navy. Once I learned about the existence of the fleet's muster rolls in the National Archives, I became even more convinced that I should write a military-social history of the Mississippi Squadron.

Being department chair slowed down my ability to complete the project. Then, like many historians, COVID-19 changed how I approached my craft. Sheltering in place with my family somehow sparked the audaciously stupid idea to create a dataset of sailors who served in the Mississippi Squadron. I recruited and trained a team of graduate students and advanced undergraduate students who breathed new life into my research. Tucker Carpenter, Evan Cocanower, Nolan Dahm, Cassie Franks, Danny Gilbert, Nick Taylor, Tobin Gold, Austin Magura, and Sean Nelson recorded information from muster rolls and pension records. I hope that their hours spent looking at a computer screen did not seem to them like being consigned to purgatory. The database of sailors that we assembled is the bedrock of this book.

The folks at Colorado State University's GIS Centroid provided assistance of another kind. Sophia Linn was a patient teacher as I fumbled around with spatial analysis. Riley Ross helped with finding historic sites of clashes between gunboats and southern forces. My son, Sam Gudmestad, created the map that appears in my article for *Civil War History*. Amanda Hastings provided the initial concepts for this book's maps, while Connor Siegfreid and Lucas Roy finished them. Even though a spatial analysis is not explicit in the narrative, the many hours that I spent in the GIS Centroid shaped my thinking about the Mississippi Squadron.

I visited many libraries and archives while researching this book. Without fail, I encountered friendly, knowledgeable, and patient staff who helped me locate materials. I met other wonderful people over email and asked them to send materials to me. Mickey deVise' Jansen at the Cincinnati Museum Center, Vicki Catozzi at the Cleveland History Center, Laura Schieb at Dartmouth, Germain J. Bienvenu at the Hill Memorial Library, James M. Prichard at the Filson Historical Society, David Kuzma at Rutgers, John C. Konzal at the State Historical Society of Missouri, Rich Aarstad at the Montana Historical Society, Cynthia Van Ness at the Buffalo History Museum, and Christine Schmid Engels at the Cincinnati Museum Center each provided materials. Jeffrey Seymour, formerly at the National Civil War Naval Museum, answered questions about naval artillery. Douglas Bell graciously sent me a CD with transcriptions of Scott Jordan's letters, while Kerby A. Miller kindly provided me with a transcription of the Murphy letters.

Many people shaped the ideas in this book. I first met Joe Beilein Jr. and Andrew Fialka at the Filson Historical Society's Hard Hand of War conference in 2014. They have had a significant influence on my thinking about the Civil War. Andrew suggested that I use GIS to track the irregular war, critiqued my spreadsheets, and read a draft of my article. Joe read the entire manuscript, and his insightful observations profoundly influenced the book. He even read a problematic chapter at the last minute—I have rewritten that chapter so many times, I feel like Sisyphus. The reader can decide if I pushed the boulder to the top of the hill or if it squashed me. The anonymous peer reviewer for LSU Press challenged me to pare down my prolixity and sharpen my analysis. Their comments pushed me to write a much better book. I have benefited from the wisdom of individuals who read conference papers or my article: Dave Danbom, Doug Sheflin, Greg Downs, Lorien Foote, Barton Myers, and Ron Peiffer.

Other folks supported the project in multiple ways. Mark Wiens graciously allowed me to stay with him while I did research at the National Archives. Thanks brother! Sarah Payne was a writing buddy while I finished the manuscript. Ryan Claycomb organized a writing group for department chairs that became a lifeline for me. Sushmita Chatterjee, Jonathan Carlyon, Greg Dickinson, and Mica Glantz were unfailing in their encouragement to keep writing. Rand

Dotson and Mike Parrish at LSU Press were sources of support and wisdom. Mike's comments were judicious and helpful. I needed the help of both Rand and Mike during the final push to finish the manuscript.

My family provided other types of assistance. Beth has been a rock of stability during the love-hate relationship that defined this project. More importantly, she encourages me every day with her generosity, kindness, and love. I aspire to be more like her. During the time it took to create this book, my children have grown so much. Sam graduated high school and college, then moved to Oregon and back. He keeps me laughing with his quick wit and keen insights. Sadie has gone from elementary school to college. She has a unique blend of ambition and compassion. It is one of my greatest joys that both Sam and Sadie have grown up to be good people. It is to them that this book is dedicated.

THE DEVIL'S OWN PURGATORY

INTRODUCTION

In the early spring of 1863, Major General Ulysses S. Grant was stuck. He had orders to capture Vicksburg, the Confederate stronghold along the Mississippi River. Union control of the city (and thus the river) would cut the Confederacy in two, open the Mississippi to commerce, and prevent the transfer of agricultural supplies from Arkansas, Louisiana, and Texas into the rest of the South. Vicksburg was the most important city in the Civil War's western theater, a huge expanse of land that stretched westward from the Appalachian Mountains to the Mississippi River and from Kentucky and Tennessee south to the Gulf of Mexico. It was larger than the eastern theater—primarily Virginia, Maryland, and North Carolina—but smaller than the trans-Mississippi theater, which encompassed Missouri, Arkansas, Louisiana, Texas, New Mexico, and other parts of the West.[1]

Grant had tried to take Vicksburg in 1862 by advancing along the Mississippi Central Railroad, but a Confederate raid on his supply base at Holly Springs forced him to retreat. Next, he attempted a series of flanking maneuvers in the swamps north of Vicksburg. Each failed, as did an effort to dig a canal that would cause the Mississippi River to bypass Vicksburg. Grant had one other possibility to take the best defended Confederate city in the western theater: cross the Mississippi south of Vicksburg and attack from the southeast. But the army could not do it alone. Grant's success in capturing Vicksburg, and perhaps his military career, depended on the U.S. Navy's cooperation.[2]

On March 29, 1863, Grant sent a deferential telegram to Rear Admiral David D. Porter, commander of the Mississippi Squadron. Porter led the Union's inland navy, which then numbered forty-four boats and was originally called the Western Gunboat Flotilla. Grant could not order the navy to assist him. He had to ask. "It looks to me Admiral as a matter of vast importance that one or two vessels should be put below Vicksburg" to enact a cross-river invasion. "Will you be good enough Admiral to give this your early consideration and let me know your determination. Without the aid of gunboats it will hardly be worth while to send troops" southward along the west bank of the Mississippi River. Despite his doubts, Porter agreed to assist Grant.[3]

Porter sent eight boats on the mission. As Grant looked on, the steamers cast loose at 9:00 P.M. on April 16, 1863. Confederate gunners unleashed a storm of shot and shell that "went whizzing shrieking howling" toward the boats "like a legion of incarnate devils from hell," as one sailor wrote. Soon after the shelling started, an impatient Grant decided to meet the fleet south of Vicksburg. Along with his son Fred and a guard of twenty cavalry, the general rode through the night. The group thundered along the Mississippi River's western bank to New Carthage, Louisiana, where the gunboats had tied up. Grant dismounted his horse, found Porter, and learned that the Confederates sank just one of the transports. The Union commander knew that he could now cross the river and advance upon Vicksburg.[4]

In his memoirs Grant wrote of the navy's importance to the Vicksburg Campaign. "Without its assistance," he judged, "the campaign could not have been successfully made with twice the number of men engaged. It could not have been made at all, in the way it was, with any number of men without such assistance." Grant knew that a conventional overland campaign would have required a much larger army and would have delayed the capture of Vicksburg by at least a year.[5]

Porter went even further than Grant in asserting the Mississippi Squadron's importance in winning the war. Writing twenty-five years after that April night, he told his former sailors that "it was the passage of the fleet by Vicksburg that sealed the fate of that stronghold." In a letter read to a sailors' reunion, Porter extolled the "Western men" who had "hearts of oak, in Western iron walls." Between them, Grant and Porter summed up this truth: the Mississippi Squadron was an essential partner in winning the Civil War because it was uniquely western and adapted to the military situation in the western theater.[6]

The West shaped the Mississippi Squadron. Its boats were unlike the ships in the rest of the Union navy. Their shallow drafts allowed them to operate on the inland waterways. Importantly, the fleet's presence on these rivers allowed it to have more influence on the freedom of enslaved people than the rest of the navy. The sailors who facilitated military emancipation were westerners. They also were the only Civil War naval personnel who fought on land against Confederate ambush squads. The squadron fought a river-based counterinsurgency war, the first of its type in U.S. history and the last until the Vietnam War. The Mississippi Squadron was unlike anything in American military history before or since the Civil War.

Adaptability was another defining feature of the Mississippi Squadron. Originally intended to batter Confederate forts, the squadron's boats also served as advance scouts for the army and provided crucial fire support in land battles. When Confederate ambush squads became a threat rather than a mere nuisance, the fleet's commanders built a new type of war boat and changed their strategy. The squadron was even malleable when it came to naval discipline. Boat captains used relatively mild punishments to mediate between the need to keep order on board, sailors' expressions of their masculinity, and the need to channel their aggression in battle.

The Mississippi Squadron, though, also had significant weaknesses. On multiple occasions the fleet got drawn into improbable joint operations with the army. These actions occurred in sinuous streams that lacked enough water to support the squadron's boats. More than once, poorly planned operations nearly led to catastrophic defeats. Disagreeable conditions on board and the difficulty of fighting guerrillas contributed to a massive turnover among its men. In the war's last twelve months, the Mississippi Squadron was less effective than at any other time in the conflict.

This book is the first full history of the Mississippi Squadron. Most previous works have focused on the fleet's attacks against southern forts, the destruction of the Confederate inland navy, the Vicksburg Campaign, and combined operations with the army.[7] A few have addressed the fleet's "irregular war" against southern insurgents.[8] Other scholarship has examined the fleet's sailors.[9] I blend these perspectives and include aspects of the brown-water navy's war that previous historians have overlooked.

One facet of the Mississippi Squadron's war that has escaped scholarly attention is the fleet's interactions with enslaved people. More than any other study, this book documents the experience of the nearly three thousand formerly enslaved men who served in the Mississippi Squadron. These men provided a crucial personnel boost between 1862 and 1864, making it possible for the fleet to expand its operations against Confederate ambush squads. These sailors left behind almost no letters or diaries, so to tell their story, I examined Black sailors' pension applications. This allowed me to include the words of formerly enslaved men and provide a description of their naval lives that has not been well documented. This book also describes how the brown-water navy amplified the efforts of enslaved people to escape bondage, if even temporarily. The army's role in the emancipation of thousands of enslaved people is well known, but that of the navy is less likely to appear in histories of the Civil War. The open rebellion of enslaved people, and the Union military's efforts to support their efforts, helped end the Confederate state.[10]

The Devil's Own Purgatory examines these themes through a blend of qualitative and quantitative evidence. Much of its social history is based on research in the *Official Records of the Union and Confederate Navies,* sailors' letters and diaries, deck logs, and pension records. But this book is the only study of a Union navy to make extensive use of quantitative evidence. Working with a team of researchers, I compiled a dataset of information for over 15,000 sailors who toiled in the Mississippi Squadron. We systematically examined the fleet's muster rolls, which contain a significant amount of demographic information. Many of the conclusions in this book are dependent on big data.[11]

Another dataset undergirds this story. Those who make their way through the *Official Record of the Union and Confederate Navies* will see that combat with Confederate ambush squads significantly affected the Mississippi Squadron. I used the *Official Records* and other government sources to create a dataset tracking the irregular war.[12]

Based on the quantitative and qualitative evidence, I believe the Mississippi Squadron's war fell into four phases. The first phase was mainly a regular war against Confederate forts and the destruction of the Confederate's inland navy. Blue-water navy and army transfers were the primary source of sailors in this period. The war shifted significantly in the second phase. While the fleet still attacked southern forts, a change in Confederate strategy forced the squadron to protect Union supply lines. Black men became a vital source of manpower at this time, as did white men from the West. The war's third phase deepened many of these trends. The fleet became more aggressive in attacking insurgents and took the war to southern civilians. It became even more dependent on African American sailors. The fleet also hastened Union victory in two important ways: it made Grant's victory at Vicksburg possible and facilitated military emancipation. During the war's last phase, thousands of men left the fleet. Their replacements were so inexperienced that Confederate attackers achieved their greatest successes in knocking out Union boats. The fleet was still powerful enough, however, to protect Union supply lines and help achieve victory.

This Union triumph was not foreordained, and it did not come easy. It depended on the efforts of ordinary men who traded their civilian identity for life in the navy. Fayette Clapp was one such American. During the Vicksburg Campaign, he confided to his wife that he dreaded going to bed and feared that he would not see her again. Hot weather, mosquitoes, and illness made life miserable on board. Rebel soldiers and guerrillas stalked the fleet. Clapp quoted an Irish petty officer who described life in the Mississippi Squadron as "the divil's own purgathory." This book tells the stories of the sailors whose entrance into purgatory was necessary for Union victory.[13]

1

CREATING THE WESTERN GUNBOAT FLOTILLA

In 1861 the U.S. government did something it had not attempted in half a century: build an inland navy. Unlike the ships that Oliver Hazard Perry commanded on Lake Erie during the War of 1812, these boats would operate on rivers. The Western Gunboat Flotilla came into existence because Union leaders recognized that control of the western rivers would be a decisive factor in winning the Civil War. A few key individuals created the fleet, which was much like the West itself: practical, improvised, and adaptable.

Rivers defined life in much of the Mississippi River valley. The Mississippi, Ohio, Missouri, Tennessee, Cumberland, Arkansas, and Red Rivers became magnets that drew white Americans to the region. Farmers in free states and cotton producers in slave states relied on waterways for communication and commerce. Smaller tributaries like the Illinois, Iowa, White, and Wabash further reinforced the notion that rivers were the connective tissue of what Americans were increasingly calling the West. Both a region and a concept, the West was closely associated with national strength, practicality, and economic vitality. Its major river towns like St. Louis, Cincinnati, Louisville, and Vicksburg connected interior residents with the Mississippi. Even though the region's free and slave states were drifting apart, "Anglo-American conceptions of the West centered on the Mississippi River."[1]

Steamboats were indispensable to harnessing the power of the western rivers. Riverboats were the most important means to transport people and cargo in the half century after the War of 1812. They powered a surge in agricultural productivity that helped turn New Orleans into the world's third-busiest port. In this interconnected, river-centric world, a steamboat could, if the water was right, travel between Pittsburgh, St. Paul, Kansas City, and New Orleans. Although railroads had gained in mileage and importance in the 1850s, steamboats were still king in the Mississippi River valley when South Carolina seceded in 1860. Decades of commercial activity indicated to even a casual observer of military affairs that rivers would be the locus of combat in the West. To control these waterways, however, new types of steamboats would be necessary.[2]

James Eads grasped this essential truth. A quintessential westerner, Eads was a visionary engineer who designed a catamaran-type boat to remove underwater obstructions. He became fabulously wealthy by convincing insurance companies to pay him to remove snags and thus make river travel safer. When the Confederacy attacked Fort Sumter, Eads was living in Missouri, a state where slavery was legal and secession was a possibility. He was a dedicated Unionist and friend of Edward Bates, who became President Abraham Lincoln's attorney general. Eads told him that he could use principles from his snag boats to build ironclad vessels of war. When Bates moved to Washington, he summoned Eads to meet with the president and the cabinet.[3]

No account of Eads's presentation to Lincoln and his advisors survives, but Eads memorialized the meeting by writing a long letter to Secretary of the Navy Gideon Welles on April 22, 1861. He argued that controlling the inland rivers was crucial to winning the war in the West because the Union could shut off river-borne commerce and starve the Confederacy into submission. Eads wanted the Union to establish a military base at Cairo, Illinois. In that secession spring, the town (its name pronounced "KAY-row") was arguably the most strategic spot west of the Appalachian Mountains. It sat at the southern tip of Illinois, where the clear waters of the Ohio River mingle with the muddy waters of the Mississippi. Union control of Cairo, Eads argued, would "effectually control the passage of vessels up or down" those two great waterways. The Union should place floating batteries—armored boats with cannons but no motive power—along Cairo's levees. Eads suggested that one or more of his snag boats would fit the bill. Although he envisioned the floating batteries as defensive measures against a Confederate attack, others would see their offensive possibilities as self-propelled gunboats.[4]

General in Chief Winfield Scott agreed with Eads's assessment of Cairo's importance, although it is unclear if he attended the meeting with Lincoln. Scott had already endorsed the president's blockade of the seceded states and proposed an advance along the Mississippi River. The Union would begin at

MAP 1. The Civil War on Inland Rivers—the Upper Rivers

MAP 2. The Civil War on Inland Rivers—the Lower Rivers

Cairo and build a chain of fortified supply depots along the Mississippi and Ohio Rivers. Twenty-five steam-powered gunboats would be needed to lead this invasion. Scott believed the bases and boats could reach New Orleans from the north and link up with the blue-water blockade in the Gulf. Although no one knew it at the time, the old general proposed building the Western Gunboat Flotilla. Critics ridiculed Scott's "Anaconda Plan," but its principles were sound. His scheme became the Union's basic blueprint for winning the war in the western theater. The Union navy would eventually use the Tennessee and Cumberland Rivers to invade the Volunteer State and would capture important cities on the Mississippi River such as New Orleans and Memphis.[5]

Eads, a man with intimate knowledge of the western rivers, and Scott, a brilliant military strategist, reached the same conclusion. They realized that, whether it was through invasion or supply, the western rivers were critical for the success of the Union war effort. Brigadier General William T. Sherman agreed. Writing from Louisville in fall of 1861, he sketched out the military situation in the West. Sherman suspected that the Confederates would advance into Kentucky, threaten Cincinnati, and then attack St. Louis. He opined, "The Power which controls the Ohio and the Mississippi will ultimately control this Continent."[6]

The Union had already taken steps to control the Ohio and Mississippi Rivers by occupying Cairo. On April 18 Secretary of War Simon Cameron urged the Illinois governor to send troops to the swampy river town. By May 10, 5,000 northern soldiers were drilling at what the army optimistically called Camp Defiance. They established several shore batteries on Cairo's levees, but Eads's floating batteries would never come into existence. A strange turn of events soon transformed those defensive weapons into the nucleus of the Western Gunboat Flotilla.[7]

With soldiers occupying Cairo, Welles brushed off Eads's plan for floating batteries. The secretary placed primary importance on blue-water ships and did not want the navy to get involved on the inland rivers. He forwarded Eads's proposal to army officials, for whom "the subject more properly pertains," he explained in a noncommittal reply to the engineer. By contrast, Cameron reacted with enthusiasm to Eads's letter. The secretary of war immediately ordered Major General George B. McClellan, the commander of the Department of the Ohio, to cooperate with Eads and a naval officer to be named later to see if one or more of his boats should be "taken by the Government and properly armed and equipped" as floating batteries.[8]

When he learned of Cameron's directive, a surprised Welles realized he had to appoint a sailor to assist McClellan. He directed Commander John Rodgers to go to Cincinnati with "regard to the expediency of establishing a naval armament on the Mississippi and Ohio rivers." Welles specified that the "interior nonintercourse" was "under the direction and regulation of the Army" and ordered Rodgers to act "in conjunction with and subordinate to" McClellan. The Union's brown-water fleet became the bastard child born of this contentious relationship between the navy and the army.[9]

Rodgers was the son of a famous naval officer and had forged a solid, if unspectacular, naval career after being appointed a midshipman in 1828. He was just as much of a scientist as he was a sailor and spent many years surveying and exploring vast expanses of oceans. At the time that Welles summoned him, Rodgers was in Washington awaiting his next assignment. He had the best qualities of an explorer: independence, confidence, and good judgment. He could also be stubborn and often failed to keep his superior officers informed of his decisions. His posting to Cincinnati would be short and tumultuous.[10]

McClellan was not interested in advancing along the Mississippi River. He proposed following the Kanawha Canal to Richmond, Virginia, or a move toward Nashville instead. If the latter, however, he would need gunboats to protect his troops. McClellan met with Rodgers and ordered him to evaluate Eads's salvage boats. If they were suitable, the commander was to buy them; if not, he was to "find others that will meet the purpose." McClellan also ordered him to "obtain all possible information as to the construction of gun boats." Rodgers interpreted these orders expansively but did not inform Secretary Welles of his enhanced job duties.[11]

Rodgers met Eads in Cairo and inspected the snag boat *Submarine No. 7*. The sailor was not impressed and dismissed the massive vessel as "old and rotten." He shifted direction and decided to purchase Mississippi River steamers for conversion into war vessels. It was a buyer's market. The establishment of Camp Defiance had effectively shut off river commerce south of Cairo. At least 150 riverboats bobbed quietly at the St. Louis waterfront. Rodgers, with McClellan's permission, purchased three sidewheelers for a total of $62,000 at the beginning of July. He estimated that it would take another $41,000 to convert them to fighting boats. Although the commander did not know it at the time, he had just acquired the first three vessels of the Western Gunboat Flotilla.[12]

When Rodgers blithely informed Welles of his purchases, the navy secretary exploded with rage. He sent an angry telegram to the officer, accusing him of overstepping his authority. Welles realized that he could not nullify the purchases, so he forwarded the information to Cameron and implied that the army should pay for the boats. The war secretary endorsed the purchases. Eventually, the Quartermaster's Department became responsible for naval purchases, construction, and operations in the Mississippi River valley until October 1862. In practical terms the army paid for and equipped brown-water gunboats, but the navy provided the officers and recruited the crews. This makeshift arrangement implied that the Western Gunboat Flotilla would be expected to cooperate with the army.[13]

The three vessels that Rodgers purchased in 1861 became the gunboats USS *Tyler,* USS *Lexington,* and USS *Conestoga.* Each was about 180 feet long and 40 feet wide, requiring a crew that ranged from 90 to 140 men. Rodgers sent the acquired boats to New Albany, Indiana, where John Lenthall, the navy's chief of the Bureau of Construction, Equipment, and Repair, supervised their conversion to war craft. It was a difficult process. Workers bolted five-inch-thick oak planks to the bulwarks, strengthened the decks to support cannons, cut gunports in the casemates, and painted the boats black. The work was slipshod and hasty. Much of the timber was green when it was installed and soon shrank, opening seams in the vessels. The dodgy planking was thick enough to stop musket balls but would be of little use against cannonballs. The planking also gave rise to the boats' nickname: the timberclads.[14]

Lenthall moved the boilers and engines from the main decks to the holds in the hopes of increasing the boats' chance of survival in battle. These high-pressure engines were dangerous even when someone was not shooting at them. Mississippi River steamboats had multiple boilers, long tubes that lay horizontally on the deck and contained pressurized steam once fires had heated up the water within them. A steam drum at the top of the boilers collected the steam before it was used to turn the boat's paddlewheels. Boilers and steam drums were notoriously finicky, and explosions plagued river steamers. A cannonball that struck a boiler or a steam drum would transform it into a bomb of scalding gasses. But putting the boilers and machinery in the hold provided slight protection from such dangers, and Rodgers knew that the timberclads would be vulnerable. "We must take our chances," he admitted.[15]

Rodgers rounded up an assortment of cannons for the timberclads. There was a wide variety of artillery available in the Civil War, and the gunboats that became part of the Western Gunboat Flotilla had an eclectic array of tubes. Civil War artillery was measured in various ways, but most guns were classified by either the weight of the solid shot they fired or the diameter of their barrel, also known as the caliber or the bore. Thus, a 10-inch gun fired a projectile whose diameter was ten inches (and weighed 128 pounds), while a 32-pounder fired a solid ball weighing 32 pounds (its bore having a 6.4-inch diameter). Artillery had two types of barrels, smooth or rifled. Prior to the war, most of the army's cannons were smoothbores, which allowed some movement of the projectile when fired. After the war started, the army started rifling its barrels, which usually involved carving grooves into the tubes to hold and spin the round when fired. Rifled guns were more accurate than smoothbores and typically had a greater range. The cannons themselves were typically made of cast iron or cast bronze and were heavier than field artillery but lighter than guns found on a blue-water ship.[16]

In less than two months, the timberclads were at Cairo awaiting orders. It was a fast turnaround. Despite critics who thought the boats were a waste of money, the timberclads proved to be durable and versatile. They lacked the firepower and the armor to slug it out with Confederate forts but excelled at infantry support, patrol, and counterinsurgency efforts. The timberclads embodied much of the western spirit, as they were improvised, practical, and imperfect. Their mere existence made up for any shortfalls—three imperfect boats were better than no boats at all.

By this time, Cairo had become the naval station for the brown-water navy. It, too, was makeshift. The navy rented wharf boats and barges for storage facilities, moored its receiving boats along the dirty levee, and built blacksmith shops, officer quarters, and a mess hall. The station grew into the fifth-largest naval base during the Civil War, becoming so unwieldy that the navy established a second base four miles upriver at Mound City, Illinois.[17]

Rodgers was forced out of Cairo before he could lead the timberclads into battle. Major General John C. Frémont replaced McClellan, who assumed command of the Army of the Potomac, in department command. Frémont was a famous explorer but was also a crony of Eads and Bates. He blended arrogance, stubbornness, and incompetence in equal portions. Frémont and Rodgers had a contentious relationship from the start. The "Pathfinder" incorrectly blamed Rodgers for construction delays on additional vessels and pushed for the commander's dismissal. Secretary Welles, who never liked the naval officer, was sympathetic and changed leadership on August 20. Rodgers deserved better. He saw the potential of the timberclads, correctly doubted the quality of Eads's salvage boats, was effective in coordinating the construction of additional boats, and energetically recruited sailors.[18]

Captain Andrew Hull Foote delivered the bad news to Rodgers. Awkwardly, Foote was also the new commander of the Western Gunboat Flotilla. Sixteen when he enlisted in 1822, Foote had a plodding career. He commanded ships in the Mediterranean, African, and East India Squadrons before commanding the New York Navy Yard. Foote was a devout Christian who led religious services as the fleet's commander and saw his naval posting as a righteous crusade. The dour warrior worked long days, built the fleet into an effective force, and established the crucial precedent that the navy would cooperate with the army. He also supervised the addition of more vessels.[19]

Timberclads were a stopgap solution until the yards could provide larger and stronger gunboats. The army's chief engineer recommended construction of sixteen ironclad vessels. Welles endorsed the plan and tapped Samuel Pook to design these gunboats. Not surprisingly, Eads won the bid to construct them. He promised to build from four to sixteen ironclads for the cost of $89,000 each by October 5, 1861, an absurdly quick schedule. The seven boats that Eads eventually built became known as the city-class ironclads because they were named after river towns: the USS *Cairo,* USS *Carondelet,* USS *Cincinnati,* USS *Louisville,* USS *Mound City,* USS *Pittsburg,* and USS *St. Louis* (later renamed *Baron de Kalb* because there was already a USS *St. Louis* in naval service).[20]

The city-class ironclads had sloping, armored casemates that were designed to deflect cannonballs and gave rise to their nickname, "Pook's Turtles." The boats' front and side casemates had 2.5-inch-thick iron plates bolted to the wooden frame, but the rear casemates had no armor. The pilot houses were only lightly armored. Pook decided that the boats needed three keels to offset the 122 tons of armor and to provide a stable gun platform. The ironclads were wider than a normal Mississippi River steamboat, 51 feet, but were about the same length, 175 feet. A single paddlewheel at the end of the center keel provided propulsion. The ironclads drew about 6 feet of water and could reach a top speed of eight knots. They were much more powerful than the timberclads. Each boat had had three forward guns, four guns along each side, and two aft guns, a total of thirteen tubes. The cannons were a heterogenous mix but most often comprised 32-pounders, 8-inch Dahlgren smoothbores, and 42-pounder rifled guns. It took about 175–200 men to operate one of these boats. A nagging variety of problems delayed construction of the city-class ironclads, but they were all commissioned by the end of January 1862. The *St. Louis* (*Baron de Kalb*) was the U.S. Navy's first ironclad, preceding the more famous USS *Monitor* by about a month.[21]

These squat, ugly, utilitarian, and industrial gunboats were part of a revolution in naval technology during the nineteenth century. Besides armor plating, the world's navies were turning to propellers, steam power, and guns that could fire high-explosive shells instead of solid iron balls. Propellers were impractical on the western rivers because of the low water levels and excessive amounts of floating debris, so the brown-water ironclads relied on paddlewheels. Even without propellers, the city-class boats were cutting-edge naval technology in 1862.

In a strange turn of events, the army added two more ironclads to the Western Gunboat Flotilla before 1861 ended. Eads successfully lobbied Frémont to purchase the salvage boat that Rodgers had rejected, receiving $40,000 to convert the massive boat into an ironclad. Frémont renamed the vessel USS *Benton* in honor of his father-in-law, Missouri senator Thomas Hart Benton. The Pathfinder also purchased the *New Era,* a ferry boat, for which Eads, of course, got the contract to convert into an ironclad. The vessel's first commander renamed it the USS *Essex* in honor of the ship his father had commanded in the War of 1812. In his typical arrogant fashion, Frémont made the purchases without permission from the War Department.[22]

The *Benton* became the fleet's flagship. It was a 200-foot-long behemoth that displaced 633 tons, sported sixteen cannons, and required a crew of about 230 men. It was so underpowered, though, that a tug often towed it into battle. The boat's comparatively deep draft of nine feet limited its ability to operate in tributary rivers. It excelled in pounding Confederate forts, but its lack of mobility was a liability during the second half of the war. The *Essex* was a poorly designed craft with a towering casemate. It turned out to be an indifferent gunboat, sturdy enough to absorb a significant pounding but not powerful enough to cause real damage to a Confederate fort.[23]

Frémont also authorized the creation of mortar boats, in part because the president pushed for them. These strange-looking craft were hexagonal barges with platforms measuring about sixty feet by twenty-five feet. Each had one 13-inch mortar that fired a 227-pound shell up to two and half miles and required a crew of thirteen men. The thirty-eight mortar boats had no means of propulsion, so gunboats towed them into position. Life on the mortar boats was miserable. Once the weapon was ready to fire, sailors hopped behind the six-foot-high bulwarks that encircled the mortar, which produced a punishing blast. After the war a mortar-boat crewman complained of being "in perfect Hell" from the effects of repeated shockwaves. "My head swims around I am dizzy and shooting pains go through my whole body," he testified in his pension application. His torment was unnecessary. The 17,250-pound mortars were wildly inaccurate and had no influence on the war.[24]

Two more boats joined the fleet in the war's first phase, which lasted until June 30, 1862. Both were captured vessels. The USS *Sumter* was a small Confederate ram while the USS *Alfred Robb* became a lightly armored boat known as a tinclad. The Western Gunboat Flotilla put fourteen boats into service in the first fifteen months of the war. It was an impressive achievement.

The Western Gunboat Flotilla's boats were both similar to and different from the fighting ships that prowled the high seas. Experienced sailors immediately recognized davits (cranes used to raise and lower rowboats), capstans (drum-like devices that raised and lowered anchors or pulled ropes), and hawsers (thick ropes) on the river vessels. And they immediately noticed important differences as well. Western gunboats had no masts, sails, or rigging in contrast to oceangoing vessels, even those with steam engines. Their main decks were on top of the sloped casemate instead of closer to the waterline. No one who looked at a brown-water ironclad would marvel at its elegance or sleek lines. Lieutenant Commander Seth Phelps, who became a capable commander, summed up the flotilla as "a mongrel service."[25]

The boats' peculiar configuration profoundly shaped the lives of those who crewed them. Simply, the men of the Western Gunboat Flotilla were not truly sailors because they did not sail. A recruit with nautical experience explained the difference to his parents when he transferred from the Army of the Potomac. "I cannot conjecture . . . what they want of Sailor men on these Gun Boats for," he wrote, "for there is no sailoring to do." He added that a landsman without naval experience was "as good as a Sailor for them." Sailors on ships had to know how to read weather conditions, adjust sails, and work the ropes. The men on the western riverboats were more like factory workers than seamen.[26]

Other aspects were unique to the Western Gunboat Flotilla. Its boats were adapted to the conditions of the inland rivers as well as the combat needs that became manifest in the western theater. The fleet's vessel's needed to be of light draft, especially when compared to the blue-water navy. A typical sloop of war drew seventeen feet of water, nearly three times as much as the city-class ironclads. Besides limiting the draft of gunboats, the rivers changed how the fleet fought. Instead of delivering broadsides like a blue-water ship, the ironclads attacked Confederate forts head-on. Thus, their heaviest armor was in their bows. Captains normally attacked upstream of Confederate forts because a disabled boat could drift to safety. The western vessels were versatile enough to slug it out with southern forts, provide infantry support, fight Confederate boats, and protect Union supply lines. This brown-water navy was unlike anything before or since in American military history.

Building a navy from scratch was an impressive achievement and testament to the energy, perseverance, and talents of the Union leadership. These vessels were durable. Eleven of the squadron's first fourteen boats still served at the end of the war. Given that Union military leaders did not know what would await them on the muddy rivers of the West, they put together an effective flotilla. But assembling a fleet was one thing; finding sailors to crew the boats was quite another.

2

THE MEN OF THE WESTERN GUNBOAT FLOTILLA

Just as the navy assembled a variety of boats for war on the western rivers, it scrounged around for men to operate them. The first men who crewed the boats of the Western Gunboat Flotilla were a motley collection of army castoffs, blue-water sailors, and new recruits. But these types changed over the war's course. Ultimately, the bluejackets who roamed the inland waters, just like the boats that carried them, were distinct from the rest of the U.S. Navy because they were mainly from the West.

In 1861 the navy had difficulty persuading men to join the Western Gunboat Flotilla. Commander Rodgers set up rendezvous (recruiting offices) in Cincinnati, Louisville, and St. Louis, but enlistments lagged. In the first half of the war, the brown-water navy was perpetually short of sailors, partly because men preferred to volunteer for the army rather than the navy. Whereas the army recruited men from the same region to join a regiment, the navy dispersed men from rendezvous into multiple vessels. This lack of opportunity to serve with brothers, cousins, and friends was out of step with the emphasis on kin and neighborhood that defined much of nineteenth-century America. Another disadvantage was that the army was able to offer enlistment bonuses early in the war. For many men, money was often the deciding factor when choosing a branch of service. Finally, those who became sailors had to face the widespread perception that service on a boat was less masculine than service in a regiment.[1]

The officers of the Western Gunboat Flotilla established a variety of methods to overcome this reluctance. They set up rendezvous near boardinghouses and saloons and sometimes used whiskey to separate men from their better judgment. Once Captain Foote took command, he distributed handbills in post offices, paid recruiters three dollars for each enlistee they corralled, advanced three months' pay to recruits, and ordered a steamer to cruise the Great Lakes and enlist men. This last measure annoyed Secretary of the Navy Welles because it siphoned off men from the blue-water service. Foote also paid each recruit below the rank of petty officer eighteen dollars per month. At a time when a seaman, the highest enlisted rank, earned sixteen dollars per month and army privates received thirteen dollars per month, it was a tempting offer.[2]

Despite these efforts, the Western Gunboat Flotilla lacked sailors. In January 1862, when the city-class ironclads were nearing completion, Foote needed another 1,000 men to crew them. He was so desperate that he convinced Major General Henry Halleck to allow transfers from the Army of the Tennessee. Major General Grant agreed to the scheme, partly because he could slough off "quite a number of soldiers in the guard-house . . . for desertion, disorderly, conduct &c." After hearing complaints from Foote, Grant later tried to send more suitable men to the navy. He distributed a circular in his army asking for "a list of river and sea-faring men" who were willing to transfer to the brown-water fleet. Foote was aware of the problematic quality of these transfers. He wrote Assistant Secretary of the Navy Gustavus V. Fox that he would take the soldiers "even if they are without brains, I only ask for muscle."[3]

The Army of the Potomac in the East also transferred men to the Western Gunboat Flotilla. As heavy snow fell on February 15, 1862, the 30th New York Regiment assembled. An officer read an order from Major General McClellan "asking for volunteers to man the gun boats on western waters," wrote John Morrison in his diary. Morrison and about thirty other men stepped forward but only he was chosen to go west. Two days later the private "shook hands with all the boys" and started his journey to Cairo. On the way seven more men from three other regiments joined the trek. Some of the transfers incorrectly believed that they were temporarily detailed to the gunboat service for thirty days, which is probably why they volunteered.[4]

Morrison arrived in Cairo about a month before Frederic Davis, who was part of a second wave of transfers from the Army of the Potomac. Davis enlisted in the 4th Rhode Island Regiment in the fall of 1861 but found out on April 13, 1862, that he and 300 other men were "going to join Commander Footes Western Fleet." It took four days for the train to bring them to Mound City. Davis reported that "only" 25 men deserted during the trip. When the remaining soldiers arrived in Cairo, they fulfilled Foote's worst fears. They found five barrels of whiskey, after which "nearly every one was drunk," according to Davis. During the wild brawl that followed, some of the army transfers cut the throats of other men and dumped them into the Ohio River. One rioter was thrown to the lower deck of the receiving boat and killed. "He died dead drunk," Davis noted. Including the deserters, he noted, "we have lost 60 [men] in all." It was a horrible introduction to the navy. "We have got into the worst place I ever imagined," Davis told his father.[5]

Foote regretted the army transfers. He told Welles that the "offscourings of the Army" were so bad that he had to use two companies of infantry to guard some mutinous men. The captain vowed to take no more soldiers and decided to "go into the action only half manned" if necessary. The next day he added that the "men sent us from the Army at the East have given us a great deal of trouble" but thought that "the strong hand of discipline and drilling" would turn them into effective sailors.[6]

Numbering from 600 to 1,000 men, some of the army transfers had negative effects on the fleet. They gave the Western Gunboat Flotilla a reputation as a destination for ne'er-do-wells. This was true only early in the war. Army transfers constituted anywhere from 40 percent to 70 percent of the fleet's crews prior to June 30, 1862. Besides the rioters at Cairo that Davis described, some of the other transfers were dissolute men. Charley Walsh, a trooper in the Fourth Illinois Cavalry Regiment who tried to kill an officer, "was given the privilege to take service on a gun-boat or stand a court martial. He chose the latter," a fellow trooper wrote.[7]

Not all army transfers were bibulous reprobates, and many of them became good sailors. Morrison earned the Medal of Honor on the USS *Carondelet* while Davis was pious and conscientious. When a large group of "Potomac draft" men left the service in the fall of 1863, their loss was significant. A sailor on the USS *Louisville* lamented, "They comprised some of the best men on the ship." Transfers were the "best men" in part because a third of them had maritime backgrounds. Sailors shipped from the army to the Western Gunboat Flotilla were an important infusion of manpower, and without these men, the fleet would have been forced to leave several ironclads idle when it went into battle in 1862.[8]

Another group of early sailors were men whom the navy transferred from its blue-water ships to the brown-water fleet. For instance, fifty-one sailors from the USS *Roanoke* and another 173 from the USS *Sabine* were sent from the East to the West. Most were working-class men from the northeastern seaboard. During the war's first phase, 82 percent of the navy transfers were residents of an eastern state, 51 percent listed their occupation as related to a maritime trade, and 28 percent were unemployed when they first joined the naval service.[9]

Men who enlisted directly into the river fleet constituted a third group of early sailors. Some of them were troublemakers. A contingent of 260 recruits from Boston got hold of whiskey when they arrived in Cairo and started a bloody brawl. Others, like thirty men who spoke no English, faced a significant adjustment to life in the navy. A few sought freedom in naval service, as over a dozen enslaved men enlisted before it became customary. Two of these men were Robert Cherry and James Hennison, who signed up near Fort Pillow on June 2, 1862.[10]

During the war's first fourteen months (phase one), the men who served in the Western Gunboat Flotilla resembled, to some extent, the sailors of the blue-water fleet. They tended to be residents of the Atlantic Seaboard who possessed maritime experience. But the types of men who enlisted after June 30, 1862, shifted significantly (see table 1). The percentage of immigrants declined noticeably, while the proportion of formerly enslaved men increased sixfold. Later recruits were also much more likely to be farmers than sailors, be residents of the West, and be teenagers. By this time, the men of the brown-water navy became distinct from the rest of the navy.[11]

The nature of recruits changed for several reasons. Captains deliberately brought runaway slaves into the brown-water navy. At the same time, the Western Gunboat Flotilla accepted few army transfers or blue-water sailors after June 30, 1862, as the Union's recruiting apparatus became robust. On July 2, 1862, President Lincoln issued a proclamation asking for 300,000 volunteers, and the government increased enlistment bonuses. By 1863, not coincidentally, the fleet's commanders stopped complaining about the poor quality of recruits. Sailors' opinions of these new men ranged from "worthless specimens of humanity" to "splendid men."[12]

Recruits who enlisted after June 30, 1862, were not necessarily better sailors or more motivated than those who joined in the first fourteen months of the war. They were not, however, openly belligerent like many of the ones who joined early. The sudden transfer of groups of men from the army or blue-water navy was a wrenching experience for the individuals that triggered wholesale dis-

TABLE 1. Comparison of Brown-Water Sailors in Phase One to Phases Two through Four

	PHASE ONE (July 1861–June 1862)	PHASES TWO THROUGH FOUR (July 1862–April 1865)
Ethnicity		
Native-Born Whites	52%	47%
Immigrants	44%	31%
Former Slaves	3%	19%
Free Blacks	2%	3%
Occupation		
Agriculture	8%	19%
Maritime	50%	21%
State of Residence (exc. Former Slaves)		
Union States, East	72%	36%
Union States, West	26%	59%
Confederate States	2%	5%
Far West States	<1%	<1%
Age		
Nineteen and Younger	13%	30%

Source: Gudmestad Sailor Dataset, N=14,442.

obedience. These men were more likely than those who enlisted directly into the brown-water navy to protest their conditions. There were no more high-profile riots, mutinies, or brawls once the navy stopped accepting such transfers.[13]

Whether they were transferred into the brown-water navy or enlisted directly into it, about 17,000 men joined the fleet during the war. These sailors can be sorted in a variety of ways, but most broadly, 48 percent of them were native-born white men, 32 percent were immigrants, 3 percent were free Black men, and 17 percent formerly enslaved (see chart 1). Their enrollments, however, varied significantly during the war. In the first phase, from the spring of 1861 through June 1862, few Black men enlisted in the fleet. From July 1862 to April 1863, the war's second phase, nearly as many Black men as immigrants enlisted. In the

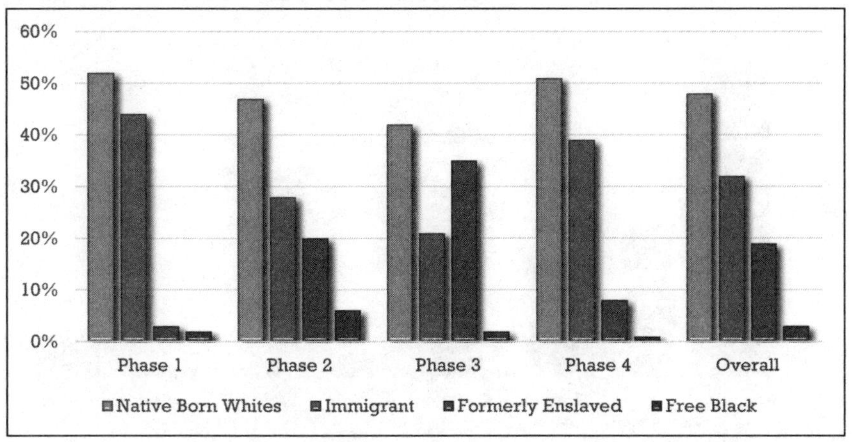

CHART 1. Enlistment Patterns, by Ethnicity
Source: Gudmestad Sailor Dataset, N=14,442.

third phase, which lasted from May 1863 to April 1864, Black men were more than a third of new enlistees. The final phase, which was the last twelve months of the war, witnessed a return to enlistments that resembled the first phase.[14]

Native-born whites, the largest contingent of free men in the fleet, hailed from all the states that existed in 1860 as well as the territories of Colorado and Nebraska. Ohio contributed one-quarter of these men, easily outpacing New York (17 percent) and Pennsylvania (15 percent). No other state contributed more than 8 percent of native-born white sailors.[15]

Immigrants were born across the globe, from the Azores to Zanzibar and even "at sea under the English Flag." Most, though, were from Europe or Canada (see chart 2). Ireland led the way at 39 percent of immigrants, a figure that constituted 13 percent of *all* sailors in the fleet. Men from the rest of the United Kingdom (England, Scotland, and Wales) were about half as numerous as Irishmen. Other notable sources of foreign-born crewmen were the German states, Canada, Norway, and France. Immigrants were part of a "roving international proletariat" who "crossed oceans and continents in search of work and respect." Service in the brown-water navy was just one more stop for these peripatetic men.[16]

A third group of crewmen in the brown-water navy was free Black men. Unlike the army, the navy had allowed such people to serve since the War of 1812. So many Black men volunteered during the early nineteenth century, however, that

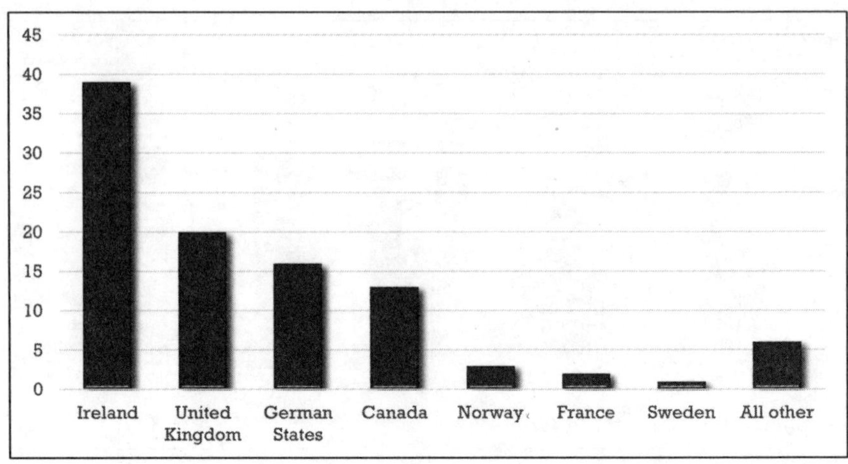

CHART 2. Immigrant Country of Origin

Source: Gudmestad Sailor Dataset, N=4,701.

the navy capped their enlistment at 5 percent. That changed with the enactment of the Militia Act on July 17, 1862. This law made it legal for Black men to enlist in the army or navy as support personnel. Of the approximately 400 free African Americans who joined the brown-water navy, 45 percent did so in the war's second phase. When considering residents of the northern states who joined the Western Gunboat Flotilla during this time, free Blacks were 8 percent of enlistments, even though they formed less than 2 percent of the northern population. These men had been eager to fight from the start but were prevented from doing so by racist policies. Once Congress cleared the way for Black enlistment, freemen proved their devotion to the Union and their desire to rid the country of slavery. Nearly half of all free Black men who served in the Western Gunboat Flotilla, 45 percent, were residents of Ohio; New York was a distant second at 13 percent.[17]

Formerly enslaved men also needed legislation to pave their way to enlistment. The Second Confiscation Act, which went into effect on the same day as the Militia Act, declared that all enslaved people of disloyal owners were free. The enlistment of former slaves in the brown-water navy had been inching up, but the twin laws of July 1862 opened the floodgates for a new source of sailors. Most of these men were enslaved in the Mississippi River valley, primarily Mississippi, Louisiana, Tennessee, and Kentucky (see chart 3).[18]

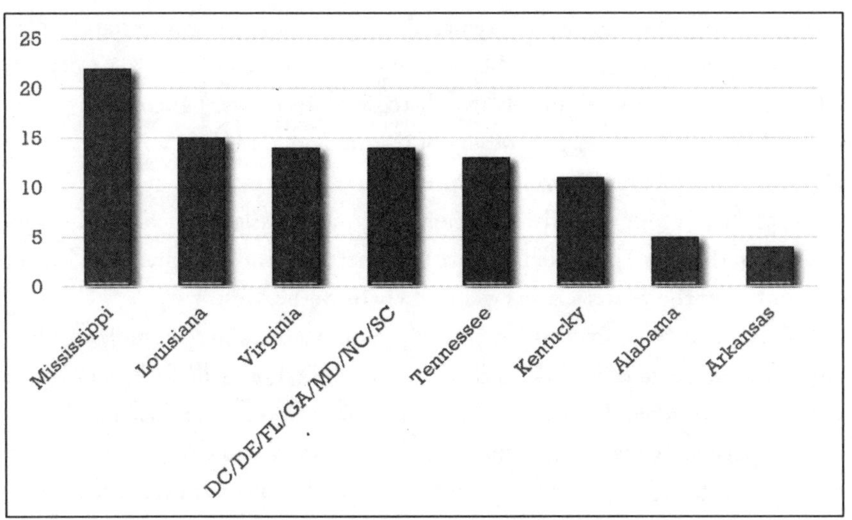

CHART 3. Former Slaves in the Mississippi Squadron, State of Birth

Source: Gudmestad Sailor Dataset, N=2,404.

Many of these men had faced the travails of forced migration. Fourteen percent of formerly enslaved men were born in Virginia, a state that sent thousands of slaves to the Deep South. Another 13 percent were from other states that contributed people to the domestic slave trade. Many of the men who were born in states near the Mississippi River had also felt the pain of sale. Brothers Walter and Joseph Perry were enslaved in Davidson County, Tennessee, but were separated when Walter was sold to a "negro trader who lived in Louisiana." The brothers enlisted independently in the Western Gunboat Flotilla. In the winter of 1863–64, Joseph was on the USS *Argosy* at Rodney, Mississippi, when the USS *Curlew* anchored alongside, and a sailor called out and asked him where he was from. When he answered Tennessee, the hailer asked who had owned him. When Joseph replied, "Lewis Overton," the man said, "You are my brother." Joseph immediately went to the *Curlew* and "fell into his [brother's] arms."[19]

The Perry brothers were like most sailors in the Western Gunboat Flotilla in that they were westerners—that is, residents of the Mississippi River valley. Data from the fleet's muster rolls indicate that 57 percent of free men—native-born white, immigrant, or free Black—who indicated a state of residence were from the West. Except for a handful of those from the Far West, residents of the

Eastern Seaboard composed the remainder of free men who gave a state of residence. The fleet's western focus becomes more apparent and rises to 62 percent by including the enslaved men who enlisted with its crews.[20] Their state of residence, however, was a category often not recorded in muster rolls. Another measure of sailors' geographic attachment is place of enlistment. Two-thirds of free men enlisted in the West. The inclusion of formerly enslaved men, all of whom enlisted in the West, pushes that figure to 79 percent. Thus, the men who fought for control of the western rivers were largely from the West.[21]

These western sailors had a variety of prewar occupations (see table 2). One-third of free crewmen indicated they were unskilled or skilled laborers. These occupations differed dramatically, from carpenters to teamsters. Men with maritime experience were another quarter of free enlistees, while those who worked on a farm totaled 18 percent. Relatively few men had prewar experience in occupations connected to a profession, the military, or a service industry. About 15 percent of free brown-water sailors were unemployed when they signed their papers, a figure that was steady across the four phases. Native-born white men and immigrants differed in one important respect, though: 25 percent of the native born came from an agricultural background, while 19 percent of them had nautical experience. Only 8 percent of immigrants worked in agriculture prior to the war, but 34 percent of those crewmen had maritime experience.[22]

TABLE 2. Occupational Class, by Ethnicity

	NATIVE-BORN WHITES	IMMIGRANTS	FREE BLACKS	ALL SAILORS (exc. Former Slaves)
Agriculture	25%	8%	8%	18%
Maritime	19%	34%	17%	25%
Military	1%	1%	0%	1%
None/Unemployed	13%	19%	19%	15%
Professional	9%	5%	3%	8%
Skilled Labor	27%	26%	29%	27%
Service	1%	1%	13%	2%
Unskilled Labor	5%	6%	10%	6%

Note: Two columns do not total 100 percent due to rounding.

Source: Gudmestad Sailor Dataset, N=11,142.

About 4 percent of native-born white and immigrant enlistees in the brown-water navy were residents of a Confederate state. It is difficult to discern the motives of these men for joining the fleet. A few were born in the North and might have wanted to save the Union. About half enlisted on board a gunboat or in a southern location and were probably Unionists. The navy also accepted some captured Confederates who traded time in a prisoner-of-war camp for life in the northern navy.[23]

Whatever their state of residence, brown-water sailors were distinct from the men who joined the Union army. Nearly half of Union soldiers were farmers compared to just 18 percent of white men in the Western Gunboat Flotilla. Immigrants were one-quarter of soldiers but one-third of the white sailors in the fleet. Additionally, Black men were overrepresented in the brown-water navy when compared to the army, 20 percent to 10 percent. The western sailors differed from soldiers in a few other ways. They averaged 24.1 years of age at enlistment, nearly two years younger than their counterparts. About 13 percent of brown-water sailors were younger than 18, compared to 11 percent of that age range for the Union army. Adult sailors were slightly shorter, too, averaging five feet, seven inches to the soldiers' five feet, eight inches.[24]

The brown-water navy accepted a higher percentage of immigrants and formerly enslaved men than the army because it had to do so. In the Civil War era, native-born white men had the widest range of employment options and, by extension, enlistment opportunities. Immigrants and Black men had fewer choices. Thus, the racial and ethnic composition of the Western Gunboat Flotilla is an indicator of how men perceived the desirability of service on gunboats. That only 48 percent of sailors who served on the western waters were native-born white men, compared to 66 percent in the army, suggests that the brown-water navy was not a desirable posting.

Brown-water sailors were also different than blue-water sailors. Historian Michael Bennett compiled a statistical portrait of sailors in the entire Union navy based on his sample of rendezvous reports. Proportionally, the brown-water navy had more men who were associated with agriculture, fewer men who were skilled laborers, fewer immigrants, and more men from the West. Sailors who toiled on the western waters were also, on average, about two years younger than those in the rest of the Union navy.[25]

The enlisted men of the Western Gunboat Flotilla, however, shared at least one important feature with blue-water sailors: they were not ideological. Brown-water sailors generally did not join the navy to protect the Union or free enslaved people. Instead, many of them signed enlistment papers because they were desperate for money. Machinist Henry O'Mahoney was broke and unemployed after the shop where he worked burned down. The Irish immigrant went to Chicago and joined the navy, primarily motivated by the $200 enlistment bonus that he could collect from the state of Illinois. An unknown number of men who had an occupation enlisted because they needed money. James C. Howe, who listed his occupation as student, was one example. His father abandoned the family, leaving behind Howe to provide for his five younger siblings. He joined the fleet, his cousin remembered, so "that he could help his mother" pay the bills.[26]

Other enlistees had mercenary motives. Unlike the army, the navy offered prize money to its recruits and touted enlistment as a way to get rich. Several sailors cited the opportunity to obtain prize money as a factor in their decision to join the brown-water navy. English immigrant John Swift, who thought that railroad work was "very hard," enlisted in the navy for the "18 dollars a month & prize money."[27]

Many men drifted into the Mississippi Squadron with no clear enlistment motives. A noticeable number merely went to a rendezvous with a friend. Hiram Martin received a medical discharge from the army for pneumonia and returned to farming, which he came to loathe. He found his way into the brown-water navy when a friend persuaded him to enlist. Walter Standish and Albert Schwab, who were lifelong friends, signed up in Cincinnati and were initially assigned to serve together on the USS *Brilliant*.[28]

Some sailors mingled notions of masculinity with military service. Eighteen-year-old Daniel Francis Kemp proudly "marched through the streets of Erie headed by the fife, drum, and bugle" after he volunteered. James Dickinson's decision to enlist was also bound up in his concept of masculinity. After he joined the navy, he spent the following day loafing around, looking at girls, and chewing tobacco "because all sailors chew tobacco." For him and probably other teenagers who joined the brown-water navy, military service was a rite of passage into adulthood.[29]

No matter the motivation, those recruits who became part of the brown-water navy had to pass a physical before they could muster in. Kemp recalled that he was "examined measured &c and entered into the service of the navy." Examinations at rendezvous and recruiting stations ranged from rigorous to perfunctory. Physical exams were so cursory at one rendezvous that a woman was allowed to enlist and only sent home when another sailor told the recruiter about her. For those who signed up on board, the boat's surgeon examined them.[30]

Most recruits traveled by train or steamboat to Cairo. Groups of men normally rode together and often established a rapport. For Kemp, that journey was his first trip away from home, and it was "wonderful." As the train chugged through Pennsylvania, Ohio, Indiana, and Illinois, the men sang popular songs and "Negro melodies"—that is, minstrel tunes.[31]

The fun stopped when the would-be sailors reached Cairo, which numbered about 2,000 residents in 1860. Visitors to the town were universally appalled by what they saw. Levees along the Ohio and Mississippi Rivers held back rushing waters. People arriving by boat had to use wooden staircases to descend fourteen feet to the town's streets. Steam pumps ran night and day but could not keep the streets dry. Sometimes the water was so deep that the only way to get around town was by boat. When these floods receded, hogs and rats roamed the streets. Cairo was a "dirty, swampy, hole, no sidewalks and mud knee deep the same as Virginia," according to a transfer from the Army of the Potomac.[32]

Recruits crossed the threshold from civilian life to military service on one of the receiving boats. An officer administered the oath of allegiance, by which sailors promised to "discourage, discountenance and forever oppose secession, rebellion and disintegration of the Federal Union." A purser then read the naval regulations, a boring process but a necessary one for new arrivals who were illiterate or did not read English. Having officially joined the navy, sailors received a canvas bag along with their uniform, a mess kit, blanket, and hammock. Uniforms were blue woolen blouses with jumper flaps that were normally tied; blue woolen bell-bottom pants; a soft, flat hat with the man's duty vessel written in gold letters across the front ribbon; and leather shoes. The blouse gave rise to the nickname "bluejackets." Sailors also received a cotton uniform to wear during the summer.[33]

Most were not impressed with their introduction to the navy. The USS *Maria Denning,* according to one recruit, was a "dirty, cold, damp Hulk." The food was no better. One sailor described his meal as "Hard Crackers and *harder Coffee.*" Kemp simply flipped his plate of rice and "salt horse" (salted beef) into the river. As they waited for a transfer to their duty vessel, recruits heard taunts of, "Oh! you fellows will be sorry you ever came here."[34]

Sometime in August 1861, the Western Gunboat Flotilla's first sailors slipped their uniform jackets over their heads and carried their canvas bags aboard the USS *Lexington.* Eighteen-year-old Joseph Cohen had crossed the Ohio River from Louisville to enlist in New Albany, Indiana. Once on board the *Lexington,* he reported to the boat's clerk, who recorded the teenager's information and assigned him a ship's number, "29" in Cohen's case. An officer examined the recruit as to his nautical and combat experience and assigned him a rating, or rank. A sailor's rating determined his payrate and was closely tied to his tasks and social status on board. Since Cohen had relevant maritime experience, he sewed a star on his sleeve to denote his rating as a seaman, designating seasoned sailors who knew the ins and outs of life aboard a sailing vessel. Cohen eventually met Joseph Preston of Massachusetts, who was an ordinary seaman, or one step below him in ratings. Preston wore a diamond insignia on his sleeve and was still learning the ropes (literally) but had some maritime experience. Cohen saw that Albert Daskam wore a rectangular strip of fabric on his sleeve, meaning he was a landsman; the Illinois resident did menial, labor intensive tasks. Holding the lowest enlisted rank of boy was sixteen-year-old Albert Lindsay. Boys, who were further divided into first, second, and third class, were normally teenagers who joined the navy and did errands or were servants of officers.[35]

Cohen also met William Daizley, a fireman. A "Boatman" from Pennsylvania before enlisting, Daizley fired the timberclad's boilers, oiled the machinery, and generally made sure that the *Lexington*'s mechanical parts were in good working order. It was atrociously hot work. The combination of being in a reinforced-timber or an iron-plated vessel that absorbed heat, working near furnaces, and being in the boat's interior with no ventilation could be deadly. A sailor on another vessel recalled how one fireman, sweat pouring off him like rain, staggered out of the firehold and collapsed. He lingered in the infirmary for a few days, laying quite still and rolling his eyes, before succumbing to heat exhaustion.[36]

Daizley worked alongside Wade Hardin, a coal heaver. Hardin was a formerly enslaved man who enlisted in, or was conscripted into, the Western Gunboat Flotilla along the Tennessee River. Men like Hardin did the most physically demanding jobs on the boat. Working in pairs, coal heavers carried wooden barrows six or eight feet down a ramp to a coal barge, where they filled the box. The men lugged the barrow, now weighing about 150 pounds, up a different ramp and dumped it in the firehold. It was so sooty, sweaty, and demoralizing that an Irish immigrant thought "death by leaping overboard would be preferable." Coal heavers spent most of their days shoveling coal, breaking it into smaller pieces, and spreading it under the boilers. Samuel Gissinger, an escaped slave who became a coal heaver, remembered: "If a man would work there 5 minutes he would be bathed in perspiration and his clothing full of water as the room was close. He could not get a breath of air." It "was very hard work for healthy men." The work was so repellent that native-born white sailors avoided duty as firemen: 60 percent of coal heavers were Black men while another 22 percent were immigrants.[37]

Cohen enlisted about a year before John Stout, a forty-two-year-old boilermaker who became a boatswain's (pronounced "BOE-suns") mate. Like other petty officers—quarter masters, captains of the forecastle, quarter gunners, coxswains, armorers, painters, and cooks—Stout was comparable to a corporal in the army and wore an eagle and anchor insignia on his upper sleeve. N. H. Miller came aboard the *Cincinnati* two months after Cohen but occupied an important position. The Indiana native was rated as a master-at-arms, meaning that he was responsible for enforcing regulations and meting out discipline. Only half of the fleet's masters-at-arms had a nautical background, suggesting that factors other than maritime experience made someone fit for the position. Below the petty officers were yeomen, mates, and stewards. They held positions of intermediate authority similar to army sergeants and also wore an eagle and anchor insignia on their upper sleeves. For all ratings, men on the starboard watch wore their insignia on their right sleeve, while men on the larboard (port) watch wore their emblem on their left sleeve.[38]

The man who commanded Cohen and the other bluejackets on the *Lexington* was Commander Roger Stembel. Like many of the squadron's early officers, Stembel had prewar experience in the U.S. Navy. He had served on ships that patrolled the waters of the West Indies, East Indies, Mediterranean Sea, Africa, and South America. Typically, most men in charge of a brown-water gunboat were rated as commanders or masters but were informally called captains, which was their onboard function as commanding officer of the vessel. They were responsible for directing the boat, making decisions in battle, and writing reports; only the captain could surrender his craft. An executive officer directed much of the day-to-day operations of the boat. He organized the watches and led drills. Staff officers included engineers, surgeons, paymasters, and the clerk.[39]

The officers of the Western Gunboat Flotilla varied in competency. Many of the boat captains during the war's first phase were castoffs from the blue-water navy. Commander William D. "Dirty Bill" Porter was court-martialed in 1841 for "scandalous conduct," disobedience of orders, neglect of duty, and contempt of a superior officer. Porter, who gained his nickname by sending his enemies letters on soiled paper, was acquitted of most of the charges but then shunted to the Reserve List, sort of a waiting room for naval officers. Two other captains, Lieutenant Commander Henry Walke and Commander Benjamin Dove, were also court-martialed prior to the war. When an officer in Rear Admiral David G. Farragut's blue-water fleet heard the names of some the Western Gunboat Flotilla's skippers, he asked "how the devil did Winslow, Dove, Walke get out here?" In a further insult, he wondered "how could such imbeciles get commands?" On the other hand, many captains were competent. Lieutenant Commander Phelps was especially aggressive, Walke grew into being an able commander, and Lieutenant Commander LeRoy Fitch became a squadron commander.[40]

A cultural and physical separation existed between enlisted men and officers. Enlisted men slept in shifts in hammocks in either a large room or, when the temperature was stifling below, on deck. Officers, on the other hand, enjoyed privacy, sleeping in either their own rooms or a shared quarters with another officer. Surgeon Fayette Clapp's room was twelve feet by ten feet and contained a bureau with four drawers, a washstand and bowl, a bed (complete with pillow, blanket, and quilt), and a spittoon "at which *visitors* shoot their tobacco juice & *in* which I shit." Another self-satisfied officer told his wife, "We shall continue to live first rate And have very easy times."[41]

Meals also reflected and reinforced the differences between enlisted men and officers. Each mess of enlisted men pooled their rations, and one member, usually under the supervision of a trained cook, prepared the group's meals. When it came time to eat, the men pulled their eating utensils out of their wooden mess chest and then used the box as a table. Most disliked or even despised their food. The men choked down a lot of salt horse or salt junk (salted beef), salted pork, beans, and hardtack. While the food was normally plentiful, it was often disgusting. One enlisted sailor told his mother that a concoction called "skouse" was so bad that "at home [you] would only think it fit for the Hogs." An Irish immigrant concluded that his food was "terrible."[42]

Mealtime was a different world for officers. They normally employed formerly enslaved men to cook and do chores for them. Such servants supported as much of an upper-class lifestyle as could be created on a vessel of war. An officer summarized his life as "very nice and snug—a comfortable room, very good provisions, and three servants to wait on our *lordships.*" In detailed letters to his wife, Acting Ensign Scott Jordan described how officers pooled their money and bought items that were unavailable to enlisted men. The breadth of their food was impressive: beef soup, boiled cabbage, Irish potatoes, stewed onions, hot biscuits, yeast bread (an important distinction from hardtack), butter crackers, pumpkin pie, custard, sweet corn, butter, honey, Worcestershire sauce, and catsup. On the USS *Marmora* Clapp shared oysters and claret wine with his peers in the wardroom. Officers were known to dine on china and gather around mahogany tables. Food that included items found in restaurants as well as the privilege to drink alcohol with no repercussions were reminders of the gulf between officers and enlisted men.[43]

Besides enlisted men and officers, each boat also carried civilian pilots. Prior to the war, pilots were well-paid specialists who memorized the features of rivers and were responsible for directing steamboats once they were under way. Rodgers, an early commander of the fleet, reasoned that it was safer to hire experts rather than train sailors to guide the boats. He negotiated the rate of $150 per month per pilot and established that each vessel would have two pilots on board. It usually was no problem to hire such men, many of whom were out of work because of the economic slowdown on the western rivers. After the first few battles, however, the fleet had to provide armor and protection for the pilot houses because Confederate sharpshooters and cannoneers targeted the structures.[44]

While the pilots in the Western Gunboat Flotilla remained consistent over time, the same cannot be said for the fleet's sailors. The squadron's first bluejackets were a short-term expedient often consisting of transferred men from the blue-water navy or the army. As the fleet grew, its sailors largely came from the West. Whatever their origin, these men often enlisted because they were unemployed, sought prize money, or wanted to prove their masculinity. Most of them lacked an ideological commitment to the war. Yet whatever their motivations, the men who joined the brown-water navy learned that adjustment to naval life would not be easy.

3

BECOMING MEN OF WAR

The adjustment from civilians to sailors was a difficult process for most of the men who joined the Western Gunboat Flotilla. Enlisted men expressed their masculinity by getting drunk, fighting, and resisting authority. Officers responded by trying to reform sailors, controlling their behavior, and building community among them. The system of naval punishment reconciled the need for order on the fleet's boats with the expressions of sailors' individuality. In the process bluejackets retained enough of their aggression to be effective in battle.

The men who joined the Western Gunboat Flotilla did not know what to expect when they signed their enlistment papers. As one historian has noted regarding Civil War soldiers, the "most individualistic society on earth now demanded that its free men submit to the control of others and subsume themselves into units that acted with the efficiency and precision of a machine." The same was true for those who joined the navy. When James Henneberry learned that his request for leave was denied, he griped that the "chords of millitary discipline" were tightening around him. How sailors adjusted to these "chords" depended in large part on their concepts of masculinity.[1]

One of the dominant strains of masculinity in 1850s America was "restrained manhood." It appealed to men who found their identities in their families, were proponents of domesticity, practiced self-control, tried to implement the teachings of evangelical Christianity, did not drink to excess, and sought success in the business world. Such Americans mastered their emotions and looked down upon working-class men and their hooliganism. Restrained manhood was often rooted in middle- and upper-class notions of respectability.[2]

Most officers and some enlisted men in the Western Gunboat Flotilla believed in restrained manhood. They were predisposed to accept the navy's emphasis on order, obedience, and avoidance of objectionable behaviors like drinking and brawling. Frederic Davis, who groused that he was sick of life in the navy, ultimately accepted his lot. He sheepishly asked his parents not to think him "extravagant" for buying a blanket with the two dollars they sent to him. Davis was so self-controlled that he spent forty-two nights wearing his coat and boots in his hammock and only bought the blanket because he was too cold to sleep. He was a devout Christian and enjoyed the church services on the boat, even if he told his mother that they were not as good as those at home. Davis was also ambitious to succeed. His good character and high scores on a promotion exam allowed him to advance to master's mate. By the standards of his officers, Davis was an ideal sailor because he conformed to their expectations of restrained manhood. Most enlisted men, though, lived according to a different type of masculinity.[3]

"Martial manhood" was the other dominant male lifestyle in pre–Civil War America. Men who exhibited it often drank to excess, reveled in displays of physical strength, and acted aggressively. They were "constantly" measuring their "achievements and skills against those of other men." The best way to establish one's reputation was through aggressive actions. While it was not necessarily class based, martial manhood had special appeal to the working class. This form of masculinity was closely tied to personal autonomy, or the ability to make decisions for oneself.[4]

The bulk of brown-water sailors adhered to martial manhood and rebelled against naval service. As an English petty officer on the USS *Silver Cloud* observed, "Americans are a very unruly lot of fellows." Bluejackets self-consciously expressed their martial manhood in ways that challenged their officer's expectations of self-control, obedience, and gentility. They commonly drank to excess, engaged in fights, defied authority, mocked others, and played cruel tricks. Edward Galligan was one such sailor. In his diary the Iowan admitted going on more than one "spree," being absent without leave, punching the first mate, fighting another sailor, getting drunk, joking about getting thrown in a military prison, whipping the captain of the Provost Guard, and stealing whiskey when he was sick. Like many of the fleet's sailors, Galligan's sense of masculinity was rooted in his fondness for whiskey.[5]

Drinking alcohol was the most common way that Civil War soldiers enacted their "masculine military culture," according to one historian. Sailors had an even greater reputation for drinking. Besides promoting a sense of camaraderie with one another, imbibing helped bluejackets endure the emotional toll of war in a way that was acceptable to peers. Knocking back shots of whiskey allowed strangers to loosen their inhibitions and for fast friends to commiserate. One measure of sailors' relationship with alcohol is the name of the dog on the USS *Tawah.* In an ironic joke, bluejackets christened the animal "Whiskey."[6]

Veteran sailors were accustomed to "splicing the main brace," or the daily grog ration. Grog was watered-down whiskey that the men slurped twice a day. Ezra Green told a friend: "We have our Rations of whiskey 2 a day. In the morning and noon 1 gill At a time." Measuring about half a cup, a gill of grog was enough to enjoy but not enough to intoxicate. Splicing the main brace was the navy's way to allow sailors to bend the rules. The Reform Act, however, banned alcohol on naval vessels as of September 1, 1862. The result, according to one sailor, put "every person in bad humor."[7]

Even before the Reform Act, bluejackets exhibited a dogged persistence in acquiring and hiding personal stashes of whiskey. Smuggling alcohol became sort of a game, with officers inspecting any boxes, bags, or packages brought on board. Their efforts were often fruitless. "But what puzzled the officers the most was how the men got their whiskey," according to a sailor on the USS *Peosta.* "If there was any whiskey around you may know the men would find it." Intoxication frequently led to fights and stupid behavior. "Several of the boys [on the USS *Carondelet*] imbibed large quantities of 'Red Eye,' which eventuated in divers pugilistic encounters," wrote one sailor. An astonished Davis watched as a drunken sailor ran around the deck, struck the boat's bell, and grappled with the quarter master. Only when a bluejacket whacked the man with a bar of iron could the master-at-arms slap irons on the drunkard.[8]

It is impossible to quantify how many sailors drank whiskey, but nearly every bluejacket who left behind letters or a diary witnessed excessive drinking. Drunkenness was rampant. When the *Tawah* stopped at Paducah, Kentucky, nineteen sailors went into town and stumbled back drunk to the boat; they constituted more than one-third of the crew. Intoxication was so widespread on the USS *Lafayette* that Alexander Miller recorded in his memorandum book, "All hands got drunk and two men deserted."[9]

Sailors were especially prone to abuse alcohol during shore leave. Teenager Dickinson visited a "rum den" and raised two glasses with his shipmates. When he returned to the boat, he "puked on the deck and could not stand up. Anderson got Isham (nigger) to clean it up." When a sailor named Sullivan went on shore in Memphis wearing his "best suit of navy clothes," he got so plastered that he returned to the boat wearing nothing but "an old piece of rug which he had wrapped around himself." Bluejackets normally roamed the shore in packs, and their consumption of alcohol was a means to reify their friendships and solidify their place within the boat's masculine culture.[10]

Drinking often led to fighting, another rebellious manifestation of sailors' martial masculinity. Fisticuffs served many purposes for sailors. On some occasions brawls were ways for groups of men to demonstrate their solidarity with one another. Provost guards were known to follow sailors because they could earn a bounty for each arrest. Bluejackets on the *Peosta* turned on such would-be captors and "licked the provost marshall guard," as one sailor proudly declared. Dickinson and two of his friends put up a good fight against other provost guards before getting thrown in jail. Even if the outcome involved bruises and confinement, it was important for a sailor to know that his buddies had his back.[11]

Some used fights to establish or maintain their reputation. Winning a fight was a way to fix one's place in the social hierarchy, which was not always equivalent to the navy's ratings. Martial men put their behavior on display in public spaces. When Galligan punched Jack Smith for touching his tools, he did more than show that no one could infringe on his property, he was showing that he was above Smith in the social hierarchy. George Washington, an escaped slave who served on several boats, did much the same thing when he fought a fellow contraband named Butler. One day their argument exploded in violence when Butler stabbed Washington with a bayonet. In a desperate fight the two men bit each other, and Washington beat Butler with lumps of coal before an officer yanked them apart. According to Washington, "everyone was glad that I had whipped Butler," and white sailors paraded him "around down stairs then up stairs" and "made quite a howl." With that fight he established his reputation as a badass among his fellow sailors.[12]

Brawling was also a means to reinforce the norms within the sailors' culture. Washington said of his fight, "Butler was a big fellow and was a bully among the negroes." Butler had violated social expectations, and Washington used violence to put the man back in his place. On the USS *Essex,* two sailors drew knives on one another. One of them was rumored to be a recent inmate in Illinois's Joliet State Prison. He ended up bleeding to death from a nasty slash to his abdomen. The perpetrator was never punished, even though many sailors watched the fight. The inmate's words or behavior were so odious that his fellow sailors protected the man who enforced the crew's unwritten social code.[13]

Many fights were simply manifestations of martial masculinity. According to a disapproving officer, John Morrison went on shore and "got beastly drunk." Back on the boat, "he had a row with the ward-room-cook, and gave him 'a shot between the skylights.'" A wild brawl involving John Ring and Edward McClain seemed to have no purpose. The two sailors were part of a shore party dispatched from the USS *Osage* on October 8, 1863. They somehow got hold of liquor and became "furiously drunk." Ring started "fighting with every one near him" and pistol-whipped McClain three times. Sailors subdued Ring but not before he called the officer in charge a "whorish son of a bitch." McClain, meanwhile, assaulted the same officer and called him "a black son of a bitch." For these sailors, their fights were small-scale rebellions against the highly structured naval life.[14]

As the example of Ring and McClain shows, defiance of authority was another feature of sailors' rough-edged culture. Insolence, disobeying orders, or other types of rebelliousness can be seen as a pattern of unthinking resistance, but the men used resistance to authority to assert their individuality and evade naval regulations. Bluejackets who pushed back against officers were attempting to impose their own terms upon the navy's structure. This resistance was widespread, according to an officer on the *Lafayette.* He tersely concluded that his boat's hold contained "several men in irons all the time."[15]

Sailors frequently lived out their defiant masculinity with their peer group. John Swift, the paymaster's steward on the *Silver Cloud,* gave orders to several men, "but they laughed at me." One "flatly refused" to comply, "and when I threatened to report him he told me to go to H—1and called me a very ugly name." Here, the sailors who mocked Swift were reinforcing their bonds with one another. On the USS *Benton,* the first watch did not finish coaling, so officers ordered the second watch to finish the job. The "whole watch mutinied," according to an officer on the boat. These men valued their solidarity with one another and were willing to be punished together to demonstrate their disgust with naval life.[16]

It is difficult to quantify the levels of drinking, fighting, and disobedience in the Western Gunboat Flotilla. One case study, though, is instructive as to the pervasiveness of sailors' rebelliousness. Since most discipline was meted out on individual boats, the vessels' deck logs often record what type of behavior triggered punishment. Between January 1863 and December 1864, the *Rattler's* log lists seventy-five incidents involving fifty different enlisted men that led to some type of punishment. In those twenty-four months, a total of 135 enlisted men served on the vessel, meaning that 37 percent of the crew got drunk, got into fights, displayed insolence, were negligent, or acted out in some other way.[17]

Yet despite the pervasiveness of drunkenness, fighting, and defiance of authority, most bluejackets were reasonably effective sailors. Whilst Galligan was drinking and fighting, he was also loading supplies, hauling anchors and chains, scraping paint, shoveling coal, bringing ammunition on board, washing the decks, and manning his gun. The navy in general, and the brown-water fleet in particular, had a set of practices, structures, and rituals that converted civilians into sailors. Officers variously tried to reform sailors, control their behavior, build a sense of community amongst them, and channel their aggressiveness in battle. These efforts often challenged men's martial masculinity.

Officers used prohibitions against swearing to force restrained manhood upon bluejackets in an effort to reform them. Fourteen-year-old George Yost found himself in formation on the USS *Cairo*'s deck on September 12, 1862. The ironclad's new captain, Lieutenant Commander Thomas O. Selfridge, wanted the crew to know that their behavior was not up to his standards. The naval veteran lectured the men that he would mete out severe punishments for anyone who engaged in "profane swearing." Yost struggled to see the connection between speech patterns and combat effectiveness because the rule seemed pointless in a war zone.[18]

Many officers tried to use religious services to knead restrained manhood into their men. Divine services, as sailors called them, varied from boat to boat and were always Christian, specifically Protestant. Some captains held no church, most made it voluntary, and a few required it. If the captain did allow or mandate a divine service, a boatswain's whistle summoned men to the main deck on Sunday morning for inspection. Once inspection was over, a sailor raised the church flag, a white triangular pennant with a blue cross. Since there were no chaplains in the Mississippi Squadron, the captain, another officer, or sometimes an invited guest led the service, which consisted of hymns, prayers, and a sermon. After about an hour, the boatswain piped down while a bluejacket lowered the church flag. Ensign Jordan liked having a short ceremony. He told his wife that he thought of "Brother Tobey" and wondered "if it would not be a good plan to have a Boatswains Mate to *pipe him down* when he gets on one of his long tracks." Whether or not the speaker droned on too long, most enlisted men were not interested in singing a hymn or becoming a devout Christian. Since such attempts at reforming sailors' martial masculinity rarely worked, the navy also implemented structures that controlled the men's behavior.[19]

The daily schedule, a petty officer observed, was designed "to keep the men out of mischief." Whistles, bells, or drums reminded sailors that they surrendered their autonomy when they signed their enlistment papers. Early in the morning, normally 5:30 or 6:00, the boatswain piped all hands to lash up their hammocks. Sluggardly sailors ended up on the "Black List" and might carry their hammock on the hurricane deck for half of the day or do some other pointless but physically demanding task. Breakfast of "colored hot water facetiously called coffee, and hard biscuits" followed. On any given day, whistles brought the men to the deck for cleaning, sent them running to their stations for target practice, called them to musket drill, summoned them to practice in repelling boarders, directed them to line up for inspection, or forced them to do other chores like cleaning the small arms. Dinner—what we call lunch—was at midday, while supper was at 5:00 or 6:00 P.M. Sailors slung their hammocks at 7:00 and then had two hours of free time. A final whistle called lights out at 9:00 P.M.[20]

Like the daily schedule, the system of watches was a constant reminder of how military life kept men busy. Twenty-five enlisted men, two quarter masters, and one captain composed a watch, and normally two watches were on duty at any given time. The entire day was segmented into various watches, each running from two to eight hours, and almost all enlisted men were in one of them. Being on such duty was sometimes miserable and often tedious. Dickinson described a watch on Christmas Day as "dirty, nasty, mean, stinking slobbering, rotten post duty." He was also on watch on New Year's Eve and "froze nearly to death." The resulting case of frostbite he contracted ended with the boat's doctor removing several of Dickinson's toenails. It was a "dam fine beginning for a New Year," he grumbled. Being on watch required self-control and vigilance, aspects of restrained manhood.[21]

Inspections reinforced the expectation that sailors needed to conform to a different expression of restrained manhood. A proper appearance was one way that men could advance in polite society. One sailor remembered how bluejackets had to "appear in neat and clean uniform, shoes polished, and his person neat and tidy" for Sunday inspection. Unkempt crewmen soon wished they had taken more pride in their appearance. On the USS *Silver Lake,* the entire crew watched as "two strong Negroes" stripped the offenders and scrubbed them with soap, sand, and hickory brooms. "It wasn't often a man needed a second scrubbing," wrote a landsman. Such spectacles were painful and humiliating reminders that sailors could no longer express their individuality in how they appeared. For those who preferred to express their martial masculinity through nonconformity, uniforms were tangible reminders of the connections between restrained manhood and the loss of their civilian identity.[22]

Scrubbing the deck was another way that officers controlled sailors' behavior. Bluejackets pumped water onto the deck and then sprinkled sand across it, but most often they scrubbed with brooms and soap. When a deep cleaning was necessary, sailors used the holystone, "a large sandstone cut square or oblong, with an iron ring fastened into each end, into which a rope is made fast," a sailor remembered. Amid a torrent of "tall swearing," two men heaved the slab back and forth across the deck, scraping off the top layer of wood. Officers on the USS *Manitou* saw holystoning as so important in keeping sailors busy that, during the siege of Vicksburg, their men even holystoned a deck they built for their land camp. Such work was "particularly fatiguing," according to one sailor. But tired men, officers hoped, would be less likely to act upon their most aggressive impulses. Besides controlling sailors' behavior, the navy also recognized the need to build camaraderie within crews.[23]

An important site for building community among sailors was the mess. In the Western Gunboat Flotilla, these consisted of groups of five to ten men. Sailors in a mess had the same watch schedule so that they could eat together. If a sailor died, his mess mates buried his body and distributed his property. Men traded their civilian friendships for short-term military ones. With a group like the brown-water sailors, who did not possess strong ideological motivations, it was necessary to build a sense of identity within the collective. In this way the navy intended that relationships with buddies on board the boats would become the social glue that held a crew together. At times these relationships also nurtured sailors' expressions of martial masculinity. James Dickinson and eight or nine other sailors—the size of a mess—swam to shore one day "and played Indian for two or three hours." The planning for this defiance likely occurred around the mess table.[24]

Efforts to reform sailors and control their behavior (that is, to work the values of restrained manhood into them) had limited success. Officers like Captain Foote were mistaken when they believed the "strong hand of discipline and drilling" would change sailors who "have given us a great deal of trouble." The service also recognized that the men needed to express their martial masculinity in acceptable ways.[25]

The navy designated a time for sailors to engage in rough play during the longstanding tradition known as skylarking, a tacit admission that the men needed to release their pent-up aggressions. On certain days the boatswain piped "all hands to mischief," and enlisted men had an organized, possibly disorganized, free-for-all. Skylarking normally took place in the evening and often involved fighting, wrestling, or an especially violent game called "Fox and Geese," in which a blindfolded sailor tried to hit his boatmates with a hammer or anvil. James Henneberry was on the receiving end of a hard blow during this rough game. He "got a very bad black Eye (in skylarking) which deprived me of the use of it for the past four days." Even though skylarking was useful in defusing martial masculinity, another activity was even more effective.[26]

Shared service on a gun crew, universally called exercising the great guns, was the most powerful activity on a gunboat because it taught lessons associated with restrained manhood and tapped into bluejackets' martial masculinity. Exercising the great guns was a brute-force ballet that required teamwork. Smaller guns had a crew of eight men, while the large cannons on the ironclads needed twelve hands. After a cannon fired, half the crew seized the ropes connected to a block and tackle on each side of the gun and pulled in unison. Naval guns and their wooden carriages weighed 10,000 pounds or more, about the same as a modern-day ambulance. Moving cannons in and out was "very hard work," army transfer Ezra Green wrote to a friend. Once the gun was run in, a sailor used a long pole with lambswool at the end to swab out the tube. A powder monkey, often a first-class boy, brought a nine-pound bag of gunpowder to the loader. The loader, sometimes leaning out the port hole, rammed the powder down the barrel. Based on the gun captain's orders, a crewmember took a shot or shell out of an ammunition box and gave it to the loader, who rammed the projectile down the tube. Once the loader stepped away, the crew used ropes to run out the weapon. The gun captain then punctured the seated powder bag with a brass spike through the vent and inserted a copper primer. He then aimed the gun, directing his crew to sidle the cannon sideways or adjust the elevation. When all was ready, he yelled for the men to brace themselves, then pulled the lanyard to fire the gun. Constant practice improved sailors' abilities and deepened their reliance on one another.[27]

Old salts passed along nuances that protected their mates from some dangers and built trust among the men. Gun captains created a vacuum in the barrel during swabbing by placing a thumb protected by a leather stall over the vent. Swabbers used only one hand in their work lest the gun accidentally fire. Loaders kept their left hands on the tube while ramming home the projectile to dispel any static electricity that might cause an accidental blast. When the cannon fired, men covered their ears and opened their mouths to protect themselves from the concussive blast. Experienced sailors usually spread sand on the gun deck before battle and fought barefoot. Blood is slippery, after all.[28]

Early in the war especially, the fleet relied on sailors with naval and combat experience to train their mates in gunnery. Through June 30, 1862, 50 percent of free men in the Western Gunboat Flotilla had nautical experience. The rate dropped to 21 percent from then on for the remainder of the war. After an early battle, Lieutenant Commander Walke observed that the "old men-of-war's men, captains of the guns, proud to show their worth in battle, infused life and courage into their young comrades." They exhibited "coolness and discretion" in battle, he thought. Morrison, who had been a sailor prior to enlisting, was one of them. He served under Walke on the *Carondelet* and demonstrated his bravery and experience on multiple occasions. Other bluejackets who provided seasoning were John Murphy, an Irish seaman on the USS *New Era* who had spent fourteen years at sea, and Joseph Johns, a native of Italy who was at sea for nineteen years before enlisting in the brown-water fleet on March 23, 1862.[29]

Competitions between gun crews affirmed a shared identity in which sailors nurtured mutual relationships *because* they were willing to fight for one another. Captains often set up targets on sandbars or picked out shoreline features and pitted gun crews against one another to see who could hit the mark. Sailors took delight in showing that they were up to the task. Galligan proudly noted that the *Essex* hit its target three times when it faced off against the USS *St. Louis.* Other types of competition nurtured gunners' pride. During a salute, the captain of the *Essex* challenged the crews of the No. 1 and No. 2 guns to "make better time" than the full crew of the USS *Richmond.* Galligan foolishly agreed to stand outside the casemate when loading his cannon because, he claimed, "my gun could not hurt me." His braggadocio is an example of how exercising the great guns fused aspects of martial masculinity and restrained manhood together. Galligan was willing to perform an individual act of derring-do that was in service to his identity within a team. Sailors learned to surrender their sense of self to a larger collective through gun drills.[30]

The bonds built during hours of exercising the cannons were meaningful to sailors. Members of one gun crew on the *Essex* thought their friendship was important enough to memorialize with a photograph. The resulting image shows four men in uniform, two of them standing and two of them sitting. The standing sailors each have a hand on the man sitting in front of them. These signs of affection show the trust they had for one another. Each faces the camera with a steady stare. Their whiskers mark them as men, not boys, while their studied nonchalance, especially the sailor with his arm propped on furniture, oozes confidence. These were confident men, ready for combat, their strong bonds formed through hours of rigorous drill and outbursts of battle.[31]

The navy reconciled the competing demands of obedience to rules and expressions of martial masculinity through mild punishments. Drinking, fighting, and disobeying officers had to be punished, but the navy also needed to retain, perhaps even reform, its sailors. With such widespread disobedience in the fleet, relatively light punishments allowed the boats to have enough men to stay in operation. Galligan, for his part, on separate occasions was handcuffed for a day, chained to a stanchion for two days, and confined in jail for two days. Immediately after being released from the stanchion, he "went to moving nine inch guns." The officers on board the *Essex* were willing to put up with Galligan's defiant actions as long as they could extract the requisite labor from him to operate and fight the gunboat effectively.[32]

Across the fleet, punishments varied immensely. The navy abolished flogging in 1850, but officers routinely doled out punishments that emphasized humiliation and physical pain. Confinement in single irons—handcuffed at the wrists—or double irons—having wrists and ankles bound—was the most common form of punishment. Another widespread punitive measure was banishment to the hold, also called the hole, brig, or sweatbox, situated below the waterline. Boats had solitary confinement there as well as cells that could accommodate multiple prisoners. Sailors were usually in the hold for a day or two, but some languished for weeks. Their diet was normally bread and water. Other punishments included being reduced in rating, wearing a shirt with "thief" painted on it, rolling a cannonball around the deck for hours, being chained together after fighting, or being put on the blacklist.[33]

More serious offenses went to a fleet court-martial. For these cases, the squadron's commander convened a court of several officers. Offenders had no legal representation, but they did respond to the charges and could call witnesses on their behalf. In 1863 the navy brought cases against twenty-two enlisted men in the Western Gunboat Flotilla. Eight trials involved desertion and seven involved sodomy. The others ranged from disobeying orders to assault, mutiny, or theft. The most common punishment was hard labor, although one mutineer was sentenced to death by hanging. The number of cases brought to a fleet court-martial in 1863 were few, given that at least 4,200 men *enlisted* in that year alone. Few sailors behaved in ways that were egregious enough to trigger significant punishment.[34]

The prevalence of mild punishments created a space where sailors could blow off steam and face consequences that were temporary and annoying. Returning to the seventy-five punishments involving enlisted men in the *Rattler*'s log, only four of them led to an onboard court-martial. In nearly all the other cases, the usual punishment was some combination of confinement in single or double irons, solitary confinement, a diet of bread and water, or reduction in rate. Conditions on gunboats were difficult—close proximity to a wide variety of individuals, stultifying schedules, continual danger, inability to leave the boat and get away from others—so it is no surprise that smoldering resentments flared into verbal and physical confrontations. Life in the Mississippi Squadron grated against sailors' expressions of martial manhood. Bluejackets who expressed their frustrations by getting drunk, fighting with one another, or mouthing off to officers knew that they would face consequences. Rolling a cannonball around the deck, being in double irons for twenty-four hours, or spending a few days in the hold were small prices to pay for assertions of individuality and masculinity.[35]

Punishments were sometimes even milder than prescribed because sailors helped their friends avoid them. Henry Holdrege, a sailor on the USS *Nymph,* casually told his commanding officer that he was not ready to report for duty. After hearing that his punishment would be forty-eight hours in the hold, Holdrege said he would not go. That earned him an additional six days, double irons, and a disrating to landsman. Holdrege, though, "spent the day[s] very pleasantly in the Hold," according to his diary entries. His friend Johnny Simons, he noted, "fetched me everything that I wanted." Holdrege bought a can of peaches, smoked cigars, read novels, played the accordion, read his mail, and "had pleasant dreams," even though he was supposed to have his wrists and ankles shackled. Upon being released, he washed up, went to the quarterdeck, and endured a "good talking to" from the captain. Likewise, when Dickinson and friends were in the hold after "licking" the provost guards, they got out of their irons and escaped when they "stove through the bulkhead."[36]

The combination of skylarking, exercising the great guns, and mild punishments preserved enough of the sailors' martial masculinity so that they would be effective in battle. Bluejackets who had a certain edge to them were capable warriors. The navy did not want to do too much to squelch their aggressiveness. Galligan, for instance, easily moved between the seeming contradictions of striking the first mate and refusing to leave his gun despite a painful hip wound. Other sailors embodied this ability to thumb their noses at naval discipline but perform heroically in battle. One day Morrison was clocking a sailor in the head, and the next he was running along the gun deck and firing each cannon at a Confederate boat.[37]

Men like Galligan and Morrison were essential to the Western Gunboat Flotilla's ability to function. They, and others like them, retained some of their martial manhood despite the efforts of officers to impose restrained manhood. While drunkenness, fighting, and insolence were widespread in the brown-water service, they did not rise to a level that impaired the fleet's effectiveness. Ultimately, enough sailors moderated enough of their behavior, subordinated themselves to authority enough of the time, and retained enough of their aggressiveness to be effective sailors and make the fleet functional. These men had the opportunity to put their martial manhood on display in battle when the gunboats started down the Mississippi, Cumberland, and Tennessee Rivers in 1861 and 1862.

4

EARLY COMBINED OPERATIONS

In 1861 and 1862, the Western Gunboat Flotilla saw its first combat. Its gunboats cooperated with army offensives along the Mississippi, Cumberland, and Tennessee Rivers. They scouted Confederate positions, escorted troops to the place of battle, provided infantry support, and attacked enemy installations. These victories proved the value of combined operations in the western theater and demonstrated the brown-water fleet's versatility.[1]

The first test for the Western Gunboat Flotilla came at Columbus, Kentucky, a site about twenty miles down the Mississippi River from Cairo. Confederate military leaders recognized the primacy of rivers in the western theater and built forts at Columbus, Kentucky; Island No. 10, Missouri; and Fort Pillow, Tennessee, on the Mississippi as well as in Tennessee, with Fort Henry on the Tennessee River and Fort Donelson on the Cumberland River. They also began fortifying Vicksburg, Mississippi. Confederate armies augmented these forts and could, in theory at least, move to whichever point seemed most vulnerable. Southerners also started building a river-defense fleet, but it would not act in coordination with their armies.[2]

Columbus sits in the southwest corner of Kentucky. In 1861 it was a strategic location for several reasons: the Mississippi River made a sweeping turn at the town, forcing boats to slow down as they navigated their way through the channel; the 150-foot-high Iron Banks Bluff on the Kentucky side commanded the river; it served as the northern terminus for the Mobile and Ohio Railroad; and it could be a staging base for an attack on Cairo, the loss of which would be devastating to the Union. Southerners established three tiers of batteries on the bluff and another battery about a mile north of Columbus. About 140 guns were embedded in these defensive works, including the "Lady Polk," a 128-pounder that was the largest gun in the Confederacy. With just over 16,000 men divided between the cannon emplacements, the camps outside of Columbus, and Camp

Johnson across the river near Belmont, Missouri, the "Gibraltar of the West" was one the most heavily defended spots in North America.[3]

In early November 1861, Brigadier General Ulysses S. Grant received orders to attack Confederate forces in southeastern Missouri. He interpreted his orders broadly and used them as a pretext to attack Camp Johnson so that his men could gain combat experience. Grant prevailed upon Lieutenant Commander Walke to bring the timberclads *Tyler* and *Lexington* as escorts for the steamers that would carry his 3,100 troops.[4]

On November 7 Walke led the small flotilla to Hunter's Farm, a spot three miles upriver from Camp Johnson. Grant's troops disembarked, formed ranks, and shambled into battle. After initial success, Union forces broke and ran under the stress of a Confederate counterattack. Blue-clad soldiers fled to Hunter's Farm, where they scrambled aboard the transports. Musket balls rattled against the sides of the boats as the loaded vessels shoved off. Walke shifted the *Lexington* and *Tyler* to get a clear line of fire at the ragged Confederate line. The paddlewheel of the transport *Belle Memphis* became entangled with some floating debris, forcing the boat to drift downstream and block the *Lexington* from firing. Commander Stembel ordered the soldiers on the damaged steamer's deck to lie down. Both timberclads then poured grape, canister, and five-second shells into the Confederates, mowing down whole ranks of southern soldiers. A Union shell struck a cannon just as it was about to fire, shattering the gun and sending its crew cartwheeling through the air. The timberclads' blasts came in the nick of time and prevented a disaster for the Union army. One of the soldiers who clawed his way on board a steamer gratefully admitted, "The gunboats was all that saved us from being shot like hogs." Grant was one of the last men to reach the transports. He spurred his horse, rode across the gangplank, and collapsed on a couch in a stateroom. The Union vessels steamed upriver to Cairo, thankful to escape. The Western Gunboat Flotilla proved its value as infantry support in its first battle.[5]

After Belmont, the timberclads also functioned as something of a riverine cavalry that scouted Confederate positions. In late 1861 Lieutenant Commander Phelps took the *Lexington* down the Tennessee and Cumberland Rivers to surveil Forts Henry and Donelson. The two posts were over 150 river miles apart but only 12 land miles distant. Together, they protected Middle Tennessee from invasion. The loss of Fort Henry would open the Tennessee River to Union attack as far as northern Alabama; allow Federals to cut the Memphis, Clarksville, and Louisville Railroad; and threaten the important rail juncture at Corinth, Mississippi. Should Fort Donelson fall, Union forces could reach Nashville with little opposition. The capture of both forts would allow the Union to occupy most of Middle Tennessee and deprive the Confederacy of much needed resources. Forts Henry and Donelson were the only obstacles preventing Federal forces from punching a hole in the Confederate's main defensive line in the West and capturing much of the Volunteer State.[6]

Phelps learned that Confederates were forcing enslaved African Americans to build the installations. On a routine scouting mission twenty miles shy of Fort Donelson, he spotted a fugitive slave hailing the *Lexington.* The man, who had been "chased by blood hounds in full cry after him," told Union sailors that Kentucky troops were "seizing the negroes of Kentuckians, [and] carrying them to Dover to work upon the fortifications." Bluejackets took the man on board and "brought him away," according to the timberclad's captain.[7]

Phelps acted in accord with Union policy. Confederates routinely compelled enslaved people to dig entrenchments, build forts, and work in military camps. Enslaved workers, though, ran to Union lines and forced the northern commanders to decide whether to return them. Congress codified policy on August 6, 1861, with the First Confiscation Act. It stated that enslavers forfeited their claim to the labor or service of enslaved people whose work benefited the Confederacy. At this point in the war, boat captains were unlikely to encounter fugitive slaves. As the Western Gunboat Flotilla penetrated farther into Confederate territory, however, it would become a force for liberation.[8]

Grant was eager to move against Forts Henry and Donelson, but he faced a daunting obstacle: Major General Henry Halleck. Having assumed command of the western theater in November, Halleck denied Grant's request to attack one of the forts. Even though "Old Brains" understood what needed to be done, his natural caution induced military paralysis. Undeterred, Grant approached Foote. The flag officer said he could provide four boats for the operation. Faced with the combined pressure of Foote and Grant, Halleck relented and on January 30, 1862, sent orders to the general to bring his troops up the Tennessee River "as far as practicable," have Foote "protect the transports with his gunboats," and attack Fort Henry.[9]

Even though Fort Henry was unfinished by the time the Federals moved up the Tennessee River, the southern installation was a significant obstacle. It had earthen walls eight to ten feet thick and four to six feet high and mounted seventeen guns, eleven of which faced the river. The cannons were adequate but not enough to compensate for the fort's wretched location. It was on low ground that was prone to flooding. Brigadier General Lloyd Tilghman, who assumed command of the area in December 1861, was supposed to construct a second stronghold, Fort Heiman, on high ground across the river from Henry, but he dallied. When the Western Gunboat Flotilla steamed into action, Heiman played no role in the battle.[10]

Foote had recently been promoted to flag officer (or commodore), a significant development for the Western Gunboat Flotilla. At his prior rank of captain, he was the equivalent of a colonel and, since the fleet was considered part of the army, was obligated to obey the orders of any military officer who outranked him. Now, Foote was the equal to a brigadier general and could resist the whims of those who might order him around. It also signaled that the Western Gunboat Flotilla was roughly equal to a Union army of this time.[11]

Foote had no opportunity to celebrate his promotion since he had to decide which boats to send into battle. He lacked enough sailors to man all of his dozen gunboats. Foote shifted bluejackets around and chose the three timberclads as well as the ironclads *Essex, Carondelet, Cincinnati* (which would be Foote's flagship), and *St. Louis.* No one knew if the ironclads would be able to slug it out with the big Confederate cannons. A pessimistic Halleck wondered if "the gunboats are worth half the money spent on them."[12]

As the flotilla steamed into action, Foote readied his men for battle. His orders reveal the musings of a cautious man who had grave concerns about his gunners' competency. The flag officer began not with a stirring call to smash the rebels, but with the obvious advice to open the gunports before firing, "otherwise great injury will result from the concussion of the guns." He further insulted the intelligence of his men by intoning that they must adjust their second shot after seeing the effect of the first one. There was to be no "firing wildly and harmlessly" because it would waste ammunition, cost a lot of money, and encourage the enemy. Indeed, Foote told his men that each shell they fired would cost Uncle Sam eight dollars, so they had to be careful to "get the worth of your money." What he and the other Union commanders did not realize was the extent to which environmental factors would influence the upcoming battle.[13]

The winter of 1860–61 in the region had been especially rainy. By the time the gunboats and transports left Paducah, the Tennessee River was at flood stage. Its swirling and gurgling water brought driftwood, lumber, fences, large trees, and even buildings bobbing downstream. There were so many hazards that Union sailors with long poles stood on the bows of the gunboats and pushed away the more dangerous debris. The high water would give Foote's gunners a better line of fire at Fort Henry because the boats would be nearly level with the Confederate cannons. The flotilla arrived in the area on February 5, 1862. Grant and Foote agreed that the navy would bombard the fort while the army surrounded it.[14]

While the infantrymen trudged their way forward, the gunboat crews prepared for battle. On the *Cincinnati* Foote spent much of his time praying. By contrast, Commander "Dirty Bill" Porter on the *Essex* assembled his crew on the spar deck and pointed to the rebel flag flying over Fort Henry. He predicted that by the time the sun set on February 6, the Union would raise the Stars and Stripes in its place. "All hands gave him three cheers," reported a sailor. The crew then swigged some grog.[15]

Coal heavers in the gunboats increased the intensity of their labors, and the firemen built up more steam in the boilers. Black smoke belched from the tall stacks, a sure sign that the attack was imminent. The gunboats surged around Panther Island and approached Fort Henry, the first time that a fleet of American ironclads went into battle. The *St. Louis, Carondelet, Cincinnati,* and *Essex* created a parallel line about a mile from the fort. The three bow guns of the three city-class boats ranged in size from 32-pounders to 42-pounders. The *Essex* also had three bow guns, but two of them were at the front corners of the vessel and did not face directly ahead, so the boat angled slightly to allow two of these forward guns to engage the fort at any one time. The Union fleet had more and heavier guns than the Confederate fort.[16]

At about 12:30 P.M., the *Cincinnati* opened fire, and its first three shots splashed well short of Fort Henry. "There was twenty-four dollars' worth of ammunition expended," a gunner on the *Essex* said sarcastically. Nearby, Jack Matthews, "an 'old Tar'" from the English navy, elevated the *Essex*'s No. 2 gun and sent the boat's first shot into the fort. When the commander of the No. 1 gun reprimanded Matthews, the old sailor merely touched his cap and "coolly replied" that he had made a good shot. When the No. 1 gun followed suit, Job

Philips, its fourteen-year-old powder boy, took a rusty nail and scratched a line in the whitewashed casemate. As Philips made more scratches, the men threw off their coats and shirts to move faster. Soon their faces were blackened with grime and powder. The cannonading was immense, despite Foote's admonitions to save money. Philips made seventy scratches that day. The *St. Louis* trailed behind with thirty-seven salvos.[17]

Even though Union gunners struck the fort and caused some damage, it was unlikely they could force the Confederates to surrender. The inexperienced bluejackets simply could not inflict enough damage. Even with experienced sailors, it was difficult for naval gun crews to hit a target, even a stationary one. Accuracy was predicated on several factors: experience, training, natural aptitude, grit, the quality of the cannon, and chance. Gun captains considered the wind and the movement of the boat when selecting their weapon's elevation and aim. Firing an exploding projectile was even more challenging. The gun captain then also had to determine the length of the fuse (normally spelled "fuze" during the war), which was lit by the explosion of the powder charge that launched the projectile. A fuse burned for a specific length of time before detonating the charge inside the round. The gun captain usually cut the fuse to length and inserted it into a wooden fuse plug in the shell. It was a tricky business to gauge the amount of time the projectile would be in the air before it should explode. Worse still, river currents ensured that gunners never fired from the same location twice. A change in position of even a few inches was magnified when firing a projectile for a mile or more.

As the Union boats pressed forward, rebel gunners started to find their mark. The rounds fired from their Columbiad let out a "wild whistle" as they screamed past the Union boats, probably because they wobbled coming out of the ancient gun. One shot came so close to Foote that it knocked the wind out of him when it rushed past. On the *Essex* a shot came through the No. 2 gunport and broke "the handle of the sponge between Jack Rogers hands," took off the top of another gunner's head, smashed through the bulkhead, and slashed open the boiler. Steam shot out of the cylinder and scalded the forward gunners. James Coffey, a shotman to the No. 2 gun, was on his knees in the act of taking a shell from the box when steam burned off his face. Both pilots were scalded to death, one of them still standing erect and holding the signal-bell rope. Porter instinctively tried to dive overboard when the boiler erupted. Sailor Jack Walker caught the badly scalded captain around the waist and steered him to the boat's stern instead. The quick-thinking Walker probably saved Porter's life, as most of the men who jumped overboard were carried underwater by the strong current. The disabled gunboat dropped out of formation and drifted downstream "like a log" until a tug towed it to safety.[18]

The burst boiler was a grim reminder of a specific danger that brown-water sailors faced. Gunner William Park, who watched his best friend die an agonizing death, said the scene was "sickening to look at. I shall not attempt to describe it." The incident resonated through the fleet. A sailor on the *Mound City,* which had stayed behind in Cairo, was stunned when the casualties arrived at fleet headquarters. He told his fiancée that he "saw most of the bodies brought back, and indeed the sight was awful." Besides the thirteen dead solemnly brought to Cairo, another forty-two sailors were wounded.[19]

Soon after the *Essex* tragedy, Tilghman ordered Fort Henry to strike its colors. The sailors on the gunboats still in action erupted in cheers. Foote, never one to cede any control over his crew, "had to run among the men and knock them on the head to restore order." Confederate soldiers rowed Tilghman out to the *Cincinnati,* where Foote received him and accepted the official surrender. Soon thereafter the army arrived, delayed by its slog through the muddy backcountry. In this important victory, which opened up Union access to the Tennessee River in the Confederacy, the navy carried the day. While Foote sent the *Essex, Cincinnati,* and *St. Louis* to Cairo for repairs, he looked to use the timberclads to cause further damage upriver.[20]

The three timberclads steamed up the Tennessee River, with wide-ranging orders to destroy a railroad bridge and capture or destroy any Confederate gunboats encountered. During the five-day mission, the boats went to Florence, Alabama, nearly two hundred miles upstream. Sailors tore up the Memphis, Clarksville, and Louisville Railroad's bridge and damaged some of the trestlework. They also seized two steamers, forced rebels to burn six steamboats, seized military supplies, and captured the *Eastport* at Cerro Gordo, Tennessee, where the rebels were in the process of converting it into an ironclad. Attempts to scuttle the *Eastport* came to naught, and Phelps towed the boat to Cairo, where northern workers finished the job of making it an ironclad.[21]

While Phelps roamed up the Tennessee, Grant wanted to immediately attack Fort Donelson. Foote refused. An impatient Grant then ordered the

Carondelet to proceed to Fort Donelson, apparently in hopes that Foote would send support for the lone boat. The latter action put Walke, newly promoted to commander and the ironclad's captain, in a bind. He was compelled to obey the general's order, but he risked infuriating his direct superior. But Foote reluctantly gave in. He shuffled crews around and dispatched the ironclads *St. Louis, Pittsburg,* and *Louisville* to join the *Carondelet* in attacking Fort Donelson. Additionally, two of the three timberclads returned from their raid in time to help the fleet on the Cumberland. Grant's pressure on Walke illustrates the importance of the brown-water navy to the main Union advance in the western theater. The general knew that he needed the fleet's help to capture the fort.[22]

The Union army and the *Carondelet* arrived at Fort Donelson on February 12. Early the next morning, a courier reached Walke and told him that Grant had the fort surrounded on the land side. The general sent orders that in a few hours Walke was to shell Donelson as a diversion while the army attacked. At about 9:00 A.M. the *Carondelet* opened fire. The ironclad's gunners fired an astonishing 139 times that day, but only the penultimate shot caused any damage, dismounting a 32-pounder and killing the commander of the river batteries, who happened to be passing by the gun at the time. The *Carondelet* took only two hits, one of which penetrated the casemate and ricocheted around the boat's interior. It knocked down a dozen sailors like so many bowling pins and "seemed to bound after the men . . . like a wild beast pursuing its prey," an engineer told Walke. Grant's army made no headway against the rebel defenses, and the day ended with no decisive results for either side.[23]

Close to midnight, Foote and the five additional gunboats "came to anchor during a heavy snow fall alongside the *Carondelet,*" as the commander of the *Pittsburg* noted. Grant got even better news: twelve transports carrying 10,000 Union reinforcements also arrived. This overnight jolt changed the battle's trajectory.[24]

Grant met with Foote and told the flag officer to hurl his ironclads against Fort Donelson and pummel the water batteries. Then, the boats would steam upriver past the fort and shell the enemy lines. With the Confederates sufficiently weakened, Grant's soldiers would fight their way into Donelson. Foote protested. He knew that his gunboats would be vulnerable to plunging fire and wanted to wait for the mortar boats to arrive from Cairo. Grant waved off Foote's objections and predicted that the navy's big guns would carry the day.[25]

Union commanders spent the next morning getting ready for battle. Walke ordered his men to stack chains, lumber, and bags of coal on the boat's upper decks as protection against plunging fire. Lieutenant Egbert Thompson, captain of the *Pittsburg,* took heed of the *Essex*'s misfortune at Fort Henry and ordered his men to pile hammocks and bread bags full of coal around the boilers. Before the ironclads went into battle a second time, their weaknesses were already apparent.[26]

As the gunboats crept forward on February 14, Grant stood on shore to watch the battle in hopeful anticipation that his predictions would come true. About a mile from Fort Donelson, the *St. Louis* opened the ball. Gun captains on the other boats immediately yanked their lanyards, and balls hurtled towards the rebel stronghold. Foote yelled into a megaphone and ordered the boats "not to fire so fast." It was no use. A sailor who had been transferred from the *Essex* to the *Pittsburg* scribbled in his diary that he and the other gunners were "loading and firing as rapidly as we could run the guns out." It was "one continual boom and roar," wrote a rebel soldier inside the fort.[27]

As the boats slowly advanced, Confederate shells came screaming out of the fort and its batteries. Some splashed in the water, others clanged off the casemates, but several caused damage. One shot ripped away the *Louisville*'s tiller ropes. The crew could hardly steer the boat as a result, and it moved out of harm's way before the ironclad sustained any serious damage. Two balls pierced the *Pittsburg*'s bow, another struck its pilot house, and a fourth penetrated its gun deck, coming so close to a sponger's head that it burned his skin and made his nose bleed. Other balls knocked the boat's flag into the water and tore away ladders, davits, and lifeboats. The *Carondelet* took a mighty beating. One shot smashed the anchor to bits and tore through a smokestack, another ripped through the pilot house and killed a pilot, and others tore off the side armor "as lighting tears the bark from a tree," according to Walke.[28]

Despite the pounding, Foote ordered the fleet to chug even closer. Union gunners had not silenced any Confederate guns to this point, and it looked like Foote was throwing good money after bad. By the time the boats were within a quarter mile of the fort, some Union gun captains switched to grapeshot. As one Confederate put it, the ironclads were trying to "run our guners away from thear Guns." But the Union bombardment was more sound than fury. Federal gunners did no structural damage to the water batteries, failed to silence any southern guns, and wounded only a few rebel soldiers.[29]

The Confederates poured it on. A blast to the *St. Louis* nearly obliterated the pilot house and carried away the wheel, making it difficult to steer the boat. Shell fragments killed one pilot and struck Foote in his left foot. As the boat reversed its engines and hove out of action, another rebel shot smashed through the casemate and sent shell fragments and splinters spinning through the air. A chunk of wood tore into Foote's left arm. The flagship dropped downstream.[30]

The *Pittsburg* and *Carondelet* gamely kept fighting but got badly mauled. The water batteries, nearly level with the Cumberland, skipped cannonballs across the river's surface into the *Pittsburg*'s hull, nearly sinking the gunboat. One exhausted sailor wrote that the crew "was all night bailing her out." Two Confederate shots entered the *Carondelet*'s bow ports, decapitating three men. By this time, there was so much blood on the sand-covered floor of the gun deck, Walke later wrote, "that our men could not work the guns without slipping." Two skip shots punched holes in the ironclad. Once Foote called off the attack, Grant aborted his planned assault, and the Federals spent a miserable night on the cold ground.[31]

Foote despondently tallied up the wreckage to the Western Gunboat Flotilla: fifty-four men killed or wounded plus significant damage to three more ironclads. The flagship *St. Louis* sustained fifty-nine hits, the *Pittsburg* withstood at least thirty shots, and Confederate gunners hit the *Carondelet* fifty-four times.[32]

Foote wanted no more of Fort Donelson and decided to take the Western Flotilla back to Cairo for repairs. He needed to tell Grant of his decision, but his own wounds were serious enough that he could not ride a horse. Instead, Grant rode eight miles to the fleet. Sailors wrapped in heavy blankets were waiting for the general and rowed him to the *St. Louis* in a skiff. Foote broke the bad news, but Grant protested that he needed the ironclads to stay while he invested the fort. They then agreed on a compromise: Foote would depart with two ironclads and leave two others to protect the Union transports. But the Confederates had plans of their own.[33]

While Grant and Foote haggled, the encircled garrison launched a desperate attack against the Union right flank. The rebels were initially successful, in part because Grant had not designated an alternate commander during his absence. The southerners dithered, however, and Grant rushed back to his army and took decisive action. He reasoned that the Confederates had pulled men from their right flank to make the attack, so he launched an overwhelming sortie against it. The *St. Louis* pitched in by lobbing shells against Fort Donelson. The fort and its garrison surrendered the next day, opening the Cumberland River as a Union invasion route. Unlike Fort Henry, the army carried the day at Fort Donelson.[34]

The twin Union victories had significant consequences. Grant captured nearly 15,000 enemy soldiers and became the nation's first great hero. Federal forces broke the Confederate defensive line in the western theater and forced the abandonment of the works at Columbus, Kentucky. Now, the army and navy could advance along the Mississippi, Cumberland, and Tennessee Rivers into the western half of Tennessee. Union forces captured Nashville within days and seemed poised to strike farther south. Corinth, Mississippi, an important rail junction near the Tennessee border that was, in Grant's words, "the great strategic position at the West," was suddenly vulnerable. To accomplish its capture, the army once again needed the navy's help.[35]

On March 1, 1862, Foote sent the timberclads *Tyler* and *Lexington,* carrying men from the 32nd Illinois Infantry, in search of a suitable landing spot on the Tennessee River near Corinth. Once again the timberclads did the work of cavalry, scouting and securing an advance position. Because of the rainy spring, there was only one reasonable choice: Pittsburg Landing in far southern Tennessee. This eastern terminus of the Corinth Road was a cleared chunk of land about 200 yards wide and a half mile long. The Confederates had tried to fortify the site, but the timberclads chased them away with grapeshot that "sent them helter-skelter over the brow of the hill." The two boats afterward escorted the Union transports that brought Grant's army to the landing. Union control of the rivers made possible this advance into Confederate territory.[36]

On April 6 the *Tyler* and *Lexington* were on routine duty near Pittsburg Landing. Early on that sunny morning, Confederate soldiers came crashing through the Tennessee forest and caught Grant's army unprepared. In what became known as the Battle of Shiloh, the Confederates pushed the Army of the Tennessee back toward the Tennessee River. Normally, an army with its back to a river was vulnerable because it had no means of retreat. The timberclads, however, functioned as heavy artillery and helped beat back the rebels' final attack of the day. They were helpful but not decisive in what the next day, after reinforcement by part of the Army of the Ohio, became a victory for the Army of the Tennessee.[37]

The fighting along the Tennessee and Cumberland Rivers revealed strengths and weaknesses of the Western Gunboat Flotilla. The iron plating on the city-class boats was stout enough to endure a terrific beating. Union gun crews proved their valor and worth in battle. But the boats were also vulnerable to a well-placed shot, normally one striking an armored seam. One round to a boiler was enough to knock out an ironclad. The peculiar conditions of the western rivers, moreover, limited the boats' ability to reduce a well-constructed fort to rubble. The rivers forced them to fight head-on instead of steaming parallel and firing broadsides, as was normal for a blue-water fleet. These cramped conditions limited the amount of metal the gunboats could hurl at a Confederate bastion and seemed to confirm the old naval adage that a ship was a fool to fight a fort.

It is no small thing that Foote and Grant cooperated with one another, but their actions were not fully integrated. The navy captured Fort Henry with little help from the army, while the opposite was true at Fort Donelson. A simultaneous advance along the Mississippi River, however, proved the value of true combined operations to success in the West.

Despite the victories at Forts Henry and Donelson, Foote was angry and frustrated. His wounded foot kept him on crutches and throbbed in pain. He needed to repair his battered fleet, supervise additional armor for pilot houses (or else his current pilots would refuse to go back into combat), and scrounge up more sailors. As the flag officer turned his attention to the hydra of problems that faced him, the military situation changed dramatically. Halleck displayed a surprising sense of urgency and sent Brigadier General John Pope's Army of the Mississippi against the Confederate stronghold at Island No. 10. Located about thirty miles downriver from Columbus in the bootheel of Missouri, Island No. 10 was so named because it was the tenth island south of the Mississippi River's junction with the Ohio River. Although the island no longer exists, in 1862 it was situated in a perfect place to obstruct river traffic. The Mississippi River made two sharp turns, creating an "S" flipped backward and turned on its side. Island No. 10 was in the middle of the river on the bottom, or southeastern, curve, and New Madrid, Missouri, was atop the second, or northwestern, curve. The low island was about a mile long and a quarter mile wide. Swamps in the pocket on the river's left bank prevented Pope's army from getting close enough to attack the garrison, while marshes on the right bank also shielded the fort. With a land assault unfeasible, the army either had to besiege the stronghold or batter it into submission. In either case, Pope needed siege guns and Foote's gunboats. He got the guns from Halleck but had less luck with the navy.[38]

Foote was in no mood to cooperate with either Halleck or Pope. He was peeved that the navy received no credit for the victory at Fort Donelson and was "disgusted" that Halleck prevented the fleet from capturing Nashville. In a letter to his wife that betrayed a tinge of insubordination, the by-the-book Foote declared that he "will not obey any orders except the Secretary [of the navy]'s and President's." He was true to his word after receiving a telegram from Halleck on March 4, 1862. Old Brains told Foote to forget about repairing his fleet but instead to move his gunboats and mortars to Island No. 10 and, "if possible," assist Pope in making "an immediate demonstration."[39]

After venting his frustration to Halleck's chief of staff, Foote decided to cooperate with Pope. He sent the ironclads *St. Louis, Carondelet, Pittsburg, Mound City, Cincinnati, Benton* (newly converted); the timberclad *Conestoga;* eight mortar boats; two ordnance boats; a coal barge; and several transports. On March 14, the day Pope captured New Madrid, Foote moved down the Mississippi River in the rain and fog.[40]

Once the fleet arrived near Columbus, Foote put the mortars in position to shell the island and went forward in the *Benton* to scout the Confederate position. What he saw was formidable: five batteries on shore, with twenty-four guns, and five more batteries on the island, with nineteen guns. He could tell that the earthen walls that protected the guns were substantial and later learned that they were twenty feet thick in spots. Foote also spotted the CSS *New Orleans,* a floating battery with nine guns. Even though the Confederates at Island No. 10 did not have the advantage of plunging fire, their fifty-two guns, which included a 128-pounder Columbiad named "Lady Polk, Jr.," were positioned in such a way as to create a crossfire. After a half-hearted attack on March 17, Foote concluded that a long-range bombardment was the best strategy. He was ready for a siege.[41]

But an impatient Pope was not ready for a siege. He wanted to put pressure on the Confederates by moving troops across the Mississippi River to the eastern shore. His chief engineer asked Foote to run an ironclad past the Confederate defenses so that it could protect the army while it crossed the river below them. The flag officer convened a meeting on the *Benton* to discuss the request, and accounts differ as to the day of the meeting and even who was present. It was clear, though, that Foote held the council of war not to hear the views of his commanders, but to reiterate his decision to continue the bombardment. One or two commanders argued for an aggressive strategy. Foote refused to budge. In a telegram to Halleck, he recited an extensive list of reasons why one or more of the gunboats should not run past the batteries: if the attempt failed, "the rivers above us . . . would be greatly exposed" to Confederate attack; the boats were ill adapted to fighting downstream; two cannons had burst on his vessels; and the fleet's shells were "imperfect." For good measure, Foote added that he himself was still on crutches and his wound was not healing. He was also dealing with a personal tragedy: his thirteen-year-old son died unexpectedly. The pressure of command, his painful wound, and this devastating personal news weighed heavily on the flag officer.[42]

Foote's caution is understandable. Besides the reasons he fired off to Halleck, a lone Union boat below Island No. 10 would be vulnerable. If the siege lasted a long time, the ironclad might run out of coal or food, and its crew would have to go ashore and get supplies. While such foraging expeditions for Union boats would eventually become common, they were untried in March 1862. Foote also heard rumors that the Confederates were building two large ironclads at Memphis; if one or both swung into action, a lone Union boat could be captured or destroyed. None of this pleased Pope, who cursed when he learned of Foote's intransigence.[43]

For two weeks, Foote resisted all pressure to "run the blockade" but finally relented at the end of March. The reasons for the change are unclear, but they might be related to Pope's telegram to Halleck to ask the secretary of war to remove the naval crews from two gunboats and turn the vessels over to the army. Foote had to take Pope's gambit seriously since the gunboats were army property. The flag officer convened a council of war a few days later and secured Commander Walke's commitment to run the *Carondelet* past the Confederate guns.[44]

Walke's men took extensive action to prepare for any number of desperate scenarios. They piled hawsers, haybales, and chains on the vulnerable deck; wound hawsers around the pilot house; built wooden barriers around the boilers; rerouted the steam pipe to muffle noise; closed all the gunports; hooked a hose to the boilers for use to scald boarders; brought twenty sharpshooters on board; and lashed a barge full of coal and hay on the port side in order to protect the magazine. An officer from the *Cincinnati* with two decades of experience on the Mississippi River agreed to pilot the vessel. If something went terribly wrong, Walke was to destroy the steam machinery, set fire to the gunboat or sink it, and send the men ashore.[45]

Fortune favored the bold on April 4, 1862. The weather during the day was clear and pleasant, but as the sun set, a storm blew in. Rain poured down in sheets, and the night was "dark as pitch" when the *Carondelet* shoved off at 10:00 P.M. When John Morrison peeked out from the gun deck, he saw flashes of lighting that "made everything look weird-like and fantastic." The ironclad drifted with the current. As the boat passed in front of Battery No. 2, flames shot from the smokestacks, but the Confederates failed to see the sparks. Minutes later another flame appeared. An irritated Walke later learned that the rerouting of the steam pipe had made the soot in the stacks more combustible. A rebel lookout spotted this second flame, and immediately five rockets screamed into the air and a cannon boomed. Walke ordered the boat to full steam ahead. Sailor Charles Wilson stood "knee-deep in the foaming water on the forecastle heaving the lead" to make sure the ironclad did not run aground.[46]

The Confederate barrage was frightening but ineffectual. Southern gunners could not track the boat's path since the driving rain obscured their vision and the brilliant lightning acted like a strobe light, freezing the boat's silhouette for a second. The wind, which was so strong that it forced one rebel soldier to hold on to a tree lest he be blown into the river, blinded the Confederates. A sailor on the *Mound City* who visited the fort after the battle speculated that the island's embankment also prevented the southerners from lowering their guns far enough to hit the boat. The *Carondelet* roared past the fort unscathed, and it was anticlimactic when the boat ran aground below it. After refloating and reaching New Madrid, all hands "spliced the main brace."[47]

A few days later Pope asked Foote to send another gunboat past Island No. 10. Despite much grumbling and complaining that the loss of a boat might lead to the downfall of western society, Foote agreed to send the *Pittsburg* through the gauntlet. Its crew took the same precautions as the *Carondelet*. Somewhat miraculously, another storm front blew through the area and "poured down one of the most tremendous deluges of rain that I ever saw," according to a sailor on the *Pittsburg*. The ironclad grounded during the run but easily ran past Island No. 10. About the same time, Union crews brought four transports through the swamps. Pope was now ready for the final phase of the battle for Island No. 10.[48]

Pope ordered Walke to silence a small Confederate fort that could threaten Union troops when they crossed the river. Walke directed that the *Pittsburg* follow him and the *Carondelet* into battle, but Commander Stembel replied that his ironclad was not ready. The tempestuous Walke went into battle anyway and methodically advanced on the fort. Union gunners worked deliberately and went so far as to wait for the smoke to clear before firing a follow-up salvo. Broadsides of grapeshot and canister sent Confederates "flying over the corn fields." As the *Carondelet* was trying to smash the last rebel gun, the *Pittsburg* joined the fray and started firing cannonballs just over its sister boat's bow. A furious Walke waved his speaking trumpet at Stembel to cease fire. When the action died down, Walke sent a small party on shore to spike the two guns that had been dismounted. Both boats then went upstream and silenced two more batteries.[49]

After the engagement, Brigadier General David Stanley came on board the *Carondelet* to congratulate Walke. While they exchanged kind words, Stembel came on board to join in the fun. Walke pounced. "D— you, I don't congratulate you, you skulked behind my boat and fired shells over my deck," recorded a flummoxed Stanley. For good measure, Walke swore again and yelled, "if you ever do such a thing again I will turn my batteries on you and blow you out of the water." A shocked Stembel gave no reply.[50]

The ironclads protected Pope's army while it crossed the river and outflanked the Confederates. Southerners at Island No. 10 started deserting in droves. As the garrison melted away, Confederate commanders simultaneously tried to withdraw their remaining forces and surrender the post. Two southern lieutenants in the rebel steamer *De Soto* reached Foote on April 7—the same day as the second day of Shiloh—with word that they wanted to discuss surrender terms. Foote sent Phelps ashore to speak to the Confederate commander, who confirmed the capitulation. The arrogant Pope took credit for the victory and was not as magnanimous as Grant in giving any credit to the navy. In a move that angered Foote, the general praised Walke's courage in running past Island No. 10 but barely mentioned the flotilla's other efforts.[51]

More so than Forts Henry and Donelson, the victory at Island No. 10 took deep cooperation between the army and navy and hinted at the future for the brown-water fleet. The runs of the *Carondelet* and *Pittsburg* past the Confederate batteries defied conventional wisdom and showed that shore-based gunners had difficulty hitting a moving target in darkness. The campaign provided a blueprint for the fleet's role at Vicksburg: run past the batteries, squelch opposition south of the bastion, and move an army across the Mississippi River.

The combat along the Cumberland, Tennessee, and Mississippi Rivers in early 1862 confirmed the Western Gunboat Flotilla's centrality to any Union advance. Foote and his gunboats largely captured Fort Henry, while the victory at Fort Donelson belonged to Grant. In both cases Grant and Foote deserve credit for working together to make the victories possible. On the Mississippi Pope needed Foote's ironclads in order to capture Island No. 10. Gunboats proved their utility in other ways. The timberclads rescued Grant at Belmont, scouted Confederate defenses, and secured the steamboat landing near Shiloh. During the same time, the Western Gunboat Flotilla also fought the Confederacy's brown-water navy. Its combat with enemy vessels once again demonstrated how Union naval forces adapted to conditions in the western theater.[52]

5

DESTROYING THE CONFEDERATE FLEET

After the victories at Forts Henry and Donelson, Shiloh, and Island No. 10, several more prizes remained. Union leaders wanted to capture the Mississippi River towns of New Orleans, Memphis, and Vicksburg. Doing so would not only open the Mississippi to commerce but also shut down the transfer of supplies from the regions west of the river to the rest of the Confederacy. Doing so required combat against a small Confederate fleet and an unusual rebel ram. Union naval efforts involved coordination between the Western Gunboat Flotilla, an improvised ram fleet, and blue-water ships that ventured into the lower Mississippi. Once again, the gunboats would prove themselves necessary for any Union advance into southern territory.

After the surrender of Island No. 10 on April 8, 1862, one more obstacle remained before Union gunboats could threaten Memphis. Fort Pillow was a series of breastworks perched on the brow of a 150-foot bluff on the Mississippi River's eastern bank. About forty heavy guns inside the hastily built emplacement had a commanding view of the river. The Confederates also had eight small gunboats sheltered beneath the safety of the cannons. Foote, recently promoted to rear admiral, had no hope of knocking out the elevated batteries with his flotilla. He called for the mortar boats to soften up the fort in preparation for an army assault. Foote brought five ironclads, several mortar boats, and some tugs to Craigshead Point, about two miles upstream from Fort Pillow. This flotilla was hidden from the fort but close enough for the mortars to go to work.[1]

Rear Admiral Foote's plans crumbled immediately. Major General Halleck ordered all the western Union armies to Pittsburg Landing in preparation for an overland advance against Corinth. A frustrated Foote, who was still on crutches, had few choices except lobbing mortar shells into Fort Pillow in hopes of forcing its surrender. Starting in mid-April, each day an ironclad would tow a mortar boat into place, the shelling would commence, and several hours later the ironclad brought the mortar boat back to safety. This desultory bombardment was wholly ineffective. Foote was stuck. He did not have permission to retreat, he could not take the fort without infantry support, and he now faced a new foe: the River Defense Fleet.[2]

The Confederacy created the River Defense Fleet in early 1862. Riverboat captain James E. Montgomery rounded up fourteen steamboats and converted them to fighting vessels. Most of the boats had cotton squeezed between thick timbers for protection and possessed some type of light armor, usually railroad iron nailed to the casemates. Four of these "cottonclads," as they were known, were fitted with iron rams. Confederate leaders intended for the fleet to protect New Orleans, but when that city fell in March, Montgomery brought eight boats upriver to Plum Point to guard Fort Pillow.[3]

The River Defense Fleet was a manifestation of Confederate desperation in the face of superior Union industrial capacity. Cotton squeezed between bulkheads and railroad iron were quick, inexpensive, and achievable ways to assemble protected vessels into a fleet in a region that was unable to manufacture iron plates in large quantities. Yet these boats were hastily thrown together, woefully underpowered, and dependent on luck and surprise. The use of rams in naval combat revived a tactic that had been dead for centuries. With the construction of southern ironclad rams lagging behind schedule, this improvised fleet was the Confederacy's best river defense against the Western Gunboat Flotilla.[4]

Life in the Union squadron was miserable. The sailors on the ironclads had little to do other than drill and swat mosquitoes. "Nothing going on," was the common refrain that John Morrison recorded in his diary during April. Symmes Browne complained that the mosquitoes were "so numerous and troublesome here that we cannot write at night." What Browne and his fellow sailors did not know was that the mosquitoes brought an epidemic of malaria to the fleet. Up to one-third of the men languishing at Craigshead Point were on the sick list on any given day. "I am sick with the ague," Morrison told his diary. "Feel bad."[5]

Foote also felt terrible. In April fleet surgeons agreed that his injury would soon render him "totally unfit" for duty. They recommended that "for the future interest of the flotilla," the admiral be sent home to recuperate. Foote suggested that Flag Officer Charles H. Davis assume temporary command of the flotilla.

The two men were good friends, having served together on the frigate *United States,* but Davis was wholly unprepared to fill in for Foote. He was bookish, unimaginative, deeply suspicious of the new naval technology, completely unfamiliar with warfare on the western rivers, and steeped in the ways of the old navy. While appearances can be deceiving, Davis's was not. With his epaulettes, gold braid, and a bodacious walrus mustache, he looked like "a character from Gilbert and Sullivan." Davis reported aboard the *Benton* on Foote's last day with the fleet.[6]

Foote was not the type to craft a stirring farewell speech to the sailors he had led for eight months. As he hobbled from the USS *Benton* to the transport *De Soto* on May 9, the ironclad's officers and men gave three cheers. All hands on the other boats stood at attention and saluted the rear admiral as he passed by. "He looked very pale and feeble," thought Morrison.[7]

Even though Foote was gone, his legacy remained. In a landscape that favored rivalry between the navy and army rather than cooperation, he worked with Major General Grant and Brigadier General Pope during what were the first combined operations of the war. Foote established that the Western Gunboat Flotilla was an equal partner with the army. He used poor tactics at Fort Donelson and was initially flummoxed at Island No. 10, but he adapted. That Foote allowed two gunboats to run past the latter stronghold was indicative of his capacity to listen to other options. He also coordinated the successful commissioning of ten gunboats and scraped together enough crews to man them all. Foote successfully combined administrative acumen with a fighting spirit and created conditions for the future success and growth of the Western Gunboat Flotilla. Sadly, he did not live to see the ultimate success of the fleet that he built. Bright's Disease killed Andrew Foote on June 26, 1863.[8]

On May 10, 1862, Davis's first as commander, the Union fleet began the day as it had for the last four weeks. The USS *Cincinnati* slipped its cable and towed a mortar boat through the fog to a position about three miles from the rest of the flotilla. As the ironclad eased its way to the bank, *Mortar Boat No. 16* fired its first shell of the day. Suddenly, several Union lookouts spotted dense clouds of smoke in the direction of Fort Pillow. It was the eight boats of the River Defense Fleet charging upriver. These cottonclads intended to ram the *Cincinnati* and, if they were lucky, sink or capture it. In the process they would swipe the mortar boat.[9]

Mortar Boat No. 16 had few options since it was a round tub with no motive power. Second Master Thomas B. Gregory, who commanded it, reported that he "trained my mortar upon" the attackers, shortened the fuse, and burst "my shell directly over them." Despite taking a 32-pounder and using dangerously short fuses, Gregory gamely kept up his barrage.[10]

Coal heavers in the *Cincinnati* desperately shoveled fuel into the bunkers to raise steam. They threw "oil and everything else inflammable into her fires," recalled an ensign on the boat. Commander Stembel, the captain, managed to swing his gunboat around and, at a distance of fifty yards, fired its four starboard guns at the CSS *General Bragg.* The barrage did nothing to slow down the ram, which struck the *Cincinnati,* gouging out a chunk of the hull twelve feet long. Water poured into the magazine as sailors rushed to contain the damage. The *General Bragg* reversed its wheels, but the two boats were locked together. Stembel saw his chance and shouted, "Give her another broadside, boys!" With a cheer, the gunners fired even though they could not run the cannons out of the gunports. The resulting salvo flicked the *General Bragg* away and "tore an immense hole in her from side to side." The cottonclad nevertheless limped to safety.[11]

Before the *Cincinnati* could move to protect the mortar boat, two more rams closed on it. The CSS *General Price* struck first and crushed the ironclad's rudders and steering apparatus. The blow swung the *Cincinnati* around, exposing its side. The CSS *Sumter* then slammed into the ironclad's midsection. Water now flooded the engine room and extinguished the boiler fires. The ironclad was now dead in the water. Minié balls from Confederate sharpshooters zinged through the air and clattered off the iron plating. Stembel went on deck to assess the damage and took a ball through the neck. A Union sailor immediately shot the assailant, and bluejackets squirted scalding water from the boilers into the Confederate boats to keep boarders at bay. Lieutenant William Hoel took command of the *Cincinnati* and rushed to the gun deck, where he shouted: "Boys, give 'em the best you've got! we ain't dead yet!" The gunners fired one last broadside because the rest of the ammunition was soaked. The pilot tried to steer the vessel toward the bank, but the *Cincinnati* soon settled in twelve feet of water. Union sailors clambered onto the wheelhouse and perched there "like so many turkeys on a corncrib."[12]

The *Cincinnati*'s desperate defense bought enough time for the ironclads *Mound City, Benton,* and *Carondelet* to beat to quarters and chug downriver. First in line was the *Mound City,* which faced off against the CSS *Van Dorn.* The ironclad's gunners "were pouring broadside after broadside" into the rebel boat, a Union officer wrote. The *Van Dorn* took a terrific pounding. Despite bearing so many holes that Union balls started flying untouched through the cottonclad, it still advanced. The *Van Dorn* crashed into the *Mound City,* tearing away the ironclad's forecastle and causing it to spin around so that it was facing upstream. The rebel ram ricocheted to the Arkansas shore but rushed through the dense smoke to attack again. This time it missed, but sailors on both boats exchanged gunfire. "The bullets whistled thick," commented one sailor on the *Mound City.* As water gushed into the ironclad, Commander Augustus Kilty steered it to shoal water, where it sank. The Confederates had knocked a second ironclad out of action.[13]

It was now up to the *Benton* and *Carondelet* to continue the fight against the remaining three Confederate boats. At least one southern ram tried to capture the mortar boat, but the *Benton*'s "shots played so fast around them that they had to let go," a Union sailor proudly told his mother. By this point, the *Benton* was amid the Confederate boats and "throwing shot & shell in every direction." The flagship's vigorous defense convinced the Confederates to go after the *Carondelet,* which promptly sent a round from its 50-pounder into the *Sumter*'s boiler. Steam rushed out "in huge jets, from an hundred different places," Morrison wrote. Scalded sailors staggered to the deck, only to collapse and die. Another rebel boat came near the *Benton,* but two well-directed shots from the stern guns hit its wheelhouse, "and for a few minutes the air was full of splinters," according to Morrison. Montgomery knew that he had no chance of sinking any more Union boats, so he ordered the remnants of his fleet back downriver to the protection of Fort Pillow's guns. The battle was over.[14]

Both sides claimed victory, but the Battle of Plum Point was a draw. Four of the southern boats "were literally torn to pieces, and some had holes in their sides through which a man could walk," claimed the *Benton*'s commander. While it was difficult to miss the fact that "the river was white with cotton," the Confederates quickly patched up their damaged boats. Union losses were also temporary. Engineers raised the *Cincinnati* and *Mound City* and sent them north for repairs. More troubling for the Confederacy, and a conclusion that Montgomery and others failed to acknowledge, was that their boats could only be successful if conditions were ideal. The rams surprised the northern fleet because of lackadaisical Union preparation. It would not happen again. Davis assigned two boats to guard the daily mortar-boat movement and ordered workers to put railroad iron on the bows and sterns and to attach logs to the boats' sides. While the southerners initially had superior numbers, the ironclads' big guns riddled the flimsy Confederate boats. In the long run, Confederate speed could not best Union brawn.[15]

Factors outside of Davis's control brought a resolution to the doldrums at Fort Pillow. The army's occupation of Corinth in May flanked the fort and made its defense untenable. At dusk on June 4, Union sailors saw heavy clouds of smoke and the bright glare of a fire in the stronghold. A "sullen boom came floating through the calm evening air," Morrison wrote, and everyone knew that a magazine had exploded. During the night, the Confederates destroyed what they could not carry out of Fort Pillow. Early the next day, northerners raised the Stars and Stripes in triumph over the fort. With the simultaneous evacuation of Randolph, Tennessee, the Mississippi River was open to Memphis.[16]

The Western Gunboat Flotilla hastened downriver, and it was only a matter of days before it faced the Confederate Defense Fleet again under the Memphis bluffs. During the rematch, a new type of Union boat ensured that the results this time would be very different.

Charles Ellet Jr. was the man primarily responsible for the new type of Union boat. A notable civil engineer, Ellet had designed a suspension bridge across the Ohio River at Wheeling, Virginia. But no one in the U.S. government took Ellet's naval ideas seriously until he correctly predicted that the ram *Virginia* would threaten the Union naval blockade. Suddenly, Secretary of War Edwin M. Stanton was interested in hearing what the engineer had to say. After meeting the energetic Ellet, Stanton appointed him a colonel of engineers and sent him to the Mississippi valley in March 1862 to "take measures to provide steam rams for defense against ironclad vessels on the western waters." Ellet's boats would become known as the Ram Fleet and later be the nucleus for the Mississippi Marine Brigade.[17]

Ellet insisted that Stanton transfer his younger brother Alfred W. Ellet from the 59th Illinois Regiment to the Ram Fleet and promote him from captain to lieutenant colonel. Alfred brought along about fifty men from his unit, including his son Edward Ellet. Never one to shy away from nepotism, Charles also brought his nineteen-year-old son Charles Rivers Ellet into the Ram Fleet. Colonel Ellet reported directly to Stanton and was not required to coordinate with the Western Gunboat Flotilla. He had a daring spirit, a sense of invincibility, and a conviction that military orders did not apply to him.[18]

Ellet purchased seven steamboats and supervised their conversion to rams. He kept the machinery on deck and directed workers to reinforce the hulls, fill the bows with oak, construct three oaken bulkheads, and stiffen the boats with iron rods, braces, and stanchions. None of the rams had armor or cannons, as Ellet believed that gunnery was ineffective for boat-to-boat combat. When it was clear that the men of the 59th Illinois were not numerous enough to crew the vessels, the colonel recruited civilians and promised them extra pay for capturing or destroying enemy vessels. Ellet brought six of his rams to Memphis and anchored next to the Western Gunboat Flotilla about two miles above the city. It was June 5.[19]

Montgomery's River Defense Fleet was the city's only protection against the Union navy. He had few options. His patched-up boats had used up most of their coal at Plum Point, and there was none to be had in Memphis because of Confederate supply problems. "In view of their overwhelming strength I would have retreated," Montgomery noted in his official report, "but only one boat had sufficient coal to reach Vicksburg." He could either scuttle his boats or fight. Montgomery chose to fight.[20]

Davis knew none of this information, but he was eager to get revenge for Plum Point. He ordered the ironclads to drift downriver stern first. It was an unusual tactic because the boat's sterns had no armor, but Davis reasoned that if a boat was disabled or badly damaged, it stood a better chance of steaming forward rather than backing out of danger. He did not incorporate Ellet's Ram Fleet into his plans, but it appears that these boats were supposed to wait while the ironclads finished off the Confederates. Yet Ellet was not the type of man to wait.[21]

Even before the sun rose on June 6, the city had a festive air. The "bluffs in front of the city were crowded with spectators who were invited by Ed Montgomery to see the Yankees getting whipped," Morrison told his diary. Davis sent the *Benton* and *Louisville* to scout the Memphis waterfront. They reported that the eight boats of the River Defense Fleet were anchored at the wharf. The Union ironclads then returned to their place in line, and Davis let the fleet's sailors finish breakfast before ordering the attack. It was 4:20 A.M. Before the bluejackets could put away their dishes, the cottonclads *M. Jeff Thompson* and *Colonel Lovell* steamed into the river and started shooting at the Federal fleet. Davis ordered his boats to fight back, and as one sailor put it, the ironclads "let loose their fiery dogs." Union coal heavers redoubled their efforts to raise steam, and between the guns firing and the smokestacks belching, a sooty black cloud enveloped the Union fleet.[22]

At the sound of the guns, Ellet sprang to the deck and waved his hat to get Commander Walke's attention. "It is a gun from the enemy! Round out and follow me! Now is our chance!" he shouted to the puzzled naval officer. Ellet, who was on his flagship USS *Queen of the West,* then signaled to three other rams to advance. Only the USS *Monarch,* under the command of his brother Alfred, responded properly. The two little rams "fearlessly dashed" through the wall of smoke as Union sailors huzzahed. The boats met the Confederate fleet far out in front of the Western Gunboat Flotilla. No one could doubt Ellet's bravery.[23]

The *Queen of the West* faced off against the *Colonel Lovell,* and both boats charged at each other in a high-stakes game of chicken. Just as they were about to crash, the cottonclad's engine failed. The Confederate boat veered and presented its side for attack. The *Queen of the West* crashed into the cottonclad. Plates, cookware, and half-eaten breakfasts flew through the Union ram's cabin, but the boat nearly sliced the *Lovell* in two. It sank so quickly that only five sailors escaped the southern coffin. While the *Queen of the West* tried to disentangle itself from the sinking *Lovell,* the CSS *General Beauregard* smashed into it, crushed its wheelhouse, and knocked the vessel out of action. Ellet rushed on deck to inspect the damage and took a bullet to his knee. His men carried him below deck.[24]

The ironclads had already started shelling the rest of the Confederate fleet by this time. With cannonballs splashing nearby, the *Monarch* slipped between the *General Price* and *General Beauregard.* The two southern boats collided and locked together. While the rebel boats tried to work free, the *Monarch* circled around and slammed into the *Beauregard.* The southern boats thereafter became unstuck but began taking heavy Union fire. The *Benton* finished off the *Beauregard* with a cannonball to the boiler, and other shots riddled the *Price,* which sank in shoal water. The *Monarch* started chasing the Confederate flagship *Little Rebel,* which had taken several shots and was moving toward the Arkansas shore. The Union ram struck it a glancing blow, and the cottonclad scudded into the Mississippi mud.[25]

This deadly game of demolition derby was enough to convince the remaining cottonclads to flee. The ironclads gave chase for about ten miles and peppered the Confederate boats. First to succumb was the *M. Jeff Thompson,* which became a flaming wreck when a Union shell hit its magazine. The explosion was "a terrific spectacle" that sent fragments whirling through the air for up to a mile. Union gunners put so many cannonballs through the *Sumter* that Confederates ran it to shore and abandoned it. Next was the *General Bragg.* Its upper works and hull were so shattered that it, too, ran aground. Confederates on the sinking boats grabbed life preservers and jumped into the muddy water, drifting as far as two miles downstream. Yet the exhausted sailors who made it to shore were not out of danger. Union sharpshooters "mowed them down . . . as they were crawling up the bank of the river," a bluejacket wrote. He estimated that 150 Confederate bodies bloodied the banks. During the melee, the Confederates' ammunition boat burned to the water's edge and then exploded. Fragments arced 900 feet in the air, and cotton bales sprinkled into the water. Only the *Van Dorn* escaped.[26]

Ezra Green, a sailor on the ironclad *Cincinnati,* dismissed the Confederate effort to defend Memphis as so paltry that it was merely "target practice" for the Western Gunboat Flotilla. Union gunners demonstrated a high level of competence, but Ellet deserves much credit for the victory. As Morrison noted, the rams "roamed about like the evil one seeking whom they might destroy." The Union boats sustained only one casualty: Charles Ellet. While in the hospital, the colonel contracted dysentery and measles and died fifteen days after the battle. Confederates lost all of their boats but the *Van Dorn.* Rebels also had to scuttle the *Tennessee,* an unfinished ironclad. Only the ironclad ram *Arkansas* escaped the debacle. Confederates towed it ninety miles up the Yazoo River to Greenwood, Mississippi. The fate of the *Arkansas* became bound up in the Union's effort to capture Vicksburg, which also involved another Union fleet.[27]

Rear Admiral Farragut led a fleet of blue-water screw sloops, gunboats, auxiliary vessels, and mortar schooners up the Mississippi River in 1862. The fleet captured New Orleans on March 25 and then took Baton Rouge, Louisiana, and Natchez, Mississippi. With this and the capture of Memphis, only Vicksburg and Port Hudson, a Confederate river stronghold in northern Louisiana, remained as significant obstacles. Farragut realized that his fleet alone could not force Vicksburg's surrender, so he took some of his ships past that city to link up with Davis. Confederate guns roared for ninety minutes as the fleet crawled upstream, but most of the ships survived the gauntlet. Farragut sent a message to

Davis requesting that he join the Union attack on Vicksburg. He also sent a message to Halleck asking him to send troops to Vicksburg. Halleck declined to cooperate, but Davis begrudgingly took the *Benton, Carondelet, Cincinnati, Louisville,* and six mortar boats downriver. They hovered between the mouth of the Yazoo River and De Soto Point in a bend of the Mississippi just above Vicksburg and out of range of the Confederate guns. The combined Union fleets shelled the town, more from a sense of obligation than a determination to force its surrender. Such was the military situation when the *Arkansas* entered the fray.[28]

The *Arkansas* was an unusual boat. Its designers intended it to operate on the rivers and the ocean. Its main offensive weapon was a nine-ton cast-iron ram that jutted four feet in front of the bow. The boat's rectangular casemate ran about half its length and protected three guns on each side as well as two in the front and two in the stern. Since the Confederacy did not have the industrial capacity to make armor plating, the *Arkansas* had railroad iron bolted to its casemate. Its power plant and means of propulsion proved inadequate. The boat had two high-pressure engines and screw propellers at a time when virtually every other steam-powered boat on the western waters used paddlewheels. The propellers were vulnerable to river debris, and the engines were unreliable. As a crew member recalled after the war, the "hermaphrodite-iron-clad" was a combination of "haste and incompetency." But Confederate leaders hoped to use the ram to wreak havoc on the Union fleet and relieve the pressure on Vicksburg.[29]

Lieutenant Isaac N. Brown commanded the *Arkansas.* He was a hard-driving Kentuckian who left the U.S. Navy in 1861 to join the Confederacy. Brown had orders to attack the Union fleet, fight his way to Vicksburg, and, according to some sources, continue to Mobile and take on Union blockaders. Brown finished the boat's construction after Memphis fell and guided it down the Yazoo River. As the *Arkansas* pushed on through the night, all "was quiet save the dull thump, thump of the propellers," remembered one sailor. Around midnight on July 14, the boat anchored at Haynes' Bluff, about ten miles from the mouth of the Yazoo—and the Union fleet. Once again the Confederates would catch the Western Gunboat Flotilla off guard.[30]

Vigilance within the two Union fleets had slipped. Despite rumors of a large Confederate boat lurking nearby, captains were lax. Most vessels banked their fires. The intense Mississippi heat was one reason to have low fires, but a coal shortage was another. The fleets were at the tail end of a supply line that started in Memphis. The low fires meant it would take the brown-water boats about thirty minutes to get underway in an emergency. Farragut's ships would take four times as long.[31]

When five southern deserters told stories that a Confederate ram was on the move, Davis decided to investigate. At 4:00 A.M. on July 15, he sent the ironclad *Carondelet,* timberclad *Tyler,* and Ellet ram *Queen of the West* to the Yazoo River. While the *Carondelet* waited at the river's mouth, the other two boats chugged through the mist that covered the sinuous stream. They soon found the *Arkansas,* which sent a 64-pounder shell screaming over the *Tyler*'s stacks. Bluejackets, who should have been at their battle stations, brushed aside their breakfasts and "sprang to the guns without waiting for the boatswain's whistle."[32]

The *Tyler* opened a noisy and ineffective cannonade. The timberclad's only success came when a curious crewman in the *Arkansas* stuck his head out a gunport and was decapitated. The rebel ram abused the *Tyler.* One sailor remembered, "Eleven shots [went] through us from stern to stem and killed several men." One of them exploded in the engine room, where bloody men staggered and collapsed; a pilot had his arm torn off. The *Queen of the West* steamed toward the rebel boat with the intention of ramming it. When the *Arkansas* fired a broadside at the unarmored boat, it skedaddled downriver. Lieutenant William Gwin, commanding the *Tyler,* bitterly resented being left alone to face the Confederate goliath and accused the ram's commander of behaving "in a most cowardly and dastardly manner." But the *Tyler* also fled, its firemen furiously shoveling coal into the fires.[33]

The timberclad soon came under protection of the *Carondelet*'s guns. Walke's men opened fire on the "formidable looking monster" as it emerged from the Yazoo River. Their initial salvo splashed into the river, and ensuing blasts clanged off the brown casemate. The *Arkansas* now concentrated its fire on the *Carondelet.* One solid shot, John Morrison wrote, punched a hole in the wheelhouse, "gutted the captain's cabin," crumpled some steam pipes, and "then rolled out on deck." The *Carondelet* spun around and chugged downriver. A low-speed chase ensued, and both boats scored hits. The *Arkansas* put at least eight balls into the *Carondelet,* but the Union ironclad responded with a "bolt" into the Confederate ram's pilot house, mortally wounding one pilot and disabling another. As he was being carried below deck, the dying man advised the survivor to "keep in the middle of the river." A sharpshooter on the *Tyler* shot Brown in the temple, but the nearly spent bullet only knocked the captain unconscious for a short time.[34]

By now the *Carondelet* was taking on so much water that all it could do was head for shallow water and wait for the *Arkansas* to strike. Walke ordered his men to get ready to repel boarders. Morrison led the men on deck. There the commander appeared next to him, "a big East Indian scimeter" in his right hand, a navy revolver in his left hand, and his toupee "on hind side fore." Not wanting to run aground, Brown ordered the *Arkansas* to sheer away. The ram's gunners depressed their cannons as far as possible and fired a broadside. The resulting blast "stove in our plating as if it was glass," noted Morrison, and rocked the *Carondelet* back so far that water shipped over its lower casemate. The half-naked Morrison ran below deck and "fired every gun that was loaded, the stern gun last." He earned the Medal of Honor for his bravery that day. As the ram moved downriver, smoke and steam poured out from gaping holes in the *Carondelet.*[35]

The *Arkansas,* however, was slowing down. Even though Union gunners barely damaged the casemate, they had put several shots through the ram's stacks. As these holes multiplied, the draft to the boilers ebbed, which reduced the steam pressure from 120 pounds to about 20 pounds. The engines now barely turned the wheels. At the same time, the temperature in the engine room soared to 130 degrees. The coal heavers could only work for ten minutes before collapsing on the main deck, their chests heaving in the cooler air. Inside the boat at least twenty-five men were dead.[36]

At about 8:30 the *Tyler* came within sight of the Union fleets. Even though sailors had heard the cannons, the vessels were not ready to fight. William Van Cleaf, a sailor on the *Benton,* reported the noise to his commanding officer, but the drunken lieutenant dismissed it as Union boats shelling the woods. "Most of our boats had no steam up," another sailor remembered after the war.[37]

When the *Arkansas* came into view, the Union crews beat to quarters, and the firemen raised steam as quickly as possible. The USS *Lancaster,* one of the unarmored rams, took the lead. A crewman cut the anchor cable and the boat steamed toward the *Arkansas.* The rebel boat's opening salvo turned the *Lancaster's* steam drum into a bomb. Scores of men were either parboiled or sent diving into the Mississippi's muddy water. A deckhand had both legs and an arm blown off while the blast broke the pilot's right shoulder, cracked several of his ribs, and blew out his teeth. Only six of the boat's forty-three Black sailors survived the blast. The ram was "shot all to pieces," its log noted.[38]

The *Arkansas* plodded along, issuing "her Broadsides at a furious rate," according to a Union sailor. It also received a terrific punishment. Brown recalled how the "shock of missiles striking our sides was literally continuous." The clanging was so intense that rebel crewmen had to communicate with hand signals. Federal shots were "skipping of[f] her Iron sides like haill," judged one bluejacket. A few Union balls ripped into the huge ram, though. One "made a piece of iron fly about a mile in the air," wrote a sailor on the *Benton.* One of Farragut's ships sent a ball through the ram's port casemate, knocking out a gun crew, breaking Lieutenant George Gift's arm, and killing another eight men at a starboard gun.[39]

Belching torrents of black smoke from its two stacks, the humongous *Benton* crept into the channel. In this clash of the titans, the *Arkansas* tried to ram the ponderous Federal craft, but the Union boat turned at the last second. As the two ironclads chugged past one another, the *Arkansas* fired a broadside. One shot came so close to killing its captain, Seth Phelps, who recalled that it "left its trace on the back of my coat." Another ball removed a sailor's head "as clean as you could of cut it with a knife," noted a bluejacket. The *Benton* gave chase, if it can be called that. The ironclad was so slow that, as Davis observed, its "usual snail's pace" rendered "anything like pursuit ridiculous." The *Cincinnati* joined in, but when the two Union boats rounded De Soto Point near Vicksburg, Confederate batteries greeted them with a salvo and ended the farce.[40]

The *Arkansas* was fortunate to reach Vicksburg when it did. Its smokestacks looked like "an immense nutmeg grinder," and several chunks of railroad iron were missing. There was no official tally of the dead, but one of the boat's officers wrote that a "great heap of mangled and ghastly slain lay on the gun deck, with rivulets of blood running away from them." One person was mashed flat, and "brains, hair and blood were all about." Somewhere between fifty and sixty men lay in its sick bay, moaning.[41]

Davis was surprisingly honest in his official report. The flag officer admitted that steam in the fleet was low and his men were "so entirely unprepared" that the *Arkansas* was able to "pass without positive obstruction." He added quickly, though, that the ram was "seriously injured by shot." Farragut tucked his tail between his legs and expressed his "deep mortification" for allowing the *Arkansas* to escape. After reading the reports, a furious Secretary of the Navy Welles sent nearly identical telegrams to both men ordering them to capture or destroy the rebel menace.[42]

Farragut and Davis had different reactions to Welles's telegram. Farragut wanted revenge "regardless of consequences to ourselves," but Davis countered that "patience [is] as great a virtue as boldness" and that he was "unwilling" to put his ironclads at risk to "indulge a momentary spleen." Privately, he complained that the admiral was "an excited, hot-headed boy." The contrast between the two men could not have been starker. The aggressive Farragut saw opportunity, while the passive Davis feared risk.[43]

Farragut also wanted to return his fleet below Vicksburg. A sortie against the *Arkansas* was a convenient reason to move his ships downriver. His fleet sprayed the Confederate vessel as they passed Vicksburg but did not otherwise engage it. Farragut thereafter kept his fleet just below the city.

Alfred Ellet also thirsted for revenge and twice asked Davis for assistance in sending one of his rams after the *Arkansas.* Davis ignored him, but Commander "Dirty Bill" Porter, who had just arrived with his repaired USS *Essex,* got wind of the scheme. He and Ellet contacted Farragut, who traveled overland to convince Davis to go after the *Arkansas.* During a lengthy and contentious council of war, Farragut, Ellet, and Porter wore down Davis. The cautious flag officer agreed to a risky scheme: while boats from both the upper and lower fleets boats bombarded Vicksburg, the *Essex* and the *Queen of the West* would attack the *Arkansas.* The ironclad would steam close to the rebel boat, secure it with grappling hooks, and hold it in place while the smaller boat punctured it.[44]

After the council of war adjourned, Porter went back to the *Essex* and called the crew on deck. He told his men that the admiral had asked him to attack the *Arkansas,* and anyone who wanted to stay behind could step to the side. Edward Galligan proudly noted that "every man said they were willing to go where he and the ship went." Bluejackets then stuffed haybales into gunports and piled them around the engines. They also loaded thousands of marbles in their guns. Fired at point-blank range, the glass projectiles might blind the enemy gun crews and sharpshooters.[45]

At about 5:00 A.M. on July 22, the *Benton, Carondelet,* and *Cincinnati* started their bombardment as the *Essex* and *Queen of the West* chugged past De Soto Point. The *Queen of the West* stopped to hear a final word of encouragement from Davis but misinterpreted the commander as ordering the ram to go back; the *Essex* advanced alone. Despite this awkward start, the Union plan had a chance of success, mainly because the *Arkansas* was in such poor shape. The boat was in extreme disrepair and had about a third of its normal crew on board. As the fruitless Union bombardment started, sailors in the rebel boat scrambled to raise steam and load the cannons. The situation was so dire that even officers went below deck to lend a hand.[46]

When the *Essex* got close to the *Arkansas,* the Union boat heaved sideways and launched its attack across the Mississippi's powerful current. The gunboat's underpowered engines could hardly keep the craft pointed in the right direction, and Brown in the *Arkansas* had plenty of time to devise a defensive strategy. By now he had enough steam to move, so he swung his boat around to present its bow to the creeping Union vessel. As the *Essex* chugged toward the *Arkansas,* the two boats exchanged salvos at point-blank range. One Union blast bounded diagonally across the Confederate's gun deck, killed six men, and wounded an equal number. Return fire merely clanged off the Union casemate. The *Essex* turned away, and the boats exchanged more cannon fire. Two rebel shells "came halfway through the casemate," wrote Galligan. Wooden fragments split a sponge handle, killed one man, and wounded five others. Galligan took a splinter in the hip, a painful wound but one that could not prevent him from staying at his gun; at breakfast the next day, a gunner's mate "took it out at the mess table." The Union ironclad continued downriver, having failed to sink the *Arkansas.*[47]

Ellet had realized his mistake, turned his vessel around, and arrived soon after the *Essex* went downriver. The little ram steamed toward the rebel boat, survived a broadside at fifty feet, and rammed the inert *Arkansas.* The glancing blow jarred loose several pieces of railroad iron and tore a small hole in the Confederate boat. The *Queen of the West* caromed off, briefly got stuck in shoal water, and then headed upriver. Every rebel gunner was determined to sink the pesky boat, but in a testament to their ineffectiveness, southern shot wounded only one sailor. The *Arkansas* had survived another attack, but its days were numbered.[48]

Essex, having continued downriver once it ran past Vicksburg, started prowling around Baton Rouge. Major General Earl Van Dorn sent a small army and the *Arkansas* to capture the Louisiana capital and chase away or seize the Union boat. Now under the command of Lieutenant Henry K. Stevens, the rebel ram chugged to a spot several miles north of Baton Rouge. It sat out the battle for the town on August 5 because its engines gave out. Porter saw his chance. Accompanied by one of Farragut's ships, he took the *Essex* in search of the ram. The *Arkansas* tried to meet the Union boats, but its engines again failed to respond. Stevens now had no choice but to scuttle the ram. The magazine's explosion destroyed the Confederacy's most powerful boat on the western waters on August 6.[49]

The Western Gunboat Flotilla's victory at Memphis and the destruction of the *Arkansas* highlight the Union's immense advantages in industrial capacity. The flotilla ultimately commissioned 101 fighting boats and twenty-six service craft. Confederates launched four ironclads, only one of which saw significant action, and fewer than ten wooden boats. Neither the River Defense Fleet nor the *Arkansas* could change the strategic situation in the western theater; southern ingenuity was no match for northern firepower. But the Union advantage and victory over the Confederate fleet was not due only to manufacturing prowess.[50]

The aggressive Union strategy limited southern efforts to build a viable brown-water navy. The Confederacy's best boat-building facilities in the West were in Memphis and New Orleans, but the Union's quick advance and capture of these cities prevented southerners from making full use of their boatyards. In retrospect, building a few large boats like the *Arkansas* was a less effective strategy than building several smaller boats. The Union made the most of its industrial advantages by fusing an effective construction strategy with a vigorous plan that smothered the Confederate boat-building campaign before it could pose a serious threat.[51]

Although it was unclear at the time, the victory at Memphis and the *Arkansas*'s destruction were crucial victories that swung the war even more in favor of the Union. The destruction of the southern fleet opened the river to Vicksburg, and the Union could not capture that city without control of the Mississippi. Once again the Western Gunboat Flotilla demonstrated its centrality to Union victory in the western theater. While the fleet had success against the Confederate brown-water navy, it now faced two new threats that once more forced it to adapt.

6

THE SOUTHERN AMBUSH STRATEGY

The Union victories at Forts Henry and Donelson, Shiloh, and Memphis as well as the destruction of the CSS *Arkansas* convinced Confederate leaders to change course in the western theater. Their shift to an ambush strategy inaugurated the war's second phase for the Western Gunboat Flotilla. Lasting from July 1862 to April 1863, this period saw an increase in irregular combat between the gunboats and Confederates who threatened the Union's riverine supply lines. This new enemy strategy demonstrated the fleet's limitations. At the same time, an environmental threat gnawed at one of the squadron's weaknesses. Ambushes and mosquitoes brought on a pair of crises in the brown-water navy.

After the Union victory at Shiloh, Major General Halleck gathered a force of 120,000 soldiers and shifted Major General Grant to a meaningless second-in-command position. Grant faced heavy criticism for being unprepared at Shiloh and suffering heavy casualties as a result. Halleck's action was equivalent to suspending his subordinate and mollified Grant's critics. Old Brains then slowly advanced toward Corinth, Mississippi, and captured the town on May 30, 1862. This important rail juncture in northern Mississippi between the Tennessee and Mississippi Rivers would serve as a supply base for a land advance against Vicksburg. Halleck then dispersed the various Union armies he had concentrated throughout the western theater and put many of them to work repairing railroads and refitting themselves.[1]

Halleck was not given the opportunity to restructure the Army of the Tennessee and march against Vicksburg. On June 11 President Lincoln promoted Old Brains to general in chief of all Union armies and summoned him to Washington. Grant now resumed command of the Army of the Tennessee and became responsible for capturing Vicksburg. Major General Don Carlos Buell remained in command of the Army of the Ohio and pushed eastward across Tennessee toward Chattanooga. Even though both major Union armies in the West would follow railroads in their advances, they still depended on army steamers for supplies.[2]

The armies stitched together a patchwork supply network that relied on steamboats, railroads, and wagons to transport their supplies and soldiers. While southerners attacked railroads and wagon trains as well, the Western Gunboat Flotilla would concentrate on threats to the riverine supply line. Army quartermasters commandeered, rented, or purchased commercial steamers and put them to work as transports. The average western river steamer carried 500 tons of supplies—enough food and forage to supply 40,000 men and 18,000 animals for nearly two days. By comparison, it took 670 wagons or fifty rail freight cars to haul the same amount. It is no wonder that steamers were a necessary method to transport food, supplies, and men in the western theater. Because these boats attracted the attention of southern guerrillas, they needed the protection of the Union gunboats. This was a new type of mission for the brown-water fleet.[3]

Between July 1861 and June 1862—the war's first phase—southern attacks on supply boats or gunboats were relatively infrequent and mild. Ambushers were part of seventeen attacks during this period, or just over one per month.[4] Even though these strikes were haphazard, Union brass was concerned. During the siege of Corinth, ambushes along the Tennessee River were enough of a problem that Halleck told Grant that transports "should in all cases be convoyed by a gunboat." Buell, now based in Middle Tennessee, thought that a gunboat would be necessary on the Cumberland River to chase away insurgents. The Western Gunboat Flotilla was limited in its ability to assist both Grant and Buell at this time. It was engaged in the Vicksburg Campaign and did not have enough boats to spread across the western waters. The fleet became even more attenuated once involved in yet another type of war in Arkansas.[5]

In June 1862 the Western Gunboat Flotilla became entangled in a joint expedition with the Union army in the trans-Mississippi. In early March Brigadier General Samuel R. Curtis's Army of the Southwest defeated a Confederate army at the Battle of Pea Ridge in northwestern Arkansas. The victory secured Missouri for the Union for the time being, but Curtis had bigger ambitions. He marched toward Little Rock in hopes of asserting Union control over Arkansas. Curtis, though, underestimated the hazardous countryside and the capabilities of Confederate defenses. Bad roads and terrible logistics delayed his advance. Rebel resistance made the situation miserable. Major General Thomas C. Hindman, who commanded the Confederate Trans-Mississippi District, rallied independent companies of partisan rangers to attack Curtis's supply lines and harass his foragers. They were so successful that the Union army hunkered down in north central Arkansas in mid-May. Curtis begged Halleck to bring in troops and establish a riverine supply line that could offer relief to his army. The nearest navigable stream was the White River.[6]

Besides the need to help Curtis, there was another good reason for a naval expedition up the White River. After Union forces captured Memphis, Confederate gunboats and transports scattered to the Mississippi's tributary rivers. Flag Officer Davis thought some cottonclads had escaped to the White River and wanted to destroy them. He selected the ironclads *St. Louis* and *Mound City,* the timberclads *Lexington* and *Conestoga,* and a tug to accompany three army transports on an expedition up the White.[7]

Getting these boats to Curtis would be no easy task. The White River originates in northwestern Arkansas and flows northward into Missouri before turning southeast and joining with the Black River near Batesville, Arkansas. From there it wanders southeast and connects with the Mississippi River about fifty miles south of Helena, Arkansas. Curtis could have hardly picked a worse river to serve as a supply line for his army. Even though it had been a wet spring, the water levels in the White were too low to support large steamboats, let alone the heavy ironclads. Worse, the river was "very narrow & crooked," as described by the paymaster on an ironclad that later joined the expedition. He added, "navigation is difficult for boats like this." The White offered perfect conditions and opportunities for ambushes. Heavy woods along the shores concealed assailants, boats were always near the shore and thus at close range for attacks, and the curvy channel slowed river traffic to a crawl. It is unclear if Davis appreciated the difficulties his men would face, but he did arrange for the 46th Indiana, under the command of Colonel Graham Fitch, to be detailed to the convoy to serve as skirmishers. The Union fleet would need the Hoosiers, as the Confederates were not willing to concede Arkansas.[8]

The Federal convoy steamed into the White River in mid-June. It chugged about 100 miles upstream until it rounded a bend just south of St. Charles. Commander Augustus Kilty, captain of the *Mound City* and the expedition's commander, paused the fleet because he spotted two 32-pounders on a bluff and obstacles in the river. He swept the area with his field glasses but saw no Confederates in the thick woods. Kilty then sent the 46th Indiana ashore and ordered it to prepare to storm the bluff. As the fleet moved forward, hidden Confederate cannons and sharpshooters opened fire. Balls clanged harmlessly against the lead ironclad's armor. Kilty ordered all hands below. Meanwhile, the 46th Indiana tramped its way to the base of the bluff and waited for the signal to storm the Confederate position.[9]

Kilty wanted to soften up the Confederates before a ground attack. The *Mound City*'s forward guns sprang to life and sent balls arcing toward the bluff top. Ere long, the rebel cannons replied and kept up a lively cannonade. At 10:03 A.M. "there was *a crack,* a rushing sound, and an awful crash" on the *Mound City,* according to an officer on another boat. A shot from the upper battery had bashed through the boat's port bow and burst its steam drum. Peter Dugan, a gunner's mate, remembered that he was in the shell room when the explosion knocked him "senseless" and paralyzed the left side of his face. Great torrents of steam immediately poured forth and scalded about a hundred men. The casualties were magnified because sailors were packed onto the gun deck due to the Confederate musket fire. Desperate bluejackets stampeded to escape and plopped into the river. The water was "full of men struggling with the swift current which was sweeping them to a speedy death," wrote one sailor. The other boats lowered launches in hopes of fishing out the survivors.[10]

The scene on the *Mound City* was sickening. Some men were so badly scalded that even their friends could not recognize them. Others were blinded. Skin from men's hands and feet, sometimes with the nails attached, was strewn about the ironclad. Sailors shrieked in agony: "Oh God, save me, save me. Oh! kill me, shoot me. Oh! do end my misery. Doctor will I live? Tell my wife how I died." Others tore at their clothing, leaving "long strings of bleeding flesh dangling from their finger ends, hand, arms, and lacerated bodies." Many called for water or ice to "quench the heat from the steam which was burning them inside." Surgeons administered chloroform to those who suffered most, and sailors tried to ease the pain of the victims by pouring oil on them, sprinkling flour on wounds, and gently covering the men with raw cotton. A few sailors, insensitive to the suffering in their midst, chugged whiskey and rifled through the bags, purses, trunks, and carpetbags that had been stowed. A disgusted officer wrote that "quarreling, cursing, and rioting, as well as robbing, seemed to rule." Eventually, enough sailors banded together to restore order.[11]

Not much could be done for the worst cases. Symmes Browne was at his brother's side when he "passed from a calm sleep in this world to immortal rest beyond the skies." He arranged for his brother's body to be shipped to Memphis. The disfigured corpses of officers were also shipped home for burial. But there were too many bodies to send them all back, so two companies of men from the 46th Indiana later had the sad duty of burying fifty-eight sailors amid a driving rain in a rebel gun trench under the Arkansas trees. As the Hoosiers were shoveling dirt on the mass grave, the speedy *Conestoga* was heading to Memphis with the wounded sailors. But the boat was not fast enough for some. It stopped about halfway between the mouth of the White River and Memphis so its crew could bury another twenty-six victims.[12]

The total casualties were staggering: 105 men killed and 44 wounded. With a crew of 175, the *Mound City* had an 85-percent casualty rate. It was the single bloodiest day of the war for the Western Gunboat Flotilla. The attack underscored the basic vulnerability of gunboats—their boilers and steam drums were potential bombs.[13]

But scalding steam was not the only danger in action. Shrapnel ripped off Kilty's left arm, so command of the expedition devolved upon Lieutenant Wilson McGunnegle, captain of the *St. Louis.* McGunnegle decided that the boats must continue upriver to rescue Curtis. The *Mound City* needed repairs, but the flotilla could not simultaneously advance and tow the crippled ironclad to Cairo. McGunnegle thus detailed a portion of the 46th Indiana to protect the immobilized gunboat while the rest of the convoy continued its mission. The boats chugged sixty-three miles upstream to Crooked Point cutoff near Clarendon, where the *St. Louis* nearly grounded. With this, McGunnegle changed his mind and wisely scrapped the expedition because of low water. The fleet headed back to Memphis.[14]

On the same day as *Mound City*'s explosion, Hindman clarified the role of partisans in defending Arkansas. Their duty, he explained, was to "cut off Federal pickets, scouts, foraging parties, and trains, and to kill pilots and others on gunboats and transports, attacking them day and night." Hindman's orders were part of a larger southern effort to choke off Union supplies. Guerrillas and partisans were already at work across the southern interior, burning railroad bridges and water tanks, tearing up track, and firing into trains, particularly in Tennessee. Most of these men were probably local citizens who had no deep allegiance to the Confederacy. Others may have taken their cue from the Confederate government, which passed the Partisan Ranger Act on April 21, 1862. This controversial law authorized commissioned officers to organize and oversee independent companies of men who were supposed to abide by the same regulations as regular troops. The act was, in effect, the Confederacy's effort to provide some control and direction to a guerrilla war that was metastasizing throughout the occupied South.[15]

The effects of Hindman's strategy were immediate and effective. Grant arranged for another rescue mission to Curtis's beleaguered army. Eight transports, three regiments of infantry (including the 46th Indiana again), the *Lexington,* and the *Conestoga* ascended the White River. The boats again failed to reach Curtis, this time because southern guerrillas hid in the brush along the banks and harassed the convoy with musket fire. The downriver trip put the Union boats through another shooting gallery. One day a guerrilla's bullet severed a sailor's tongue. A day later another attack punctured the chief engineer's aorta and severely wounded a fireman. The *Conestoga* fired grape or canister every fifteen minutes to suppress any hidden attackers. Sailors who went on deck risked their lives. Frederic Davis told his father how he was on the "Bow Port, (a dangerous seat)" talking with a friend when he decided to go somewhere safe. Not fifteen minutes later, "Pop, Pop, Pop against the side of the boat came the bullets." His friend tumbled on the deck, dead. Another ball hit the chief engineer "not six feet from me," Davis wrote, and killed the man. In words that certainly did not reassure his worried parents, the bluejacket concluded, "We did not know when we arose in the morning wether we should be alive at night or not." The Union boats made it back to Memphis, but not before leaving behind several dead sailors. Those men died in vain because Curtis's army finally escaped by slogging overland to Helena.[16]

After the 1862 White River Campaign, the Confederacy shifted its strategy. Attacks against transports and gunboats became a regular feature of life in the western theater for two reasons. Hindman's partisans demonstrated that ambush squads could deter Union boats if the conditions were right. Confederates became particularly adept at identifying choke points along rivers and finding favorable ground. Additionally, Union river traffic increased. The amount of shipping rose during the war's second phase as Federal armies became larger than ever before and were dispersed across the Upper South. Confederates sent infantry, cavalry, and artillery units to promising locations along the western rivers. These ambush squads carried out most of the attacks on riverine supply lines.

Confederate ambush squads were part of a larger strategy of resistance that is often described as irregular warfare. Instead of "regular" fighting that takes place between armies on a traditional battlefield, irregular warfare uses small units to carry out hit-and-run raids. The intention is not to inflict a catastrophic defeat, but to hector, harass, and demoralize the opponent. Anyone can carry out an attack anytime and anywhere. The unpredictability, or the terror, of irregular warfare is one of the things that makes it so effective. Often the threat of an attack is enough to change behavior.[17]

Ambush squads used similar tactics as partisans and guerrillas. Partisan forces, like the ones that Hindman encouraged in Arkansas, were locally constituted and legally obligated to serve the Confederacy. They were not quite Confederate soldiers and generally were local defense units that did not travel great distances from their homes. Guerrillas were civilians who were locally constituted, often fought for personal gain, and did not have to obey orders from the Confederate government. While southern officials generally sanctioned and even encouraged guerrillas, they did not control their actions. Since all three irregular groups used similar tactics, Union sailors usually did not distinguish between them in their writings and often described Confederate soldiers in ambush squads as guerrillas.[18]

Southern attacks against the Union supply system and the boats protecting it increased dramatically from the war's first phase to the second phase, from an average of 1.3 per month to 6.4 times per month. These ambushes paid immediate dividends. During the war's first phase, southerners captured, burned, or sank two unarmed northern boats; both were probably commercial steamers. In the second phase, southerners knocked out fifteen unarmored boats. Tables 3 and 4 summarize this irregular warfare as well as the boats lost to such action.[19]

Some of these attacks were along the Cumberland and Tennessee Rivers. During the winter of 1862–63, over 100 riverboats chugged back and forth to supply the Army of the Cumberland. Major General William S. Rosecrans, who replaced Buell, complained that guerrillas were knocking out too many of the transports supplying his army. The fleet's commander shot back that he had to

TABLE 3. Irregular Warfare along the Western Rivers

	PHASE ONE (July 1861–June 1862)	PHASE TWO (July 1862–April 1863)	PHASE THREE (May 1863–April 1864)	PHASE FOUR (May 1864–April 1865)
Mutual Attacks	7	19	30	26
Northern Unilateral Attacks	18	63	95	63
Southern Unilateral Attacks	10	45	65	70
Monthly Average, Northern Unilateral and Mutual	1.9	8.2	10.4	7.4
Monthly Average, Southern Unilateral and Mutual	1.3	6.4	7.9	8.0

Source: Gudmestad Irregular Combat Dataset.

TABLE 4. Northern Boats Sunk, Burned, Captured, or Destroyed by Irregular Warfare

	PHASE ONE (July 1861–June 1862)	PHASE TWO (July 1862–April 1863)	PHASE THREE (May 1863–April 1864)	PHASE FOUR (May 1864–April 1865)
Transports & Merchantmen	2	15	7	25
Gunboats	0	0	2	7

Source: Gudmestad Irregular Combat Dataset.

"protect the whole line of [the Cumberland] river against guerrillas." Rosecrans was "doing nothing" to stop the rebels from putting batteries along the river, "which the gunboats have to silence."[20]

Confederates sprung more attacks, though, along the Mississippi River in the hopes of protecting Vicksburg. Inspector General Samuel Cooper sketched out Confederate plans in an order to Brigadier General Richard Taylor, directing him to use artillery to "embarrass the enemy in the navigation of the Mississippi River." A Confederate officer later recalled that he had orders to "prevent, as much as possible, reinforcements from reaching General Grant," who moved against Vicksburg in late 1862.[21]

Captain William Ritter led a Confederate ambush squad that sank at least one boat bound for Grant's army. His Third Maryland Artillery (CS) arrived at the Mississippi River in January 1863 and split into three groups, which were "scattered up and down the river." One joined with artillery units from Georgia, Louisiana, and Missouri and did most of their damage while operating from the Fish Lake camp near Greenville, Mississippi. Ritter's group had about 250 men and four cannons, including one christened "Black Bess." Other squads were as small as a few dozen men.[22]

Confederates studied the environment carefully and set up camps that made the best use of the landscape. These sites were anywhere from one mile to twenty-five miles back from the riverbank and typically in well-concealed locations. Ritter's Fish Lake camp was "snugly inclosed on all sides by a deep and primitive forest of cottonwood, magnolia and live oak." Favorable ambush sites like this one were near sinuous stretches of river where rebels could stage multiple attacks. Fish Lake was just back of Carter's Bend, a lazy loop in the Mississippi about three miles above Greenville. Ritter could spring an ambush, pack up when outgunned, scamper a mile across the peninsula formed by the bend, and set up for another attack. About the time he got his guns in place, Federal boats had chugged their way around the fifteen-mile loop. The best ambush sites shared other features: concealment (usually brush, a cane brake, or woods), good roads to the interior, readily available food, and sympathetic civilians.[23]

Ambush squads often switched locations, either in response to Union shipping patterns or to keep from being discovered. Rebels developed a network of supporters and were in close communication with helpful southern civilians. Squads commonly squatted for a few nights in barns or sheds. Colonel Colton Greene, another Confederate who led attacks on Union boats, explained to his superior officer that his men bivouacked at Campbell's plantation on a Monday, moved to Daniel Session's plantation the next day, set up at Leland's plantation later that day, made a stop at Sunnyside plantation, and finally ended up at Smith's plantation by the following Monday.[24]

Confederate camps depended on sympathetic families for all manner of assistance. A few civilians took up arms and became guerrillas themselves, but most just provided food, shelter, information, and encouragement. In some cases, entire households supported Confederate soldiers as resistance became tribal. Old men shared military intelligence, women nursed the ill or injured, boys served as guides through the woods, enslaved people were forced to carry notes to nearby plantations, and children dug up unexploded ordnance and sold the gunpowder. Civilians sometimes boosted the morale of cavalrymen who attacked Union transports by fixing meals and bestowing gifts on the troopers. Rebels also perched in the buildings of friendly civilians and plucked away at gunboats.[25]

Civilian sympathizers and rebel camps were part of an unseen yet sophisticated network. Hidden observation posts, Ritter noted, "lined the river" and served as tripwires for the backcountry encampments. Members from Parsons's Cavalry, a unit from Texas, set up a "good stand on the Mississippi River" in the thickly wooded bank and studied the river traffic for patterns. It is unlikely that the ten transports that passed on April 4, 1863, knew the rebels were spying on them. Insurgents who crouched in these stands signaled other encampments through a "regular system of signal fires," rockets, and "overland runners."[26]

A portion of this network kicked into action on May 6, 1863. On that day Ritter's men were lounging around when scouts pounded into the Fish Lake camp with news that a transport "heavily laden with stores" and pulling two barges was coming down the river. The Confederates hitched up their cannons and headed to Argyle Landing. Ritter set up his guns in the brush "at a point where the current ran in near the bank." Geography would funnel the unsuspecting boat close to shore.[27]

Soon enough, the *Minnesota* came puffing into view. When the transport steered close to shore, Ritter's 12-pounders opened up. One of the first shots severed the tiller rope, while another shattered a piston rod. The *Minnesota*'s crew hoisted a white flag, and Ritter boarded the stricken vessel once it touched the shore. The boat's captain asked him to have a drink in "true western style," but Ritter refused. Hungry Confederates swarmed aboard, wolfed down a "luxurious dinner," and then broke into the $40,000 worth of supplies. It was a scene reminiscent of Christmas morning. During their celebration, someone grabbed a bottle of wine and merrily broke it over the barrel of Black Bess. The Confederates toted "flour, bacon, potatoes, pickles of all sorts, sugar, coffee, rice, ginger, syrup, cheese, butter, oranges, lemons, preserves, canned oysters, whiskey, wines, musquito [*sic*] nets, clothing, stationery, tobacco, etc. etc." ashore. Some men brought food back to camp, others hitched up the guns, and a few torched the steamer. As flames consumed the unlucky boat, the tinclad USS *Rattler* hove into view and chased away the "rascals."[28]

Back at the Fish Lake camp, Ritter's men chatted around fires, reclined on their elbows, "sipped the aromatic beverages with great enjoyment," and reveled in their glory. The captain also sent a courier to the nearby Willoughby plantation (and likely others as well) with cans of oysters and blackberries. The Worthington family, who lived at Willoughby, were strong supporters of the local insurgents. Sixteen-year-old Amanda Worthington recorded in her diary how her family fed soldiers, gave them a place to sleep, nursed sick ones, and provided them with local information. One day her father brought in eighteen soldiers and urged them to stay for dinner. "He will never let one pass without either taking a meal or staying all night," Worthington wrote with pride. Ritter knew the value of staying on friendly relations with civilians. It took only one disgruntled person to seek out a Union boat and lead northern sailors to a hidden Confederate camp.[29]

Less than two weeks later, Ritter struck again. On May 18, Confederate scouts from a riverside stand thundered into camp with news that "a number of transports laden with reinforcements for General Grant's army" were coming down the river. The Army of the Tennessee had just pushed the Confederates back across Big Black River in Mississippi, and reinforcements would help the Yankees creep closer to Vicksburg from the east. Men in the camp jumped to their feet, and all was immediately "life and bustling activity." Soldiers hooked horses to cannons, and they went clattering toward Carter's Bend. Near the river, the Confederates rode through openings they had previously hacked in the levee. After setting up their guns in the heavy brush, the dismounted cavalrymen fanned out along the bank. After checking their weapons, Ritter's men coolly munched on blackberries and waited to strike.[30]

It was nearly 1:00 P.M. when Confederates sighted the telltale plume of smoke in the distance. Soon the transport *Crescent City* came around the bend. Men from the 3rd Iowa Infantry were "packed and crowded" on the hurricane deck, laughing and joking like they were on a holiday. The tinclad USS *Linden* trailed about a mile behind the steamer, and behind it were the transports *Luminary, Ohio Belle, Gladiator,* and *Sultana.* All told, perhaps 4,000 bluecoats were jammed into the transports. It was a high-risk, high-reward situation for the rebels. If Ritter could sink one or more of the transports, perhaps he could derail Grant's advance. But the Federals could also land and overwhelm the small

Confederate force. Ritter knew that launching an attack would invite Union retaliation against the local civilians. But he decided that the reward was worth the risk, in part because the river's channel forced the *Crescent City* to steam close to the shore and increased the likelihood that he could sink the transport.[31]

A sudden volley of shell and canister stopped all merriment on the *Crescent City*. The panicked Iowans stampeded to the opposite side of the boat, their combined weight causing the steamer to tip sideways and expose its vulnerable hull. Another shell slammed through the boat, and it looked like the Union infantrymen were about to go for an adventure swim. Union officers "yelling and swearing" herded their men back into place, and the boat righted itself. Some soldiers had the presence of mind to shoot back at the Confederates, and a brief firefight erupted. The *Linden* hurried forward and started blasting away at the ambushers. By the time the *Crescent City* puffed out of range, fourteen soldiers lay wounded on its deck.[32]

Ritter had no desire to linger once the other transports veered toward the riverbank and threw out their gangplanks. Federal infantry and cavalry streamed ashore, hungry for revenge. Ritter's men limbered up their guns and stampeded away from the levee. Union cavalry bore down on the southern artillery, but Confederate horsemen counterattacked and bought enough time for the guns to get away. The southern cavalry soon fled, their commander emptying his revolver into the faces of the Federals on his heels. Rebel horsemen galloped across a bridge and found protection behind their cannons, which had hastily deployed in a line. The guns barked once more, "sweeping the road clear for a distance of more than three hundred yards" and emptying many saddles. While the Federals regrouped, the southerners limbered up again and fled. As the rebels raced across a bridge spanning a bayou, now six miles inland, Ritter recalled how "white balls of foam from perspiration had formed on the backs of the artillery horses." Union forces chased the Confederates another three miles before ending their pursuit. The troopers, now nine miles inland and increasingly vulnerable to an ambush, headed back to the boats "without accomplishing the purpose of our landing," as their commanding officer admitted. The Confederates trotted back to their camp, relieved that they had lived to fight another day but disappointed that they had not inflicted more damage.[33]

The proliferation of ambush squads like Ritter's group exacerbated an ongoing problem within the Western Gunboat Flotilla: a manpower crisis. The fleet needed more boats and the requisite crews to deal with this new threat. Yet it continued to struggle in recruiting men and lost hundreds of bluejackets when epidemics malaria or other diseases swept through the fleet.

Female mosquitoes, *Anopheles quadrimaculatus,* are the most common carriers of malaria in the United States. Transmission usually occurs when the insect bites an infected victim, ingests the parasites, and then injects them into a person's bloodstream. The parasites then move to the liver. Eventually, infected red blood cells surge through the body. Victims experience fever, chills, sweating, and nausea. Malaria is usually not fatal, but it often incapacitates victims for weeks or months and makes them more susceptible to respiratory infections or death from other causes. Ezra Green avoided service in the White River Expedition because he became so weak from malaria that he could not sit up for more than an hour. His weight plummeted to 137 pounds, becoming so emaciated that he received a medical discharge from the navy. Malaria also spread through the army, with estimates that 1.3 million Union soldiers contracted the disease during the war.[34]

Malaria was a serious problem because the Western Gunboat Flotilla often lingered in swampy areas that were ideal breeding grounds for mosquitoes. Transmission occurred more readily where people crowded together, so the presence of a fleet of boats packed with sweaty men was a blood buffet. While the USS *Cairo* was trying to force Fort Pillow's surrender, George Yost concluded, "*Musquitoes* [were] worse than the Rebels." Frederic Davis on the *Lexington* agreed. While the timberclad idled upriver from Vicksburg, he complained to his brother that the "mosquitos are busy eating us up."[35]

Mosquito-borne malaria was not the only medical problem that beset bluejackets. River water caused all sorts of intestinal distress in the fleet. Davis complained that drinking from the Ohio River "gives us Deorahea." James Dickinson noted that the "Mississippi is awful muddy and it made all of us sick to drink the water." Several sailors believed that bad water permanently ruined their digestive health. In his pension application, sailor Francis James indicated that he was "very sick" with "Diarrhea, [and] misery in the stomach, and bowels" because of the water he drank while on the USS *General Lyon.* Twenty-five years after he packed away his uniform, he still had chronic diarrhea.[36]

Davis, Dickinson, James, and the other sailors with gastrointestinal maladies probably ingested bacteria—*Shigella, E. coli,* or other types of salmonella—by drinking water that was contaminated with fecal matter. Flies might also have infected them. Diarrhea was more than an annoyance when the illness became extreme. Sailors who suffered from dysentery might have blood or mucus in their stool and became susceptible to dehydration. Their weakened state also made them less likely to survive other threats to their health. Like malaria, diarrhea and dysentery were rife in Civil War armies. One medical historian has speculated that every Civil War recruit probably suffered from bowel problems. Diarrhea or dysentery afflicted at least 1.75 million Union soldiers and killed at least 45,000 of them. Other diseases struck bluejackets as well. Scurvy, dengue (or break bone) fever, smallpox, and yellow fever afflicted sailors but did not reach near-epidemic levels like malaria and diarrhea.[37]

Each boat had a physician or surgeon, and these men tried various means to treat diseases. Rowland Stafford True, a farmer from Pennsylvania, remembered that his boat's doctor had a dispensary. Sick sailors would "take our turns at the little window," state their symptoms, and get some type of medicine. Doctors usually prescribed quinine for malaria. Quinine was derived from the bark of tropical plants, and the navy had an ample supply of it during the Civil War. Sailors did not like the drug because of its bitter taste, so they sometimes mixed it with whiskey. Morrison, for instance, at first tried to treat his malaria with twelve unknown pills, then drank "grog thickened with pepper," but eventually knocked back a dose of quinine. Doctors also doled out opium pills and a mysterious blackberry syrup, often with no rhyme or reason. Medicine did not always have the desired effect. One night True was so desperate for help that he woke the doctor. Without lighting a lamp, the physician poured some blackberry syrup into a glass and gave it to him. As the sailor gulped it down, he noticed that there was something else in the glass: "I spit out about a half dozen cockroaches" that had been feasting on the sweet medicine.[38]

Disease ravaged the brown-water navy in 1862. According to one sailor, the *Lexington* had 150 men on the sick list on May 6; most of them had diarrhea. A month later Morrison, on the *Carondelet,* told his diary: "A great many of our crew sick with the ague. In fact, all hands look dull and stupid." By the end of July, 40 percent of brown-water sailors were unfit for duty. The navy also discharged an unknown but significant number of medically disabled men from the fleet.[39]

Many malaria-stricken bluejackets were transferred to the USS *Red Rover,* the navy's first hospital boat. The *Red Rover* had distinct operating and amputating rooms, large rooms for the recuperation of 200 men, a steam boiler for laundry, three elevators, and storage for 300 tons of ice. Besides surgeons and stewards, the boat had at least two Roman Catholic nuns, Sisters Mary Adela and Veronica. They were listed on the boat's records and were the first women acknowledged as nurses on board a U.S. naval vessel. Several formerly enslaved women also worked as chambermaids on the *Red Rover*. One of them, Ann Bradford Stokes, became the first woman to receive a U.S. pension for military service as a woman. The boat entered service on June 10, 1862, and remained in operation for the duration of the war.[40]

Even as disease was whittling down the number of able-bodied sailors, the government was not providing replacements for these men. In February 1862 about 300 new bluejackets joined the fleet. That number dwindled to about 20 in May and 30 in June. Lieutenant Commander Alexander Pennock, who oversaw the fleet's logistics from Cairo, glumly concluded on July 30, "Can not obtain men here."[41]

The lack of sailors and the increased responsibility to protect Union supply lines left the Western Gunboat Flotilla in a difficult position. A portion of the fleet was just north of Vicksburg in hopes of capturing the city. It was cooperating with Rear Admiral Farragut's fleet, which had an army contingent that was too small to assault the town. After one month of ineffectual bombing, the assistant surgeon on the flagship *Benton* bluntly told Flag Officer Davis that it was time to abandon the Vicksburg expedition. The flotilla commander wrote in his diary that he decided to "yield to the climate and postpone any further action at Vicksburg till the fever season is over." At the end of July, Farragut returned to New Orleans, and Davis steamed upriver to Helena.[42]

The twin crises in the summer of 1862 showed the weaknesses of the Western Gunboat Flotilla. Southerners waged an effective insurgent war in part because large ironclads were not suited to suppressing ambushes. The paucity of sailors, due to both tepid recruitment and the ravages of malaria, limited the fleet's ability to respond to the new rebel threat. But its boats and men changed significantly after June 30, 1862.

Timberclads like the USS *Conestoga* were versatile boats that suppressed insurgents, provided support to infantry ashore, and scouted enemy positions.

NH 55321, courtesy of Naval History and Heritage Command, Washington, DC.

The USS *Cairo* was one of seven city-class ironclads, which were the backbone of the Mississippi Squadron.

NH 61568, courtesy of Naval History and Heritage Command, Washington, DC.

Civil War sailors, like this landsman on the USS *Benton,* wore a distinctive uniform, which included their boat's name on the hatband and a blouse that gave rise to their nickname "bluejackets."

WICR 30264, courtesy of Wilson's Creek National Battlefield.

The crew of the USS *Choctaw.* Over the course of the Civil War, the 17,000 men who served in the Mississippi Squadron earned a reputation for drunkenness, fighting, and disobedience to their officers.

From Francis Trevelyan Miller, ed., *The Photographic History of the Civil War,* vol. 6, *The Navies,* by James Barnes (New York: Review of Reviews, 1911), 211.

Between Decks—Serving the Guns, after a sketch by Rear Admiral Henry Walke. Firing the large naval cannons required training and teamwork, but even the best-trained crews had difficulty hitting their targets with any consistency.

From Johnson and Buel, *Battles and Leaders of the Civil War,* 1:365.

Brown-water sailors, like this cannon crew,
formed intense bonds while "exercising the great guns."

Gunner's Crew of the USS *Essex,* PO232-2304, courtesy of Missouri History Museum, St. Louis.

The Great Naval Battle Opposite the City of Memphis, June 6, 1862,
by Alexander Simplot. The Mississippi Squadron, with the assistance of the Ellet rams, destroyed the Confederacy's River Defense Fleet at Memphis on June 6, 1862.

ICHI-069961, courtesy of Chicago History Museum.

Tinclads like the USS *Cricket* were the most numerous type of vessel in the Mississippi Squadron. They were effective at both protecting Union supply boats and fighting insurgents.

NH 63377, courtesy of Naval History and Heritage Command, Washington, DC.

David D. Porter took command of the Mississippi Squadron in October 1862 and cooperated closely with Ulysses S. Grant and William T. Sherman, particularly during the Vicksburg Campaign.

NH 47394, courtesy of Naval History and Heritage Command, Washington, DC.

George Washington Moseby was one of about
3,000 formerly enslaved men who served in the Mississippi Squadron.

Moseby Pension Application, C 2,581,691, Record Group 15, courtesy of
National Archives and Records Administration, Washington, DC.

Robert Walker, an eleven-year-old fieldhand when he enlisted, likely became a servant to officers on the USS *Pittsburg.*

WICR 32071-L, courtesy of Wilson's Creek National Battlefield.

7

THE MISSISSIPPI SQUADRON'S WAR OF EXHAUSTION

In 1862 the Western Gunboat Flotilla built a new type of boat, found new leadership, implemented a new strategy, relied on a new source of sailors, and took on a new name. Once again, the brown-water navy adapted to the changing military conditions in the western theater.

Before it ventured into the White River, the Western Gunboat Flotilla had minimal contact with insurgents, partisans, or Confederate ambush squads. Between July 1861 and June 1862, it carried out twenty-five attacks against insurgents or suspected insurgents, or about 1.9 per month. Union boat captains, moreover, were restrained in these early interactions. On the Tennessee River, the captain of the USS *Conestoga* was fed up with "riflemen concealed in the woods" who shot at the timberclad. He warned residents of Tobacco Port, Tennessee, that he would hold them responsible for any further attacks on his boat. Such restraint vanished after southerners implemented their ambush strategy.[1]

After July 1, 1862, the Western Gunboat Flotilla became more aggressive in attacking rebels, civilians, and Confederate resources. During the war's second phase, Union gunboats carried out at least 82 attacks, or 8.2 per month, a fourfold surge from the war's first phase. About 40 percent of these attacks involved sending sailors ashore on raids (see table 3).[2]

Many of these raids were retaliatory. The vengeance meted out after the ambush of the *Minnesota* is instructive of Federal methods. Late in the day on May 7, 1863, sixty-seven soldiers from Company D, 101st Illinois Volunteers filed onto the USS *General Bragg*. The boat cast off into the Mississippi River and met up with the tinclads *Cricket* and *Rattler*. While the three boats chuffed downriver, ten "scorchers" checked their supplies: haversacks with a bottle of coal oil, some tar, and a piece of port fire (similar to a flare, it was normally used to touch off a cannon). At about 4:40 A.M. the next morning, the soldiers and twenty-nine sailors, including the scorchers, landed in Washington County, Mississippi, near Chicot Island. They immediately drove back some enemy pickets and marched about a mile inland to the Blantonia and Roach plantations.[3]

The scorchers then got to work. They set a "fine and spacious mansion" ablaze and watched as the "magnificent and costly furniture, splendid library, etc." disappeared in the crackling flames. While a line of pickets stood guard and the *General Bragg* occasionally lobbed shells into the woods, the scorchers torched a cotton gin, a huge pile of cotton, an overseer's house, a large barn containing 5,000 bushels of corn, a still larger barn containing 20,000 bushels of corn, slave quarters, cottages, storehouses, and several other buildings. Perhaps sixty structures became charred rubble that morning. The men returned to their boats by 9:00 A.M. For good measure, the scorchers also set fire to buildings on Chicot Island and at Argyle Landing.[4]

While the visit to the Blantonia and Roach plantations was well planned, many other Union retaliatory attacks were immediate and improvised. Somewhere along the Mississippi River south of Memphis, for instance, rebels pumped five musket balls into a Union sailor on the USS *Cairo.* Crewmen instantly went ashore and "burned up all the houses barns and everything combustible near the scene of the assassination," wrote sailor George Yost. Likewise, the USS *Essex* rained down shells on the town of Bayou Sara, Louisiana, after guerrillas sabotaged the boat's coal heap.[5]

The increase in Union retaliatory attacks came even though the Western Gunboat Flotilla was ill suited to go after ambush squads. On July 1, 1862, it had only fifteen vessels in the water, ten of them ironclads. These big boats had awesome power; their 64-pounders could shake the earth during a bombardment. One young Mississippian was in the woods when a gunboat let loose a barrage. The first salvo tore through the forest "like a drove of wild hogs" and ensuing blasts shredded trees, sent shrapnel careening through the air, and generally created mayhem. Ironclads typically did not have to worry about conserving their ammunition and often walked their salvoes inland, sometimes throwing "near one hundred bombs" at suspected rebels.[6]

An ironclad's bombardment, though, usually just sent insurgents scurrying out of range. Worse yet, the large boats were expensive, ponderously slow, crewed by large concentrations of sailors, and not usable in shallow water. The three timberclads were better suited for chasing popup attackers, but their wooden walls were of indifferent quality. If the Union hoped to take the war to the guerrillas, it needed a new type of boat. As one captain remarked in June 1862, "We think that the [ironclad] gunboats have nearly finished their work, and that a different kind [of boat] will be required for the future." That new type of boat was the tinclad.[7]

The Western Gunboat Flotilla put twenty-seven tinclads into service during the war's second phase and commissioned a total of seventy-one such boats during the war.[8] No two were exactly alike. A few were captured Confederate vessels, but most were riverboats that the navy purchased. They ranged in size from the diminutive USS *General Pillow* at 38 tons to the jumbo USS *Black Hawk* at 902 tons, but the median size was 190 tons. Workers bolted one-inch-thick boiler plates to the casemates to make them "rifle proof" and usually added extra armor and wooden planking near the engines and the pilot houses. Tinclads sometimes had cotton bales or hawsers to reinforce weak points and normally carried six to eight cannons or howitzers, none of which was larger than a 32-pounder. Each boat was assigned a number, which was painted in two-foot-high black numerals on the forward part and sides of the pilot houses. Sailors slept on the main deck in hammocks, while the officers' quarters were on the upper deck. Magazines, storerooms, and lockers were in the hold. The tinclad was an improved version of the timberclad.[9]

Tinclads had numerous advantages over ironclads. They drew three to four feet of water unlike an ironclad's six-foot draft, allowing them greater reach up tributary streams. It took about $15,000 to purchase a steamer and another $8,000–$10,000 to convert it to a tinclad. That was much more affordable than the $90,000 price tag for an ironclad. Tinclads averaged 80 men per boat, whereas it normally took 150 men to operate an ironclad. The smaller crew size meant that the fleet could disperse its sailors in a larger number of boats instead of concentrating them in a few vessels. Tinclads became the ubiquitous northern war vessel because they were well suited to suppressing insurgents.[10]

But Tinclads were not the only new type of boat added to the Western Gunboat Flotilla in the war's second phase. The navy also commissioned the USS *Osage,* the first of seven river monitors. All monitors had at least one revolving turret with two guns. These cannon tended to jam the turret when fired, however, so none of the monitors compiled an impressive service record. During

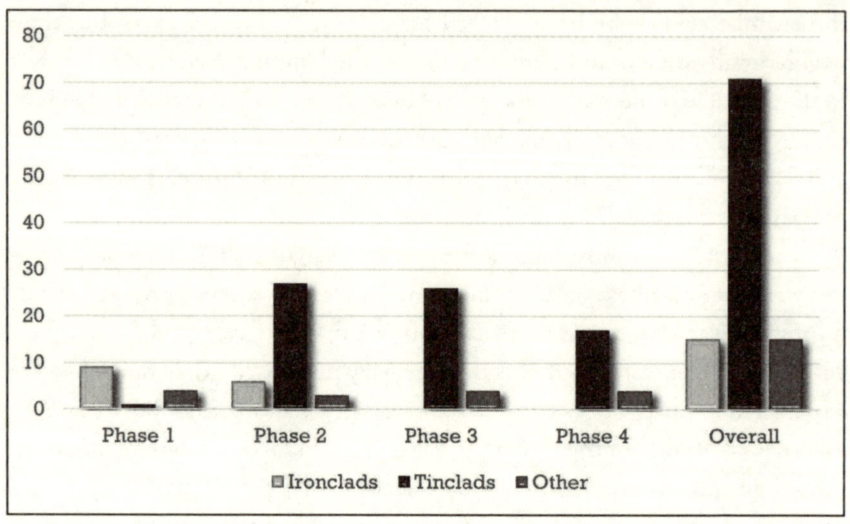

CHART 4. Fighting Vessels in the Mississippi Squadron
Source: Compiled from Silverstone, *Warships of the Civil War Navies.*

the second phase, the fleet added a total of thirty-six fighting vessels, the largest increase in any phase for the brown-water navy in terms of total boats and boats per month (see chart 4).[11]

A new fleet commander was responsible for this surge in boat building. Flag Officer Davis was slow to see that the war was changing, had limited capacity for strategic thinking, and lacked an aggressive spirit, so Secretary of the Navy Welles transferred him to the Bureau of Navigation. Rear Admiral David D. Porter, who came from a famous naval family and had enlisted as a midshipman when he was only ten years old, became commander of the western fleet. He had commanded the mortar boats in Farragut's fleet during the operation to capture New Orleans, so he had some knowledge of the war on the western rivers. Porter was talented, aggressive, and energetic. He was also "casual with the truth" and actively undermined Davis. In gossipy correspondence with Assistant Secretary of the Navy Fox, Porter opined that Davis "deserves to lose his command" because he allowed the CSS *Arkansas* to escape. Welles had his doubts about the admiral but chose the brash self-promoter because he had few other options. More than any other person, Porter shaped the direction of the brown-water navy. He took command of the Western Gunboat Flotilla on October 15, 1862.

At the same time, the War Department transferred control of the flotilla to the navy and renamed it the Mississippi Squadron.[12]

Despite his faults, Porter was just the man to use tinclads to, as he put it, "beat back the rebels from the river banks." If southerners attacked, the admiral told his captains that it was their "duty" to "fire back with spirit, and to destroy everything in that neighborhood within reach of his guns." They would snuff out this unconventional war by demolishing buildings that provided shelter "to rebels." Should innocent people be harmed, "it will be their own fault."[13]

Porter blurred the traditional distinction between home front and battlefront. He preferred to think of people as being either loyal or disloyal. His use of "neighborhood" and "localities" implies that he understood, at least on a basic level, the interlocking relationship between households, guerrillas, and Confederate soldiers in opposing the Union armed forces. Even though Porter was willing to chastise civilians supporting the irregular war, his hard-war strategy had its limits. He tried to set boundaries on his sailors' actions and prevent indiscriminate attacks. Porter clarified that sailors should only burn houses if the guerrillas used them as protection when firing on gunboats. The burning, he explained, "must be done at the time the firing takes place; not any length of time afterwards." Surviving records indicate that Union attacks on civilians were mainly confined to property—burning houses, confiscating cotton, and stealing or destroying possessions, for instance. Civilians were not the same as soldiers. While sailors did kill men actively engaged in attacks on gunboats and sometimes summarily executed guerrillas, there is no evidence that they killed civilians who abetted the rebellion.[14]

The Mississippi Squadron's methods were part of a broader Union tendency to efface the distinction between Confederate soldiers and civilians and often regard the latter as legitimate military targets (short of death). Major General William T. Sherman, who is usually remembered for his attacks on civilians in Georgia, was another early advocate for the need to chasten civilians and destroy their property. On September 25, 1862, he sent a portion of the 46th Ohio Regiment to Randolph, Tennessee, to "destroy the place" after guerrillas used the town as a platform for an attack on the transport *Eugene.* Sherman struck up a friendship with Porter, and their attitudes toward southern civilians were similar. In November 1862 Porter told him that he wanted to carry "the war into the heart of the [enemy's] country" and "give them (the rebels) a taste of devastation that may bring them to their senses." Sherman would do that very thing when he marched from Atlanta to Savannah.[15]

To bring the rebels to their senses, brown-water sailors needed training through small-arms drills. Sailors in ocean-going ships rarely left their vessels to fight on land. On the western rivers, however, small-group combat became a regular feature of life in the Mississippi Squadron during the war's second phase. A sailor on the USS *Silver Lake* remembered, "we were put through a course of drill every day, cannon drill on [the] boat and musket drill ashore." Besides learning how to fight as a member of a landing party, sailors practiced with cutlasses, revolvers, and pikes. "We were thoroughly drilled in the use of *all* these arms," the sailor noted.[16]

Porter also wanted to create a "naval brigade" that would "operate against the numerous guerrilla bands and other scattered rebel forces along these rivers." He met with Lieutenant Colonel Alfred Ellet, who now commanded the Ram Fleet, and suggested that Ellet lead the counterinsurgency force. This "self-contained anti-guerrilla army" was a "revolutionary concept," according to one military historian. Porter endorsed the idea in a letter to the secretary of the navy, thinking that the brigade would report to him. But Ellet had different plans.[17]

Like his late brother, Alfred Ellet was not the kind of man to be content within a chain of command. He convinced Secretary of War Stanton to promote Charlie Ellet, his nineteen-year-old nephew, to colonel and put him in charge of the Ram Fleet. The result of all this was the Mississippi Marine Brigade. Even though the new outfit was supposed to be under Porter's command, it operated as an independent unit. The admiral eventually got the marine brigade transferred to Major General Grant's command, but that officer was not interested in working with the Ellets.[18]

Recruiting for the Ram Fleet steered lazy, indifferent, and undisciplined soldiers toward the brigade. "Soldiering Made Easy! No more Marching No Carrying Knapsacks!" advertised one broadside. It also promised no picket duty, no trenches to dig, no muddy camps, and plenty of food. Another broadside said the brigade was "especially attractive to old soldiers." Recruiting nevertheless lagged, but enough men joined the fleet to make the unit viable.[19]

The army added five fighting vessels to the existing Ram Fleet. Workers installed heavy timbers around the boilers, put two-inch oak planking on the cabin level, bolted sheets of iron to the pilot house, installed an extra-wide stage (gangplank) especially for the cavalry, and hooked hoses to the boilers so that crewmen could repel boarders with scalding water. Each boat carried about 125 cavalrymen, twice as many infantrymen, and a few field cannons.[20]

Done properly, the Mississippi Marine Brigade could have helped suppress the rebel insurgency. But the whole enterprise was mismanaged from the start, and the brigade probably hurt the Union war effort more than it helped. Neither Alfred nor Charlie Ellet were ones to take orders from anyone, and after the fall of Vicksburg, there was no oversight or accountability for the marine brigade. The Ellets instead used it as their private army. The poor quality of its troops, indifferent officers, and a lack of training meant that the unit often antagonized southern civilians. Men came to resent service in the brigade, and a riot occurred on at least one boat. Its antiguerrilla operations often turned into pillaging expeditions.[21]

Even before the Mississippi Marine Brigade confirmed its incompetence, Porter realized that merely playing Whack-a-Mole would not suppress the insurgency. The Mississippi Squadron needed a persistent and broad application of force to separate rebels from the civilians who supported them. Changing the environment became one way to destroy the civilian infrastructure that nourished the irregular war. The Mississippi Squadron turned the levees, or more precisely, the waters the levees held back, into a weapon. In January 1863 the admiral ordered the USS *Tyler* to drown out guerrillas near Greenville, Mississippi. The timberclad drew near the bank, and its sailors hacked away at the levee "so that the whole country may be overflowed." Two months later the *Conestoga* and the *General Bragg* brought a group of contrabands with picks and shovels to Bolivar, Mississippi. The men scratched away fifty feet of the levee to "drown out Mrs. Monley and Old Topp," who were likely sympathetic to the guerrilla cause and thus paid dearly for their loyalty. Water was soon "pouring through [the opening] very rapidly," noted the *Conestoga*'s captain.[22]

When the navy harnessed the power of nature against guerrillas, it was restoring the landscape to its condition prior to the levee system. The rushing waters washed away fields, farms, and produce that had stood in comparative safety behind the levees. By altering the landscape, Union sailors were turning nature against the Confederacy and converting the region into a swampy wilderness. Northern gunboats struck a powerful blow against the southern agroecosystem. Southern planters had worked for years—or at least forced their enslaved people to work for years—to establish an agricultural economy that drew sustenance and wealth from the land. Union gunboats interrupted or destroyed this complex system and thereby sapped the Confederate ability to sustain war.[23]

A more elaborate use of environmental warfare involved digging a cutoff channel near the confluence of the Mississippi and Arkansas Rivers. There was a sizable isthmus in a Mississippi's loop there that harbored a "very bad Guerrilla Station," according to Lieutenant Commander Thomas O. Selfridge, the *Conestoga*'s new captain. Guerrillas, or "those pests of the human race" as Porter called them, could make multiple attacks on boats chugging around Beulah Bend, as it was known, which cradled the isthmus. Selfridge brought the timberclad to the spot and dug a cutoff that partially flooded the isthmus and eventually led to the demise of nearby Napoleon, Arkansas. Not only did guerrillas no longer use the spot for attacks, but the navigable river was also about ten miles shorter afterward and allowed the squadron to concentrate its forces more quickly in case of an attack.[24]

Porter put other policies in place. On December 2, 1862, he ordered his captains to shut down commerce along the river unless it occurred in Union-occupied areas or the seller had a permit from him. The regulation signaled the Union's attempt to extend the blockade to the inland rivers. Two months later Porter sanctioned the confiscation of food from southern civilians. Next, the admiral declared war on civilians who actively fought against the Union, noting how men in plain clothes "lurk in the woods" and fire at people on steamers "without caring or knowing whether it is friend or foe they are about to murder." In a notice that the fleet apparently distributed along the Mississippi River, Porter warned that such people "will be treated as highwaymen and assassins, and no quarter will be shown them." If this "savage and barbarous Confederate custom" did not stop, he pledged to "try what virtue there is in hanging." It was his plainest statement that the Mississippi Squadron would attack civilians if necessary.[25]

Under Porter's command, the Mississippi Squadron spent most of its time protecting Union supply lines and attacking southern ambushers and their supporters. By the spring of 1863, the admiral had sketched out a strategy for fighting this war: wear down Confederate military resistance, starve Confederate civilians, separate rebel soldiers from the civilians who nourished them, and suffocate southern commerce. Porter's war of exhaustion would last until 1865, and it fundamentally altered the brown-water navy's activities. The irregular war became *the war* for the squadron, especially after the capture of Vicksburg.

There was another crucial change that happened to the fleet in the war's second phase. The Mississippi Squadron enlisted Black men in large numbers. These recruits provided a necessary jolt of manpower that allowed the fleet to suppress the irregular war and protect Union supply lines.

In 1862 the navy tried to supply enough sailors for the Mississippi Squadron, particularly by turning on the recruiting spigot that was Cincinnati. In the war's first fourteen months, 6 percent of free sailors enlisted in Cincinnati. That figure jumped to 31 percent between July 1862 and April 1863. Even with this new source of bluejackets, Porter complained, "We can get the vessels faster than we can get crews."[26]

Since the navy could not provide enough sailors, the fleet recruited formerly enslaved men. In a private letter, Porter bluntly admitted, "I could get no men so I work in the darkies." As noted earlier, formerly enslaved men went from 3 percent of enlistees in the war's first phase (through June 1862) to 20 percent in the second phase (July 1862 to April 1863) and 35 percent in the third phase (May 1864 to April 1864). The Confiscation and Milita Acts created the opportunity for Black enlistment, but it took the ravages of malaria, tepid enlistment of white men, and the fleet's expansion to push commanders to allow large numbers of former slaves to become brown-water sailors.[27]

Boat captains often enlisted enslaved men in groups, usually from plantations or temporary camps. For instance, a dozen enslaved men joined the USS *Carondelet*'s crew on July 22, 1862, while six contrabands from the Vicksburg area began service on the USS *Great Western* two days later. Another source of recruits was government contraband camps. Most of these were temporary communities within Union lines where formerly enslaved people had minimal protection but endured overcrowding, poor sanitation, and miserable conditions. The 370 former slaves who listed Cairo as their enlistment location during the war's second phase were probably living in the contraband camp near the fleet's headquarters when they joined the service.[28]

The enlistment of significant numbers of Black men came at a crucial time in the Mississippi Squadron's history. The fleet was becoming responsible for protecting Union supply lines and suppressing guerrilla activity. It added dozens of boats and careened toward an aggressive strategy. Soon it would be more active in the Vicksburg Campaign. Arguably, the fleet would have failed without the labor of formerly enslaved men, and had no freedmen served, the success of the Union armies in the western theater would have been jeopardized. Black men, however, faced significant hardships when they put on a blue uniform.

8

BLACK SAILORS

The penetration of the Mississippi Squadron by river into the slaveholding states was an opportunity to enlist thousands of formerly enslaved men. White sailors exhibited racism toward these new recruits in many ways, including forcing them to do the worst jobs, giving them the lowest ratings, and enforcing segregation as much as possible. Life in the Mississippi Squadron for Black sailors was not far removed from slavery. A few sailors, though, carved out small pockets of relative equality.[1]

About 2,900 African American men joined the Mississippi Squadron, composing 17 percent of the fleet's total crews, a percentage that probably equaled the blue-water navy.[2] In their efforts to join the service or escape bondage, enslaved men broke through the "geography of containment" that had constrained them for years. This impressive mobility signaled a firm determination to improve their lives. Andrew Lusk was enslaved in Monroe County, Tennessee, northeast of Chattanooga. In April 1863 the teenager and his friend John Washington "left there together and enlisted on the U.S.S. Rattler at Rosedale Landing Miss.," he remembered. It was a 450-mile journey across the Volunteer State. Free cities across the river from slave states were common points of enlistment. About 150 enslaved men fled to Cincinnati and there joined the fleet. A few traveled from the Deep South, but most were from Tennessee, Kentucky, and Virginia.[3]

Some enslaved men became sailors despite their enslavers' best efforts to shore up their property claim. George Washington Moseby—self-described as "ginger cake color"—worked as an enslaved teamster for Joe Moseby in Memphis when the Civil War erupted. Joe Moseby saw the peculiar institution dissolving before his eyes and forced his enslaved people to cross the Mississippi River to St. Francis County, Arkansas. This effort to prevent escapes did not work, as George Moseby explained in his pension application: "I left my master and went to Helena Ark. and joined the navy." In a final act of defiance, the self-emancipated man dropped "Moseby" from his name when he enlisted on August 8, 1862.[4]

The motivations of Black men to serve in the Mississippi Squadron ranged from the practical to the abstract and overlapped with reasons why native-born whites and immigrants enlisted. Preserving the Union and destroying slavery rested alongside economic opportunity and youthful exuberance. Some men saw gunboats as their best opportunity to escape from slavery. Bill Keys and Allen Turner were enslaved in Bolivar County, Mississippi. "We left the farm together," Turner explained after the war, "and went to the mouth of White River, where we stopped, with [the] intention of enlisting on one of the U.S. Gunboats lying there." Turner enlisted on the USS *Prairie Bird,* but Keys was rejected because of an injured hand.[5]

Enslaved men also had good reasons *not* to enlist in the Mississippi Squadron. Service on gunboats was not desirable for white men, so it is reasonable to assume that Black men felt the same way. The uncertainty of life aboard an ironclad, concerns about ill treatment, the possibility of death or dismemberment, and the lack of autonomy were concerns that enslaved men shared with others who looked upon brown-water naval service with suspicion. Fugitives from slavery wanted economic independence, and many saw the cultivation of land as the primary way to get it. Moreover, men with wives and children often saw their paramount duty as protecting their families. The pressure to enlist forced them to choose between competing notions of masculinity. In one, they could achieve empowerment within the body politic through violence. In the other, they cared for their families. Many men chose the latter form of masculinity by staying in contraband camps or plantations instead of enlisting.[6]

Some men were compelled to serve in the Mississippi Squadron. Captains forcibly enlisted former slaves from government contraband camps, improvised refugee sites, and cities. While George Washington said he "joined the navy" at Helena, he went on to imply that he was dragooned into service. "Jerry Irvin was first mate and it was he who came ashore at Helena and took me and two other colored fellows named Harrison and John, strangers to me." Officers also made a habit of taking enslaved men from riverside plantations, partly because they did not have to compete with the army for bodies. John McCoy, who served on the USS *Curlew,* remembered after the war how sailors "took us off a plantation." There is even evidence that officers used alcohol to persuade fugitives to enlist. On May 17, 1863, three contrabands came on board the USS *Lafayette* and "joined the U.S. Service," according to an officer on the boat. "The Capt. emptied the ale bottle to one of them. In an hour, they were rigged up in 'Navy Uniform.'"[7]

Enslaved men, whether enlisting voluntarily or forcibly, normally underwent a physical examination before mustering in. Charles Olden, who was enslaved near Vicksburg, "ran away and joined the US ship Benton in July 1863 at the mouth of the Yazoo River." He noted, "I was stripped of all my clothes and thoroughly examined as to my being able to do the work in the vessel." Such examinations sometimes revealed the brutal reminders of slavery lacerated into a man's body. December Haskell, John Haskell, and Joseph Haskell, who enlisted on the USS *Marmora* with three other men named Haskell, each had lash marks on his back or butt.[8]

Despite the brutality inherent to slavery, most white sailors generally opposed emancipation and held negative racial attitudes. On January 1, 1863, the day the Emancipation Proclamation went into effect but before news of it reached the fleet, a sailor denounced President Lincoln as a traitor to the Union soldiers and sailors who had died in the war. He predicted that if the proclamation went into effect, the result would be a "total destruction of the Union and a bloody war of Extermination." Elias Smith, one of the few sailors who demonstrated abolitionist sympathies, admitted that prejudice against contrabands was common, "particularly among the Irish." Also, the majority of native-born white men were from the Midwest, a region that was among the most racist in the North.[9]

In their correspondence sailors portrayed formerly enslaved men in condescending and stereotypical ways common in the mid-nineteenth century. They described Black sailors as lazy, grinning all the time, jolly, ludicrous dancers, childlike, impertinent, dishonest, and simpleminded. Sailors also made negative comments about Black men's physical features. In a typical passage, one sailor on the USS *Silver Lake* described Black crewmen as "a happy-go-lucky set" who danced to the fiddle every night. He and his fellows called one of the men "Lippy," and he noted, "We had much sport with him." White sailors also fastened demeaning nicknames on contraband crewmen, including "Coast of Africa Nigar Go James," "Goodfer Nothing," and "Abe Linkum."[10]

Rear Admiral Porter shared and affirmed these negative racial attitudes. In a general order that is astonishing to modern eyes, he justified the use of contrabands in the fleet because "white men can not stand the southern sun." Black sailors should be used to defend the vessels only in cases of emergency, he noted, believing that in a pinch they would be "efficient men." They should be issued only enough clothes "to make them comfortable until they are out of debt," presumably because they could not manage finances. In a racist crescendo, the admiral added that officers would have to closely monitor the cleanliness of the Black recruits, "as they are not naturally clean in their persons."[11]

Between emancipation and the influx of contrabands into the fleet, white sailors felt a sense of racial demotion. One on the USS *Cincinnati* complained, "niggers are treated so much better than white men." Since President Lincoln issued the Emancipation Proclamation, he thought, "some of our niggers have become very saucy and independent. Why! One of our coal heavers had the impudence to tell one of our firemen that the day would come when they (the blacks) would be masters and the white men would be their slaves." White sailors were in constant and close contact with former slaves, and they did not like it. Soon after the fall of Vicksburg, an officer on the USS *Louisville* grumbled that he had "shipped several contrabands as lands[men]. It begins to look as though we are going to have a whole crew of negros." At the time that he wrote those words, 36 of the ironclad's 173 enlisted men were African American recruits.[12]

Sailors, though, simultaneously held paternalistic attitudes and could be magnanimous toward individual Black sailors by helping them in personal ways. George Black, a contraband, was a blacksmith on the USS *Essex.* He enlisted on July 25, 1862, but a month later wanted to free his twelve-year-old son. When the *Essex* was near Vicksburg, Black secured the help of two white sailors, Edward Galligan and William Park. The three men went in a wagon "3 miles back in the bush" to find the boy. They located Black's son, who was working alongside several other enslaved people. The sailors also discovered some who were confined in stocks; Galligan used an ax to "let free three wenches and one buck nigger." The sailors took Black's son, who left without saying goodbye to his mother, but refused to take the other enslaved people, claiming, "we had more of them on board than we had provision for." It is impossible to know how Galligan and Park perceived Black and other contrabands, but their writing was free from overt racial stereotypes, something that stands in stark contrast to most other surviving materials.[13]

The hostile racial attitudes pervading the Mississippi Squadron undergirded the blatant discrimination against Black sailors. Even a bluejacket who was "glad" to have such men in the fleet saw them as useful for labor instead of combat. His attitude aligned with the intentions of the Militia Act, which limited African American men to support roles. On April 30, 1862, Secretary of the Navy Welles reinforced such assumptions by specifying that contrabands who enlisted in the navy must be rated as "boys at $8, $9, or $10 per month and one ration." This policy was doubly discriminatory. In 1862, at least, the brown-water navy paid every recruit below the rank of petty officer eighteen dollars per month but specified that contrabands "will in no case, whatever may be their employment, receive a higher rating and pay than that of first-class boys."[14]

The subordination of Black men into lower ratings was pervasive. Four out of ten such crewmen were rated as some type of boy, compared to 5 percent for whites. White "boys" were nearly all teenagers, whereas Black men of that rank were often adults. Henry Clay, who enlisted when he was sixty-two, was one such "boy." The disparity between the number of white and African American coal heavers was also significant. Six out ten coal heavers were Black sailors and were three times more likely to be shoved into that rating than native-born white recruits. In fact, white sailors took it for granted that Black men would be assigned to these subservient and hard-labor roles. "Enlisted six niggers—runaways. They were assigned as coal-heavers," a white sailor wrote casually in his diary. Taken together, 57 percent of Black sailors were assigned ratings that reflected a labor or service role: boy, coal heaver, cook, or steward. The practical effect was the establishment of white dominance and a clear racial hierarchy within gunboats.[15]

African American sailors also did all sorts of menial and unpleasant tasks that were reminiscent of enslavement. During the Red River Expedition of 1864, former slaves commonly moved cotton bales on and off barges being towed behind Union gunboats. Four contrabands on the USS *Carondelet* had to go ashore and dig a grave for Joseph Brown, a white sailor from Ohio. Later in the same day, more contrabands went ashore to cut wood. Hundreds of Black men were forced to be servants of officers. Routinely engaged in hard labor or service jobs on gunboats, they had little opportunity to develop skills that would benefit them after the war.[16]

This intense physical labor led to a variety of health problems for African American sailors. Since Charles Olden was "stout and able bodied," he became a shell passer. When the *Benton* attacked Fort DeRussy in Louisiana, Olden was passing shells to the gunners. He picked up a 100-pounder shell and "got a wrench in my groin," which caused him to fall and sustain a concussion. When he awoke in his hammock, he had a lump in his right groin the size of a "large egg." The rupture made him unfit for duty. After the war Black sailors were more likely than white sailors to report a rupture or hernia in their pension applications, suggesting that they were more likely to have performed heavy manual labor while employed in the navy.[17]

Black men were also overrepresented on support vessels. The Mississippi Squadron had twenty-six nonfighting craft, including three receiving boats, seven tugs, and a hospital boat, among others. About 850 sailors served on these boats, and 47 percent of them were Black men. This discrimination paralleled the Union army, where African American soldiers were overrepresented in support roles like guard duty, manual labor, or work along supply lines.[18]

Robert "Bob" White had a different type of support role in the Mississippi Squadron. White was a biracial man from Georgia who worked as Rear Admiral Porter's personal servant. Many formerly enslaved men became personal servants of officers. It is unclear if they volunteered for such assignments or if white sailors forced them into menial positions that were a few steps away from slavery. Regardless, serving officers was a condition resembling enslavement and reinforced notions of Black inferiority. Servants of navy officers ranged widely in age, and they normally appear on muster rolls as first-, second-, or third-class boys.[19]

It is difficult to recover the experience of these men. Percy Davis was one of four Black sailors who worked for eight officers on the *Carondelet*. The fourteen-year-old boy kept the officers' staterooms "in good order," blackened the officers' boots "every morning," repaired clothes, and waited on tables, according to one officer. Such employment of African American sailors was a matter of convenience. William Bock, a signal officer on the USS *Lexington,* liked having a "negro boy" as his servant: "I have no cooking to do, no bed to make."[20]

Officers likely held paternalistic attitudes toward the men they forced to be servants, as Robert Walker probably learned firsthand. Walker was eleven years old when he shipped on board the USS *Pittsburg.* The former fieldhand became a first-class boy and likely a servant to a group of officers. Remarkably, a photograph of Walker survives. He posed for a carte-de-visite at Mound City, wearing his uniform. At the bottom of the image, someone (likely an officer) wrote "Our Bob." The occasion of the photo is lost, and there are many reasons why Walker might have taken the time to have his likeness captured: pride at serving in the navy, peer pressure, or a sense of why his enlistment was important. Another explanation, however, is that an officer, his pseudo-master, wanted a memento of him. The phrase "Our Bob" might indicate that the sailors whom he served saw him as something of a mascot or a pet.[21]

A few Black women also worked in service roles on boats. Bock told his wife that a chambermaid "does all of the washing of all the officers." She and her husband, a carpenter's mate, were "colored folks." Ann Stokes was a nurse on the fleet's hospital boat. Like the unidentified chambermaid, she worked alongside her husband and inhabited a complex world. As women in a decidedly masculine space, they might have been subject to taunts, verbal harassment, and sexual assault. But couples who worked on the same boat were able to stay together during the war, earn steady pay, and eat regular meals even if they were in a space that exerted conflicting pressures on their marriage.[22]

Besides treating Black men as laborers and servants rather than sailors, the navy also tried to keep them separate from white sailors. The *Rules and Regulations for Vessels of the Light Draft Flotillas in the Mississippi Squadron* was clear: "Contrabands must be messed by themselves, and also be kept in gangs by themselves when at work. They are not to be mixed up with the crews of the vessels, nor are they to be included in the general exercises." On at least one ironclad, Black sailors endured an inspection at 8:15 A.M., while the general inspection occurred at 9:30. There were limits to what could be enforced, however. Enlisted men slept in shifts in hammocks in a common area and ate in a shared space, so there was no way for Black men to be relegated to their own location. The exact sleeping arrangements are lost to history, but it seems that white and Black men were in close proximity. Henry Coffinberry, who was a master's mate on the *Louisville,* was trying to sleep when he "heard a nigar reading his letters a little to loud." Coffinberry stepped out of his room "and gave him a good blowing up." It is unclear if white and Black sailors ate at the same time. What is clear, though, is that messes were usually organized by race. Rowland True remembered after the war that the "thirty Negroes" aboard his tinclad had their own "mess and [their] mess cook was entirely separate from ours."[23]

An additional type of segregation involved burial rites. It appears that African American men were buried separately from white men. At Hard Times Landing, sailors from the *Carondelet* reinterred men killed on board the *Benton* whose graves had washed away. Two days later the boat's acting master supervised the burial of Jacob Lewis Haskin, who had died of typhoid fever. Haskin's messmates, all of whom were probably Black men, went to Joseph Davis's plantation and buried Haskin "in the Servants burial ground." A sailor named Murphy read the funeral service over the grave. This incident may be read any number of ways. The navy could have mandated segregated burials, Haskin may have had a connection to the planation, or Black sailors may have insisted that they be interred in a slave burial ground.[24]

African American men may have preferred certain types of onboard segregation because they could recreate fragments of their slave community. Many had escaped in small groups and, when they enlisted, typically served on the same boat. Hilliard, Sam, and Thomas Dunlap left a plantation in Mississippi and enlisted in Memphis on October 1, 1862. They were fifteen, twenty, and twenty-four years old respectively when they joined the navy and served together on the USS *New Era.* On board the boats, former slaves had their own religious services. A white officer noted disapprovingly, "Evening—there is a negro prayer-meeting on the spar-deck—a notable commentary on religion—consistent thoughts and inconsistent actions." On the *Carondelet* Black men were allowed to go ashore after the boat's divine service and attend a prayer meeting, presumably at a contraband camp.[25]

If the uncertain walls of segregation were breached, white sailors were quick to defend what they saw as their racial privilege. On the receiving boat *Clara Dolsen,* about fifty "darkies from Mississippi" were shipped as coal heavers. They were "messed with the white boys, much to our disgust," wrote one sailor. When a mess cook "gave the darkies the fat meat and the white boys the lean," the white sailors attacked the Black men.[26] William Bock, who employed a servant, told his brother that when a Black sailor "acts saucy or impudent," he "stands on the *capstan* a few hours with a large chunk of coal under his arm. Sometimes they stand in the pilot house all night." James Dickinson hit an African American sailor with a marlinspike when the man laughed at him. Dickinson and a friend later "cut down the nigger's hammock" so that "his head got a bully bump." Such abuse was widespread, judging from the conclusions of a surgeon in the fleet. He believed that Black sailors in the Mississippi Squadron were merely trading one exploitative master for one who was "almost *always* selfish & mean."[27]

Despite the intimidation, threats, and violence, Black sailors persevered and forced small changes on the fleet. When the coal heavers on the *Cincinnati* told white counterparts that their former enslavers would be punished, they were asserting a claim to be recognized as men. Even Porter begrudgingly recognized that Black men could be good sailors. In a general order to the fleet on July 26, 1863, the admiral decreed that qualified Black sailors could be promoted to landsmen or ordinary seamen "but not to petty officers." The change in policy came after an excuse-making preamble in which he argued that the "increasing sickness in the squadron, and the scarcity of men" were reasons why contrabands were employed with such frequency.[28]

There were other flashes of equality. Despite Porter's orders to the contrary, African American sailors manned cannons on many boats. Former slave William Johnson, for instance, became the first loader on one of the USS *Tyler*'s guns; officers on the *Essex* put Black men on cannon crews prior to its fight with the CSS *Arkansas;* and an officer on the *Pittsburg* routinely "engaged drilling Contrabands with big guns" as well as small arms.[29]

A few Black men rose above the discrimination and assumed positions of authority. Henry King was a captain of the after guard, a rating that gave the former slave authority over the starboard watches. John Moore was another Black man who obtained a position of authority. He was a coxswain on the *Pittsburg,* where he directed the crew of a cutter as they rowed to shore. A fieldhand according to the boat's muster roll, Moore was born in North Carolina and shipped on board the *Pittsburg* when he was thirty-three. But these men were exceptional: most Black sailors remained stuck in the lower ranks.[30]

African American sailors also had a slight measure of equality in the navy's court system. Unlike the judicial system in southern states, where Black people, enslaved or free, were routinely barred from bearing witness, Black sailors testified in the fleet's court-martial cases. For instance, Peter Dunker and Christopher Gibson, African American firemen on the USS *Lilly,* were sworn in as witnesses in a desertion case. Black sailors appeared to receive the same legal treatment as their white comrades when appearing in court-martial cases. Ordinary Seaman Richard Cornelius one day went on shore and got drunk. When he returned to his boat, he used "abusive and profane language" toward the acting master's mate and, once Cornelius was put in irons, struck the man. After Cornelius pleaded guilty, the court questioned three of the boat's officers about his character. They described him as having a "very good character" and being a "very respectful, trustworthy man." The court prescribed a sentence of death by hanging, most likely for striking an officer, but also recommended mercy for Cornelius.[31]

In another small step towards equality, Black sailors received prize money and were eligible for military pensions. The navy auctioned contraband property it seized, most of which was cotton, and distributed the proceeds among the crew of the boat or boats that seized the material. One's share depended on his rating, not his race. African American sailors who received prize money probably had greater opportunities in post–Civil War America to own land than Black men who did not receive such cash transfers. Likewise, a sailor's race did not affect his pension amount. The U.S. government created the pension system in 1862 and expanded its operations over the second half of the nineteenth century. While it is true that African American men had more difficulty than white veterans in obtaining a pension, those sailors who secured payouts had more mobility and economic security than those who did not.[32]

Although they were not as celebrated as the men who joined the U.S. Colored Troops, the Black men who served in the Mississippi Squadron were just as important to the Union's war effort. They were a necessary source of labor for the brown-water fleet, and it is no coincidence that their surge in enlistment started during a manpower crisis. The squadron was expanding its reach in the western theater. Black sailors helped its gunboats take the war to the doorsteps of their former owners during the campaigns to capture Vicksburg.

9

THE YAZOO PASS AND STEELE'S BAYOU EXPEDITIONS

In the fall of 1862, the Union military got serious in its attempt to take Vicksburg. No more would two undersized naval squadrons try to capture the city with next to no army support. Instead, the army took the lead in the campaign and brought the Mississippi Squadron into its efforts as an auxiliary. Effective Confederate defensive measures and hostile environmental conditions ensured that Federal forces would not achieve their objectives. Ironically, the failures of 1862–63 confirmed that the navy would have to be central to capturing the rebel stronghold.

Vicksburg was the best defended southern city west of the Appalachian Mountains. Confederate engineering took advantage of the region's geography. The city sat atop a huge bluff on the Mississippi River's eastern bank, making an attack from the west impossible. East, north, and south of town, the loess soil created a naturally defensible barrier. The ground was unusual in that millennia of runoff had created a series of sharp ridges whose slopes were remarkably steep. Migrants to the region cleared the black walnut trees atop these ridges and established farms and plantations. Some of the farmland washed into the gullies, turning them into boggy sloughs that nurtured a jungle of cane, cat's-claw vines, greenbriers, and honeysuckle. It was an easy task to defend these narrow approaches. In addition, any army advancing from northern or central Mississippi would have a long and vulnerable supply line behind it.[1]

Federal efforts to take Vicksburg became bound up in the politics swirling around the Union armies in the West. Major General John McClernand, a man with a gift for raising troops but no skill in leading them, weaseled his way into the western command structure. A friend of President Lincoln, McClernand had presidential approval to lead an independent assault on Vicksburg. Major General Grant, who was recently promoted to overall command in the West, rightly resented this intrusion on his authority. He accelerated a partially thought-out scheme to attack Vicksburg before McClernand arrived. Grant proposed that two Union armies advance overland to Vicksburg. The first, under his direct command, would strike south along the Mississippi Central Railroad and establish a supply depot at Holly Springs. It would then follow the railroad to Jackson and from there veer west to Vicksburg. The second army, under Major General Sherman, would depart from Memphis and meet up with Grant near Oxford.[2]

At the same time, Grant was also considering a combined army-navy operation up the Yazoo River, a sluggish stream that emptied into the Mississippi nine miles north of Vicksburg. If the Mississippi Squadron could bring soldiers up the Yazoo, they might be able to get north of the Confederate defenders and outflank the city. Grant and Rear Admiral Porter met on the USS *Black Hawk* on November 20, 1862, to discuss matters. Porter and his staff wore their dress whites and enjoyed French champagne and roast duck. Grant, true to form, wore shabby clothing. The general presented his plan, and the admiral agreed to send some boats into the Yazoo. Union gunboats would first secure the river and then later carry troops upstream and land them northwest of Vicksburg.[3]

Porter selected Commander Henry Walke, one of his most experienced commanders, to lead the small Yazoo naval expedition. Walke was to scout the river and "prevent the rebels from raising forts right under our noses." In a measure of the campaign's importance, Walke had command of the seven Pook's Turtles, the tinclads *Signal* and *Marmora,* and the ram *Queen of the West.* On December 8 the fleet steamed the short distance to the mouth of Yazoo, where it paused. The prudent Walke sent the *Marmora* and the *Signal* into the greenish-brown waters of the river to check the depth and scout enemy defenses.[4]

The two tinclads chugged single file up the narrow stream for about twenty miles and then halted. Sailors had noticed an alarming amount of "small scows and stationary floats of various kinds along the channel." The Union gunboats were in a minefield.[5]

These torpedoes were better designed than the ones Confederates had deployed at Fort Henry. Most of them were a five-gallon glass demijohn bottle stuffed with gunpowder. Each had an artillery friction primer attached to a wire that passed through a watertight seal of gutta percha, beeswax, beef tallow, and/

or plaster of paris. They were either anchored to the river bottom or tied to a line stretching underwater from shore to shore, typically floating a few feet below the surface. The weapons could be detonated in two different ways. When a boat snagged a line, it pulled the torpedo to its side, causing the line to go taught and pull the friction primer. Other torpedoes had a copper line running to shore, and Confederates in rifle pits there detonated them with a battery or by pulling the line taught. Additional rebels along the shoreline were poised to pick off any sailors who were on the bow looking for torpedoes or those unfortunate enough to be blown into the water when one of the "infernal machines" exploded. Torpedoes tended to leak and were easy to spot when they became unmoored but were devastating on the few occasions when they worked as intended.[6]

The Yazoo minefield was well placed. It was around a bend in the river so that a lead boat would be physically separate from the rest of the fleet when it entered dangerous waters. Nearby Johnson's plantation was a convenient location for making torpedoes and for sheltering rebel soldiers tending them. The minefield was also close to a series of hills on the eastern bank of the river collectively known as the Chickasaw Bluffs. The outcroppings began on the northern edge of Vicksburg and arced toward the Yazoo, where they terminated at Drumgould's, Snyder's, and Haynes' Bluffs. The hills were only about ninety feet high but were excellent defensive positions. The Confederates had eight guns on the top of Drumgould's Bluff that could attack any boat stuck in the minefield.[7]

The sailors on the two tinclads had probably not encountered a torpedo before and decided to improvise their response. One of them took aim at a glass demijohn about fifty yards away and "casually" fired his musket. At the same time, a rebel on the bank triggered a different torpedo. The explosion lifted the *Marmora*'s stern out of the river, sent water shooting fifty feet in the air, and showered the boat with glass shards. Confederates on shore opened up with a furious volley that sent Minié balls splattering against the tinclads. They triggered another torpedo close to the *Signal,* but the explosion caused no damage. Lieutenant Robert Getty, commanding the *Marmora,* had seen enough. The tinclads backed downriver out of range, their guns ineffectively barking at the unseen Confederates.[8]

When he returned to the fleet, Getty told Walke that there was enough water in the Yazoo for the ironclads. He also explained that any expedition would need heavy guns to provide covering fire for the crews removing torpedoes. Walke decided to send the USS *Cairo,* USS *Pittsburg,* and the three lighter boats upriver to clear the minefield. The tinclads and the ram would lead the way "to scour the shore . . . and haul the torpedoes on shore, and destroy them." The ironclads were to stay well back and "shell the banks of the river above them if necessary." If there was any "apparent danger," the expedition was to return to the other boats waiting near the Yazoo's mouth. It was a reasonable plan. Unfortunately, the Union captains venturing upriver would not stick to it.[9]

The five boats entered the Yazoo on December 12 and spread out in single file as they steamed upstream. The *Marmora* was in front with the *Cairo* next in line, despite Walke's orders to the contrary. After about four hours, the *Marmora* found a torpedo. "We were nearly on it before we saw it," the tinclad's captain reported. He backed the boat downstream a bit and sent a cutter to investigate. The tinclad was in a vulnerable position—in a mine field, separated from the other boats, and out of sight of them around a bend.[10]

What happened next is a matter of dispute because the Union commanders did their best to deflect blame for the first western gunboat being knocked out of the war. The most likely story is that sailors on the *Marmora* started shooting at torpedoes, hoping to detonate them, while Getty dispatched a cutter to snip the wires that tethered others. The *Cairo* surged forward despite Walke's admonition to hang back. Its captain, Lieutenant Commander Thomas O. Selfridge, was new to the brown-water navy and mistook the musketry of the *Marmora*'s sailors for a Confederate attack. He was a career naval man who had commanded the USS *Cumberland* when the ironclad CSS *Virginia* sank the wooden vessel at Newport News, Virginia. Selfridge was transferred to the Mississippi Squadron because of poor performance, which would soon become evident once more.[11]

By the time Selfridge realized the *Marmora* was not under attack, the *Cairo* was in the minefield. The boat was in more danger than the tinclad because of its deeper draft. Selfridge quickly realized he had made a terrible mistake and started backing the *Cairo* downriver. A strong wind made the huge boat difficult to manage, and the ironclad ended up sideways in the channel. Confederate artillery on Drumgould's Bluff started shooting at the gunboat. Selfridge returned fire, righted the ironclad, and then inexplicably ordered it forward. The vessel soon snagged an underwater line and pulled a pair of torpedoes to its side. As a fellow officer remarked drily after the war, "Selfridge of the *Cairo* found two torpedoes and removed them by placing his vessel over them."[12]

The first torpedo exploded under the port quarter, launching the *Cairo*'s anchor several feet in the air and knocking the crew to the deck. As sailors struggled to their feet, another volcanic blast rocked the boat. This one, under the starboard bow, knocked a heavy gun off its carriage. Inside the boat George Yost saw dark water rushing into the hold with the roar of Niagara Falls. Selfridge ordered the boat to make for the shore and told his sailors to man the pumps. A gun crew fired one last defiant shot at the bluff as the *Cairo* chugged toward the bank.[13]

The other Union boats rushed toward the minefield to help the stricken ironclad. Confederate musket balls slammed against the boats as shells from Drumgould's Bluff splashed into the water. The *Pittsburg* hammered the levees, forcing rebels there to keep their heads down. The boat's steady cannonade, Yost thought, prevented the enemy from "coming down on us."[14]

Nothing could be done to save the *Cairo,* however, so Selfridge gave the order to abandon it. Soaked sailors scrambled to get out of and off the boat. The "water was all over the Gun decks," Yost wrote, "when the Ram 'Queen of the West' came alongside." Bluejackets had only a few minutes to salvage what they could. Yost grabbed two revolvers and his diary before scrambling to safety. "We moved just in time to escape being swallowed up in the seething caldron of foaming water," he wrote later. Less than fifteen minutes after the explosions, the *Cairo* slipped beneath the dark waters of the Yazoo, leaving only its jackstaff and chimneys to mark the location of the first successful use of a torpedo in the Civil War. All the crew survived the attack. After knocking down the sunken ironclad's jackstaff and chimneys and destroying some torpedoes, the flotilla glumly steamed downriver.[15]

Walke, who was not one to suffer fools, was angry at Selfridge's disobedience of orders and sent him to Porter. The admiral was aboard his command boat, which was stuck on a sandbar in the Mississippi River. Surprisingly, Porter rewarded Selfridge's incompetence by giving him command of the timberclad USS *Conestoga.* Perhaps he had no other choice. The Union was building new boats, and the brown-water fleet's commander was desperate for men to crew the vessels and officers to lead them.[16]

Things were not much better for the two Union armies. Sherman's troops were bogged down in the mud near Oxford, while Grant was growing nervous about his vulnerable supply line. Grant sent Sherman's army back to Memphis to link up with the Mississippi Squadron. Sherman and Porter met on December 18.

The admiral wore his dress uniform for the occasion and looked like a "drum-major," as he recalled. The general wore a plain blue uniform that was greasy and dirty. Sherman explained that he needed the navy to bring his army up the Yazoo River so his men could land near Johnson's plantation. The Federals would then attack Chickasaw Bluffs while the gunboats shelled the rebel positions. If things went as planned, Sherman would invest Vicksburg from the northwest while Grant attacked from the east. Porter agreed to help.[17]

Two days after this meeting, the Confederacy effectively ensured that the Union's jaunt up the Yazoo would fail. Major General Van Dorn, in an uncharacteristically competent move, attacked and destroyed the Union supply depot at Holly Springs. This forced Grant to abandon his march on Vicksburg and return to Tennessee. He informed Sherman of this but issued no recall orders, so Sherman and Porter unwisely decided to continue their mission. Confederates defeated the paltry Union attack on Chickasaw Bluffs.[18]

The failed attempts to capture Vicksburg in 1862 demonstrated the flaws of an overland campaign in Mississippi. Grant's plan was utterly conventional in that it called for concentrating forces, maneuvering to take geographic points, securing lines of communication and supply, and advancing along a railroad. The Mississippi Central, though, was too long and too vulnerable to be his forces' sole means of supply and communication. Grant needed to move his logistics back to the Mississippi River. In January 1863 he shifted his army to Young's Point, which was directly west of Vicksburg on the Louisiana side of the Mississippi. This move signaled a greater role for the Mississippi Squadron and confirmed the navy's importance in capturing the Confederate citadel.[19]

While the Army of the Tennessee was moving across the Mississippi River, Sherman secured its western flank. He wanted to "thrash out Arkansas Post," situated on the Arkansas River about twenty-five miles from its mouth. The little town supported nearby Fort Hindman, which could be used as a staging base for Confederate raids on Young's Point. Sherman wanted to put his defeat at Chickasaw Bluffs behind him by achieving a quick victory in Arkansas. He convinced Porter to help him.[20]

Sherman got his quick victory. The USS *Baron de Kalb,* USS *Cincinnati,* and USS *Louisville* pounded the poorly built fort into submission on January 11 as Sherman's troops made slow progress toward it over swampy land. A Union soldier was amazed at the Union bombardment. The shelling was "one incessant roll of thunder" that "seemed to make the earth cave in." Confederates did not have enough guns to stave off the Union fleet. By the middle of the afternoon, the ironclads had silenced most of the southern artillery. They also inflicted gruesome casualties. After the battle one sailor inspected the position and told his parents that the "interior of the fort was covered with legs arms head[s] brains &c." Late in the day, Porter climbed into what was left of the fort to obtain its surrender.[21]

The capture of Fort Hindman was a rarity: federal gunboats stood up to a Confederate fort without the army's help and forced a surrender. The Union success, however, was partly due to Confederate mistakes. The few cannons in Fort Hindman were improperly positioned. A sailor on the *Cincinnati* noted that as the Union boats got close to the fort, the rebels could not depress their guns far enough to do any damage. The victory was also due to the stronghold's relatively low position. As at Fort Henry, noted a sailor after the war, "the elevation [of Fort Hindman] was just right for the boats."[22]

Grant thought the whole affair was a wild goose chase and excoriated McClernand, who technically commanded the expedition as senior officer, for exceeding his authority. When he learned that Sherman and Porter planned the attack, Grant quietly let the matter drop. Victory at Fort Hindman removed a threat to the Union supply line and allowed him to gather the Army of the Tennessee at Young's Point. He now had 50,000 men, hundreds of transports, and a growing pile of supplies mere miles from Vicksburg. Most of Porter's boats were nearby, either at the mouth of the Yazoo River or suppressing ambushes. It was unclear, however, where Grant would lead his army.[23]

After a failed attempt to dig a canal that would change the course of the Mississippi River and bypass Vicksburg, Grant settled upon traversing the Yazoo Delta. Heavy rains made it possible to steam across the delta, get into the Yazoo River northeast of Vicksburg, and then go *downstream* to the city. Using this route would put Sherman's army on high ground east of the city. It would not be easy. The delta was a jungle-like forest of densely packed trees in a swamp that had an old water route in its midst. An old steamboat cutoff connected to Moon Lake, the gateway to the Old Channel, once part of the Mississippi River. The Old Channel wound its way to the Yazoo River. Light-draft steamers had used this route to reach cotton plantations deep in the delta until the state of Mississippi built a huge levee to control flooding. An old steamboat pilot told Porter and Sherman that Union boats could reach the upper Yazoo via this route, so the two commanders decided on a combined operation. The resulting expedition, however, reinforced the Mississippi Squadron's inability to overcome harsh environmental conditions.[24]

Porter chose Lieutenant Commander Watson Smith to lead the expedition and gave him the ironclads *Baron de Kalb* and *Chillicothe;* the tinclads *Forest Rose, Marmora, Petrel, Rattler, Romeo,* and *Signal;* and the rams *Lioness* and *Fulton.* He also had three coal barges and numerous transports that carried 6,000 of Sherman's men. Smith had led the attack on Fort Hindman and was an obvious choice for the mission. He was, however, an uninspiring selection because he was naturally cautious and stuck to naval protocol when boldness and imagination were required. Watson was also sick, which contributed to his inability to sufficiently push the Union fleet forward. Brigadier General Leonard L. Ross commanded the ground troops, while Grant's topographical engineer, Lieutenant Colonel James H. Wilson, sent reports from the expedition back to Union headquarters.[25]

The *Chillicothe* was untested and the product of a new builder. While James B. Eads had built the Pook's Turtles and modified other ironclads like the *Essex,* Joseph Brown built the 385-ton *Chillicothe* in Cincinnati. Veteran sailor John Morrison was not impressed. He thought it was "the queerest-looking specimen for a war ship that ever I seen." The city-class gunboats had been beaten up, so Porter's decision to send the *Chillicothe* into action was a sound one. What he did not know was that the boat was so poorly built that it sabotaged the mission.[26]

The only way to get into the Yazoo Delta was to blow a hole in the Mississippi River levee, which was twenty-eight feet high and three hundred feet wide at its base. On February 2, Union soldiers hacked out a divot, then sailors from the *Forest Rose* placed a fifty-pound keg of gunpowder in the cavity. The ensuing explosion sent earth shooting in the air. A torrent of chocolatey water raged into the gap and then plummeted nine feet into the Old Channel. Soldiers then cut three more "shafts," packed gunpowder in them, and set them off simultaneously, "completely shattering the mound." The rushing waters wore away enough of the levee to create a hole seventy-five yards wide and sent humans and animals scrambling for higher ground. It was "like nothing I ever saw except Niagara Falls," wrote one Union officer. "Logs, trees, and great masses of earth were torn away with the greatest ease." When the waters calmed, survivors found debris scattered wantonly, dead livestock, damaged buildings, flattened crops, and a brownish slime coating buildings and fences.[27]

Smith's fleet entered the flooded delta in late February. The one-mile trip to Moon Lake was a wild ride as the waters of the Mississippi continued surging through a small channel. One Union soldier wrote: "Our boat was whirled round and round like a toy skiff in a washtub. We all held our breath as the steamer was hurled among floating logs and against overhanging trees." Ten white-knuckle minutes later, the steamer arrived, backward, in Moon Lake. While the Union flotilla paused to prepare for the campaign and distribute sharpshooters among the boats, sailors took cotton bales from the "fine plantations" along the lakeshore and piled them on the upper decks of the boats to protect the riflemen.[28]

In a driving rainstorm on February 25, the fleet left Moon Lake and entered the Old Channel. The ironclads led the way and crashed ahead like icebreakers. Progress was torturously slow. Intertwined trees impeded progress. Surgeon Fayette Clapp, who was on the *Marmora*, estimated that every five minutes sailors had to loop a cable around a tree and use the capstan to pull the boat forward. He constantly heard "Crash! Crash!! Crash!!" as tree limbs fell on the deck. "Again, we are litterally *working* our way through this narrow, crooked *Pass* through trees so close on either [side] as just barely to admit the passage of the boat," he wrote, amid "over hanging, over reaching limbs, great stout, brawny arms that seem to reach & *grab* at every thing on the boats & particularly spiteful at chimney stacks." The branches knocked escape pipes and davits into the water and shredded pilot houses. Logs got stuck in paddlewheels, and snags tore off rudders. Some boat crews lopped off their chimneys at the hurricane deck so they would not get destroyed. Soot coated everyone on board. The fleet crawled forward a few miles per day.[29]

Dangers were everywhere. The serpentine river and dense woods prevented visibility, and Union lookouts could only see the vessels immediately ahead of and behind them. Confederate soldiers shadowed the fleet in hopes that one of the boats would become separated from the rest. Union commanders were so concerned that they developed a special code. One whistle meant go ahead, two whistles meant stop, three whistles meant attack an enemy boat, four whistles meant destroy enemy property, and five whistles meant "destroy our own boat."[30]

The fleet entered the Coldwater River on February 28 and headed south into cotton country. Soldiers and sailors dragged bales back to the boats, prompting planters to burn their crops rather than see the Yankees steal them. Massive blazes greeted the Union vessels as they steamed downriver. Yost told his diary that one inferno was so large, "our roof caught fire several times. . . . [A] Blazing Shingle fell into the muzzle of one of our Guns" and almost caused it to explode. Farther downstream, a rebel steamer with 2,000 bales of cotton lay burning to the waterline. "Cotton was floating all around her. We have passed over 6 million dollars worth," noted a sailor on the *Baron de Kalb*.[31]

Guerrillas and Confederate soldiers pestered the fleet and slowed its progress even more. Once, a person on shore hailed the *Rattler* and called for the captain, saying he had a letter to deliver. As the tinclad paused, Yost recorded, "a volley of Musket Balls . . . flew around us pretty lively I can tell you. [T]he men were up in a very few minutes and were shelling the woods and Cane Brakes at a terrible rate." Although there were no casualties that day, another band of rebels attacked the boat the next day and killed a bluejacket. Rebels hoped such tactics would impede the fleet's progress long enough so that they could finish building a fort farther downstream.[32]

Fort Pemberton, as the Confederates called it, or Fort Greenwood as the Federals named it, was at the spot where the Tallahatchie and Yalobusha Rivers joined to form the Yazoo. It was an excellent location. The river juncture created a pocket of land that looked like a horseshoe tipped on its side. Fort Pemberton was at the open, or western, end of the horseshoe. Confederates had forced enslaved men to dig earthworks, muscle cotton bales into place, chop down trees, brace timbers against the bales, and heap dirt upon the cotton and wood. Its eight cannons had a perfect line of site northward up the Tallahatchie, which was so narrow that two Union ironclads could barely squeeze next to each other to make an attack. And a land assault across the marshy ground was unthinkable. Confederate obstacles in the Old Channel and the slow pace of the Union advance allowed the rebels to finish the fort. The friction of war had caught up with Lieutenant Commander Smith.[33]

On March 11 Smith took the *Chillicothe* downstream to test Fort Pemberton's defenses. Sailors "slushed [the] Tower and placed Bales of cotton against our Turrett" in hopes of deflecting Confederate balls. The ironclad steamed to within 800 yards of the fort when a steel-pointed rifle shell told Smith what he needed to know, as the projectile cracked an armored plate on the *Chillicothe*. Soon, another slug penetrated the forward port slide and struck its gun as sailors were loading it. The resulting blast flung one of the 1,600-pound slides into the brown water, set protective cotton bales on fire, left four men dead, and wounded another seventeen sailors. One poor soul had a "violent concussion of the brain," and several others sustained powder burns in their eyes. After getting "battered and hammered" for seven minutes, the gunboat withdrew. The Confederate's rifled 68-pounder was the perfect weapon to exploit the Union vessel's weakness.[34]

In its first battle, it was obvious that *Chillicothe* was "a perfect failure as a fighting vessel." The boat's builders had cut corners and used nine-inch instead of twelve-inch framing. They also used spikes instead of screws to secure the armor to this wooden backing, which was made from pine instead of oak. The *Chillicothe* was unable to absorb any direct hits because the impact of cannonballs either broke the spikes or caused them to fly out. Wilson concluded that the *Chillicothe* was a "great cheat and swindle upon the Government."[35]

With a land assault impossible, Smith twice more tried a naval attack. On the first occasion, rebel gunners hit the *Chillicothe* about thirty times, breaking the boat's beam and again setting cotton bales aflame. Inside Fort Pemberton, Major General William Loring encouraged his men, "Give 'em blizzards boys!" The *Baron de Kalb* was similarly abused and had its wheelhouse and steerage knocked to pieces. One round crashed into a gun crew, killing its captain and leaving gunner James Duke blind in his left eye, deaf in his left ear, and without use of his left hand. The second day's attack was no better. Each time the Union boats failed to inflict any damage on Fort Pemberton.[36]

Brigadier General Ross and Lieutenant Colonel Wilson were disgusted. In a scathing letter to Brigadier General John Rawlins, Grant's chief of staff, Wilson accused the naval commanders of avoiding "a close and desperate engagement." He claimed that he talked to them "and tried to give them backbone, but they are not confident." Wilson saved his highest criticism for Smith, whom he mocked as "His Excellency Acting Rear-Admiral Commodore Smith." He added sarcastically that Smith was not "the equal of Lord Nelson."[37]

The army officers would not have to contend with Smith much longer. He could not bear the strain of the expedition and resigned his command due to ill health, which probably included dysentery. Lieutenant Commander James P. Foster, captain of the *Chillicothe,* now took charge of the naval group. Foster and Ross agreed that there was no point in continuing the expedition. The flotilla slunk back through the Yazoo Delta. According to one sailor, it was only the "timely assistance of volunteer slaves, who cut and cleared away the trees which had been felled across the bayou," that allowed the Union boats to escape. John Morrison, a veteran sailor, saw the fleet return. It looked "awfully used up, some of the boats being minus their smokestacks, hammock nettings, and boats."[38]

The Steele's Bayou Expedition developed out of this Yazoo Pass failure and involved an even more circuitous route to get upstream of Haynes' Bluff. Steele's Bayou emptied into the Yazoo River near its juncture with the Mississippi River on the southern end of the Yazoo Delta. Any boat using this route would have to zigzag northward on Steele's for about thirty miles. It would then steam eastward on the Big Black Bayou for four miles before reaching Deer Creek and squiggling northward. Once the boat reached the Rolling Fork, it would then travel eastward until it turned southward on either the Little Sunflower River or the Big Sunflower River. Traveling south on either of the Sunflowers would take the boats to the Yazoo in between Yazoo City and Haynes' Bluff. It was a roundabout trip of about one hundred miles that, if using only the Yazoo River, was about fifteen miles direct from the Mississippi. The scheme was possible only because of the heavy spring rains.[39]

Porter decided to lead this mission himself and selected the ironclads *Carondelet, Louisville, Cincinnati, Mound City,* and *Pittsburg* to chug into the delta. He also had four tugs pulling mortar boats and a coal barge, which almost proved the expedition's undoing. Sherman followed a few days later with several transports that carried one of his corps. Some of his soldiers would march on land so they could chop down obstructions, scout for any enemy forces, and provide protection for the fleet.

The task force steamed into the "muddy, stagnant" waters of Steele's Bayou on March 15. After an easy ten-mile cruise, it became apparent that the environment would thereafter make things difficult. The ironclads entered an unreal world in which cypress trees and willows grew out of the dark waters, snakes and snapping turtles swam the waters, and stinging insects buzzed through the air around the boats. Limbs from the primeval trees "were so dense that a ray of the sun rarely penetrated them," wrote one sailor after the war. Like during the aborted Yazoo Delta expedition, tree limbs tore away boats' woodwork, snapped jackstaffs in half, and sent chimneys crashing to the deck. Oftentimes, there was no clear path in the channel, so the *Carondelet,* the lead gunboat, had to clear the way by "mowing down large trees like grass."[40]

Things got worse when the expedition turned north again into Deer Creek, which proved to be a mere "ditch," as Porter scoffed. The "large trees that lined the banks were so near together that men had to hew down the sides of many of them to allow the boats to squeeze through." In doing so, "a multitude of vermin would be shaken out on the deck—among them rats, mice, cockroaches, snakes, and lizards, which would be swept overboard by the sailors standing ready with their brooms." By this point, Sherman's men either marching on land or aboard the transports had lost touch with the admiral's boats.[41]

Porter needed these soldiers because southern civilians were actively opposing the Union expedition. "All along, as far as the eye could see, there was nothing but cotton fires burning up, and many dwellings consumed with it," he noted with some satisfaction. Rebels also used cotton as a weapon. They stacked bales on the levee and set them ablaze when the expedition came near, hoping to damage the vessels or injure the sailors. Near one inferno, sailors doused the boats with water, closed gunports, and stood ready with buckets of water. "Ring the bell and go ahead fast," Porter ordered the captains. Intense heat blistered the ironclads' paint, and the thick white smoke sent sailors into spasms of coughing. "It was a red-hot undertaking, but the vessels got through slightly scorched and a few men blistered," one sailor remembered. Once past this "fiery gauntlet," the expedition stopped for the night.[42]

As the day faded away, sailors noticed that the enslaved Americans who had flocked to the levee to see the gunboats "mysteriously and suddenly disappeared." Worse, "faint strokes of axes were heard in the dim distance." Confederate cavalry were on the scene. Enslaved men, "with pistols and guns to their heads," were felling trees across the ditch. Porter put a howitzer in the tug and sent it forward. A few shells from the 12-pounder dispersed the work crews and cavalrymen. Porter felt such a sense of urgency and concern that he had sailors walk on shore with lanterns to guide the boats forward. He was eager to push ahead because the flotilla was only a few hundred yards from the wider waters of Rolling Creek.[43]

But the vessels did not make it to Rolling Creek because they got stuck in Deer Creek. Thousands of willows no wider than a man's pinkie snagged the joints of the *Cincinnati*'s armor plating and paddlewheels. The lithe plants, which local enslaved people used to make baskets, "held us as the threads of the Lilliputians held Gulliver," Porter complained. Sweat-soaked firemen raised steam to alarming levels, and the paddlewheel spun forward and backward, but it seemed like the gunboat was held in a vice. Daring sailors jumped into the water and sawed the little plants with jack-knives. After four hours, the *Cincinnati* finally wrenched itself free, but moving forward was no longer an option.[44]

Porter sent a desperate note to Sherman asking him to "shove up troops to us at once. . . . [I]t takes all my men to defend the position I have taken." As if he did not do enough to convey the urgency, the admiral ended his message with a strong appeal: "Please send on troops." Sherman, who received the letter at midnight, had problems of his own. One transport had a crippled rudder, another had lost its smoke pipe, and the rest were stuck in Black Bayou. "I will do all that mortal can to push troops" forward, he explained to Porter, "but as to our getting the number of men you ask up to Rolling Fork is a simple impossibility." The troops could not go overland because "men can not march, for the whole country is submerged."[45]

Confederates took advantage of Porter's lack of infantry support. Lieutenant Colonel Samuel W. Ferguson set up a crossfire with cannons and sharpshooters. The *Cincinnati*'s guns were "utterly useless" for defense because the enclosing levee was too high. The next day Brigadier General Winfield Featherston's Confederate brigade arrived. Porter estimated that he now faced 800 men and seven cannons. He also learned that rebels were felling trees downstream to prevent an escape. "This looked unpleasant," he noted.[46]

The Confederates had a good opportunity to capture five city-class ironclads. Featherston and Ferguson decided to rush the boats and capture them in hand-to-hand fighting. Late in the afternoon of March 21, rebel guns hidden in the woods opened up against the sailors who were on shore. Shell and grape rained down on the bluejackets and set off a stampede. "Each man seemed to try and get to the boat before the others," Daniel Kemp wrote to his sister. "Some left their muskets and cartridge boxes and off they started like deers." Just as Ferguson was getting ready to storm the ironclads, he learned that Featherston had backed out. The brigadier's dithering bought the fleet some time.[47]

Porter ordered the rudders unshipped in preparation for the boats to back downstream. Both sides spent a sleepless night warily eying each other. Porter sent another desperate note to Sherman: "Hurry up, for Heaven's sake." The major general sent Colonel Giles Smith and 800 men from the 8th Missouri on a twenty-mile double-quick march to relieve the Union gunboats.[48]

About the same time that Smith's men started their march, Confederates musket balls began clanging off the ironclads. Most of the Union sailors hunkered down. "We dare not go on the Spar deck for as soon as a man made his appearance he was fired at by some of the rebel sharpshooters who were skulking on the bank," wrote Kemp. Here, one sailor felt a chunk of lead rip through his thigh. There, another bluejacket lost use of his hand when a ball mangled it. Porter's first lieutenant took a slug in the head and fell at the admiral's feet. In all, at least twenty bluejackets became casualties that day.[49]

The gunboats, now with the *Louisville* in the lead, slowly drifted downstream. As the huge ironclad crept backward, it struck the expedition's coal barge and sank it, "bottling up the gunboats as successfully as a million trees." Confederate fire was too effective to permit Union sailors to refloat the barge. Porter ordered the ironclad to repeatedly ram the boat in hopes of smashing it to pieces. It was a futile effort.[50]

Porter prepared for the worst. If commanders saw rockets or blue lights from the *Louisville,* they were to destroy their boats. Sailors would use turpentine, oil, camphene, coal oil, and anything else flammable to build a fire and then spread gunpowder in the magazines and leave the doors open. Gunners were to load the cannons, prime them, and point them to the deck. Other bluejackets would wreck the machinery. Once the sabotage was complete, sailors would "arm themselves with muskets, pistols or pikes and form together back in the edge of the woods," Porter instructed his men, "where we will try and retreat to the place we started from." It did not come to that, however, thanks to the infantry's day-long march.[51]

The 8th Missouri reached the area at about 4:00 P.M. and fought their way to the gunboats, much to Porter's relief. "I never knew before how much the comfort and safety of ironclads, situated as they were, depended on the soldiers." The Missourians drove the Confederates back far enough to allow the sailors to remove the coal barge.[52]

With the barge out of the way, the fleet inched downstream. It took the boats nine hours to go three miles because of all the downed trees in the channel. At about 3:00 P.M., the expedition came to a bend in the river where the rebels had created a significant barrier of felled timber. Just as the *Cincinnati*'s men started pulling up the trees, Confederate artillery and infantry blasted away at the boats. The Pook's Turtles, now in a part of the river where they could use their guns, "poured a destructive fire" into the rebel position. The Confederates, Porter wrote with glee, "scarcely waited to hitch up their horses" during their skedaddle.[53]

Sherman's main body arrived about the same time. His men had ridden in an empty coal barge, marched during a driving rainstorm, and waded through swamps. The red-haired general hailed Porter and said: "Why the deuce did you get into such an ugly scrape? So much for you navy fellows getting out of your element. This is the most infernal expedition I was ever on." His troops drove away the rest of the Confederates, and the expedition withdrew to the Mississippi River.[54]

Both the Yazoo Delta and Steele's Bayou Expeditions were desperate improvisations that asked gunboats and their crews to do nearly impossible tasks. The vessels were too big, the water was too shallow, and the flora was too forbidding. Importantly, Confederates were active in fighting off the expeditions and turned environmental factors in their favor. They felled trees, situated a fort in an ideal location, and sprung ambushes. While the expeditions were not doomed to fail, they could only succeed if everything went smoothly for the Union forces.

The twin expeditions, though, did have some successes. They signaled a turn to aggressive tactics by which bluejackets destroyed food, stole property, and helped liberate enslaved people. Hungry sailors and marines foraged at plantations. "We destroyed a large amount of Confederate corn and captured a large number of mules, horses, and cattle," Porter reported to Secretary of the Navy Welles. Marines on the *Cincinnati* went ashore and, after chasing away the planter who was plowing his field, ransacked his buildings and confiscated 150 chickens, 600 pounds of bacon, a young bull, some geese, and a couple of guinea hens. The food that Union troops captured or destroyed would not feed Vicksburg's soldiers. Rebels, the admiral estimated, themselves burnt over 20,000 bales of cotton, while the rumor among enlisted men was that the fleet destroyed about a million dollars of the fleecy staple.[55]

These operational failures in the Yazoo Delta demonstrated that the Mississippi Squadron was vulnerable when caught in unfavorable environmental conditions. The near disasters also persuaded Grant that he needed a different strategy to capture Vicksburg. He slowly embraced a plan that had been turning over in his mind for some time. The new scheme was difficult and dangerous. More importantly, it could only succeed with the navy's help. Even though the brown-water fleet would have to do something (again) that seemed impossible, Porter had no choice but to comply.

10

CAPTURING VICKSBURG

After the Yazoo Pass and Steele's Bayou debacles in early 1863, it seemed as if the Union might never capture Vicksburg. Major General Grant was down to one final option: cross the Mississippi River below the city and attack it from the south. For the audacious effort to succeed, he needed some gunboats and transports to run past Vicksburg and then bring his men across the river. Rear Admiral Porter agreed to help. In doing so, he not only proved the value of combined operations but also demonstrated that the Mississippi Squadron was essential to victory in the western theater.

About the same time that the Mississippi Squadron ventured into the Old Channel, Porter initiated a series of events that anticipated Grant's final gamble. The admiral wanted to cut off the flow of supplies from the mouth of the Red River to Vicksburg. The USS *Essex* had been patrolling the area since it faced off against the CSS *Arkansas,* but the ironclad needed assistance. Porter ordered Colonel Ellet, commanding the Mississippi Marine Brigade, to run past Vicksburg in his ram *Queen of the West.* The impetuous Ellet was the direct opposite of Lieutenant Commander Smith, who was then gingerly creeping through the Yazoo Delta. "The only trouble I have is to hold him in and keep him out of danger," Porter prophetically told Navy Secretary Welles.[1]

Any Union boat running past Vicksburg would encounter several dangers. The swirling waters of De Soto Bend, the spot where vessels would first come under fire, were notoriously tricky to navigate. If a boat ran aground, it was likely to be blown to bits. Should it succeed with this perilous navigation, it would then face fire from thirty-seven large cannons and another dozen smaller guns. Most of the artillery was in well-protected parapets about thirty feet above the waterline.[2]

Porter ordered Ellet to cover *Queen of the West* with "two thicknesses of cotton bales." Just after dawn on February 1, 1863, the boat roared downstream. Vicksburg's guns burst into action, and one shell struck the *Queen* and set its cotton ablaze. The thick black smoke forced sailors out of the engine room. Ellet ordered his men to cut loose the fiery bales, which tumbled into the water. The ram sped downstream and made it safely through the gauntlet. In all, twelve shots struck the boat during its fifty-minute run. Damage was light: some charred wood, a few holes in the casemate, and a dismounted gun. The *Queen of the West* reached Union troops on the western bank that afternoon, and its crew set about repairing the boat.[3]

Ellet had orders to go as far as the Red River to "capture and destroy all rebel property" he could find and to "sink and destroy all vessels" he encountered. The uninhibited colonel captured three boats laden with 110,000 pounds of pork, 500 hogs, salt, 200 barrels of molasses, ten hogsheads of sugar, 30,000 pounds of flour, and forty bales of cotton, proof that rebels were using the Red as a conduit to supply Vicksburg. But his recklessness also allowed the Confederates to capture *Queen of the West,* after which he burned the loot, torched two captured boats, and fled in a third.[4]

Porter assumed that Ellet would commit some grievous mistake, so he sent the new ironclad USS *Indianola* downriver on February 17 even before word reached him of the *Queen of the West's capture.* The *Indianola* began its run at 11:10 P.M. by drifting downstream in a fog. "The weather was all that I could desire," its captain, Lieutenant Commander George Brown, wrote. The boat floated silently in the darkness past the first battery. When an eagle-eyed Confederate lookout spotted the ironclad, Brown gunned the engines, and the *Indianola* chugged downriver. Eighteen different guns fired at the boat, but none of the balls connected, as Confederate gunners aimed too high. After a brief stop, the *Indianola* went in search of Ellet.[5]

Brown soon found Ellet, who was now in a captured boat. Behind him, three rebel rams were in hot pursuit. The pursuers stopped when they saw the huge ironclad and hovered just out of range. While Brown dithered, the Confederates planned a night attack under the assumption that the limited visibility would neutralize the *Indianola*'s advantage in firepower. In the inky darkness, the CSS *William H. Webb* rammed the *Indianola* so hard it looked "as if it were going to pass entirely through" the ironclad, its commander exulted. The ram crushed the ironclad's starboard paddlewheel, disabled a rudder, and tore off the boat's bow. Soon, another rebel boat slammed into the *Indianola* and ripped a second gaping hole in its side. With water pouring into the boat, Brown gave the order to strike the colors. Confederates captured most of the crew as well as the ironclad, which sank in ten feet of water. Like the USS *Chillicothe,* the *Indianola* was a dreadful failure in its initial voyage.[6]

A few Union sailors escaped from this debacle and returned to the Mississippi Squadron. They told their story to Porter, who was livid. Welles was equally furious. If the Confederacy could raise the *Indianola,* it would have a strong ironclad to use against the *Essex* or any northern boats that might run past Vicksburg. The navy secretary believed that any Union push against Vicksburg had to come from south of the city, and Brown's mistake threatened future operations. Welles roared that the *Indianola* "must be destroyed."[7]

Porter "set the whole squadron at work" building a "cheap expedient" fake boat. Sailors took an old coal barge and framed up scrap wood to simulate paddlewheel boxes and a casemate. They added logs for guns, a privy for a pilot house, and pork barrels for tall stacks. At the top of the stacks, bluejackets put iron pots full of tar and oakum that would burn slowly and give the appearance of smoke. An American flag at the stern completed the ruse. Creative sailors also put a skull and crossbones flag at the bow, painted "Deluded Rebels, Cave In!" on a wheelhouse, and christened the creation the "Black Terror." Porter estimated that the whole thing cost $8.23.[8]

On February 26, sailors towed the dummy gunboat to De Soto Point, lit the iron pots, and watched the craft drift downstream. Confederate guns opened fire but failed to inflict any significant damage. The Black Terror glided to shore below the city. There Union soldiers, aware of the ruse, shoved the raft back into the river. The *Queen of the West,* still in rebel hands, was on an errand to fetch some salvage equipment for raising the *Indianola* when its captain saw the Black Terror approaching. Fearing that he was about to be blown to bits, the *Queen*'s captain turned and fled. Panicked Confederates sent word to the salvagers to blow up the *Indianola.* The rebels did such a thorough demolition job that bluejackets north of Vicksburg heard the explosion. But by doing so, they had ruined one of their best chances to impede or stop the next phase of the Vicksburg Campaign.[9]

A few days later, Rear Admiral Farragut decided on his own initiative to seek out and destroy the *Queen of the West.* He led seven of his deep-water ships upriver, but only the *Hartford* and *Albatross* made it past Port Hudson's guns. Farragut knew that he lacked enough vessels to hunt down the *Queen,* so he sent a message to his foster brother asking for help. Rear Admiral Porter was busy in the Mississippi willows, so Farragut contacted Lieutenant Commander Walke, the Mississippi Squadron's second in command; Walke declined to act. He then turned to the loose cannon known as the Mississippi Marine Brigade. Its commander was not one to turn down a chance at adventure.[10]

Brigadier General Alfred W. Ellet, uncle of Colonel Ellet, jumped at the opportunity to help Farragut and asked permission from Walke. The austere commander, somewhat surprisingly, sent his "hearty good will and sincere prayer" for Ellet's success. The brigadier and a guard walked eleven miles across De Soto Peninsula and met with Farragut aboard the *Hartford.* They decided to send two rams, the USS *Lancaster* and USS *Switzerland,* to hunt for the rogue Confederate boat. Charles Rivers Ellet, who had returned to the Mississippi Marine Brigade, would lead the expedition.[11]

Once again, Colonel Ellet acted with more courage than sense. He did not pack cotton around the rams' boilers, steampipes, or pilot houses for protection. He also started at dawn on March 25, meaning that Confederate gunners could easily spot the boats. A Union sailor on the ironclad USS *Lafayette* watched the rams steam into danger. He counted thirty-nine flashes from rebel guns at Vicksburg. The results were terrifying. "Shot after shot struck my boat," Colonel Ellet wrote in his official report, "tearing everything to pieces." A 10-inch rebel shell tore open the *Switzerland*'s boiler and sent clouds of steam rushing through the boat; three unlucky sailors were badly scalded. The ram's engines stopped, and the vessel floated downstream with the current. Miraculously, it sustained no further damage.[12]

Things were worse for the slower *Lancaster.* After rounding De Soto Point, a Confederate shot slammed through the ram's smokestacks. Five minutes later "a heavy shot" ripped away the steps leading from the cabin to the pilot house; it also tore off the foot of the steersman standing on the steps. By this time, Vicksburg's water batteries "poured a very active fire" into the ram, and another shot punctured the steam drum. Engineers, firemen, and gunners fled the "excruciating tortures of the hot steam." As men scurried to the bow, another rebel ball gashed a hole in the stern and severed the tiller ropes. The *Lancaster* was "sinking very fast" as it spun around in an eddy. Ellet ordered the men to abandon ship, and they rowed to the Louisiana shore in cutters. Some fled to the woods as others watched the ram sink bow first.[13]

When they learned of the results, neither Farragut nor Porter were pleased. Farragut sarcastically commented that Ellet's decision to travel during the day "afforded the enemy nothing but target practice." Porter, still stinging from his close shave in Steele's Bayou, fired off a tersely worded telegram to General Ellet asking him by what authority he sent the rams past Vicksburg "in open day" and without additional protection. He was not surprised, Porter added, that the "unfortunate affair" ended with one ram resting on the Mississippi's bottom and the other riddled with holes. Farragut, despite his disappointment, took responsibility for initiating the expedition.[14]

Porter calmed down and ordered the *Switzerland* repaired and attached to Farragut's command. When the *Hartford, Albatross,* and *Switzerland* left for the Red River, Porter advised his foster brother to keep Colonel Ellet on a short leash or "he will go off on a cruise somewhere before you know it and then get the ship into trouble." Ellet did not get into trouble because Farragut received reinforcements from his fleet, hunted down the *Queen of the West,* and destroyed it. The *William H. Webb* subsequently fled toward the Gulf of Mexico and sank. They were the last operational Confederate boats below Vicksburg.[15]

The strange sojourns of the *Queen of the West, Switzerland, Lancaster,* and *Indianola* once again demonstrated the uncertainties surrounding attempts to send boats south of Vicksburg. A daytime run was madness. A nighttime run was the better option, even if it increased the chances of running aground. Union sailors also learned that Confederate gunners were no marksmen. Just as importantly, Farragut seemed to put to rest any rumors that the rebels had any more surprise gunboats awaiting Union forces. If any southern war vessel of moderate power had existed below Vicksburg, it could harass and possibly sink Union boats. And lost gunboats, whether captured or sunk, could be turned against the Federal effort. The runs past Vicksburg in February and March, even though they were short-term failures, prepared the Mississippi Squadron for bigger things.

Yet Porter did not see the value of subjecting his fleet to Vicksburg's guns. In a confidential letter to the secretary of the navy, the admiral thought there was "but one thing now to be done, and that is to start an army of 150,000 men from Memphis, via Grenada," Mississippi. Grant had come to the opposite conclusion. Intrepid Confederate defenses and geography eliminated all but one line of advance: cross the Mississippi below Vicksburg and attack the city from the southeast. He decided to send the Army of the Tennessee south along the western bank of the Mississippi River to New Carthage, Louisiana. According to Grant's original plan, his men would cross the river and link up with Major General Nathaniel Banks's army and take Port Hudson. This combined force would then turn and attack Vicksburg.[16]

On March 29 Grant sent an apologetic and deferential telegram to Porter. "It looks to me Admiral as a matter of vast importance that one or two vessels should be put below Vicksburg" to protect a cross-river invasion. "Will you be good enough Admiral to give this your early consideration and let me know your determination. Without the aid of gunboats it will hardly be worth while to send troops" southward into Louisiana. Grant could not order Porter to assist the army with his naval vessels. The canny general counted on friendship, mutual respect, shared experiences, and military necessity to carry the day. He also lowballed the Mississippi Squadron's commitment by asking for only one or two boats.[17]

Despite his doubts, Porter replied that he would assist Grant. But he warned the general, "when these gunboats once go below [Vicksburg] we give up all hopes of ever getting them up[river] again." This statement could be read as a way to preemptively shift the blame for any future defeat onto the general's shoulders. Porter, though, supported him because he trusted Grant's judgment, knew that he could count on Farragut to keep any Confederate resistance bottled up in the Red River, and had received intense pressure from Secretary Welles to go downriver. It was perhaps the finest example of interservice cooperation in the war.[18]

While Grant's men trudged southward through the Louisiana mud, Porter readied his fleet for its mission. In early April 1863, he stationed several boats at the mouth of the Yazoo River. Rumors had been circulating that the Confederates were completing a powerful ram in Yazoo City, and Porter wanted to make sure that it did not interrupt the upcoming attack. He chose eight boats to test Vicksburg's guns: the city-class ironclads *Louisville, Mound City, Pittsburg,* and *Carondelet;* the casemate ironclads *Benton* and *Tuscumbia;* and the rams *General Price* and *Lafayette.* About one-third of the Mississippi Squadron was directly involved in Grant's last-chance operation against Vicksburg. Three transports—*Forest Queen, Henry Clay,* and *Silver Wave*—and one tug completed the flotilla.[19]

Porter ordered extensive precautions be taken to minimize damage to the boats. Sailors stacked haybales around machinery. They also spread bales "over the tender parts of the boat and saturated [the hay] with water." A tired bluejacket wrote in his diary that sailors "covered the forecastles with ranges of chain and greased our port side with a heavy coat of pork grease. Covered our quarterdeck and fantail with loose sheets of iron and then coiled hawsers on top of them." Engineers added extra iron to the *Pittsburg*'s port bow. The *Lafayette* shielded *General Price,* a vulnerable ram like the *Lancaster,* by lashing the boat to its starboard side. Other boats had coal tenders attached to their port sides as added protection. These expendable craft could absorb some shells and then be cut loose if they became a liability.[20]

Porter hoped that darkness and silence would conceal the fleet as it drifted south. He ordered the boats to float silently downstream after the sun went down, display no lights, and keep their gunports covered until the rebels fired at them. Once discovered, they would engage their engines and steer toward the Louisiana bank in hopes of blending in with the trees. The gunboats could fire at either the batteries or the town. Each vessel would be about fifty yards apart, with the *Tuscumbia* at the end of the line as the "whipper." Its mission was to ensure that the transports, which were civilian boats, did not turn around.[21]

Most sailors considered the run past Vicksburg to be a suicide mission. Edward Goble, a bluejacket whose father served on the *Pittsburg,* begged to go with his kin. He got nowhere, so he volunteered to take his father's place. "He was deaf to that," Goble wrote his uncle, "saying that he was an Old Man and that if he was killed they would not cheat him many days any how." Many civilians were not as brave as Goble's father. One captain and the entire crews of two boats balked at the mission. More than enough of Grant's soldiers volunteered to take their places.[22]

The weather was "clear and pleasant" on April 16. Spectators, including Grant and his family, packed onto thirty vessels to watch the passage. At 8:45 P.M. Porter came aboard the flagship *Benton,* and about fifteen minutes later, the ironclad ran up two white lights, the signal to cast loose. "All lights were extinguished and [the boats] floated down the river in silence and darkness," Master's Mate Coffinberry wrote in his diary. Union gunners waited silently at their posts. The mammoth *Benton* immediately became unmanageable without any motive power and "persistently refused to point her head downstream." After two hours of cajoling, the ironclad nudged around De Soto Point and drifted into danger. According to the boat's log, the lights of Vicksburg were then "plainly in sight."[23]

Confederate sharpshooters sent musket balls zinging toward the *Benton,* then rebel cannons joined in. Southern gunners unleashed a storm of shot and shell that "went whizzing shrieking howling" for the *Benton* "like a legion of incarnate devils from hell," as one sailor wrote. A Texan on shore recalled that the "booming of Cannon" woke up his men. "Such a grabbing for Boots Pants & [etc.] you never did see." Confederate soldiers rushed to the levee and aimed their muskets at the gunports. On the west side of the river, sentries lit tar barrels, buildings, and bonfires. The captain of the *Mound City* thought these made it "almost as light as day."[24]

The *Benton* engaged its paddlewheels and "and went ahead at full speed." Contrary to Porter's orders, the pilot steered toward the Confederate guns on the east bank. The ironclad got within forty yards of the levee, a perilously close distance. Union gunners blasted the city with enough accuracy to "hear the rattling of falling walls," a sailor remembered. The *Benton* made it through the gauntlet relatively unscathed and came to anchor south of Vicksburg at 2:10 A.M. It suffered minimal damage and only five men were wounded, including Charles Doss, who had his "left leg shot away."[25]

The *Lafayette* and *General Price,* which were lashed together, were next into the breach. They "steered very awkward" because the *General Price* was a faster boat but the *Lafayette* had the bigger engine. The vessels veered so close to the Mississippi shore that they nearly ran aground. The *Lafayette*'s pilot then overcorrected and became confused by the bonfires and steered upriver, exposing the vulnerable *General Price* "to the full rake of the Rebel batteries." At least eight solid shots slammed into the tandem, and one shell burst so close to the boats that sparks showered on the *Lafayette*'s pilot. Confederate gunners "set up a fiendish yell of triumph" thinking they were about to sink the boats. The *Lafayette*'s pilot found his bearings and turned the boats downriver, but a new threat suddenly appeared.[26]

This was the *Louisville,* the next gunboat in line. The flames on the far shore so confused the ironclad's pilot that he made two full turns in the river. During one of these, the *Louisville* was firing a broadside when "suddenly something came crashing on our port side." It was the *Lafayette* and *General Price.* At this time sailors cut the two boats loose. They endured "a heavy concentrated fire for nearly an hour" but made it past the batteries. The *Lafayette* took no significant damage and had four men slightly wounded, a circumstance the captain chalked up to the boat's "fortunate pirouette." The unarmored *General Price* was a different story. Two rifle shells exploded inside the ram, "destroying the officers' quarters and setting the vessel on fire twice," its captain reported. The boat was "badly cut up in her upper works," with one sailor dead another three wounded. Still, the ram would be repaired and sent back into action.[27]

But the unfortunate *Louisville* was not done banging into things. As soon as it got clear of the *General Price,* the ironclad ran into a coal barge. Then a transport came across its bow with a crash "that started everybody off their feet," according to a sailor on the gunboat. Just as the *Louisville* passed Vicksburg's last battery, it collided with yet another Union craft. The *Tuscumbia* struck its bow with "a very solid rap with her solid iron sides." Despite pinballing its way downriver, *Louisville* sustained only light damage. An equal number of Union boats and rebel cannonballs hit the ironclad—four.[28]

Mound City, Pittsburg, and *Carondelet* had relatively easy passages. Their only scare came when the *Carondelet* grounded on a sandbar. The "devils cheered and yelled, thinking that we were done for," wrote John Morrison. "For 15 minutes it was truly awful. Whiz, thump, and again and again we are struck." A dozen shells slammed into the boat, but only three of them penetrated the casemate. The Irish-born sailor sarcastically thanked "our *neutral* English cousins" for the duds. *Carondelet* worked itself free and chugged down the river without further incident. *Mound City* was the only boat from this trio to sustain casualties when a "heavy shot" smashed through the port casemate and wounded four men.[29]

While the ironclads plunged forward (or sideways), the pilots in the *Henry Clay* and *Forest Queen* lost their nerve and turned upstream. Like a giant border collie, the *Tuscumbia* herded the two transports back in line. Confederate shells thereafter made short work of the *Henry Clay,* which went up in flames, much like the presidential aspirations of its namesake. The barrage knocked cotton bales into the Big Muddy, and "the river was covered with bits of burning cotton, looking like a thousand lamps," Porter wrote. The *Tuscumbia,* even though it was a new boat, had difficulty steering. It struck the Louisiana shore and, while backing off, "got foul" of the *Forest Queen.* "This collision," wrote the *Tuscumbia*'s captain, "caused the rebels great rejoicing, and was made evident to us by their loud cheering." Confederate gunners concentrated their fire on the two boats, and a few balls clanged off the *Tuscumbia*'s casemate. One well-placed shot severed the *Forest Queen*'s steampipe, rendering it powerless. Another ball gouged a hole below the transport's waterline. The helpless craft drifted downstream but took no further damage. *Forest Queen* carried fourteen inches of water in its hull when the *Tuscumbia* took it in tow south of Vicksburg.[30]

Once south of Vicksburg, boats paused to assess the damage. As sailors inspected their vessels, someone in a small boat yelled out, "Benton ahoy!" It was Major General Sherman. He ribbed Porter about being at home on a big river instead of a ditch and then went to check on the rest of the flotilla. Sherman learned that all the boats, save the *Henry Clay,* had safely run the gauntlet with minimal casualties.[31]

The fleet was then at Diamond Bend, about twelve miles above New Carthage, Louisiana. Union sailors were ecstatic. "All praise to the Lord and Admiral Porter," wrote Elias Smith on the *Carondelet.* A sailor on the *Louisville* declared: "It seems little short of a mirical the way we came out, suffering less than any other boat. We were the third boat into the hell and the last boat out." While taking stock of the damage, the sailors saw burning driftwood and blazing cotton bales drift past. Once it was clear that the vessels were in good working order, the fleet pressed on to New Carthage, where Grant greeted Porter. Union soldiers from Indiana serenaded the two commanders.[32]

This success was due to effective Union planning and poor Confederate execution. Cotton, hay, lard, extra armor, hawsers, and other protections reduced the chances of a catastrophic hit. Running at night made it difficult for rebel gunners to hit the boats, partly because of the darkness but more because of the fires on the western bank. Several northern captains mentioned a glare or reflection from the blazes that caused confusion. As the dancing flames reflected off the river, it was difficult for southern gunners to track the Union boats as well. Confederates also put many of their cannons in poor spots. Gunners could not depress their tubes low enough to hit those boats that came close to the eastern shore.

Many years later Porter wrote, "Grant had turned the enemy's flank with his army, I had turned it with the gun-boats." Now "Grant had to cross the river and trust to his brave soldiers" to capture Vicksburg. While the campaign to capture the Mississippi stronghold was not over on April 17, it was clear that

Grant had outmaneuvered the hapless Lieutenant General John Pemberton. The Union general jettisoned plans to link up with Banks and decided to advance on Vicksburg immediately. But to secure victory, he needed even more help from the navy.[33]

The main obstacle to a river crossing was the Confederate position at Grand Gulf, a point about thirty miles below Vicksburg. It had good roads to Mississippi's interior and was Grant's preferred jumping-off point for a land campaign. The town was situated on a circular bay, or gulf, located at the foot of a one-hundred-foot-high ridge. Southerners had built two earthen forts, one above the town and the other below it. Fort Cobun, the upper fort, sat forty feet above the water line and had four heavy guns nestled in a thick parapet. Railroad iron protected its magazine. Fort Wade, the lower position, was only twenty feet above the shore and had less firepower. A line of rifle pits connected the two forts.[34]

Porter scouted the defenses and did not like what he saw. The Confederates were, according to one sailor, "working like beavers" to improve the already strong position. Porter advised Grant to find a different place for his cross-river invasion. The general made a personal reconnaissance of Grand Gulf on the *Benton* and believed the navy was up to the job. Porter, once again despite his reservations, agreed to help Grant. He sent four boats against the weaker lower battery and three against the upper battery. Transports jammed with Grant's men would hover upstream, waiting to disembark once the Union gunboats reduced the Confederate forts.[35]

At about 7:30 A.M. on April 29, the *Pittsburg* led the *Louisville, Carondelet, Mound City, Lafayette, Tuscumbia,* and *Benton* into battle. The city-class ironclads attacked Fort Wade, forcing its surrender around noon. It took about 1,500 rounds to do the job. One of the Confederate casualties during the barrage was Colonel William Wade, the fort's namesake. Wade was at his gun "when a piece of shot struck him in the head, killing him instantly." The surrender came at a cost, though. The *Carondelet* was "badly cut up," one of its officers judged, and at least thirty sailors died in battle.[36]

The *Benton, Lafayette,* and *Tuscumbia* were not having any such success against Fort Cobun. Not only was it higher and better built, but the strong six-knot current and eddies near the fort were treacherous. The swirling waters turned the ironclads "round and round, making them fair targets." Somehow, one of the *Benton*'s shells knocked down the fort's flag, but the rebels quickly put it back up. Confederate guns were devastatingly effective. The "whole hillside was one continued line of flame," wrote a bluejacket. One enemy shell penetrated the *Benton*'s starboard quarter and exploded in a stateroom, setting the bedding on fire. Then another shell passed through the pilothouse, wounding the pilot and shattering the wheel. The boat, now unmanageable, got caught in an eddy and then ran into the bank. Before being knocked out of the fight, the *Benton* took forty-seven shots.[37]

The *Tuscumbia* fared even worse. It bobbed around like a cork, going "round and round, exposing her at every turn," wrote a disgusted Porter. A shot struck the ironclad's port shutter and jammed it shut. Another well-placed shell exploded in the forward turret and "threw sparks of fire into the shell room and magazine passages." Sailors worked frantically to prevent the boat from exploding. At least eight sailors died during the battle, and an astounding eighty-one projectiles battered the *Tuscumbia*. The captain concluded it would need "extensive repairs."[38]

Only the *Lafayette* challenged Fort Cobun. It braved the eddies and got within nine hundred yards of the position. The bow gunners energetically worked their guns, firing two or three times a minute. "And then didn't the sand fly, but it was no use as we could not dislodge them," wrote Morrison. Confederates shot away just about everything that was not nailed down on the gunboat. Even though the city-class ironclads joined in the fight, the Union flotilla inflicted almost no damage on the fort. The boats were running out of ammunition, and the crews were "almost tired out," noted the *Lafayette*'s surgeon. Porter called off the attack at about 1:00.[39]

The Union sailors fought with all their might, but they had almost no chance to defeat the rebels. "I may safely say it was the hardest fight I ever was in," wrote an "extremely tired and sore" Morrison at the end of the day. He personally fired eighty-five rounds. All this effort had little effect against an elevated and well-designed fort. Despite pouring about 800 rounds into Fort Cobun, the gunboats inflicted almost no damage. "Huge shells would strike the surface of the high banks above our feeble batteries, explode, and cover guns and gunners with piles of sand, out of which the latter would work themselves like moles or gophers, and cheerily clear their pieces again for action," wrote one rebel Missourian in the fort. The Union guns created much sound but dispensed little fury.[40]

Confederate gunners killed eighteen sailors or soldiers stationed on the Union boats and wounded another fifty-seven. Fred Grant, who accompanied his father on board the *Benton,* was horrified at what he saw. "The deck was covered with blood and pieces of flesh; several dead men torn and lacerated, lay about us. Some of the gunners, with still bleeding wounds, were standing firmly by their guns," he marveled. Porter was among those wounded, the only injury he sustained during the war. His "face was colorless and expressed great agony; he leaned forward, using his sword as a cane for support," according to the young Grant. It turned out to be a superficial, if painful, wound.[41]

General Grant, meanwhile, consulted with Porter. They agreed that a cross-river attack here was too risky. They decided to send the transports past the Confederate guns once it was dark and find a different landing point. About 9:00 that night, the weary crews of the Mississippi Squadron were back in action. They provided enough covering fire so that the transports made it downriver unscathed and landed about four miles below Grand Gulf. Grant had effectively outflanked Fort Cobun. As he did for most of the Vicksburg Campaign, the general improvised again. An enslaved man told Union soldiers that Bruinsburg, about ten miles downriver from Grand Gulf, had good roads leading into Mississippi's interior. A nearly deserted plantation with a good steamboat landing would be where Union soldiers set foot on the eastern bank of the Mississippi River.[42]

On April 30 the U.S. military carried out its largest amphibious invasion until World War II. Transports, gunboats, and barges carried the Army of the Tennessee across the river. The soldiers were "full of zeal and fire to carry the War until the Rebellion is crushed out," wrote Thomas Lyons on the *Lafayette.* His boat took about 1,500 men across the river that morning. Fittingly, Grant crossed the river in the *Benton* with Porter. As the ironclad reached the shore, a band started playing "The Red, White, and Blue." Troops cheered and waved their muskets when they saw their commander disembark. By the end of the day, Master's Mate Coffinberry estimated that Union boats landed "something like thirty thousand men on the eastern shore."[43]

As Grant's army moved inland, the Confederates realized that their position at Grand Gulf was untenable. At about 5:45 A.M. on May 3, Morrison was startled to hear four massive explosions shake the citadel. His boat got underway and steamed up the river. Sailors spotted smoke and then fired a few shells into the forts. They received no response. The boat edged to shore and put out its stage. Marines and sharpshooters "went racing up the bluffs at railroad speed to see who would gain the fortification first." Someone reached the summit and hoisted the Stars and Stripes. Sailors on the ironclad saluted the flag with "three rousing cheers."[44]

Part of the reason that Grant's men landed unopposed at Bruinsburg was because Pemberton was completely befuddled. Colonel Benjamin Grierson had led 1,700 Union cavalrymen on a raid through central Mississippi that diverted attention from the river campaign. The Mississippi Squadron also caused the inept Confederate commander to be concerned about an attack along the Yazoo River. On April 30, at Grant's insistence, Lieutenant Commander Kidder R. Breese took eight boats into that waterway, protecting Sherman's men, who were on transports, and towing three mortar boats.[45]

The USS *Choctaw* and USS *Baron de Kalb* made a noisy demonstration against Drumgould's Bluff while the USS *Tyler* and USS *Black Hawk* attacked rebel artillery emplacements. As usual, the mortar boats ineffectively sprayed shells in the general direction of the Confederates. The Union gunboats were not supposed to take any risks, but the *Tyler* steamed too close to the southern position and took a shot "between wind and water," forcing it to withdraw and patch the hole. The *Choctaw* foolishly neared the bluff and absorbed forty-six shots. A southern soldier saw one cannonball strike the heavy ram "right between the chimneys & the steam that came in quite a cloud showd that some vital part had been reached." The boat ducked back to safety. "I could plainly see them at work trying to repair the damage that she sustained," the soldier noted. While the Union boats were exchanging greetings with rebel gunners, Sherman landed his men in essentially the same place where they had tasted defeat four months earlier. The soldiers tramped around a bit and withdrew the next day without incident.[46]

Sherman and Porter had opposite opinions about this attack. The general shared a bottle of good wine with the *Louisville*'s surgeon. He believed his feint "helped draw the rebs away from Grand Gulf." Porter, on the other hand, was furious with Breese. In a sharply worded telegram, he bluntly concluded that "the affair will be considered a defeat." The southern position was too strong to attack. "A feint means a pretended attack, whereas yours was a real one. . . . I never intended the vessels to go under fire." Porter was correct. Neither the *Tyler* nor the *Choctaw* should have gotten within range of the southern guns.[47]

The Mississippi Squadron remained on duty for the rest of the Vicksburg Campaign. Grant's men marched to Jackson, Mississippi, and defeated a Confederate army. They then turned west toward Vicksburg and besieged the city on May 18. While Grant's men dug trenches outside the city, Porter's boats made sure that no troops or supplies reached the Confederates via the river. The general commanding Confederate forces in the town concluded three months before the city's surrender: "I regard the navigation of the Mississippi River as shut out from us now. No more supplies can be gotten from the trans-Mississippi department." A Union commander confirmed those words when he proudly told Porter that the "crossing of the cattle" south of Natchez "appears to have been stopped."[48]

Ironclads also shelled the town with uncertain effectiveness. On one occasion the *Benton, Tuscumbia, Mound City, Carondelet,* and *Louisville* duked it out with Vicksburg's lower batteries for five hours. The "guns are so heavily casemated that we cannot damage them much," one sailor informed his brother. Mortar boats regularly lobbed shells into the town. The navy, still short of sailors, transferred men from its hospital boat to do this miserable job.[49]

Gunboats above Vicksburg also helped with the siege. Grant and Sherman asked Porter to attack the town's northern defenses because a Confederate battery was preventing Sherman from attacking a hilltop fort. Porter dispatched the USS *Cincinnati,* which had just returned to service after being mauled in the Yazoo River. Confederates rained down fire on the patched-up boat. According to one sailor, "every battery at Vicksburg was pouring shot and shell into our poor doomed gunboat." The cannon fire was so accurate that rebel gunners shot down the boat's flag three times. At least five shots penetrated the vessel, three of which passed through it and opened up huge holes. As foamy brown water flooded the ironclad, more shots blasted the pilot house, clipped the tiller, and shot away the staffs. There were many casualties. One of the blasts cut a carpenter's mate in two while he was trying to plug the holes; his dying words were, "Chuck me overboard." A shorn-off bolt buried itself in the pilot's back. Splinters lacerated a quarter master and tore open his chest.[50]

Lieutenant George M. Bache, commanding the *Cincinnati,* ordered the boat to make for the far bank. When the stricken ironclad got close to shore, sailors threw out a stage, and Bache gave the order to abandon the boat. Under a withering fire, sailors carried wounded men ashore. Unfortunately, the sailors who were supposed to tie the boat's hawser to a tree got stuck in the mud before they could finish the job, so the ironclad drifted back into the river. As the gunboat was sinking, Quarter Master Frank Bois nailed the flag to the stump of the fore-staff so it could go down with its colors flying. The *Cincinnati* sank in about eighteen feet of water.[51]

Bache told the remaining sailors to paddle to shore, but many of the men could not swim. Sailors Thomas E. Corcoran, Henry Dow, Thomas Jenkins, and Martin McHugh swam between the boat and the bank, rescuing their crewmates while under heavy fire. They then repaired a cutter and used it to tow Bache and several wounded sailors to shore. These four crewmen, along with Bois and Thomas W. Hamilton, were awarded the Medal of Honor for their valor. The short firefight resulted in at least five sailors killed, twelve wounded, and fourteen drowned.[52]

About a month after the *Cincinnati* sank, Union troops marched into Vicksburg. Grant had alerted Porter that the Confederate surrender was imminent, so the admiral was ready. He had a fast steamer with its steam up ready to dart to Cairo, which had the nearest telegraph connection to Washington. Once Federal soldiers raised the Stars and Stripes over Vicksburg on July 4, 1863, Porter sent the boat. He also ordered the ironclads to blow their whistles and fire cannons and rockets to celebrate the good news. Bluejackets cheered wildly. Fittingly, Grant rode to the levee with his corps commanders and met with Porter on the *Black Hawk*. Porter, who always seemed to have alcohol on hand, offered fine wine to Grant, his corps commanders, and the ironclad captains. Grant demurred, preferring instead to puff on an excellent cigar. He had, Porter remembered, a look of "quiet satisfaction on his face."[53]

Most people recognized what Porter and Grant knew: the capture of Vicksburg was a huge victory for the Union. The Confederacy lost weapons and equipment that it could not replace. Many of Pemberton's men were paroled; some returned to fighting but others did not. Port Hudson surrendered a few days later. The Union now firmly controlled the mouth of the Red River and could stifle the flow of supplies across the Mississippi River. Cotton, salt, and cattle from Texas would no longer assist Confederate armies east of the river.[54]

The Union would not have captured Vicksburg in 1863 without the assistance of the Mississippi Squadron. Had Porter refused to send his boats past the rebel stronghold, Grant would have been forced to march overland as he attempted the prior year. But he did not have enough troops in 1863 to guard his supply lines *and* besiege the city. Without Porter's cooperation, Grant would have had to postpone his advance until 1864. The city's capitulation was a crucial turning point in the western theater, arguably the war's decisive theater. The Mississippi Squadron was necessary for the Union's victory.[55]

A week after Port Hudson surrendered, a steamer from St. Louis docked in New Orleans and unloaded its freight. Commerce had been restored. As Lincoln put it on August 26, 1863, "The Father of Waters again goes unvexed to the sea." It was easy to assume that the Mississippi Squadron's war was over. But after July 4, the Mississippi Squadron nearly doubled its number of boats and enlisted an additional 10,000 men. Bluejackets devoted their efforts now to suppressing a guerrilla war that was growing in strength and effectiveness. In this way Confederates vexed commercial steamers, Union transports, and the boats of the Mississippi Squadron.[56]

11
THE PATROL SYSTEM

Two months before Vicksburg surrendered, the Mississippi Squadron's war entered its third phase, which lasted from May 1863 to April 1864. During this time, the irregular war between the brown-water navy and Confederate insurgents became more intense. The squadron established patrol districts for its boats and accelerated its war of exhaustion. While the patrol system was effective in protecting Union supply lines, it also created conditions that led to unjustified attacks against southern property.

Soon after the Yazoo Pass and Steele's Bayou Expeditions, Lieutenant Commander Selfridge suggested a new strategy to protect Union supply lines. After rebels captured the transport *Minnesota,* he complained to Rear Admiral Porter and Lieutenant Commander Kidder R. Breese that the Confederates had too many men and guns near Greenville, Mississippi, "to be guarded by boats." The supply line for Major General Grant's army ran past Greenville. If the Confederates could capture or destroy enough transports, they might impair the then-ongoing Vicksburg Campaign. Selfridge recommended that the Mississippi Squadron establish "a system of convoys for this river" that would escort steamers twice a week between the White River and Milliken's Bend, Louisiana.[1]

Simultaneously, the fleet had difficulties protecting steamers on the Tennessee and Cumberland Rivers. Major General Rosecrans was amassing supplies in Middle Tennessee in preparation for an advance against Chattanooga. Lieutenant Commander LeRoy Fitch was responsible for protecting Rosecrans's supply lines and had his hands full. Rebels initiated attacks at multiple points along the rivers and exploited the thickly wooded shores, winding streams, and hills overlooking the banks. Without more boats, Fitch could not keep the Tennessee or the Cumberland "free to the head of navigation." Yet he pointed out that since taking command there in January 1863, he had initiated a regular patrol system to protect Rosecrans's supply line. Fitch's boats had helped over 180 steamers and thirty barges laden with government freight arrive safely in Nashville.[2]

In May 1863 Porter combined Fitch's system with Selfridge's suggestion and organized the Mississippi Squadron into six patrol districts. He stuck the ironclads at hotspots, blockaded the mouth of the Red River, and scattered the other boats along the rest of the western waters. The admiral put his most experienced officers in charge of the districts, which expanded to eight and then ten zones within a year. The district system was a tacit admission that the Mississippi Squadron was transitioning from an invading navy fighting a conventional war to a quasi-occupying force whose primary foes were small groups of Confederate soldiers, guerrillas, and armed civilians. It also meshed with the army's efforts in the region. Major General Edward R. S. Canby, commander of the Military District of West Mississippi, had orders to use armed patrols and garrisons to protect both banks of the Mississippi River. He cooperated with the fleet to chase down guerrillas.[3]

Under the patrol system, Union boats cruised back and forth on the same stretch of river (usually about fifteen miles in length), monitored known ambush sites, kept an eye on ferry crossings, suppressed rebel trade, escorted commercial vessels and transports past danger, prevented the construction of artillery emplacements, and battled rebels. Like a policeman on a beat, commanders were supposed to "cultivate good feelings with the inhabitants." This system was a comprehensive way to implement the strategy of exhaustion: wear down Confederate resistance, starve hostile southerners, separate rebels from the civilians who nourished them, and suffocate southern commerce.[4]

Porter needed more boats and sailors to make the patrol system effective, so he asked Secretary of the Navy Welles for both. During the war's third phase, the fleet commissioned thirty fighting vessels, down slightly from the second phase's thirty-six boats but still a robust rate. Twenty-six of the new gunboats were tinclads, indicative that the fleet was going to concentrate on suppressing insurgent attacks. With seventy-one fighting vessels in the water, the war was far from over for the Mississippi Squadron.[5]

These boats needed sailors. About 4,200 men joined the fleet during the war's third phase, a large increase above the 2,600 in the second phase. The monthly average of enlistments went up as well, from 237 to 323 new sailors. It

MAP 3. Mississippi Squadron Patrol Districts

proved difficult to recruit native-born whites and immigrants during the war's third phase. The bloody battles at Gettysburg and Chickamauga, continued opposition to emancipation, and an economic recovery in 1863 suppressed Union enlistments. The draft and hefty enlistment bonuses convinced some to enlist, but the fleet became even more dependent on the blood, sweat, and labor of Black men. An astonishing 35 percent of new enlistees in the third phase were formerly enslaved, up from 20 percent in the previous phase. It is likely that the fleet had a deliberate strategy of enlisting large numbers of formerly enslaved men. On July 21, 1863, Wesley Goode, Robert Morgan, and George Washington enlisted onboard the timberclad USS *Conestoga* while it was on the Red River. Ranging in age from twenty-one to thirty-five, they were shipped as first-class boys. The patrol system, by spreading boats along the western waters and keeping them in place for long periods of time, enhanced the enlistment of former slaves. At a time when the Mississippi Squadron was once again expanding its reach and aggressiveness, such Black men were necessary for the fleet's continued operation.[6]

These recruits signed on as the Mississippi Squadron became even more aggressive in attacking rebels, civilians, and the environment. In the war's third phase, Union gunboats waged 125 known attacks. This rate of 10.4 per month surpassed the average of 8.2 per month in the war's second phase. Those figures, drawn from official records, seriously undercount the actual number attacks. Sailor correspondence and boat logs make it clear that the fleet was even more active in its fight against insurgents (see table 3).[7]

With the patrol system in place, Porter implemented a reasonably effective inland blockade of the Confederacy. First, he wanted to deprive rebel soldiers and southern civilians of food. As Porter bluntly told a treasury agent in late 1862, "if I had my way, the whole rebel population should be starved into submission." Two months later he made starvation an official policy. The admiral directed the USS *Tyler* to venture out "and procure for the use of the squadron 40 head of cattle, plenty of forage for them, 100 bushels of corn, some corn meal, chickens, turkey, ducks, geese, and eggs." Commanders and sailors were eager to carry out this policy. Less than a week later, bluejackets on the USS *Forest Rose* swarmed onto a plantation in search of rebels who had fired at the tinclad with a 12-pounder. George Yost reported that these sailors swiped "all the Provisions" during their shore excursion.[8]

When bluejackets denuded riverside farms and plantations of sustenance, they were not only augmenting their larder and punishing civilians but also degrading the ability of guerrillas and Confederate soldiers to sustain themselves. Sailors understood that each calorie from a rebellious farm or plantation that found its way onto a Union boat was one less calorie that could nourish the body of an enemy. In the sixteen months between October 1861 and January 1863, a Union vessel confiscated food only once. Boats grabbed food eleven times over the next nine months, which straddled the second and third phases of the war. The Mississippi Squadron then made food a prize in a three-cornered struggle between sailors, rebels, and civilians.[9]

Southern families felt the pinch. The combination of Union raids, guerrilla activity, white migration away from the Mississippi River, and the exodus of enslaved people created a scarcity of food and other vital resources in some areas. Two raids on the same location tell the story. In April 1863 the USS *Switzerland* came upon thirty hogsheads of sugar, 500 sacks of corn, corn meal, and 100 bushels of potatoes meant for the Confederate army. The crew had so much food that they destroyed some of it. Things were different ten months later. The best a foraging expedition could do then was to round up one cow. Conditions were similar just north of Natchez. In September poultry was scarce on riverside plantations because of, as one officer noted, "the frequent drafts upon them made by our gunboats."[10]

A second facet of the blockade was shutting down trade in hostile territory. Porter banned the sale of military clothing, food, men's shoes, salt, men's clothing, saddles, medicines, and munitions in these regions. The object, he explained, was "to break up the carrying of anything into rebel ports." He also mandated that all commercial steamers must have a legal trading permit and ordered his captains to stop commerce at all points along the rivers except for points "occupied by United States troops." Porter authorized Union gunboats to seize any vessel and its contraband from anyone who lacked a trading permit and turn them over to a prize court. Around the same time, the Treasury Department began issuing trade licenses to northern merchants to purchase cotton from southerners who pledged loyalty to the Union. In return, the merchants could sell all manner of goods to the person providing the bales.[11]

These policies shut down some contraband trade. The USS *New Era,* for instance, seized the steamer *Rowena* for carrying quinine and 2,900 pairs of "rebel uniform pants." Union boats limited the Confederacy's ability to use agricultural produce from Arkansas, Louisiana, and Texas to feed its armies east of the Mississippi River. Other bootleg trade, though, was tantalizingly out of reach, as Acting Master A. F. O'Neil learned in October 1863. O'Neil commanded the tinclad USS *Silver Cloud,* which was on patrol near Randolph, Tennessee. On October 8 he was "on the track of 70 Bales Cotton to be crossed" from Arkansas into Tennessee. The smugglers eluded detection. Three days later the *Silver Cloud* stopped near Island No. 35 and "found Bale & Bag of cotton" on the Arkansas bank. There was evidence of a "large quantity of cotton having recently shipped" at the site. Not coincidentally, a band of guerrillas had been in the area that night "but had gone back to the hills."[12]

The *Silver Cloud*'s failure is evidence that insurgent groups obtained food and supplies from what Porter admitted was an "extensive system of smuggling . . . out of the sight of the gunboats." Rebels and their sympathizers bribed officials to obtain trading permits, paid off agents to look the other way while they sold illegal goods, sold (for instance) twenty barrels of salt when they had a permit to sell two, and allowed their boats to be robbed knowing the goods would go to rebels. Guerrillas bought supplies with the profits, distributed food to helpful civilians, and funneled military supplies to the Confederate army. Rebels in Waterproof, Louisiana, supposedly earned $6,000 per month from a store and used the money to buy guns and whiskey for guerrillas. According to a sailor on the USS *Rattler,* "every kind of crime is committed on this river."[13]

While the Mississippi Squadron was trying to smother contraband trade, it was also protecting legitimate trade. Commercial shipping, especially cotton, picked up in 1863, and passenger travel also revived. Trade had numerous benefits for the North. The reestablishment of commerce on the Mississippi River demonstrated to citizens in the Midwest and Upper South that the Federal government was doing what it could to promote their financial well-being. Cotton trade gave white southerners a reason to collaborate with the Union, at least conditionally. Riverboats began to carry anywhere from 1,500 to 2,500 bales of cotton to Cairo. From there, trains carried the fiber to the eastern mills. In some patrol districts, the navy advertised its escort schedule. Three hours before departing, the escort boat hoisted a white flag with a blue cross and fired a gun.[14]

Such precautions were necessary because guerrillas and Confederate ambush squads attacked civilian commerce. According to a northern correspondent who visited the White River, guerrillas had an organized campaign "to put a stop to the navigation of the Mississippi." Their main tactic was to "open fire from the points where the boats pass nearest the shore, on occasions where they are least expected." These attacks were equivalent to the Confederacy's commerce raiding on the high seas, which had as its object bringing harm to the northern economy. Such attacks, if frequent and effective enough, would raise shipping rates, increase insurance rates, and deter passengers from boarding steamboats.[15]

Measuring guerrilla attacks against western-river commerce is difficult, but judging by newspaper stories, they were frequent. In October one river traveler thought guerrillas were "operating pretty freely" on the Mississippi River. During one week at the end of the month, a group of fifty to sixty guerrillas attacked four different steamboats fifty miles south of Memphis. They killed one man on the *Adriatic* and two more on the *Diligent.* Another passenger casually remarked that the river below Memphis was "guerrilla country," and he likened surprise attacks to lightning strikes in a thunderstorm. People knew they were inevitable and sought safety until they were over. At one point the captain of a riverboat assured guests that guerrillas had not been sighted for six weeks, only to have a "sharp thwack and a handful of splinters" send the passengers ducking for cover.[16]

Of course, gunboats on the patrol system protected army transports. After the fall of Vicksburg, the Army of the Cumberland crept into southeastern Tennessee while the Army of the Tennessee moved upon Chattanooga. Supply lines for both armies were tenuous due to low water levels on the Tennessee and Cumberland Rivers, and rebel attacks on Union railroads. Still, Porter tried to cooperate with Major Generals Grant and Sherman. He sent tinclads to the Tennessee River, where they fought Confederate troops. The Mississippi Squadron provided crucial protection for Union supplies making their way to the Army of the Tennessee and the Army of the Cumberland.[17]

James Dickinson nearly died protecting those supplies. The teenager, who was a first-class boy on the tinclad *Tawah,* kept a diary of his one-year stint in the brown-water navy. The number of enemy attacks that he recorded is sobering. Between February 20 and March 30, 1864, rebels attacked the *Tawah* at least fifteen times as it patrolled the Tennessee River. Dickinson reported many firefights: guerrillas fired at the gunboat from 3:00 A.M. until daylight; sailors skirmished with rebels all day; two boatloads of sailors went ashore and drove rebels out of a log house; a ball from a guerrilla's pistol wounded Dickinson in the knee; the boat was "bushwhacked for over two miles"; sailors fought about 200 rebels at Savannah, Tennessee; bluejackets went ashore to forage, but guerrillas drove them back to the tinclad; and Dickinson nearly got "salted" when fighting rebels on land. The picture that emerges is a desperate fight to keep the Union supply line open in Tennessee.[18]

Gunboats had other duties as well. They responded to various Confederate raids and provided protection for Union forts and supply depots. When Brigadier General John Hunt Morgan led a Confederate cavalry foray into Indiana and Ohio in the summer of 1863, Union tinclads on the Ohio River responded. Lieutenant Commander Fitch, in the USS *Moose,* placed six tinclads in a dragnet along the river. When Morgan tried to cross into Kentucky, the tinclads, in concert with Union cavalry, prevented his escape and forced his surrender. The Union also increased its footprint in occupied territory by building a series of forts, strongholds, and blockhouses that sheltered detachments of Union troops or served as supply depots. Some of these posts were inland, but many were along the rivers. Most of them were small and were vulnerable to guerrilla attacks. One of these was Fort Anderson, a small earthen stronghold near Paducah, Kentucky, that faced the Ohio River.[19]

In March 1864 Major General Nathan Bedford Forrest tried to capture Fort Anderson. The Confederate cavalry commander, who had a knack for disrupting Union supplies and communication, was looking to inflict a quick defeat on the small garrison. The tinclads *Peosta* and *Paw Paw,* which were on patrol in the area, came to the support of the beleaguered Federals. George Vance, on the *Peosta,* reported that he and his fellow sailors poured "shell grape + canister . . . at a terrible rate" into the rebels attacking the fort. Forrest's men drifted back into Paducah and took up positions in houses, from which they "just rained the lead into us so that we could hardly serve our guns," Vance wrote. Despite the rebel onslaught, Union gunners destroyed one-quarter of the town, including the City Hotel, a brewery, and many houses. It was a long and dangerous day for the bluejackets. Over 200 musket balls struck the *Peosta,* and Union sailors fired so many rounds that a "worn out, stiff, [and] tired" gunner Vance wearily crawled into his hammock at the end of the day.[20]

The patrol system also accelerated the Mississippi Squadron's destructive war. Pillaging and plundering became more widespread at the end of the war's second phase and gained strength in the third phase. When the USS *Cincinnati* stopped at a plantation in March 1863, sailors and marines went ashore and grabbed a huge cache of food. They also, according to a bluejacket on the boat, helped themselves to bed clothes, pictures, crockery, "&c. &c. &c. &c. &c. &c."—a clear implication that they took all kinds of personal possessions. Two months later Union sailors "gloriously pillaged" the homes around Bruinsburg, reported fourteen-year-old Fannie Murdoch. They tore open drawers, rifled through trunks, threw clothing on the floor, danced in the parlor, stole photographs, and tore letters to shreds. One sailor cheekily left a daguerreotype of himself behind. At another plantation sailors found a piano hidden on a flatboat near the manor house. They blew it to smithereens.[21]

A sailor's rank influenced what articles he pilfered. Enlisted men usually stole small items. Quarter gunner William Park of the USS *Essex* noted in his diary how he took "a good number of valuable Books" and his shipmates carried off "a great many valuable things" before burning Bayou Sara, Louisiana. Enlisted men did not have the space or privacy to cart away large things or items of great monetary value. Their officers, however, shared private rooms and could protect their stolen goods. Scott Jordan, an ensign on the *Carondelet,* bragged to this wife that the costly carpeting in his room "came *very cheep* as it was some which we confiscated." Other pillaged articles that made Jordan's life more comfortable were a large mirror, a picture of a terrier and a mastiff with a bouquet of roses in its mouth, two large vases, linen curtains, a bookshelf, a writing desk, and a costly bed, "which we got up the Red River."[22]

Through Union raids, bluejackets released their frustrations and escaped, if however briefly, the navy's rigid schedule and the tedium associated with patrolling. As one man put it, destroying things was "considerable fun." Onshore sprees sometimes descended into a "highly ludicrous scene," according to another sailor. He laughed as he watched one crew member with a drawn cutlass chase a chicken and another holding an empty horse pistol hunt an old gander. Sailors experienced a sense of release as they swarmed out of their iron hives and onto southern plantations, farms, and towns. Since there were no conventional battles that occurred during the war's third phase, brown-water sailors used onshore raids to distract themselves from life inside the belly of their beasts.[23]

These forays created hardships for white southerners. One sailor archly observed that residents along the western rivers were "living between two fires," as rebels and Union sailors used increasingly aggressive means to bend neutral civilians to their side, vacuum up food, settle scores, or enrich themselves. Some whites tried to escape the tumultuous conditions by moving farther inland. When Confederate cavalryman Henry Orr arrived in eastern Arkansas to attack Union boats on the Mississippi River in June 1862, he noticed many of the plantations there were already abandoned. Whites who skedaddled, recalled one migrant after the war, squatted in abandoned houses, slaughtered cattle and hogs they found in the woods, and spun or wove their own cloth.[24]

Other white southerners fled *to* Union gunboats. At the end of 1863, a sailor on the *Peosta* told his wife that people were "coming out of the [Tennessee] River on rafts by the hundred times." A noticeable number of white men were fleeing from Confederate conscription. When the ironclad *Cincinnati* arrived at the mouth of the Red River, sailor Daniel Francis Kemp remembered after the war that a "large number" of refugees were just a few steps ahead of Confederate draft hunters. There was no consistent Union policy for handling white refugees, but captains generally facilitated their movement to a nearby Unionist town.[25]

The bulk of white southerners, though, stayed in place and supported the Confederacy's irregular war. The Worthington family, who received some of the fruits of the captured *Minnesota,* remained in their Willoughby home even though their world was dissolving around them. Several of their enslaved people had seized their opportunity for freedom, including Harry Higgins, Porter Hunter, Anderson Hyde, and Henry Jackson, all of whom enlisted on the USS *Romeo* on January 5, 1863. The family, though, placated Union sailors while simultaneously sheltering southern soldiers. On July 25, 1863, four or five officers from a gunboat held an uncomfortable conference with the family. While several family members "talked strong secession talk," according to young Amanda Worthington, the officers responded with "strong union" comments. During this debate, sailors raided the henhouse and slaughtered chickens. When the family matriarch asked the officer in charge to stop the theft, he did so and recalled his men to the gunboat. Less than a month later, the family sheltered eighteen Confederate soldiers. Union sailors likely suspected the family was up to no good, but why they did not raze Willoughby is unclear.[26]

Raids against plantations like Willoughby anticipated the actions of Union soldiers in Georgia and in Virginia's Shenandoah Valley in 1864. Both Sherman and Major General Philip Sheridan allowed their men to pillage southern plantation households, "acts of war" that specifically targeted southern elites as secessionist leaders. Like the Mississippi Squadron, some of the army's forays had military purposes, such as taking food or encouraging enslaved people to run away, as they narrowed the margin of survival for plantation households. Other attacks were symbolic, like destruction or confiscation of expensive personal property that they did not affect the ability to survive. Along the Mississippi River as well as in Georgia, pianos were a symbol of class privilege, so soldiers took special pleasure in destroying them.[27]

The increase in raids led to a rise in pillaging and plundering in 1863. Porter's General Order No. 44 tacitly acknowledged that the brown-water navy engaged in a significant amount of pillaging. On April 10, 1863, he forbade his captains from landing sailors "for the purpose of taking property of any description from plantations along the river." If that was not clear enough, he further explained, "No person will be allowed to pillage, burn, or destroy (unless from military necessity, which must be shown)." But the admiral had little power to enforce his orders. If anything, the symbolic decree loosened discipline and reinforced the tendencies of a population of sailors who wanted to act upon their martial masculinity.[28]

The Mississippi Marine Brigade was even more committed to pillaging than the Mississippi Squadron. Although the brigade's men occasionally hunted guerrillas, they were relentless in their pursuit of plunder and mayhem. On various occasions they threw a family carriage into the river, stole furniture, confiscated livestock, pocketed silver, broke fruit trees, tore up gardens, got enslaved people drunk in order to learn the locations of valuables, took personal clothing, and, in an action worthy of the Grinch, took knives and forks off the table while a family was eating. At one point they reputedly told one shocked plantation owner that "your booty" was their pay. The actions of the brigade became so egregious that the military deactivated the unit.[29]

Plundering along the western waters, whether at the hands of the Mississippi Squadron or the Mississippi Marine Brigade, was widespread enough to catch the attention of the president. In early 1864 an unnamed correspondent sent a letter to Lincoln alleging that men in the "Mississippi Flotilla," especially in the tinclads, behaved as if their "sole object has been plunder." This person alleged that sailors stop at plantations "and carry off everything of value, from the piano to the tea urn." Porter dismissed these charges as "libel" and deflected the blame to the Mississippi Marine Brigade. In a separate letter he angrily argued that the men of the Mississippi Squadron "never entered a house without orders or took so much as an egg without permission of the owner."[30]

Despite these sprees of thievery, there were limits to such actions. Most of the sailors' and marines' efforts were directed against structural property. Captains normally warned civilians and allowed them to escape before burning buildings. There are no known incidents where bluejackets executed noncombatants. Sailors restrained themselves, in part, because the navy, Federal government, and northern population demanded it. The Civil War was a contradictory combination of violence and restraint. Both the Union and Confederacy sanctioned military violence but demanded their armed forces demonstrate discipline, especially toward civilians. For the most part, citizens were not the targets of lethal violence.[31]

The Mississippi Squadron, however, did execute some southern guerrillas. Dickinson casually noted in his diary that men on his boat, the tinclad *Tawah,* had "two prisoners whom we are to execute as soon as it gets warmer. Meanwhile they are fattening for the sacrifice." Less than two weeks later, bluejackets shot the men. "One died like a man, the other like a dog," Dickinson thought. Two months after this, ten sailors from the tinclad shot three more guerrillas. Officers who authorized the execution of guerrillas were probably acting without explicit authorization but were within Federal policy. General Orders No. 100, also known as the Lieber Code, clearly stated that guerrillas "are not entitled to the privileges of prisoners of war."[32]

A few officers pushed the bounds of acceptable behavior in other ways. Late in 1863 the USS *Mound City*'s beat was near Lake Providence, Louisiana. The boat's officers became familiar with the residents. Acting Master Ferdinand Coleman, his brother Acting Ensign Silas Coleman, and three other officers stole chinaware, furniture, books, oil paintings, silk dresses, a crucifix of ivory and wood, a hanging hall lamp, two bells, a buggy, and goblets from civilians. The officers then forced a carpenter's mate to build a corral and an armorer to make horseshoes and stirrups so that they could sell stolen horses and mules to people in the area. Someone even alleged that Ferdinand Coleman had a torrid affair with a Miss Blackburn.[33]

The officers' actions were so outrageous that Porter brought charges against five of the *Mound City*'s officers. On December 14, 1863, four officers convened the court-martial proceedings on the USS *Conestoga* at Skipwith's Landing, Mississippi. Charges ranged from pillaging to destruction of property, disobeying orders, riotous and excessive conduct, withholding pay from sailors, and "acts of tyranny and oppression" toward the *Mound City*'s crew. Even though the boat's officers did their best to exonerate each other, the court found the Coleman brothers guilty of disregarding Porter's orders and "permitting pillaging on shore, going on shore seven miles from the river bank, and permitting officers to go on shore and take things from the houses of the inhabitants." They also were guilty of violating naval rules with regards to punishment of enlisted men.[34]

In a general order that captains read to their crews, Porter reported that the Coleman brothers made the *Mound City* "an instrument of tyranny." They deserved "the severest punishment," the admiral intoned, and pledged to prosecute any future instances of pillaging. His words were, to use naval jargon, "gundecking," or a shoddy job that covered up defects. There is no evidence that either brother experienced any significant punishment. Indeed, Ferdinand once again became acting master of the *Mound City,* while Silas was promoted to acting commander of the tinclad *Naumkeag.* The failure to punish either malefactor in any serious way probably undermined respect for authority within the fleet. If officers were not held accountable for their actions, why should enlisted men obey them and restrain their own impulses?[35]

One hundred miles south at Rodney, Mississippi, occurred another shocking breakdown in discipline, this time involving piety rather than thievery. The *Rattler*'s beat took it past Rodney, and the boat's acting master, William E. Fentress, got into the habit of attending church in the small town every Sunday. At 11:00 A.M. on September 13, 1863, he and twenty-two officers and crewmen went ashore to worship at the Presbyterian church. A few minutes into the service, congregants heard the thundering of horses' hooves and the scrape of spurs on the brick walkway. A Confederate officer burst into the packed church, pointed a revolver at the sailors, and said, "Surrender, you are my prisoners." Fentress stood and agreed to the surrender, but Second Assistant Engineer A. M. Smith, who was sitting in a different pew, pulled out his revolver and sent a ball through the Confederate's cap. Pandemonium ensued as civilians screamed and rushed in every direction. The rebel officer returned fire, but in the confusion seven bluejackets escaped. Confederate cavalry captured the other sixteen men and put them in a carriage that was waiting outside the church. When the crew on the

Rattler heard the gunfire, they beat to quarters and shelled the town. But it was too late—the Confederates had escaped with their prisoners.[36]

As the capture of the *Rattler*'s bluejackets demonstrates, Confederates were still a dangerous force along the rivers during the war's third phase. Indeed, rebels increased the pace of their attacks after the implementation of the patrol system. Southerners tangled with Union gunboats, transports, or commercial steamers at least 95 times between May 1, 1863, and April 30, 1864, an average of 7.9 actions per month. That was a higher rate than the 6.4 times per month in the previous phase. Despite the increase in rebel attacks, the patrol system was effective in protecting Union supply lines. Shipping losses in the third phase were half that of the second phase (see table 4).[37]

With the advent of the patrol system, the Mississippi Squadron implemented a coherent system to counter the Confederate ambush strategy. The fleet protected the Union's supply line and ensured that its armies would have enough supplies for their deep advance into enemy territory. Sailors punished civilians by taking their food and personal property. And bluejackets also undermined the social order in another important way: they facilitated the destruction of slavery and helped thousands of enslaved people escape bondage.

12

MILITARY EMANCIPATION

The Vicksburg Campaign created opportunities for the Mississippi Squadron to increase its involvement in military emancipation—that is, the ways that soldiers and sailors assisted fugitives to attain a measure of freedom. Bluejackets brought enslaved people to contraband camps, protected them from Confederate attacks, and provided them other types of assistance. Sailors' actions, however, were limited and reluctant.[1]

Waterways were important to the liberation of enslaved people in the decades before the war. Enslaved men working as roustabouts or waiters on steamboats used their mobility to escape. Eliza Harris, the character in *Uncle Tom's Cabin* who jumped across icefloes in the Ohio River to reach free soil, was based on a real story. Many fugitives crossed the Great Lakes to put themselves farther from the clutches of slavecatchers and to remove themselves from the pervasive racism in the Midwest. Runaways sometimes waited on the south shore of Lake Erie for ships to smuggle them to Canada.[2]

Initially, the Mississippi Squadron was reluctant to amplify these water-centric visions of freedom. In the summer of 1862, when the fleet was cooperating with the failed attempt to capture Vicksburg from the north, enough fugitives approached Union boats that Lieutenant Commander Charles H. Davis issued instructions that "contrabands" were "not to be received promiscuously on board the ships of the squadron." In practice, the fleet brought men on board if they enlisted in the navy or if they could be put to work as short-term laborers. Bluejackets on the USS *Essex,* for instance, forced fugitives (who had not enlisted) to shovel coal onto a flat boat and later used them to break down the door to the Natchez jail and set free Union captives.[3]

Once President Lincoln issued the Preliminary Emancipation Proclamation on September 22, 1862, enslaved people became more assertive in seeking sanctuary on Union boats. In late November the commander of a timberclad told

Porter, "All those who came on board the *Lexington* tell me that they are to be free on the 1st of January, but that their owners are getting ready to move them back from the river as soon as possible." He added that fugitives did everything in their power to "get to the river." Captains, though, routinely barred women and children from boarding their boats. Through the end of 1862, the Mississippi Squadron was not actively working to unravel slavery.[4]

Policy and practice changed in response to political events and the actions of the enslaved. Most obviously, Lincoln issued the Emancipation Proclamation on January 1, 1863. It imposed military emancipation in territory under the control of rebel armies while also exempting portions of the Confederacy, like much of Tennessee, then occupied by Union forces. When thinking about the western waters, most of the Cumberland and Tennessee Rivers thus were exempt, as was the Ohio River. The Union patrolled some of the Mississippi River above Vicksburg, but it was unclear if the presence of gunboats constituted control. Such fine distinctions did not matter to boat captains. By early 1863, they assumed that any enslaved person who reached a Union vessel could be freed no matter the location. Two weeks into the new year, Rear Admiral Porter complained to Secretary of the Navy Welles that fugitives, "among them many women," were "continually" claiming protection on gunboats. He added, "I cannot reject them under the law," by which he probably meant the Emancipation Proclamation. Fugitive agency intersected with the navy's presence to create conditions for limited freedom.[5]

By this time, gunboats had penetrated into Confederate territory that the army could not reach on its own. During the Yazoo Delta and Steele's Bayou Expeditions, the vessels of the Mississippi Squadron offered refuge to enslaved people within their iron walls. Along Steele's Bayou, crowds of runaway slaves seeking freedom started trailing the expedition. An officer on the USS *Cincinnati* saw people walking, riding horses or mules, and shouting that they were "going to freedom, sure." It was too far and too difficult for them to walk out of the delta, so sailors brought many of them on board the boats or crowded them onto flatboats or barges. Daniel Kemp groused that he was on half-rations because the *Cincinnati* sheltered contrabands who "eat our rations. I never was so sick of niggers in all my life you can hardly step for them they are always in the way." Another sailor estimated that the expedition "captured 800 Niggers," many of whom were placed on a barge. The changes in Union policy, coupled with the assertive actions of fugitives, were eroding slavery.[6]

But not all fugitives who made it to a Union boat or barge tasted freedom. Crewmen in the transport *Silver Wave* tossed a line to a rickety flatboat, and someone tied it fast. There were people of all ages on the flatboat, perhaps seventy total, reported correspondent Franc Wilkie. When the sternwheeler surged forward, waves from its paddlewheel swamped the flatboat. As the *Silver Wave* picked up speed, the flatboat's bow "was drawn under [the water], and the entire boat with all its human freight . . . disappeared under the greenish waters of the Yazoo." Wilkie looked for signs of life, but the "cruel waters held them fast." The *Silver Wave* did not even slow down. "Nothing that I saw during the war shocked me as did this occurrence." The incident only highlighted the often-callous attitude of soldiers and sailors toward fugitives hoping to escape slavery.[7]

The flight of slaves from the Yazoo Delta influenced the Vicksburg Campaign by causing a drop in southern agricultural production. After the Yazoo and Steele's Bayou Expeditions, Porter observed that there would "be no more planting in these regions for a long time to come" because the labor force was much smaller. The *New York Times* agreed. "The slaves thus brought of the Yazoo region," it argued, "would raise corn and pork enough to feed a whole brigade of rebel soldiers." The Mississippi Squadron's presence farther into the Deep South would erode slavery even more.[8]

The failed expeditions into the Yazoo Delta were one-time events, but the Vicksburg Campaign altered how the army and navy interacted with fugitives. Federal forces became more apt to use Black men and women in support of military operations. The navy relied on them to chop wood and operate woodyards for gunboats and transports. Exploitation of formerly enslaved people accelerated in the spring of 1863. First, a significant portion of the fleet was below Vicksburg after April 16. By this time, almost 75 percent of plantation-sized households in the Mississippi River valley were within fifty miles of a waterway accessible to northern vessels. Second, Porter instituted the patrol system. As the squadron became a familiar presence in these heavily populated areas, enslaved people had more opportunities to seek refuge. Everywhere the Mississippi Squadron went, it threatened slavery. This can be seen in June, when two ironclads were part of a significant exodus of enslaved people that left behind a remarkable written record.[9]

Once Major General Grant's army was safely across the Mississippi River, Porter sent the USS *Lafayette* and USS *Pittsburg* to Angola, Louisiana, at the mouth of the Red River in West Feliciana Parish. Their mission was to bottle up any Confederate supplies or gunboats on that river that might be used to assist southern armies at Vicksburg. The gunboats entered an area where slavery thrived prior to the war. About 9,500 enslaved people were held captive in West Feliciana Parish, along the river's east bank, while another 14,400 enslaved people lived across the state line in Wilkinson County, Mississippi. Farragut's boats had briefly passed through the region, but the enslaved people living here were largely untouched by military emancipation until the arrival of the two ironclads.[10]

The *Lafayette* was near the mouth of the Red River on May 26. At 11:00 P.M. a "skiff with two contrabands" came alongside the boat. Alexander Miller, a sailor on board, recorded in his diary that "Negroes began to come on board." This was not as easy as it may seem. The ironclad was floating in the river and was heavily secured. People did not come on board without the permission and assistance of the crew. Enslaved people, unless they enlisted, normally did not stay on the ironclad.[11]

This move to freedom did not escape the notice of the local slaveholders. On of them, according to Thomas Lyons, an officer on the ironclad, "comes on board and wants the Capt. to surrender five of his negroes that have escaped on board our boat." Lyons did not report what transpired between the two men, but it seems that Lieutenant Commander Henry Walke did not allow the fugitives to be returned. The next day Joseph Acklen, who owned five plantations and enslaved about 650 people, met with Walke on board the *Lafayette.* According to Lyons, the forty-seven-year-old enslaver had a "Southern 'aristocratic air,' about his manner" and argued with Walke about "his private rights, loyalty &c." During the lengthy meeting, which included "considerable profanity" on Acklen's part, the two men struck a deal, according to Lyons. None of Acklen's enslaved people would be brought on board the ironclads. In exchange, it is likely that Walke received permission to establish a hospital and to bury bluejackets on Acklen's property.[12]

Further actions of enslaved people forced bluejackets to consider the link between slavery and the Confederate war effort. At about 10:00 A.M. on June 10, fifteen enslaved men came to the shoreline and asked to be taken away. They were "dressed in miserable rags," according to Lyons. Elias Smith, the *Lafayette*'s clerk, recorded the men's names as well as the identity of their enslavers in the boat's log. Eleven fugitives had run from Colonel William Brandon, "who had his leg shot off in the Rebel Service in Virginia." The others escaped from a Confederate recruiting officer, a rebel private, and a man who had sent provisions to southern soldiers at Port Hudson.[13]

The next day, as the sun's rays were peaking over West Feliciana Parish, the crew of the *Lafayette* became aware of a crowd of fugitives from slavery who had gathered on shore. Lyons noted they were "signalling for us to take them away." The crowd "seemed to be in great consternation about something," and "all took some luggage with them." During the next three hours, sailors brought 170 enslaved people on board the *Lafayette,* a boat that normally had a crew of about 200 men. Many of them were women and children. During the next three weeks, sailors brought nearly 1,000 additional fugitives on board the two ironclads and then sent them along to refugee camps. Groups of enslaved people walked to shore, paddled in canoes, and even floated on logs just to get within sight of the Union gunboats.[14]

Surviving records do not indicate the reasons for the stunning decision to bring hundreds of enslaved people on the ironclads. Bluejackets had no compelling military reason to allow the people on board their boats. The *Pittsburg* had been in the Yazoo Delta, and the *Carondelet* was part of the Steele's Bayou Expedition, so perhaps the precedent of taking enslaved people out of that region convinced the captains to change course. It is also possible that because the men who sought refuge on June 10 were closely connected to active rebels, officers realized that weakening slavery in the area would undermine the Confederacy.

Beginning with the fifteen men on June 10, Smith recorded the personal information of the enslaved people in the boat's log. At first, he noted their name, place of birth, age, hair color, eye color, height, and occupation. In the following days, the crush of people seeking sanctuary became too great, so he reduced the biographical data to name, age, place of birth, and enslaver. Smith's decision to record the names of the fugitives is exceptional for several reasons. Demographic information on enslaved people is scarce. Most were listed in census records by age and gender without any other identifying information. Surviving records from plantations are spotty. Clerks on other boats did not record the information of enslaved people who were brought on board. Smith was opposed to slavery, and he likely realized the historical importance of the events unfolding in Louisiana. The *Lafayette*'s log (preserved in the National Archives) is a rich and unusual source of information about enslaved people.[15]

Smith recorded the enslaved people in family groups. More than a third of the fugitives were children, and most arrived at the Union boats with relatives. A typical family was Tom and Patience Green, both aged forty, and their children Eleck, Mary, Lovey, Manny, and Thomas. The oldest refugee was ninety-seven-year-old Ned Beaufort, but the median age of adults was twenty-six. These people had suffered much in slavery. Most obviously, the domestic slave trade had ravaged families. Of those who had birthplaces listed, 42 percent were born outside of the Louisiana-Mississippi region. They fled from seventy-five different enslavers, including the notorious Acklen, whose wife was the widow of the South's most successful slave trader. The sailors had become "practical emancipators" like the officers in the Union's western armies.[16]

Over the next few weeks, news about the gunboats traveled along the slave grapevine to the region's African American communities. For example, at 3:00 A.M. on June 15, a bluejacket on the *Lafayette* spotted a fire on shore with "a number of contrabands around it." The officer on duty sent a cutter to shore with some sailors, who reported the fugitives "claimed protection from us for cruelty from their masters and wanted to come on board." Three hours later "two dug outs came down the Miss river with some contrabands." The *Lafayette* received sixty-two fugitives that day, including some from Natchez and Adams County, a distance of fifty to sixty river miles. During the ironclads' time offshore at Angola, about seventy enslaved people journeyed from Natchez or Adams County. Nearly twenty more came from Woodville, Mississippi, which was forty miles distant. Two men, Delany Simpson and Jacob Haywood, claimed that someone from Texas named Reed enslaved them. Like a pebble dropped in water, the gunboats stationed at the mouth of the Red River made ripples that affected enslaved people in increasingly distant locations.[17]

It was not feasible for the *Lafayette* and *Pittsburg* to provide shelter for hundreds of civilians and still function as fighting vessels. Walke put the refugees in a coal barge. Sailors tore down a shed and used the boards to build a roof over the barge. In essence, the navy created a temporary, floating contraband camp.[18]

Contraband camps, although miserable, disease-ridden environments for freed people, were sites that nurtured Black culture. The coal barge was no different. Enslaved people from a variety of locations mingled and created a small, temporary community even as the big guns at Port Hudson boomed in the distance. Lyons disapprovingly observed, "Last night there was a wedding ceremony and dance in one end of the Barge, a religious prayer meeting in the middle and a birth in the other end." It was also common for "fiddleing and dancing" to take place on it.[19]

The barge also presented challenges to military discipline, as did contraband camps on land located near Union army forces. Several sailors from the *Lafayette* were "condemned to ride on the 'Slag-Chain' for flouring a saucy negro," Lyons noted. It is unclear if the sexual relations were consensual or a gang rape.[20]

Almost immediately, the boats' commanders decided that they had to move the fugitives from the barge to another location. On June 11, 1863, the same day that the first large group of escaped slaves arrived, the transports *Laurel Hill* and *Empire Parish* came alongside the barge "and took all the 'Contrabands' on board and went on down to Port Hudson," Lyons wrote. Port Hudson was forty-seven miles downstream and the site of a Union siege against a second Confederate strongpoint on the Mississippi River. The navy later sent fugitive groups to Bayou Sara, thirty-seven miles from Angola.[21]

The sources are silent as to what happened to the fugitives when they arrived at Port Hudson and Bayou Sara. Those at Port Hudson were probably placed in a temporary camp within or near the Union lines. It is possible that some of the men were forced to enlist in the Union army or work in some capacity during the siege. There is no record of a contraband camp at Bayou Sara. The crew of the USS *Essex* shelled and burned that town in 1862, and the site became a supply depot for Union troops investing Port Hudson.[22]

Enslaver Acklen was growing concerned that people from Angola would end up at Port Hudson or Bayou Sara. He colluded with local guerrillas, and on June 29 several "mounted Rebels" arrived on his plantations and started "driving the colored people back to the hills," according to the *Lafayette*'s log. Acklen probably meant to move his chattel to Texas or somewhere beyond the navy's reach. If so, he was mirroring the actions of hundreds of other enslavers. Historians estimate that at least 250,000 enslaved people were forced to walk to Texas during the war to escape the reach of the Union military. The guerrillas also captured seven sick men in the onshore hospital at one plantation, including Luke Walker, a contraband. They eventually released all but Walker, who they "maltreated" and threatened to hang.[23]

Instead of walking westward, Acklen's enslaved people forced their way to the gunboats. At least 284 of them found shelter with the Mississippi Squadron on that summer day. Union sailors assisted with the freedom of at least 336 enslaved people who lived on Angola, numbering half of the chattel property Acklen had claimed on the 1860 census. The presence of the Mississippi Squadron and the collective action of enslaved people challenged Acklen's power as well as that of other enslavers in the region.[24]

At least six of the refugees from the region took the war against their former masters by enlisting in the Mississippi Squadron. One of them was George Davey, who escaped the clutches of Orrick Metcalfe. The thirty-seven-year-old Davey was born in Kentucky and was probably sold to a slave trader who transported him to Mississippi. It seems he ran away from his enslaver's plantation near Natchez and traveled sixty miles to the mouth of the Red River. Davey enlisted on June 16, 1863, and became a cook on the *Pittsburg.*[25]

The *Lafayette* remained at the mouth of the Red River until early July, when it received orders to return to Vicksburg. As the ironclad steamed upriver, fugitives encamped along the shore asked to be taken away. By the time the boat reached Vicksburg, it had taken another fifty or sixty refugees on board. Sailors probably brought the people to a contraband camp near the city.[26]

The emancipation activity at the mouth of the Red River was unusual for its particular intensity, but it reflected historian Joseph Reidy's observation that "emancipation was a complex and uneven process rather than a specific event." Freedom unfolded over several weeks, and not all enslaved people in the region became free at the same time. The presence of gunboats was necessary, but freedom also depended on enslaved people to force a deeper and more consequential series of actions. There is evidence that others in the region sought refuge with the navy. The log of the USS *Richmond,* a ship in the West Gulf Blockading Squadron, notes that on June 4, 1863, "a large steamer came up to-day to take away the contrabands who had accumulated on the bank opposite the ship—about 1,200 in number." The *Richmond* was stationed at Port Hudson, about thirty miles away from the *Lafayette.* Enslaved people were actively working to bring down slavery from the inside. Freedom, though, was tenuous, and the military had no long-term plan to protect the self-emancipated from Confederate or guerrilla retribution.[27]

Outside of the Red River, bluejackets acted in contradictory ways toward small clusters of enslaved people who established riverside encampments. There were thousands of refugees along the Mississippi River between Natchez and Helena. Many of them created their own camps, which were literal constructions of freedom. Two such sites were near Grand Gulf. On June 13, 1863, a sailor told his diary that fugitives were "camping" on both sides of the Mississippi and that about a dozen people on the Grand Gulf side had smallpox. A few days later, the USS *Louisville*'s captain reported that about 120 fugitives were living at Grand Gulf. They had no food because "guerrillas and jayhawkers have driven everything off." He added, "I will be forced to supply them." Sailors on the *Cincinnati* had a different response to an improvised camp. Daniel Kemp wrote that enslaved people built a "collection of huts" along the shore that became a "sort of rendezvous for contrabands." Bluejackets "cleaned the place out several times." He did not estimate how many people were in the camp, but it must have been significant. There were so many refugees in the spot that they "made a tremendous noise singing and preaching" when Kemp was trying to sleep.[28]

The Federal government, though, preferred that fugitives live in contraband camps. Women in such camps could be put to work, while the men could be recruited or conscripted. These centers ranged in size from a few hundred people to nearly 10,000 refugees. Contraband camps were often rife with disease, poor sanitation, and appalling living conditions. Guerrillas and Confederate cavalry raided several of these places, squeezing "the perimeters and terrain of freedom." Some camps were so insecure that the army relocated refugees to islands in the Mississippi River.[29]

There were other types of refugee sites along the lower Mississippi. The army established a series of government plantations stretching across 4,000 acres on the western bank of the Mississippi River near Lake Providence. The concept was deceptively simple: pay formerly enslaved people, mainly women and children, to work on abandoned cotton plantations. Refugees, according to the day's conventional wisdom, would learn self-sufficiency while growing a product that would benefit the northern economy. The government confiscated the land from its rebel owners and leased it to northern investors or southerners who swore loyalty to the U.S. government. These people managed the plantations, organized the labor, and paid the workers. In order to guard against attacks from Confederate cavalry and guerrillas, the army stationed Black regiments next to them. The system re-envisioned the plantation as a fortified village but was shot through with greed, violence, poor medical care, defaults on wages, high taxes, and starvation. There was so much government fraud and abuse that many formerly enslaved people refused to work or left the plantations.[30]

Yet another type of encampment emerged at Davis Bend, the site of plantations formerly owned by Confederate president Jefferson Davis and his brother. After the Union captured Vicksburg, Porter established a type of colony for formerly enslaved people at Davis Bend. Residents cut wood for gunboats and tended cattle, which they provided to naval crews. Later the government leased out the land to former slaves but eventually took over and converted the area to government plantations.[31]

The Mississippi Squadron became partially responsible for transporting people and supplies to these sites. The USS *Curlew* routinely brought fugitives to Lake Providence. Whether the formerly enslaved people requested to be taken there or the bluejackets arbitrarily decided to dump them at a plantation is unknown; the latter seems more likely. Crews probably took refugee groups to a location that was convenient for the bluejackets. Sailors on the USS *Rattler,* for instance, noticed some large fires at a plantation near Grand Gulf and went to investigate. Fugitives "came pouring down to the boat," according to the acting master's mate, as gunners "poured a lot of Broadsides over into the fields" to keep the pursuing enslavers at bay. The tinclad took sixty-four enslaved people on board as well as the "body of a colored soldier who had been shot by the rebels." The *Rattler* brought the fugitives and the body to Davis Bend, which was within its normal beat.[32]

The fleet also provided protection for the government-sanctioned plantations. In June 1863 Confederates targeted the Union supply base at Milliken's Bend as well as nearby government plantations in the hopes of drawing Union pressure away from Vicksburg. Grant had transferred troops from that area to his lines, and the Black troops remaining near the plantations were inexperienced and poorly trained. Their only advantage was a garrison site on top of an old Native American mound, which rose about fifty feet above the alluvial plain.[33]

On June 29 Confederate forces attacked the plantation at Goodrich's Landing. They quickly overwhelmed the garrison and started burning "mansions, cotton gins, and negro quarters as far as the eye could see," according to one sailor. The garrison's commander managed to send word for help, and Porter dispatched the Mississippi Marine Brigade's ram *John Raine* as well as the tinclad *Romeo* to the scene. Cavalry from the *John Raine* chased the Confederates, while the *Romeo* followed them along the riverbank and fired nearly a hundred rounds. The rebels fled for fifteen miles, "setting fire to everything as they went along." Either the 1,400-man raiding force was strong enough to simultaneously ward off attacks and burn property, or Union sailors had no stomach for landing troops.[34]

The gunboats arrived too late to prevent a series of atrocities. Confederates carried away from 1,200 to 2,000 enslaved people and "restored them to their owners," according to one rebel officer. An unknown but significant number of formerly enslaved people were executed. At Goodrich's Landing Union sailors found the "charred remains of human beings" whom the raiders had burned. One officer from the Mississippi Marine Brigade also alleged that Confederates nailed several white officers to trees crucifixion style and set them on fire.[35]

Confederates committed crimes at Milliken's Bend as well. Rebel forces overwhelmed the garrison there and clubbed and bayoneted Black soldiers who tried to surrender. Others murdered African American troops execution style, with a bullet to the head. It was racially motivated killing and not war. A few Black soldiers were able to fall back to a levee and were only saved from annihilation by the arrival of the USS *Choctaw* and USS *Lexington.* Bluejackets from the *Choctaw* sent a cutter ashore and brought nineteen wounded soldiers to the boat. Eventually, the naval guns convinced the Confederates to withdraw, but not before a shocking 43 percent of Union troops were killed or wounded.[36]

The establishment of the government plantations reversed the old order because they symbolized free labor and loss of control within southern society. White southerners could not brook such impudence and escalated their violent acts once it became apparent that Union armed forces threatened slavery. The widespread violence of guerrillas and Confederate soldiers continued the actions of the slave patrols and provided a bridge to the Ku Klux Klan of the postwar South.[37]

Guerrillas and Confederate soldiers attacked enslaved Americans in other ways. One southern officer threatened to "hang every negro that he could catch going to or coming off" a gunboat, one Union officer discovered. About sixty enslaved Americans approached the *Essex* near Baton Rouge on the same day that Lincoln signed the Emancipation Proclamation. According to a sailor on the boat, a "Band of Guerillis" interrupted this bid for freedom when they "came down and shot one of them and tied another one both hands and feet then threw him into the River." The sailor concluded the obvious: "That is what they call making an example to prevent the Niggers from running away." Bluejackets chased away the guerrillas and brought the remainder of the people across the river to a contraband camp. Several months later "Jayhawkers" near Grand Gulf tried to snatch fugitives from the temporary contraband camp.[38]

Such attacks continued into 1864. The shift of Union troops away from the river over the winter of 1863–64 emboldened ambush squads and guerrillas. An accumulation of smaller attacks that ranged widely across space increased the vulnerability of enslaved people living in contraband camps and plantations. Lieutenant Commander Frank Ramsay, who commanded the Mississippi Squadron's Third District, noticed this change. He had been forcing fugitives to cut wood for his coal-starved boats. In December 1863 he sent them away, "as it is not safe to keep them on the bank now." Near the end of the war, the tinclad *Huntress* came across a family of forlorn-looking fugitives near Fort Pillow. They were trying to get to Memphis because "white men were killing negroes," they told a sailor.[39]

Despite these limitations, the Mississippi Squadron helped bring about the end of slavery. When sailors sheltered slaves and handed out food to refugees, they were nurturing what some historians have called the largest slave revolt in history. Bluejackets, though, saw the uneven demise of slavery in pragmatic terms. When sailors forced enslaved people to coal boats or cut wood, they indicated that they valued their labor but did not seek to liberate them in any meaningful way. Aid and shelter were afterthoughts, not priorities. Sailors brought these attitudes to northwestern Louisiana from late 1863 into 1864, when they became ensnared in yet another combined operation. The Mississippi Squadron assisted with the freedom of enslaved people along the Red River, but the poorly planned expedition nearly had catastrophic consequences for the fleet and the overall war effort.[40]

13

THE RED RIVER EXPEDITION

By the beginning of 1864, the conventional war was over for the Mississippi Squadron. Its boats were primarily patrolling their sectors, protecting transports, and suppressing insurgent attacks. The army, however, had one final request of Rear Admiral Porter. It needed the brown-water navy to accompany Union troops into Louisiana. What Porter did not anticipate is that the ensuing campaign up the Red River would repeat the mistakes of the failed White River, Yazoo Pass, and Steele's Bayou Expeditions. In each case the Union gunboats advanced in enemy territory, encountered hostile environmental conditions, and faced irregular attacks. The navy would face new complications—cotton confiscation, falls in the river, and inconsistent protection from the army—that would nearly result in the loss of a third of the fleet. The campaign underscored the Mississippi Squadron's vulnerability when facing difficult environmental conditions.

The ill-fated Red River Campaign arose from a curious collection of factors. Shreveport, in northwestern Louisiana, was now the Confederate capital of Louisiana and an important supply depot. The city was also the headquarters for the Army of the Trans-Mississippi and a natural gateway to Texas. President Lincoln wanted the army to occupy the region so the government could hold elections in the area and send Republicans to Congress. Union politicians also wanted to capture cotton and send it to northern mills, an action that would stimulate the economy, pacify industrialists, and shore up support for the war. Major General Sherman was enthusiastic about the scheme and wanted to lead the expedition, perhaps because he had lived near Alexandria when he was superintendent of the Louisiana State Seminary of Learning and Military Institute. Porter signed on as well, assuming that he would work with his friend.[1]

Even before any Union soldier marched toward Alexandria, the campaign encountered trouble. Ulysses S. Grant, now wearing a third star as general in chief of the U.S. Army, doubted a campaign into Louisiana was a wise use of resources. He wanted to capture Mobile and Atlanta and needed Sherman to carry out those plans. Worse, Major General Banks thereafter got involved. Banks was a political general from Massachusetts who outranked by date of commission every Union general west of the Appalachian Mountains. He also aspired to become president in 1864 and craved a decisive military victory that would launch his campaign. Banks elbowed his way into the operation and informed Sherman that, as senior officer, he would command the expedition. The best that Sherman could do then was to send 10,000 of his troops to accompany Porter. Brigadier General A. J. Smith, a skilled commander, led these veterans.[2]

Banks, who was out of his depth, devised a plan that depended on skill, speed, and cooperation. While Porter ascended the Red River with the troops from Sherman, Banks would tramp through the Louisiana countryside toward Shreveport with 20,000 men. Simultaneously, Major General Frederick Steele would march a Union army from Little Rock and threaten Shreveport from the north. Coordinating the movements of these military groups would prove to be impossible. Moreover, Major General Halleck, now U.S. Army chief of staff, refused to name an overall commander for the expedition. Sherman insisted that his men were loaned to Porter, not to Banks. The confusing command structure hobbled the campaign.[3]

Porter chose to bring twenty-five gunboats into northwestern Louisiana. Several Mississippi Marine Brigade rams, a hospital boat, tenders, tugs, supply vessels, and numerous transports were also part of the expedition. If it seems that twenty-five fighting vessels was an excessive display of force, it was. Most of the boats were not there to fight the Confederates but to haul away cotton taken from previously untouched plantations. Cotton had legitimate military purposes: sailors stuffed it into gunboats to shore up weak spots, it protected boilers, and the navy could woo Unionists by protecting their cotton from destruction or confiscation. But Porter and his men also knew that they could seize it, haul it to a prize court, and receive a share of the profits once it was sold. Better yet, they could sell it on the black market and receive even more money. The confiscation—perhaps more accurately, the theft—of cotton became a get-rich-quick scheme. Even Porter privately admitted in 1863 that a "cotton mania" infected his fleet. The thirst for cotton would distract the sailors of the Mississippi Squadron during the Red River Campaign.[4]

The expedition began on March 7, 1864. Porter's boats quickly forced the surrender of Fort DeRussy, an earthen structure about twenty-five miles upstream from the Red River's mouth. Porter left the USS *Benton* and USS *Essex* to destroy the fort and sent the monitor *Osage* ahead with the army transports to capture Alexandria. On March 15 the gunboat pulled up to Alexandria's wharf, and its captain demanded surrender of the town; civilian authorities readily complied. Soon thereafter, the rest of the fleet, except the *Benton* and *Essex*, were in Alexandria waiting for Banks to arrive. One sailor noted with satisfaction that "the Stars and Stripes wave in triumph over this Rebel hot bed to the great joy and satisfaction of the Negroes." Bluejackets were overjoyed to get out of their boats and naturally headed for the town's whiskey joints. A marine officer complained that his men "arrested all drunken sailors and sent them to the blockhouse." Banks finally breezed into town and prepared for the campaign's next phase.[5]

The destruction of Fort DeRussy and the capture of Alexandria cleared the lower Red River of Confederate resistance, meaning that the army and navy could focus on collecting cotton there. Porter admitted as much after the war. "There is no use blinking at the cotton question," he wrote. "Cotton was king all the way through the expedition." He simultaneously deflected the blame to his men: "Naval officers complained to me that they were losing a chance of making prize-money, and they thought they were at least entitled to the cotton along the banks of the river. I unwisely consented to that." More likely, the admiral and his captains knew from the beginning that they would slurp up as much cotton as possible.[6]

The army and navy could legally take cotton from rebellious southerners but were supposed to ignore bales that belonged to loyal citizens. It was difficult to tell one from another, and in practice, the navy indiscriminately seized cotton from everyone. Sailors were also supposed to confine their attention to cotton along the shore and not venture inland. Again, bluejackets largely disregarded that directive.

Sailors in the expedition had a pecuniary interest in stealing cotton. A quarter gunner on the USS *Lafayette* wrote in his diary: "Gen order was reced on the quarter deck to the crew. Stating that all the Vessels in this expedition Shall share alike in the Cotton Captured by any Vessels in the expedition." That news excited an officer on the USS *Carondelet*. "I expect to make a *Fortune lacking a few cents* out of this Expedition," he wrote his wife. Captains were supposed to surrender the confiscated cotton to Treasury agents, who then would sell it on the commercial market in Cairo or Mound City. Half of the proceeds went to a fund for disabled sailors, while the other half went to the captors. Officers received more than enlisted men, and Porter received 5 percent of the amount that went to his fleet.[7]

Bluejackets on the *Benton* and *Essex* confiscated cotton on the lower Red after they leveled Fort DeRussy. On March 16, sailors from the *Essex* took 24 bales from a "Mr. Brochard," whose loyalty was "doubtful." Twelve days later they swiped 18 bales from the plantation of a "bitter rebel." Sailors also took 10 bales from G. W. Snoddy's place. Snoddy was "said to be loyal," but that was not good enough for the bluejackets. Within two weeks, a man on the *Essex* estimated that the navy had already sent 2,000 bales of cotton to Cairo as prizes for the fleet.[8]

Farther upriver, bluejackets were also at work. On April 5 the *Osage*'s captain "sent all hands ashore after cotton." Sailors sometimes went five or six miles inland in their quest for the white gold. They "seized wagons and animals wherever they could find them, and they were using those wagons and horses and mules to draw in this cotton," one army officer remembered. Crewmen were known to stencil "C.S.A." on a bale they found and then promptly mark "U.S.N." on the reverse side. They did this so often that even the straitlaced Porter joked that "U.S.N./C.S.A." stood for "United States Navy Cotton-Stealing Association."[9]

Sailors forced enslaved people to assist these shoreline raids. The *Ouachita* stopped at a "large plantation" because of rumors that "a quantity of Cotton stored back in the woods about half a mile, in great piles," one sailor wrote. "We pressed into service all of the darkies and old mules and carts we could get and had them haul the cotton to the banks of the river."[10]

Once the bales were riverside, the USS *Black Hawk*'s log observed, the "crew [was] employed loading [a] barge alongside with captured cotton." Often, white sailors forced their Black crewmates to tote the bales. Nelson Bailey, a formerly enslaved man from Tennessee, strained his shoulder and suffered a hernia loading cotton on the *Ouachita*. When barges were not available or were full, sailors just left the remaining material in great heaps along the bank. Since the caches were so valuable, ironclads anchored nearby and placed "sentries over the cotton . . . and armed the watch." Soon enough, a tug or transport came by and left an empty barge. When that barge was full, another boat hitched up to it and hauled it to Cairo.[11]

The confiscation of cotton slowed down the fleet at a time when it needed to move quickly. Sherman had told Porter that the Red River rose every spring and that there would be enough water for the large gunboats to chug up to Shreveport, another 200 miles past Alexandria. But 1864 saw the driest spring in two decades, and instead of rising, the river was falling. Wellington Withenbury, the local river pilot who gave advice to Porter, cautioned the admiral not to take the large boats any farther because there was not enough water flowing over the sandstone boulders that made up two sets of falls just above Alexandria. Unbeknown to Porter, the Confederates manipulated the environment to further reduce the water level by destroying an upriver dam used to keep water in the channel. Water that normally went downstream thereafter flowed into a floodplain. The river was at a historic low level and would create continual headaches for Porter and the fleet.[12]

Banks, meanwhile, had troubles of his own. Grant urged the general to capture Shreveport as quickly as possible because Sherman's men had to be returned by the middle of April. Banks, who thought he had all the time in the world, had dallied in New Orleans and recruited Unionists to vote in the upcoming state election. The political general now suddenly realized that he need to hurry.[13]

Porter dutifully sent eleven of the squadron's gunboats past Alexandria. On April 1 these vessels caught up with Banks's army and reached Grand Ecore, about 100 miles from Shreveport. Porter reveled in the lack of Confederate resistance and speculated that the rebellion in Louisiana was dying. He could not have been more wrong.[14]

At Grand Ecore Banks asked Withenbury about the best way to approach Shreveport. The pilot, who wanted to protect his own cotton from confiscation, directed the general to march *away* from the river for about fifteen miles and then follow a road that ran parallel to the Red. What he did not mention was that a road *next* to the river was a better choice. Banks betrayed his lack of training and experience by not scouting the various routes. His decision to trust Withenbury's word alone was a blunder that nearly led to the destruction of the Union fleet. Deep in enemy territory, the navy needed the army to fend off rebel attacks. Banks's decision was unsurprising, however, because the navy and army had been operating independently during the expedition. Porter did not have the same level of trust in Banks that he demonstrated toward Grant or Sherman.[15]

In self-serving testimony before the Joint Committee on the Conduct of the War, Banks blamed Porter for the decision to bring the fleet past Grand Ecore. He said it was up to the navy to decide if there was enough water to support the ironclads, even though it "was conceded by everybody that it was impossible to navigate the river." Further, Porter had bragged that "wherever the sand was damp he could run his boats." The admiral had a different recollection. He testified that he opposed the movement upriver and pointed out that Chief of Staff Halleck had ordered him to cooperate with the army. Once Banks left for Shreveport, Porter "could not very well decide not to go upriver" and had to risk losing his fleet. He was correct in this. Once Banks marched westward out of Alexandria, the navy was obligated to support the army and go upstream.[16]

Deciding which boats would embark on the last stage of the expedition was another matter. Upstream from Grand Ecore, the Red River narrows considerably, and its natural features favored the Confederates. Scott Jordan on the *Carondelet* told his wife, "I never had any idea of what crooked was until I got in to Red River." There was a "right Angle turn on every 200 feet," another sailor wrote in his journal, "and the river is so narrow a person in some places might jump [from a boat] on either shore." The Red also had banks as high as thirty-five feet along this stretch, from which rebels could shoot down on the boats at close range. Porter sent seven boats, a couple of tugs, and about 2,300 men past Grand Ecore. The navy was supposed to rendezvous with the army at a steamboat landing near Shreveport, but environmental conditions and canny Confederate resistance made sure that did not happen.[17]

Confederates had decided to cede no more ground without a fight. The gunboats crept upstream for three days, often dispersing guerrillas with howitzer blasts. As the water level got lower, the banks got higher, often above the pilot houses. The fleet then encountered an obstacle near the rendezvous point, as Confederates had sunk the steamer *New Falls City* across the channel by filling its hold with mud. Sand also piled up against the tightly wedged boat due to the current. A rebel prankster left a sign in large letters inviting Porter to attend a ball in Shreveport. The Union fleet was stuck.[18]

As Porter contemplated how to remove the steamer, a courier arrived with the news that Banks had been badly whipped. Lieutenant General Richard Taylor, though his Confederate forces were outnumbered, had inflicted twice as many casualties as he sustained and forced Banks to abandon the land campaign. There was no word from Steele's army, and Porter correctly assumed that it was still in Arkansas and nowhere near Shreveport. The admiral knew that he must retreat immediately because Taylor's army would be racing to the river, hoping to capture or destroy the Union fleet. Banks's incompetence put Porter's gunboats in peril.[19]

As the boats went downriver, rebels seemed to be everywhere. It was nearly impossible to see them because the twisting river limited visibility and the air was "filled with smoke from the cotton which is burning on every plantation," as a marine recorded. Sailors fought off ambushes nearly every day. On April 11, for instance, 200–300 Confederates attacked the convoy. Marines on the *Black Hawk* coiled a large hawser, piled fence rails around it, and added hammocks to make a "splendid barricade" on the hurricane roof. They would need its protection.[20]

At the high banks near Coushatta, the *Osage,* at the back of the line and towing the transport *Black Hawk,* ran aground. Confederates pounced. Brigadier General Thomas Green's men rained down a "terrific musketry fire" from only one hundred yards distance. So many musket balls hit the *Black Hawk* that its crew had to flee to the metal confines of the *Osage.* When rebels poked their heads over the nearly perpendicular banks, gunners on the *Osage* fired shrapnel with fuses cut to one second. The USS *Lexington* rushed into action and delivered a devastating fire on the "poor deluded wretches," who, Porter sneered, smelled of "Louisiana rum." The grape and canister gave the *Osage*'s crew enough cover to work their boat free. Lieutenant Commander Selfridge, captain of the monitor, cut the line to the transport and got underway. Confederates renewed their attack and got within twenty yards of the *Osage* when a blast of canister sheared off the top of Green's head. His mortal wounding ended the Confederate threat. Porter was so desperate to escape that he kept the fleet moving at night by torchlight.[21]

The convoy fended off multiple attacks the next day. First, "a party of bushwackers" harassed the boats and then about a hundred Confederates attacked. They "were sending a perfect shower of ball and shot over us," according to a marine. He and his buddies on the hurricane deck of their gunboat fought back with a 24-pound howitzer. The piece got so hot that it exploded when another marine rammed a cartridge down the barrel. The blast threw the man to the forecastle: "He had his whole right arm completely mashed to jelly and filled with powder." A rebel shot hit the steam drum on one of the transports. The *Chillicothe* finally drove off the attackers, and the crew managed to coax their stricken boat downstream. After another day of close calls, the Mississippi Squadron reached the relative safety of Grand Ecore on April 14.[22]

Porter mounted his horse and galloped through the dark to find Banks. Writing after the war, the admiral recalled that the general was wearing a robe, a nightcap, and slippers while reading *Scott's Tactics.* He unloaded his frustrations on Banks, who insisted that he had won the Battle of Mansfield on April 8 but retreated for lack of water. A frustrated Porter left and returned to his boat.[23]

Soon after the fleet resumed its withdrawal, the USS *Eastport* detonated a torpedo. The ironclad now leaked so much that Porter had no choice but to destroy the boat. Sailors put eight barrels of cannon powder beneath its forward casemate and rigged an insulated wire to trigger the blast. But before the bluejackets could destroy the big metal slug, Confederates swooped in, "rising suddenly from the bank." They tried to board the *Cricket,* but the gunboat's heavy dose of grape and canister drove them off. The other ironclads laid down a punishing crossfire that convinced the rebels to run away. As the sailors caught their breath, Lieutenant Commander Seth L. Phelps, captain of the *Eastport,* tried to use a galvanic battery to detonate the powder charge. It failed. He then spread loose powder on the deck and rigged a long cotton fuse. Phelps lit the fuse, scrambled across the deck, and leapt into a cutter as it pulled away. He barely reached the safety of the *Fort Hindman* before "flames burst forth in every direction," and eight consecutive explosions rocked the *Eastport.* After the war Porter remembered how "great pieces of the hull fell around us."[24]

After commanders made sure the *Eastport* was fully destroyed, the beleaguered flotilla resumed its journey. Rounding a bend near Cane River, the boats steamed into a Confederate ambush. Southerners had dug rifle pits and concealed four cannons. Hundreds of muskets laid down a "pelting shower of shot and shell" that sent sailors ducking for cover. The rebel cannons joined the cacophony. Porter urged the *Cricket*'s pilot to run the gauntlet and then rushed to the gun deck because his gunners were not laying down a suppressing fire. He came across a grisly sight. A Confederate shell had killed or disabled every man in one gun crew, and another projectile had "swept away" the crew from the forward gun. Porter ordered Black sailors, including his personal servant Robert White, to man the guns. Some refugees from slavery on board also pitched in. The admiral then went to the engine room and discovered that Confederate bullets had struck down most of the firemen. As Porter surveyed the scene, a "fireman standing by his side was cut in two, and his chambermaid was literally quartered." The boat began losing power because its steam was low. Porter put an assistant engineer in charge of building up the fires, and soon the *Cricket* was surging forward again. After the gunboat limped to safety, surviving crew members took inventory. Rebel balls had struck the tinclad thirty-eight times and, along with effective musket fire, inflicted twenty-five casualties. "The decks were a perfect slaughter pen," remembered one soldier on board.[25]

The other boats took a terrible beating as well. The pilot for the *Champion No. 3* lost his nerve when the shooting started and tried to turn around and go back upriver. A Confederate battery drew a bead on the pump boat and sent a ball into its boiler. It was a fatal blow in more ways than one. Massive clouds of steam rushed through the vessel's interior, where nearly 200 formerly enslaved men, women, and children were huddled together. With no way to escape, the victims could only scream in agony as they were scalded to death. The blast killed an estimated 150 refugees as well as several crewmen. The crippled boat drifted downstream "enveloped in steam" and scudded against the shore. Confederates captured most of the survivors.[26]

At about the same time, bluejackets on the *Juliet* lashed the tinclad to the *Champion No. 5*. Confederate shells crushed the *Juliet*'s steam pipe and cut its tiller ropes. They also tore a hole in the rudder of *Champion No. 5*. That last shot was severe enough to convince the pump boat's pilot to abandon his post. As he fled, the crew panicked and started hacking at the hawsers holding the vessels together. They had chewed through all but one rope before the *Juliet*'s captain, J. S. Watson, forced them to stop. With bullets and shells flying all around, William Maitland, one of the tinclad's pilots, leapt on board *Champion No. 5* and steered the two boats upstream.[27]

During this wild melee, some sailors on the *Fort Hindman* were panic stricken. Phelps, the no-nonsense captain, went to the gun deck, put his hand on his revolver, and promised that "the first man who should flinch from his gun would receive its contents." Despite the bravado, the *Fort Hindman* followed the *Champion No. 3*'s lead and went upstream. When it met the other boats about a mile above the batteries, crew members discovered a gaping hole in their boat's hull. They crammed cotton bales in the opening to keep the tinclad afloat. The boats would try again to transit this stretch the next day.[28]

At 9:30 A.M. on April 27, the boats set out. Confederates struck once more, sinking the *Champion No. 5* and severely damaging the other boats. The *Fort Hindman, Juliet,* and *Cricket* steamed to Alexandria and safety—or so their bluejackets thought.[29]

The situation at Alexandria was dire because of low water. Porter had ten boats above the town and was also loosely responsible for the several transports and several thousand soldiers waiting there. The Union boats would have to ride over the upper falls (called the falls), navigate through a mile-long stretch of huge sandstone boulders that created rapids, and then go over the lower falls (called the dam). The ironclads needed about seven feet of water to attempt a run through the rocks, but only about three was flowing over the falls and the dam. The transports could traverse both but could not safely travel farther without an escort because Confederates had established ambush sites downriver from Alexandria. Between the growing rebel threat and the shrinking volume of water in the Red River, Porter contemplated the unthinkable: destroying his fleet and having his sailors and marines march out of Louisiana with the army.[30]

Before taking such drastic action, Porter sent some of the lighter boats through the rapids. On May 4 the tinclads *Covington* and *Signal* as well as the transport *John Warner* scraped over the rocks. South of Alexandria, Confederates sprung an ambush at Dunn's Bayou. Rebel cannons knocked out the *Warner*'s rudder, forcing the transport to drift into the bank about 100 yards from the southern battery. Colonel George Baylor, commanding the Confederates, was able to set up a crossfire despite the tinclads' "hot fire." Rebel gunners "did their work well," a bluejacket admitted. After about three hours of fighting, the captain of the *Warner* hoisted a white flag.[31]

With the *John Warner* a useless heap of wood, the Confederates concentrated their fire on the tinclads. They hit the *Covington*'s steering gear and then the *Signal*'s rudder. Both boats crashed into the bank. Hundreds of musket balls zinged off their thin outer armor. The Confederates shifted their cannons around to get better angles of attack. Gray gunners soon poured more than forty shells into the *Covington*'s upper works and perforated the *Signal*'s steam pipe and port engine. Finally, as the gunboats ran out of ammunition, both captains ordered their crews to abandon ship. Sailors on the *Covington* spiked their guns and set the boat on fire. As smoke billowed out of the tinclad, its crew escaped, as Baylor approvingly noted, "under a hot fire from our Enfields." Only thirty-two of the seventy-four men on board made it to shore. Confederates also poured "incessant volleys" into the *Signal*'s hurricane deck. There was no way for its crew to escape, so the captain surrendered the boat. Several of the *Covington*'s sailors snuck back to Alexandria, a dangerous journey of about thirty miles, and told Porter the bad news.[32]

Porter had his own troubles there, but an enterprising soldier thought of a clever way to help the navy. Joseph Bailey, an acting engineer in the Nineteenth Army Corps, was part of the Union land force marooned at Alexandria. Before the war, Bailey had worked in the lumber camps of Wisconsin and was familiar with coaxing logs over river obstructions. He suggested that soldiers build a dam above the falls with a removable boom of logs in its center. The dam would raise the water level, and when sailors destroyed the log boom, the squadron's boats could ride the resulting rushing wave over the rocks. Porter thought the idea "looked like madness" but was so desperate that he gave the go ahead to Bailey. Banks also approved the plan.[33]

Sailors and soldiers worked on several simultaneous projects. The *Mound City* towed four coal barges to a ledge of rock above the falls and positioned them lengthwise across the channel, two on each side, about forty feet apart. Soldiers fastened them to the riverbed by driving iron spikes through the hulls like nails. Next, they filled the barges with heavy material, including dirt-filled coal boxes and deck buckets. Soldiers also built conventional dams from the shore to the barges. Men from the 29th Maine, 100th New York, and 110th New York Regiments built a wooden dam from the left, or north, bank. They tied together large trees, brush, planks ripped from local sawmills, furniture, and scavenged wood. Skeptical observers watched as the wooden pier extended about 300 feet into the river. Because there was not much wood on the other (south) bank, soldiers from the 97th and 99th U.S. Colored Troops (USCT) built huge cribs, floated them into place, and filled them with rocks, bricks, machinery from local sugar mills, and whatever other heavy objects they could lay their hands on. They fastened them to the riverbed in the same fashion as the coal barges. The USCT soldiers did the hardest work. Many of them were injured and a few were killed in their efforts to help save Porter's fleet.[34]

Sailors from the *Carondelet, Pittsburg,* and *Chillicothe* as well as around 3,000 soldiers worked in six-hour shifts around the clock. They slipped in and out of the water under the "broiling sun" for eight days. Teamsters used 200–300 wagons to haul materials to the river. It was backbreaking work.[35]

The dams channeled water into the center of the river. With the water level raised enough, Porter decided not to build the boom and instead sent his lightest boats over the falls. About 2:15 P.M. on May 8, the tinclad *Fort Hindman* made it safely downriver. The monitors *Osage* and *Neosho* followed, the former receiving minor damage in transit. Buoyed by that success, Porter ordered the rest of his crews to wake at 4:00 A.M. the next morning and be ready to go over the falls.[36]

Before the big boats could test their luck, the pressure on two of the barges became too much, and the current swept them away. The barges bobbed downriver for nearly a mile before ramming into some large boulders. Porter jumped on a horse and rode to where the fleet was anchored. At 5:40 A.M. he ordered the *Lexington* into the resulting chute. The timberclad, according to Porter, "with a full head of steam on, pitched down the roaring torrent, made two or three spasmodic rolls, hung for a moment on the rocks below, [and] was then swept into deep water." When the timberclad tied up below the falls, "thirty thousand voices rose in one deafened cheer," Porter reported, with some exaggeration.[37]

By now, Banks was ready to leave Alexandria. His army was running low on supplies, and foraging was increasingly difficult. Porter told Banks that he needed just a few more days to build new dams that would free the rest of the fleet. The general relented. Bailey proposed that soldiers now build a series of wing dams above the falls to force the water again to the center of the river. Lieutenant Colonel Uri Pearsall, who supervised construction of the crib dams, had originally advocated for wing dams, but Bailey rejected the idea as being too time consuming. Now, he had no other choice.[38]

Work began that same afternoon. Soldiers built a series of "light log cribs lashed together with rope and filled with brush and bricks" and sunk them in the river. The wing dams caused a noticeable rise in the water level.[39]

While soldiers continued their construction work, Porter ordered his crews to lighten the ironclads as much as possible. Bluejackets on the *Carondelet* spent the day "passing out shot & shell, Provisions, and cutting iron plating off the sides to lighten up the ship." They lugged "barrels of beef, pork, boxes of pressed meat, barrels of apples, beans, kegs of pickles, [a] barrel of vinegar, molasses, kegs of butter, barrels of sugar, [and] bread" on shore. Sailors on the *Mound City* worked all night "cutting off bolt heads to casemate iron" and throwing their older cannons overboard. Crews then coated the sides of the boats with tar or black paint so the boats looked like they still had armor. By the time the sun rose, the gunboats had iron only on their bows and a couple of cannons.[40]

The decision to remove the armor was a necessary risk. The *Juliet, Covington,* and *John Warner* proved that the Confederates below Alexandria were dangerous. It was entirely possible that the large boats could make it over the falls but then fall prey to Confederate guns. Porter, though, had no other choice—it proved to be the correct decision.[41]

Early on May 10, heavy rains pelted the sailors. It was an auspicious sign. Porter sent the *Chillicothe* through first. At 5:15 A.M. it "dropped down stream stern first" and promptly ran aground on the falls. Sailors sent a rope from the stern to the left bank and a rope from the bow to the right bank, then strained at the capstans to drag the boat forward. After five hours of grueling work, the gunboat scraped over the falls. At 2:30 P.M. the *Carondelet* weighed anchor and immediately got stuck. Bluejackets threw hawsers out and worked all night "to get the ship over the falls." At 10:00 the next morning, the *Carondelet* finally scraped free but ran "hard aground" once more. Attempts to drag it forward with the windlass failed. The *Mound City* also tried to shoot the rapids but only managed to run aground near the *Carondelet.* Porter now had three boats stuck on the rocks.[42]

In "hot haste" Bailey rode to the scene. Pearsall was already there. Postwar accounts differ, but the men agreed that the army would build wing dams in the stretch of river between the upper and lower falls. They now realized that they had to raise the water level along the entire series of obstacles, not just the upper falls. Overnight, Pearsall moved his men across the river.[43]

At sunrise on May 11, Pearsall's soldiers started making two-legged trestles out of logs. Working out from the left bank, they anchored the trestles in the riverbed. It was difficult work, and the strong current swept away several soldiers, although none drowned. Drenched men nailed the planks into place, creating a bracket dam. Sailors were simultaneously doing a different type of work. Starting at midnight, "all hands" on the *Carondelet* were straining at the capstans to pry the boat free. At 10:00 A.M. the stripped-down ironclad finally "moved past the upper dam but stuck below." Meanwhile, sailors on the *Mound City* ran hawsers to an anchor on one shore and a tree on the other and dragged their boat forward. It came unstuck only to drop down to the "wing dam where the ship grounded." Bluejackets coaxed the gunboat free once more, but as it slid downstream, its "side stuck on the iron bolts on Carondelet." Bluejackets pulled out wedges and cleared their boat, but it was still "hard aground."[44]

The next day dawned foggy and cold, with water levels slightly higher than the previous day. At about 1:15 P.M., sailors on the still-stuck *Chillicothe* used their steam capstan to work the *Mound City* and *Carondelet* free. By 6:30 P.M., all of the other boats, including the luckless *Chillicothe,* were over the falls. Passage over the dam was easier. There was enough water there for most of the boats, but the *Mound City* nearly ran aground and the *Pittsburg* broke its starboard rudder when it struck a boulder. By the next morning, all the boats were finally below Alexandria. Banks's exhausted army left later that day, though not before setting fire to the lower part of the town.[45]

The remaining journey down the Red River was not easy. "We fought our way all the time while coming down" from Alexandria, an officer told his wife. Sharpshooters near the site of Fort DeRussy shot at sailors on deck and targeted pilot houses. One rebel sent a slug six inches from a boat captain's head. The fleet still had enough guns to scare away any serious Confederate threat and reached the mouth of the Red River on May 20. A marine quietly remarked in his diary, "all got out of the Red this afternoon."[46]

When hearing about the Red River Expedition, Sherman judged it was "one damn blunder from beginning to end." Banks deserved most of the blame. His scheme was too complicated and his insistence on marching past Alexandria obligated Porter to continue upstream, even though the falling river levels were a clear signal to turn around. The ill-conceived operation caused the Mississippi Squadron to lose three fighting vessels, three auxiliary boats, and an unknown number of men. It also demonstrated that effective combined operations between the navy and the army depended on personal relationships instead of institutional arrangements. Porter trusted Grant and Sherman but distrusted Banks—for good reason. The army and navy acted independently during the campaign, and Banks had no regard for the navy's safety. Thankfully, enterprising army officers and hardworking enlisted men helped save the Mississippi Squadron.[47]

Even though the Confederacy did not capture or destroy the Union gunboats and monitors, the Red River Campaign hampered the Union war effort. It prevented a more important effort to capture Mobile at that time. The movement of Union soldiers into Louisiana also allowed the Confederacy to shift troops to the defense of Atlanta. Banks's fiasco was the first of several Union defeats in the spring and summer of 1864 that jeopardized Lincoln's ability to win the 1864 presidential election.[48]

The only tangible gain from the expedition was the capture of cotton. Even then, the amount was fewer than the hundreds of thousands of bales Union leaders had anticipated. Ledgers in the National Archives reveal that the Mississippi Squadron put 3,032 bales of cotton from the Red River into prize court. Its estimated value was nearly $243,000 (about $4.3 million in 2024). The prize court distributed about $219,000 to the navy (about $3.9 million in 2024). Porter probably earned about $5,500 (about $97,000 in 2024). The amount distributed to each sailor was based on his rank. Hiram Martin, a first-class fireman on the tinclad *Ouachita,* was satisfied with his share, which equaled about three months of his salary. "Cotton in those days was worth big money," he wrote after the war. "In 1865 I received over $100.00 as prize money for the cotton we took up this river." It was a good haul for a member of the United States Navy Cotton Stealing Association.[49]

The Red River Expedition was a tragedy of errors. Banks's casual disregard for basic military doctrine put the Mississippi Squadron at great and unnecessary risk. For his part, Porter sent too many boats on the expedition. Cotton mania impaired the fleet's performance. And while the bluejackets were happy that they would be receiving payments from cotton sales, they now returned to the grind of the patrol system, protecting transports, and battling insurgents. The war was wearing down the spirit of the men in the brown-water navy.

14

CONFEDERATE RESURGENCE

The war's last phase, which lasted from May 1864 to April 1865, narrowed the Mississippi Squadron's duties to protecting Union supply lines and smiting insurgents. While it might seem that the war was winding down for the fleet, that was not the case. The enlistment rate went up dramatically in the war's final twelve months, and the number of boats also increased. The Mississippi Squadron needed these men because it failed to retain most of its sailors. Miserable onboard conditions ensured that most brown-water sailors chose not to reenlist. At the same time, rebel ambushes reached their greatest volume and achieved their best success. The western waters remained a battle zone.

By May 1864, Union land forces were clearly winning the war in the western theater. They controlled Tennessee, much of Mississippi, and had a strong presence all along the Mississippi River. Rear Admiral Porter's friend Major General Sherman was leading a 100,000-man army group in northwestern Georgia with the goal of capturing Atlanta. One of Sherman's biggest problems was a reliable supply line. Supply boats steamed from Louisville on the Ohio River, turned into the Tennessee River at Paducah, and traveled upriver to a depot at Johnsonville, Tennessee. From there, the U.S. Military Rail Road brought the cargo eighty miles to Nashville and then to the front lines. Heavily laden transports also paddled along the Cumberland River.[1]

The Confederacy committed a significant number of men to stopping the flow of these supplies. The volume of southern attacks reached a crescendo in 1864. Guerrillas and cavalry units tore up tracks, burned bridges, and inflicted other damage on the rail system. Rebels also targeted the riverine supply line. In June the commander of the Cumberland beat (Patrol District Ten) reported, "I find the guerrillas very thick everywhere along the [Ohio] river, from Louisville down, and also up the Cumberland." The situation was the same on the Tennessee River. An experienced captain complained that his seven tinclads and one ironclad were barely adequate to "protect the large amount of supplies going to General Sherman's army."[2]

There was significant fighting in other patrol districts. More than half of the southern attacks during the war's last phase took place along the Mississippi River. Union transports that brought supplies to Union garrisons along the Big Muddy remained tempting targets. Nonmilitary commercial traffic, which was growing in volume, also attracted rebel attacks. Acting Master James Marshall, patrolling the Mississippi, told his superior officer in June 1864, "the guerrillas are growing too thick here for one boat to handle."[3]

A notable group of rebel attackers were clustered around Greenville. Brigadier General John S. Marmaduke described a chaotic scene: "the country was filled with independent squads, deserters, skulkers fleeing from conscription, and speculators (detestable animals in any country)." He tried to impose Confederate control in the area, in part by ordering Colonel Colton Greene to attack transports. Greene claimed that he successfully stopped shipping for two weeks. In one of his attacks, rebel gunners opened fire on the tinclad *Curlew*. Acting Master's Mate De Witt C. Morse scrambled below deck to one of the boat's cannons and fired several rounds before the lock string broke. He moved to a second gun, another 24-pounder, "and fired it as fast as the men could load it," even as a solid shot smashed through the boat's flimsy casemate and almost made Morse a double amputee. Another three balls entered the tinclad and sent shrapnel and splinters "flying all around [the] decks." Minié balls rattled against the *Curlew*'s sides as southern sharpshooters targeted the gunports. Suddenly, the shooting stopped; the assailants limbered their guns and fled from the scene. As he thought about the thirty-minute firefight six days later, Morse concluded wryly, "Not all Quiet on the Mississippi yet."[4]

This stubborn resistance convinced the Union military to pour even more resources into the Mississippi Squadron's antiguerrilla efforts. The fleet added another twenty-one boats during the war's fourth (and last) phase. The monthly pace was lower, but at a time when the war seemed well in hand, a 25-percent increase in boats was substantial. These extra vessels and men converted the Mississippi Squadron from a medium-sized fleet into one of the Union's largest squadrons. By war's end, the brown-water navy had commissioned 101 fighting boats and twenty-six service craft. The squadron was about the same size as the North Atlantic Blockading Squadron, which is normally considered the Union's largest fleet, when measured by number of vessels.[5]

Even more notable was the huge influx of men into the fleet during the war's final twelve months. Over 6,200 men enlisted in the Mississippi Squadron between May 1864 and April 1865, or about 521 per month. That was significantly higher than the war's average of about 294 new recruits per month. In August and September alone, about 3,200 new sailors joined the fleet. In fact, 43 percent of *all* bluejackets who served in the Mississippi Squadron enlisted during the war's final twelve months.[6]

The composition of men who joined the fleet in the war's final phase changed markedly from the third phase. Only 8 percent of those who enlisted after May 1864 were formerly enslaved, a massive plunge from the 35-percent rate of the previous phase and well below the aggregate average of 17 percent. This drop was connected to a surge in immigrant and native-born white enlistment. The proportion of immigrants jumped from 21 percent in the third phase to 39 percent in the final phase, while the corresponding figures for native-born whites increased from 42 percent to 51 percent. The reasons for the changes are unclear but might correspond with Lincoln's call for 100-day volunteers in April 1864. The increased enlistment of northern men likely led to a reduction in the forcible enlistment of enslaved men. At the same time, the navy was paying bounties by 1864. The bonus money might have convinced so many northern residents to enlist that the navy no longer needed to dragoon Black men in the South.[7]

This fourth phase saw the first explicit notation in the muster rolls of men who received a bounty to enlist or who were substitutes. Union enlistment bonuses for the army and navy soared in 1864. On the USS *Rattler,* the acting master's mate observed that recruits received bounties of $800 or $900. Some of the men, he editorialized, "are not *worth any* thing." Fifty sailors on the USS *Oriole,* most of them immigrants, were listed on the muster roll as "Volunteer. Entitled to Bounty." Joseph Stockle was one of them. The thirty-year-old German enlisted in Chicago on January 28, 1865. Four of Stockle's boat mates were substitutes—paid to take the place of a man who had been drafted. According to the muster roll, substitutes and bounty men composed 60 percent of the tinclad's ninety-man crew. In the fleet as a whole, at least twenty-one men enlisted as substitutes in the war's last phase. Three of them were Black recruits. Former slave Austin Fisher was born in Alabama and enlisted in Cairo on March 11, 1865. The navy posted him to the USS *Collier* as an ordinary seaman.[8]

The squadron needed this infusion of men because it struggled to retain its sailors. The accumulation of the navy's rigid schedule, sailors' lack of autonomy, miserable conditions on board, and officer arrogance meant that most bluejackets in the Mississippi Squadron came to dislike their time in the brown-water service. Frederic Davis, who transferred from the Army of the Potomac, complained, "I am sick enough of this, And if ever I get out of the service I'll never enter it again I tell you." He had been in the navy less than a month when he wrote those words to his father. William Van Cleaf told his brother that he was tired of being treated like a dog and advised him not to join the navy. An Irish sailor summed up the nettlesome nature of life in brown-water navy during a conversation with Surgeon Fayette Clapp: "If any man believes there is no *purgathory,* let him come into this western flotilla & then he'll believe in it. For with the rebels on one side & the guerillas on the other & the '*dammed*' miskitiys' [mosquitoes] forever bothering & biting us, it's the divil's own purgathory."[9]

Bluejackets demonstrated their disdain for life in the Mississippi Squadron in several ways. One of them was leaving the fleet as soon as their enlistments expired. John Morrison had transferred from the Army of the Potomac and had become an effective sailor. He was a coxswain, a position of some responsibility and respect, by 1864. When his time was up in the Mississippi Squadron, he "shook hands with almost every one on board," including the captain, and went back to New York. A year later he enlisted in a Union cavalry regiment.[10]

The scattered nature of naval records makes it impossible to calculate reenlistment rates for brown-water sailors. It is possible, however, to calculate a persistence rate and use it as a proxy for reenlistment. The persistence rate uses the records of men who enlisted by December 31, 1863, and whose initial enlistment expired prior to April 1, 1865. In other words, these men had the opportunity to reenlist before the war ended. The persistence rate for these bluejackets was 20 percent. Since some of the sailors became casualties, it is possible that the Mississippi Squadron's reenlistment rate was as high as 25 percent. But that figure is far less than the 60-percent rate that is sometimes cited for the Union army.[11]

A high turnover rate on individual boats might have contributed to low reenlistment rates and vice versa. An examination of the muster rolls for nine boats reveals that their three-month turnover rates varied from 15 percent to an astounding 47 percent, with an average of 24 percent. In a typical boat, which had about ninety sailors, that meant there were about twenty-two new faces on board every ninety days. There are several likely reasons for the high turnover: dislike of the navy, disease, boats knocked out of action, and desertion. The movement of men on and off vessels led to changes in messes and watches and likely dissolved some of the relational glue that held men together. Since brown-water sailors had a low ideological commitment to the war's causes, men with relatively weak attachments to one another were less likely to reenlist.[12]

Those sailors who reenlisted did so primarily because of promotions, bounties, and furloughs that the navy offered. Herbert Saunders, a carpenter's mate on the *Peosta,* mulled over whether to re-up. After noting that "a number of the crew are getting their discharges," he observed that "several of the old crew are enlisting over again for another year—they got petty officers billets by doing so." While Saunders reenlisted, bounties were not enough of an inducement for most sailors. On the *Tawah,* James Dickinson thought that he and three other sailors would renew "providing we get a bounty and a furlough." Dickinson ultimately decided to serve only his one-year hitch and leave the navy. Judging from the boat's muster rolls, his friends did likewise.[13]

Other sailors took more drastic actions to get out of the Mississippi Squadron. Seaman James Walker, for instance, was convinced that he had enlisted for one year, but the navy insisted that he had signed up for the war's duration. Walker refused to do any duties after he served 365 days. When given the opportunity of being released from irons and returning to duty, he told his commanding officer, "I will roast in hell first!" Walker earned ten years hard labor in a federal penitentiary. Likewise, Eugene Daily claimed that he could not be detached to the Mississippi Squadron for more than a year and refused to do his duty. He convinced a dozen other army transfers to do the same. They were all arrested and confined, but only Daily stood trial for making a mutinous assembly. He was sentenced to four years' hard labor.[14]

Another avenue of escape was desertion, defined as leaving the military with no intent to return. Like reenlistment, it is impossible to calculate a desertion rate for the fleet, but surviving records make it clear that desertion plagued the brown-water navy. Rear Admiral Porter speculated, "Men come here expecting to get prize money, and claim that they have been misled; others come expecting petty officers' berths. . . . [T]he consequence is continued desertion." He recognized dissatisfaction as the root cause and could have added low morale and the odious nature of naval life as likely contributing factors. Charles Word, who probably fled from slavery with his brother, was so desperate to escape life in the Mississippi Squadron that he deserted three times. After being recaptured twice, it appears that his third effort succeeded.[15]

It is possible that the Mississippi Squadron had one of the highest desertion rates of any organization in the war. The blue-water navy's desertion rate was a relatively low 6 percent, largely because it was difficult to flee a ship that was at sea. The Union army's rate was about 10 percent. Union soldiers likely viewed desertion as a last resort, as many of them came from a single locality and feared the stigma that came with leaving their neighbors, friends, and relatives in a regiment. Brown-water sailors, though, had frequent access to the shore and did not have the same type of geographic unit cohesion that army regiments enjoyed. An examination of the *Rattler*'s deck logs and muster rolls indicate that thirty men deserted in 1863 and 1864, a rate of 22 percent. Given the tinclad's checkered service record, its desertion rate was probably higher than the fleet's average. It is reasonable, though, to assume that the desertion rate in the Mississippi Squadron was robust because of the unique problems that beset the fleet.[16]

The enlistment of so many new sailors, coupled with the exodus of veterans, meant that in the war's final year, the bluejackets in the Mississippi Squadron were woefully inexperienced. A look at the USS *Lafayette*'s crew underlines this situation. During one week in August 1864, sailor Alexander Miller noted in his diary that the boat received drafts of 52, 56, and 60 men. He exaggerated a bit, but not by much. By the end of the year, 106 of the boat's 209 sailors had enlisted after May 1, 1864. The *Lafayette*'s experience was common. When examining muster rolls from the war's last phase, only 39 percent of brown-water sailors enlisted prior to May 1, 1864. A small fraction, 7 percent, enlisted in 1862 or before.[17]

The fleet's officers also underwent some turnover. Porter departed the Mississippi Squadron in October 1864. Secretary of the Navy Welles wanted the North Atlantic Blockading Squadron to capture Fort Fisher, North Carolina, and thought that its commander, Acting Rear Admiral Samuel P. Lee, was not up to the task. Welles transferred Lee to the West and sent Porter to the Atlantic, effectively swapping the two men. Prior to his post in the North Atlantic Blockading Squadron, Lee had participated in the New Orleans campaign and the blue-water navy's efforts to capture Vicksburg. He was a competent commander who largely followed Porter's precedents.[18]

Several of Porter's most trusted lieutenants remained in place. Lieutenant Commander LeRoy Fitch, Lieutenant George Bache, Commander Robert Townsend, and Lieutenant Commander James Shirk were veterans who provided much needed stability. But there were also many officers who were novice commanders. In October 1864 35 percent of the men who captained fighting boats had assumed their first command within the last twelve months. These commanders sometimes had to rely on green subordinate officers. In June Acting Ensign Scott Jordan told his father, "Some of the officers who came into the service at first are resigning and going home." Just like the enlisted men, many of the officers of the Mississippi Squadron during the war's last phase were inexperienced.[19]

The high turnover, abundance of short-timers, and lack of experience contributed to the Mississippi Squadron's reduced aggressiveness during the war's last phase. Even though the fleet increased in size, had more transports to protect than ever before, and faced increasingly aggressive Confederate resistance, Union attacks decreased over this period. The average of attacks went from 10.4 per month in the third phase to 7.4 per month in the fourth phase (see table 3). Also, the percentage of attacks where sailors went on shore dropped from 40 percent to 20 percent. At least one officer noticed the change. The "rebels have ceased to have the respect for tinclads they once had," he thought. This decrease in aggressiveness most likely came from inexperienced captains, green sailors, and short-time bluejackets who wanted to minimize their chances of getting killed or wounded. Brown-water sailors in the war's last phase were ill prepared to carry out raids against an experienced, numerous, and wily foe.[20]

Southern attacks during the war's final phase, by contrast, became more numerous and more effective. Their rate increased slightly from the third to fourth phase: 7.9 percent to 8.0 percent per month. More importantly, Confederates achieved their greatest success in knocking out Union boats during this last phase. In those twelve months, southerners burnt, destroyed, or captured twenty-five commercial boats or transports as well as seven gunboats. Their previous bests were fifteen commercial boats or transports in the second phase and two gunboats in the third phase (see table 4).[21]

The breadth of southern resistance is notable. From May 1864, about half of southern attacks were on the Mississippi River, while another 20 percent were on the Tennessee and Cumberland Rivers. Such strikes, though, took place across the South. On the White River, for instance, the tinclad *Silver Cloud* got beat up in June and had to leave the river because "the Rebs" were "thick as peas everywhere," as a sailor told his sister. Elsewhere, when an officer from the USS *Gazelle* went on shore near Raccourci, Louisiana, he "was murdered by guerrillas and horribly mutilated." Things were so chaotic near Bayou Sara that a Union captain put placards along the river announcing his intention to shoot a southern prisoner in retaliation for "each person killed by rebels firing on transports." During the war's last phase, Confederates sprung ambushes on the Arkansas,

Atchafalaya, Big Black, Big Sandy, Cumberland, Hatchie, Mississippi, Missouri, Ouachita, Tennessee, and White Rivers.[22]

Many reasons contributed to this surge in Confederate attacks. Commercial shipping was on the rise and was spread out over a greater area than ever before. Military transports were as busy as ever. Not only was a massive amount of supplies flowing to Sherman's army group, but thousands more Federal troops were stationed across the western theater. These men needed a steady supply of food and other war matériel. Southern attackers had also accrued valuable experience, both in traditional combat and in ambush tactics. With the regular war going poorly for the Confederacy, participation in an ambush squad was more enticing than ever.

Many Confederate soldiers drifted into partisan or guerrilla groups to avoid service in the army. A rebel who had served in Walker's Greyhounds, a brigade of Texas troops, admitted to a Union sailor that men in his regiment preferred to keep up "guerrilla warfare with Walker and his friends" rather than mark time in a Confederate army. Battle-tested rebels such as these augmented ambush squads rather than just quitting the war altogether. They could fight at least part time because of the loose cords of discipline in these irregular rebel units.[23]

Other southerners joined ambush squads because they could not bear to see the destruction of slavery or the presence of Black troops. Lieutenant Commander Fitch, who oversaw a patrol district, learned that some of the guerrillas along the Cumberland River were "men who were drafted for our service." Ambush squads were "thick" in the area partly because the Union was using "negro soldiers . . . to conscript every negro they could find." Supposedly, the Black soldiers stole property, insulted women, and entered "ladies' bedrooms." These tales were spurious. The accusation about Black men insulting women and entering their bedrooms drew upon longstanding sexual fears in the antebellum South. Such stories were rumors intended to whip up white southern resistance to Union occupation.[24]

Shrinking Union competence and growing Confederate abilities explain two notable incidents in the war's last phase. In late October 1864, Lieutenant General Taylor ordered Major General Forrest to attack Union transports supplying Sherman's forces. Forrest moved his 3,000 men and twelve guns into Tennessee. He occupied the abandoned Fort Heiman just north of the Kentucky-Tennessee line and then scattered his artillery toward Paris Landing on the Tennessee River. On October 28 the heavily laden *Mazeppa* steamed upriver. Once the transport churned past Fort Heiman, Confederate gunners made short work of the boat. Forrest's men took some of the 700 tons of cargo and burned the rest.[25]

Two days later the tinclad *Undine* escorted the empty transport *Anna* downriver to a spot unknowingly near Forrest's guns and then turned back toward Johnsonville. The *Anna* steamed into Forrest's trap. When Jonathan L. Bryant, the *Undine*'s acting master, heard the cannons fire, he cleared for action and headed back to rescue the transport. The lightly armored tinclad got the worst of the ensuing exchange but made it past the Paris Landing batteries and sheltered against the shore. But it was now between Forrest's two largest batteries, one at Paris Landing and the other at Fort Heiman.[26]

The *Undine*'s crew was working to repair the damage to their boat and simultaneously shooting back at Forrest's skirmishers when the transport *Venus* steamed downriver. Ignoring signals from the gunboat to turn around, the *Venus* came under fire. Confederate gunners killed the transport's captain, but the boat somehow managed to anchor near the *Undine.* Twenty minutes later the *J. W. Cheeseman* came downriver and repeated the *Venus*'s mistake. Rebel gunners turned that transport into Swiss cheese, however, and its captain surrendered.[27]

As the *Undine* and *Venus* huddled against the shore like ducks in a storm, Confederate gunners moved in for the kill. They set up a crossfire and peppered the boats. Union gunners gamely fired canister at the range of 100 yards but could not beat off the attack. When a steam pipe cracked and sent hot gas into the engine room, it was clear that the *Undine* was doomed. Bryant ordered the boat to the eastern bank. In the meantime, the crew was supposed to spike the guns and prepare to burn the vessel. They failed on both counts. As soon as the *Undine* came to rest on the bank, the crew made a mad dash for the shore. Confederates captured the tinclad as well as the Union's signal codes. The *Venus* surrendered a few minutes later. Both boats were in good enough condition that the rebels patched them up and put them into service.[28]

The *Undine*'s bluejackets lacked experience, which likely contributed to the failure to destroy the tinclad and its capture. Of the fifty-two sailors listed on the boat's muster roll, five of them enlisted in 1863, while the rest joined the navy in 1864; nearly 80 percent of the men enlisted in April or May. With only about six months experience, these bulk of the tinclad's sailors were not prepared for an emergency.[29]

Union commanders sent the tinclads *Paw Paw, Fairy, Curlew, Brilliant, Victory,* and *Moose* from Paducah to punish Forrest. They arrived too late, as Forrest had already moved his forces about forty miles upriver with the *Undine* and *Venus* to threaten Johnsonville. A second squadron of tinclads, consisting of the *Key West, Tawah,* and *Elfin,* was already at that town and had gotten word of Forrest's approach. On November 2 both tinclad squads advanced toward the rebels, who seemed to be trapped between them. Forrest, though, had set up a particularly strong defensive position in an area of the river known as "the Chute." The tinclads could not dislodge the rebels because of their heavy guns but were enough of a threat to capture the *Venus* and convince the Confederates to burn the *Undine.*[30]

Thinking that they had neutralized Forrest, the *Key West, Tawah,* and *Elfin* returned to Johnsonville. Forrest, though, moved ten guns into the heavy woods across the river from the Union depot. From there the Confederates spied piles and piles of supplies that were intended for Sherman's forces and watched as officers strolled the wharf. At 2:00 P.M. on November 4, rebel artillery opened fire on the three tinclads, which were tied up to the bank there. What happened next was pathetic. The *Key West* immediately fouled its stern wheel when pulling up its anchor, forcing the *Tawah* to take it in tow. The boats slowly moved upstream, desperately trying to chug out of range. Edward M. King, who commanded the *Key West,* reported that he fired almost all of his ammunition as rebel cannon fire knocked out the *Tawah*'s guns, a questionable assertion. He thought it "impossible to hold out longer" so the two crews "burned the boats reluctantly." For some unexplained reason, the crew of the *Elfin* followed suit. It took only fifteen minutes to eliminate the three tinclads. "We have done the best we could," King lamely explained.[31]

Forrest's gunners next turned their attention to the seven Union transports moored at Johnsonville. Within minutes, the boats were burning wrecks. Thoroughly panicked Federals set fire to their warehouses and supplies lest the Confederates lunge across the river and capture it all. By nightfall, Forrest reported that the "wharf for nearly one mile up and down the river was one solid sheet of flame." At least $2.2 million worth of supplies went up in smoke that day, but Forrest's efforts were too late to make a difference in Georgia. Sherman would not have used those supplies anyway, as he was about to cut loose from his supply line and march from Atlanta to Savannah.[32]

A high level of bluejacket inexperience helps explain the brown-water navy's poor showing at Johnsonville. Like the men in the *Undine,* the sailors who abandoned their tinclads on November 4 were not battle tested. Two-thirds of the enlisted men on the *Elfin, Key West,* and *Tawah* had enlisted in 1864 and the rest in 1863. They made a variety of rookie mistakes: fouling the stern wheel, not having enough ammunition (even as they waited at a supply base), and not being able to move quickly enough to escape danger. There is no guarantee that experienced bluejackets would have been able to repel Forrest, but it is likely that they would have put up a more spirited defense and escaped to fight another day.[33]

The fleet's shrinking competence also became manifest when one of its officers tried to sell a tinclad to the Confederates. In August the *Rattler* was on patrol near Hurricane Island, about fifteen miles downriver from Vicksburg. The boat's captain, Acting Master Daniel W. Glenney, continually sent the crew ashore. While the bluejackets kept busy, the captain spent his days negotiating with Joshua James, a notorious rebel. During several visits to James's plantation, Glenney agreed to sell the gunboat for $2,000 and 100 bales of cotton.[34]

On September 4 Glenney allowed several officers and many of the boat's "*best men*" to have liberty on shore, according to William Bock, the acting master's mate. Their departure, he thought, left "the vessel almost helpless." At about 8:30 P.M., the *Rattler* landed about two miles downriver from James's plantation. Glenney sent another twenty-two men ashore with the ostensible mission of capturing James's son. The captain, however, was sending them men a trap, as Confederates were waiting in ambush. Worse yet, twenty of those bluejackets had only reported to the tinclad *earlier that day* and had no combat training.[35]

Acting Third Assistant Engineer J. H. Hume, the officer in charge of the expedition, left two Black sailors in charge of the skiff and led the rest of the men along the shore toward the plantation. About 9:00, Confederates attacked the guards. The men "fought like devils" but died protecting the boat. Hearing the gunshots, Hume and his party rushed back toward the cutter. Before they got too far, rebels surrounded them and demanded their surrender. The sailors fought briefly but laid down their arms, an unsurprising action given that they were green recruits. In the confusion Hume and two other men eluded capture.[36]

The tinclad's crew cleared for action when they heard the gunshots. Acting Ensign Henry N. Wells and four armed men rowed a skiff toward shore. They saw a boat coming toward them and hailed it, believing it to be Hume. Instead, it was the Confederates, who responded by yelling "Aye! Aye!" That was not the correct response, so Wells started firing at the boat and yelled for the *Rattler* to "blow them out of the water." Glenney refused to give the order to fire, even though Bock was standing at a gun "with the lock string in my hand." Instead, the captain waited about twenty minutes, enough time for the Confederates to escape, before he ordered the tinclad to slip its cable and go upstream to James's plantation. Glenney, without an escort, went ashore, met with James, and then returned to the boat. On its way back downriver, the *Rattler* picked up Hume and the other two bluejackets who escaped the ambush.[37]

The next day Glenney ordered the boat back to James's plantation and met once more with James. This time the two men plotted how to cover their tracks. Glenney took Bock, Hume, and another officer on shore with him. They soon encountered a "guide," who led the bluejackets to the "enemy camp," which was about ten miles inland. While Glenney engaged in sham negotiations with a Confederate officer, the other sailors passed the time with "rebel officers" and "*two ladies*" originally from Annapolis, Maryland. Glenney then announced that the captured sailors would be paroled and led his small party back to the *Rattler*. The prisoners returned to the boat the following day.[38]

Glenney pretended that nothing unusual had happened and resumed his duties. On September 11 an army tug came alongside the *Rattler* and put Acting Master Nicholas B. Willets aboard. Willets had orders from Lieutenant Commander Selfridge, who commanded this district, to place Glenney under arrest and take command of the tinclad. About a week later, bluejackets from the *Rattler* arrested James and destroyed his plantation. The next step was to hold a court-martial for Glenney.[39]

Glenney bided his time in the hold, where he wrote a sanctimonious letter in which he admitted he was guilty of some "little transactions," claimed he upheld the dignity of the "*noble old flag,*" and asked his fellow officers to acquit him because he had to provide for his wife and baby. His peers never had the chance to make that decision. On November 4 Acting Ensign E. P. Nellis relieved the officer on deck during the first watch, which began at 8:00 P.M. He then gave the quarter master permission to go below and told the watch to "turn in." In effect, only Nellis and the pilot remained on duty. Nellis then freed Glenney, and the two men snuck into a skiff and escaped. Rumors flew through the fleet that Confederates had helped Glenney flee to Mexico. Neither Glenney nor Nellis were heard from again.[40]

Like the defeat at Johnsonville, the near-sale of the *Rattler* revealed deficiencies in the Mississippi Squadron. Glenney took advantage of his crew's inexperience and turnover to weaken the boat when he stacked the shore party with recruits. His escape demonstrates lax discipline on the boat. It is shocking that such a high-profile prisoner could slip away so easily from a navy vessel. That the quarter master and an entire watch would go below while near the plantation of a known Confederate violates all protocol related to vigilance. The bluejackets were either poorly trained or so lacking in motivation that they did not care that they went against standard procedure.

Nevertheless, the Mississippi Squadron was effective enough during the war's final phase. A cadre of veteran officers provided leadership, especially as commanders of patrol beats. There was also a small core of sailors whose experience was invaluable. Of the 7 percent of last-phase bluejackets who enlisted prior to 1863, 44 percent of them had nautical experience prior to joining the brown-water navy. Their knowledge of maritime practices, familiarity with naval discipline, and accrued experience meant that there were at least a few competent sailors on each boat.[41]

Union industrial might and aggressive northern efforts that wiped out the Confederate's brown-water navy in 1862 also helped mask weaknesses among the Mississippi Squadron's late-war personnel. Gunboats, even if they did not have the same degree of intimidation that they once had, were still more powerful than most ambush squads. The large number of boats compensated for their inconsistent performance. Not every vessel was effective, but enough of them were. The patrol system spread Union boats along the western waters, thus ensuring that they were a presence in problem areas. These gunboats, sometimes in cooperation with infantry, chased attackers away and always restored the flow of men and matériel along the rivers. Southern ambushes were dangerous and deadly in the short term but did nothing to shift the war's outcome.[42]

The Mississippi Squadron faced a variety of difficulties during the war's last year: massive turnover, inexperienced sailors, and a veteran foe. Southerners achieved their greatest successes in destroying gunboats and transports. Yet the fleet's constant presence along the western waters facilitated its ability to protect Union supply lines. Once the guns fell silent in the spring of 1865, the navy dismantled its inland fleet and sent those sailors back to civilian lives. Some of these men spent their postwar years tending to the brown-water fleet's memory.

EPILOGUE

The U.S. Navy and U.S. Army built the Western Gunboat Flotilla from literally nothing into a powerful fleet numbering 127 boats: 101 fighting craft and 16 auxiliary vessels. When the war ended, the navy reduced this fleet to whence it came. Authorities recalled all western naval vessels to Cairo, where each sailor reported to the receiving boat USS *Great Western* for his discharge papers. Rowland Stafford True remembered that men rushed to the quarter deck: "In about two hours we came back with our [discharge] papers and a roll of Uncle Sam's greenbacks in our pockets, smiling and happy." Soon after they were "homeward bound." Once a crew left their boat, workers stripped off its armor, removed its cannons, and moved the heavy equipment such as anchors and cables into storage. The navy then put the boat up for auction. In total, eighty-four vessels fetched about $700,000 for the sea service. Once the final gavel sounded, the Mississippi Squadron ceased to exist.[1]

The squadron, though, continued to influence its sailors who were now civilians. Whether they mustered out in 1865 or, more likely, left the fleet before the war ended, some former bluejackets dealt with emotional pain and struggled to make sense of their service in the Mississippi Squadron. William Murphy served about one year. At some point after the war, he lost his job in Erie, Pennsylvania, during a general strike. He "tramped all over Ohio" but could not find work. "I often in my black moods have wished that some Southern bullet had stretched me along side my fallen Shipmates on the banks of the Cumberland Tennessee or Mississippi river," Murphy confessed, "but Im getting over all that." William Palmer, a free Black man born in New York, became an inmate at the New Haven Alms House after the war. According to one witness, he was called "Crazy William and was always locked up at night." John Anderegg, a Swiss immigrant, had such serious emotional trauma from the war that he required a guardian to protect him from self-harm.[2]

Other sailors remembered their wartime service with pride, particularly after a few decades dulled the negative aspects of their time in the Mississippi Squadron. A few bluejackets created informal or formal networks that nourished memories of their time in the brown-water service. In 1895 J. E. Robinson invited a few of his boatmates to dinner at Christmas. William Bock kept in touch with some of his fellow officers, and in correspondence between them, they reminisced about their time in the navy. James Laning told Bock twenty-five years after the war ended, "we can now look back with pride & justification" on the "very best government on which the Sun of Heaven shines which we helped to save from destruction."[3]

A few years before Laning wrote those words, sailors who served on the USS *Carondelet* gathered in Cincinnati. As part of their commemoration of the twenty-fifth anniversary of the Mississippi Squadron's run past Vicksburg, they invited their commanders to reflect on the fleet's meaning for the war. David D. Porter sent his regards in a letter read to those in attendance. He first extolled the "Western men" who had "hearts of oak, in Western iron walls." In words that probably drew applause, he then noted that "it was the passage of the fleet by Vicksburg that sealed the fate of that stronghold."[4]

The men who listened to Porter's musings on the Mississippi Squadron met each April in Cincinnati. By the early twentieth century, the Carondelet Association was working with ex-congressman Jacob H. Bromwell to erect a monument for the "victories and heroes of the Mississippi Squadron" in Vicksburg. Although Bromwell was not able to secure funding for the memorial, either the Carondelet Association or another group was able to erect the Navy Monument in 1917. The 202-foot-high obelisk is the tallest monument in Vicksburg National Military Park and features statues of Porter, Charles H. Davis, Andrew H. Foote, and David G. Farragut. A plaque in front of the obelisk summarizes the Mississippi Squadron's efforts during the campaign. Near the Navy Monument is the Battery Selfridge monument, which commemorates a land battery that sailors manned during the investment of Vicksburg. It features a bust of Thomas O. Selfridge, who commanded the USS *Cairo* when it was sunk. The National Park Service later raised and preserved the *Cairo,* which is on display at Vicksburg. The ironclad, the only surviving brown-water vessel of the Civil War, and its accompanying museum serve as another type of memorial to the Mississippi Squadron.[5]

Yet no amount of memorials can capture the complex and contradictory nature of the Mississippi Squadron. The fleet was created to destroy Confederate forts in a regular war but spent most of its time protecting supplies and fighting an irregular war. It was a strange hybrid between the army and navy and demonstrated that success in the western theater depended on cooperation between the two armed services. The fleet's size and strength illustrated the North's industrial advantage, but its vulnerabilities remind us that technology alone did not win the war. Union commanders needed a strategic vision and adaptability to finish the job. The brown-water sailors, most of whom came from the West, were tough men who were known to drink too much whiskey and veer into insubordination. But they fought their boats courageously. While the bluejackets who toiled in the Mississippi Squadron endured a sort of purgatory, their efforts were necessary to destroy slavery and win the war for the Union.

APPENDIX 1

GUDMESTAD SAILOR DATASET

There is no single source of information that contains a systematic record of the names and information of the sailors who composed the Mississippi Squadron. I led a team of graduate and advanced undergraduate students at Colorado State University to assemble a dataset that would provide insight into the sailors of that fleet. The team was Nolan Dahm, Evan Cocanower, Cassie Franks, Danny Gilbert, Tobin Gold, Austin Magura, Sean Nelson, and Nick Taylor. Our work is similar to the African American Sailors' Research Project, which Joseph Reidy coordinated.[1]

The team examined U.S. Navy muster rolls digitized and made available online at the National Archives website. I gathered data on about 70 percent of the sailors in the aggregate dataset and trained the team to replicate my process for the remaining 30 percent of bluejackets. We compiled a final dataset of 14,754 sailors and have information for at least 85 percent of the men who served in the Mississippi Squadron. It is likely that another 1,000–2,000 men served in the fleet and were listed on a muster roll that we did not examine, so we suspect that about 17,000 men in all served in the Western Gunboat Flotilla / Mississippi Squadron.

Muster rolls are large, preprinted sheets that a boat's paymaster filled out every quarter. They ask for a plethora of information: name; enlistment date, location, and term of enlistment; place or vessel received from; rank; place of birth; state of which a citizen; age; occupation; eye color; hair color; complexion; height; and additional notes. The earliest muster rolls that I located were recorded in October 1862, which corresponds to the time when the navy took official control of the Mississippi Squadron. Not all muster rolls survived the war, although most did.[2]

I found muster rolls for 112 of the fleet's 127 vessels, and the team consulted 226 muster rolls to compile an aggregate list of 16,676 names. I removed entries that had minimal information and consolidated entries of the 1,322 sailors who served on multiple boats. The muster rolls contain information about enlisted men. Those for four boats also include information for men who were engineers, petty officers, and pilots. Most of those sailors are included in the final list.

Not every muster roll had complete information on each sailor. For instance, a paymaster might fail to record occupation or place of enlistment. Other times the information was illegible or torn. For that reason, the total number of sailors in the various categories that are used for analysis, like age or height, is not equal. Nearly all sailors had complete information or were missing only one or two items. Additionally, we searched for missing information in key fields such as enlistment date, enlistment location, place of birth, and occupation by examining one subsequent or previous muster roll if one existed.

At first I examined the first known muster roll as well as the final roll from the war's end, usually March 31, 1865. While doing further research into whether Black sailors were promoted, I found a substantial number of sailors who were not on the first and last muster rolls. I decided to examine a middle muster roll if it was at least nine months from both the first and last rolls. This switch happened about halfway through the project, so I went back through each entry that was affected and verified the information. At the end of the project, the student researchers went through each entry and verified the sailors' names and spot-checked their information.

We recorded the information in Excel spreadsheets, one for each boat. Then we copied the information from all of those into an aggregate spreadsheet. The information is not a literal transcription of material in the database. Instead, we coded the data for consistency across the dataset. For instance, some entries listed "C. H." as a man's rating. When this occurred, we recorded "Coal Heaver" in the spreadsheet. Or, for example, paymasters recorded "Tin Smith" and "tinsmith" as an occupation. In these instances, we recorded "Tinsmith" as the occupation. We also converted height to inches. Thus, we coded 5 feet 6 1/2 inches as 66.5. We did not record eye color or hair color and only noted complexion if it indicated a sailor was a Black man.

Consolidating duplicate entries was as much of an art as a science. Many times the entries contained identical information, but in at least a third of the cases, there was conflicting information. These ranged from minor errors, like enlistment dates being a few days off, to differences in citizenship.

APPENDIX 2

GUDMESTAD IRREGULAR COMBAT DATASETS

I created two datasets for this project, one titled "Northern Attacks" and the other named "Southern Attacks." My procedure involved reading volumes 22–27 of the *Official Records of the Union and Confederate Navies* (*ORN*) in their entirety, consulting *War of the Rebellion: A Compilation of Official Records of the Union and Confederate Armies* (*ORA*), and reading through Lewis B. Parsons's postwar report about shipping losses. The limitations of the *ORN* and *ORA* are well documented, but they provide consistency across time and space. The "Northern Attacks" dataset has 230 entries, while the "Southern Attacks" database has 191 entries. There were 177 unilateral attacks in the northern database, 108 unilateral attacks in the southern database, and 83 mutual attacks—a total of 368 unique episodes.

The datasets track the source, date, boat(s) involved, type of boat(s), physical location, river, whether it was a mutual or unilateral fight, the initiator of the event, if it was a joint operation with the army, and if the attack was against rebels or civilians. I also noted attacks on the following: towns, farms/plantations, and the environment (gunboats often fired into the woods if they suspected guerrillas were nearby). Other categories recorded if sailors captured or destroyed personal property, military supplies, food, or cotton and if they destroyed buildings.

The datasets do not include attacks on Confederate fortifications (for example, Island No. 10), participation in battles (for example, Vicksburg), boat-to-boat combat (for example, Memphis), or the expeditions in the White River, to Chickasaw Bluffs, or in the Yazoo River, Steele's Bayou, or Red River. They do not track the activities of the West Gulf Blockading Squadron or the Mississippi Marine Brigade. Most of the boats in the datasets were part of the Western

Gunboat Flotilla / Mississippi Squadron, although there were some incidents involving commercial steamboats and river transports included. I used one name for boats with variant names (for example, USS *Robb* / *Alfred Robb* and USS *Hastings* / *Emma Duncan*).

For the "Northern Attacks" dataset, Union sailors often targeted multiple things in one incident. For instance, if they burned a barn, captured cotton, and confiscated cattle in the same event, I noted the results in several categories (attack on a farm/plantation, building, cotton, and food). The incidents often involved one boat but did range up to six boats attacking one target. If multiple vessels were involved, I treated it as one incident. Boats often made multiple attacks in one day, so I created a separate incident for each time the boat moved, even if it was just a few miles.

"Southern Attacks" includes any attack on a northern boat no matter who was involved, as the sources made it difficult to distinguish between soldiers, guerrillas, and civilians. Like the "Northern Attacks," I tracked the source, date, boat(s) involved, type of boat(s), physical location, river, whether it was a mutual or unilateral fight, and the initiator of the event. Other data categories were whether it involved a battery (artillery) or torpedo and the result (if any) of the attack: casualties to the crew, physical damage to the boat's structure, damage to the boat's machinery, or sinking, capturing, or burning of the vessel. As in the other database, there were often multiple consequences of an attack—for instance, sailors might be wounded and the boat burned. Incidents ranged from an attack on one boat up to seven boats. If multiple vessels were involved, I treated it as one incident.

It is clear from working with the sources that the *ORN* and *ORA* vastly underrepresent the number of incidents. In combing through primary-source materials, I found another 139 incidents. For example, James A. Dickinson served a one-year term on the USS *Tawah*. He recorded that guerrillas fired at his vessel ten times in the two weeks after April 12, 1864, including four separate attacks on the nineteenth. None of these appear in the *ORN,* nor did they make it into the boat's deck log, preserved in the National Archives. I did not comprehensively read through the deck logs of all boats, but I did read many of them. They report many combat episodes.

It is problematic in GIS to measure scale, so the categories only indicate whether an attack took place, not the amount of the damage or harm. For example, the confiscation of one bale of cotton appears to be the same as the confiscation of ten bales.

The datasets are not as exact as they appear at face value. Some boats had abstract logs in the *ORN,* meaning that their activities were covered in more detail. Sometimes the material was imprecise or missing. An *ORN* entry might mention an ambush that took place somewhere on a river, reference an obscure steamboat landing, or use language such as "just upriver" or "near." In such cases I plotted the GIS point using reasonable inferences. The rivers, particularly the Mississippi, have also shifted over time, so I have moved the location of some of the incidents to the modern-day river course. Thus, the datasets are suggestive rather than precise in some of their locations. The overall picture, then, should be treated more like a pointillist painting, where the viewer has to step back to see the larger image rather than focusing on the individual dots.

APPENDIX 3

BOATS OF THE MISSISSIPPI SQUADRON

NAME	COMMISSIONED/ ACQUIRED	TONNAGE	SUPPORT TYPE
	Timberclads		
Conestoga	June 3, 1861	575	—
Lexington	Aug. 12, 1861	362	—
Tyler	June 5, 1861	575	—
	City-Class Ironclads		
Baron de Kalb/St. Louis	Jan. 31, 1862	512	—
Cairo	Jan. 25, 1862	512	—
Carondelet	Jan. 15, 1862	512	—
Cincinnati	Jan. 16, 1862	512	—
Louisville	Jan. 16, 1862	512	—
Mound City	Jan. 16, 1862	512	—
Pittsburg	Jan. 16, 1862	512	—
	Ironclads		
Benton	Feb. 24, 1862	633	—
Chillicothe	Sept. 5, 1862	395	—
Choctaw	Mar. 23, 1863	1,004	—
Eastport	Jan. 19, 1863	570	—
Essex	Oct. 15, 1861	355	—
Indianola	Jan. 14, 1863	442	—
Lafayette	Feb. 27, 1863	1,193	—
Tuscumbia	Mar. 12, 1863	575	—
	Tinclads		
Abeona	Apr. 10, 1865	32	—
Alexandria	Dec. 1863	60	—
Alfred Robb	May 1, 1862	86	—
Argosy	Mar. 20, 1863	219	—
Black Hawk	Dec. 6, 1862	902	—
Brilliant	Aug. 3, 1862	227	—
Champion	Apr. 26, 1863	115	—
Collier	Mar. 18, 1865	176	—
Colossus	Dec. 8, 1864	183	—
Covington	Feb. 13, 1863	224	—
Cricket	Nov. 18, 1862	178	—

(*continued*)

NAME	COMMISSIONED/ ACQUIRED	TONNAGE	SUPPORT TYPE
Curlew	Dec. 16, 1863	196	—
Elfin	Feb. 23, 1864	192	—
Exchange	June 1863	211	—
Fairplay	Sept. 6, 1862	162	—
Fairy	Mar. 1863	173	—
Fawn	May 11, 1863	174	—
Forest Rose	Dec. 3, 1862	260	—
Gamage	Mar. 23, 1865	187	—
Gazelle	Dec. 21, 1863	117	—
General Burnside	Aug. 8, 1864	201	—
General Grant	July 20, 1864	204	—
General Pillow	Aug. 1862	38	—
General Sherman	July 27, 1864	187	—
General Thomas	Aug. 8, 1864	184	—
Glide	Dec. 3, 1862	137	—
Grosbeak	Feb. 24, 1864	196	—
Hastings	Apr. 1863	293	—
Huntress	June 10, 1864	211	—
Ibex	Apr. 4, 1865	235	—
Juliet	Dec. 14, 1862	157	—
Kate	Apr. 2, 1865	241	—
Kenwood	May 24, 1863	232	—
Key West	May 26, 1863	207	—
Linden	Jan. 3, 1863	177	—
Little Rebel	Jan. 9, 1863	161	—
Manitou/Fort Hindman	Mar. 14, 1863	280	—
Marmora	Oct. 21, 1862	207	—
Meteor	Mar. 8, 1864	221	—
Mist	Mar. 8, 1865	232	—
Moose	May 1863	189	—
Naiad	Mar. 3, 1864	185	—
Naumkeag	Apr. 16, 1863	148	—
New Era	Dec. 1862	157	—
Nyanza	Dec. 21, 1863	203	—
Nymph	Apr. 11, 1864	171	—
Oriole	Mar. 22, 1865	236	—

NAME	COMMISSIONED/ ACQUIRED	TONNAGE	SUPPORT TYPE
Ouachita	Jan. 18, 1864	720	—
Paw Paw	July 25, 1863	175	—
Peosta	June 13, 1863	204	—
Peri	June 20, 1864	155	—
Petrel	Feb. 2, 1863	226	—
Prairie Bird	Dec. 19, 1862	171	—
Queen City	Apr. 1, 1863	210	—
Rattler	Dec. 19, 1862	165	—
Reindeer	July 25,1863	212	—
Romeo	Dec. 11, 1862	175	—
Sibyl	June 16, 1864	176	—
Signal	Oct. 1862	190	—
Silver Cloud	May 4, 1863	236	—
Silver Lake	Nov. 15, 1862	236	—
Siren	Mar. 11, 1864	232	—
Springfield	Nov. 20, 1863	146	—
St. Clair	Sept. 24, 1862	203	—
Stockdale	Nov. 13, 1863	188	—
Tallahatchie	Jan. 23, 1864	171	—
Tawah	Oct. 1863	108	—
Tempest	Apr. 26, 1865	161	—
Tensas	Jan. 1, 1863	62	—
Undine	Apr. 1864	179	—
Victory	May 1863	160	—
	Monitors		
Chickasaw	May 14, 1864	1,300	—
Kickapoo	July 8, 1864	1,300	—
Milwaukee	Aug. 27, 1864	1,300	—
Neosho	May 13, 1863	523	—
Osage	Jan. 13, 1863	523	—
Ozark	Feb. 18, 1864	578	—
Winnebago	Apr. 27, 1864	1,300	—
	Cottonclads		
General Bragg	July 9, 1862	1,043	—
Sumter	June 6, 1862	524	—

(*continued*)

NAME	COMMISSIONED/ ACQUIRED	TONNAGE	SUPPORT TYPE
	Rams		
Avenger	Feb. 29, 1864	410	—
General Price	Mar. 11, 1863	633	—
Vindicator	May 24, 1864	750	—
	Support Vessels		
Abraham	Sept. 30, 1862	405	Storeship
Clara Dolsen	1862	939	Receiving
Dahlia	Sept. 30, 1862	54	Tug
Daisy	Sept. 30, 1862	54	Tug
Fern	Sept. 30, 1862	45	Tug
General Lyon	Sept. 30, 1862	390	Ordnance
Grampus	July 22, 1863	230	Receiving
Great Western	Feb. 20, 1862	429	Receiving
Hyacinth	Sept. 30, 1862	50	Tug
Ivy	Sept. 30, 1862	47	Tug
Judge Torrence	Dec. 25, 1862	419	Ordnance
Laurel	Sept. 30, 1862	50	Tug
Lavinia Logan	Aug. 31, 1864	145	Powder
Lily	May 5, 1862	50	Tug
Maria Denning	1861	870	Receiving
Mignonette	Sept. 30, 1862	50	Tug
Mistletoe	Oct. 1, 1862	38	Tug
Myrtle	Sept. 30, 1862	60	Tug
Nettle	Sept. 30, 1862	50	Tug
New National	June 6, 1862	317	Supply
Pansy	Sept. 30, 1862	46	Tug
Red Rover	June 10, 1862	625	Hospital
Sallie Wood	Feb. 8, 1862	256	Transport
Sovereign	Jan. 1, 1863	336	Commissary
Thistle	Sept. 30, 1862	50	Tug
William H. Brown	Sept. 30, 1862	200	Dispatch

Source: Silverstone, *Warships of the Civil War Navies; ORN.*

NOTES

ABBREVIATIONS

Bock Papers	William N. Bock Papers, Abraham Lincoln Presidential Library, Springfield, IL
Clapp Diary	Fayette Clapp Diary, State Historical Society of Missouri, Columbia
Davis Papers	Frederic E. Davis Papers, Emory University, Atlanta, GA
Dickinson Diary	James A. Dickinson Diary, Rutherford B. Hayes Presidential Library and Museum, Fremont, OH, http://www.rbhayes.org/hayes/mssfind/285/dickinsonjames.htm
Coffinberry Diary	Diary of Henry D. Coffinberry, Western Reserve Historical Society, Cleveland, OH
FHS	Filson Historical Society, Louisville, KY
FTFWN	John D. Milligan, ed., *From the Fresh-Water Navy, 1861–64: The Letters of Acting Master's Mate Henry R. Browne and Acting Ensign Symmes E. Browne* (Annapolis, MD: Naval Institute Press, 1970)
Galligan Diary	Edward M. Galligan Diary, 1861–1863, Montana Historical Society, Helena
Henneberry Journal	James E. Henneberry Journal, Chicago History Museum, Chicago, IL (photostat)
Jordan Letters	Eleanor Jordan West, [ed.], *Dear Judith! Letters home from a Civil War Gun Boat to family in Maine.* (n.p.: self-published, 2007)
Kemp Letters	Daniel Francis Kemp Letters, Buffalo History Museum, Buffalo, NY
Kemp Reminiscences	Daniel Francis Kemp Civil War Correspondence and Reminiscences, Buffalo History Museum, Buffalo, NY
Laning Papers	James Laning Papers, Chicago History Museum, Chicago, IL
Lyons Journal	Thomas Lyons Journal, Library of Congress, Washington, DC
Miller Diary	Alexander R. Miller Diary, Hill Memorial Library, Louisiana State University Baton Rouge
Morrison Diary	"The Civil War Diary of John G. Morrison, 1861–1865," New York State Military Museum and Veterans Research Center, https://museum.dmna.ny.gov/application/files/8615/5059/7442/30thInf_Diary_Morrison.pdf
NARA	National Archives and Records Administration, Washington, DC
ORA	*War of the Rebellion: A Compilation of Official Records of the Union and Confederate Armies,* 128 vols. (Washington DC: Government Printing Office, 1880–1901) (all citations to series 1 unless otherwise noted)

ORN	*Official Records of the Union and Confederate Navies in the War of the Rebellion,* 30 vols. (Washington, DC: Government Printing Office, 1894–1922)
RG	Record Group
RG 24–LB	RG 24, Log Books
RG 24–MRS	RG 24, Muster Rolls of Ships
Squadron Letters	RG 45, Letters Received by the Secretary of the Navy from Commanding Officers of Squadrons, Mississippi Squadron
Van Cleaf Papers	William Van Cleaf Papers, Special Collections and University Libraries, Rutgers University, New Brunswick, NJ
Yost Diary	George Robert Yost Diary, Abraham Lincoln Presidential Library, Springfield, IL

INTRODUCTION

1. Hess, *Civil War in the West,* 2–3.

2. Smith, *Early Struggles for Vicksburg,* 246–61; Miller, *Vicksburg,* 328.

3. Ulysses S. Grant to David D. Porter, Mar. 29, 1863, *ORN* 24:517 (quotations); David D. Porter to Ulysses S. Grant, Mar. 29, 1863, ibid., 518; Glatthaar, *Partners in Command,* 173–74; Glatthaar, "Lord High Admiral of the U.S. Navy," 14.

4. Coffinberry Diary, Apr. 16, 1863 (quotation); Report of David D. Porter, Oct. 1862–May 1863, *ORN* 23:409; Miller, *Vicksburg,* 149–50.

5. Grant, *Personal Memoirs,* 574.

6. David D. Porter to John H. Dorman, Jan. 27, 1888, John H. Dorman Papers, Ohio History Center, Columbus (quotations); Smith, *Bayou Battles for Vicksburg,* 393–94; McPherson, *War on the Waters,* 8–9. The navy renamed the Western Gunboat Flotilla when it took control of the fleet in October 1862. The new name was consistent with the designations of the blue-water squadrons.

7. Milligan, *Gunboats down the Mississippi;* Joiner, *Mr. Lincoln's Brown Water Navy;* Tomblin, *Civil War on the Mississippi.* See also the books by Myron Smith Jr.

8. Smith, *After Vicksburg;* Smith, *Tinclads;* Patrick, "Fighting Sailor on the Western Rivers."

9. Bennett, *Union Jacks;* Still, "Common Sailor"; Merrill, "Cairo, Illinois."

10. Brewer, "African American Sailors and the Unvexing of the Mississippi"; Reidy, "Black Jack"; Reidy, "African-American Sailors' Project"; Reidy, "Black Men in Navy Blue during the Civil War"; Ramold, *Slaves, Sailors, Citizens;* Bruns, *Black Sailors in the Civil War.* Despite its promising title, Bruns's book has virtually no information on Black sailors in the Mississippi Squadron.

11. The Civil War Bluejackets Project will provide an even bigger dataset. Its goal is to use artificial intelligence to transcribe the cursive writing for all of the Union navy's muster rolls. The first part of the project is reliant on citizen-volunteers to transcribe portions of the muster rolls so that the software has a model for how to interpret nineteenth-century writing. See Civil War Bluejackets, https://civilwarbluejackets.com/.

12. Notable works that have examined the fleet's irregular war are Bennett, *Union Jacks,* 86–98; Smith, *Tinclads;* Smith, *After Vicksburg;* and Patrick, "Fighting Sailor on the Western Rivers."

13. Clapp Diary, July 3, 1863 (emphasis in original). Clapp transcribed letters to his wife into

his diary. The war broke his health. Clapp resigned soon after writing these words and died about a year later.

1. CREATING THE WESTERN GUNBOAT FLOTILLA

1. Woods, *Arguing until Doomsday,* 13 (quotation); Hess, *Civil War in the West,* 3–5.

2. Gudmestad, *Steamboats and the Rise of the Cotton Kingdom,* 117–58.

3. Joiner, *Mr. Lincoln's Brown Water Navy,* 16–18.

4. James B. Eads to Gideon Welles, Apr. 22, 1861, *ORN* 22:278; Milligan, *Gunboats down the Mississippi,* 3–5.

5. Hess, *Civil War in the West,* 10–11; Joiner, *Mr. Lincoln's Brown Water Navy,* 9–10.

6. William T. Sherman to Salmon P. Chase, Oct. 14, 1861, in Simpson and Berlin, *Sherman's Civil War,* 149; Engle, *Struggle for the Heartland,* 3–9.

7. *Harper's Weekly,* June 1, 1861, 350; Hughes, "Town between the Rivers," accessed June 11, 2022.

8. Gideon Welles to James B. Eads, May 14, 1861, *ORN* 22:280 (first quotation); Order of Simon Cameron, May 14, 1861, ibid., 279 (second quotation).

9. Gideon Welles to John Rodgers, May 16, 1861, *ORN* 22:280; Joiner, *Mr. Lincoln's Brown Water Navy,* 18–20.

10. Milligan, *Gunboats down the Mississippi,* 5; Smith, *Timberclads,* 11.

11. George B. McClellan to John Rodgers, May 19, 1862, in Sears, *Selected Papers of George B. McClellan,* 22.

12. Rodgers as quoted in Milligan, *Gunboats down the Mississippi,* 6; John Rodgers to Gideon Welles, June 8, 1861, *ORN* 22:283.

13. Gideon Welles to John Rodgers, June 12, 1861, *ORN* 22:284; Joiner, *Mr. Lincoln's Brown Water Navy,* 20; Milligan, *Gunboats down the Mississippi,* 7–8. The situation changed in October 1862, when the War Department transferred control of the Western Gunboat Flotilla to the Navy Department, which changed its name to the Mississippi Squadron.

14. Seth L. Phelps to John Rodgers, July 25, 1861, *ORN* 22:292; Smith, *Timberclads,* 64–65; Joiner, *Mr. Lincoln's Brown Water Navy,* 21–22.

15. John Rodgers to Gideon Welles, June 8, 1861, *ORN* 22:283; Gudmestad, *Steamboats and the Rise of the Cotton Kingdom,* 106.

16. Ripley, *Artillery and Ammunition,* 14–15, 75; Olmstead, Stark, and Tucker, *Big Guns,* 59–68, 73–99; Joiner, *Mr. Lincoln's Brown Water Navy,* 23–24; Silverstone, *Warships of the Civil War Navies,* 158–59. The *Conestoga* carried four 32-pounder smoothbores, while the *Lexington* and *Tyler* each had two 32-pounder smoothbores and four 8-inch smoothbores.

17. Wegner, "Old Navy," 74–76.

18. Joiner, *Mr. Lincoln's Brown Water Navy,* 25; Milligan, *Gunboats down the Mississippi,* 19.

19. Tucker, *Andrew Foote,* 7, 14–15, 116–18.

20. Smith, *USS* Carondelet, 9–17.

21. Smith, *USS* Carondelet, 20–32; Joiner, *Mr. Lincoln's Brown Water Navy,* 24–29. Eight knots is about 9.2 miles per hour. I base the crew size on the averages in the muster rolls.

22. Joiner, *Mr. Lincoln's Brown Water Navy,* 23–26.

23. Joiner, *Mr. Lincoln's Brown Water Navy,* 26–27; Milligan, *Gunboats down the Mississippi,* 15–17; Smith, *Old War Horse,* 57–67.

24. Pension application of William Rose (aka James Funk), WC 812,489, RG 15, NARA; Tucker, "Armaments and Innovations."

25. Seth Phelps to Elisha Whittlesey, Oct. 10, 1861, quoted in Slagle, *Ironclad Captain,* 146; Bennett, *Union Jacks,* 82–85.

26. Frederic Davis to Parents, May 6, 1862, Davis Papers (quotations); Bennett, *Union Jacks,* 39, 82–85.

2. THE MEN OF THE WESTERN GUNBOAT FLOTILLA

1. Bennett, *Union Jacks,* 2–5.

2. Charles H. Davis to Gideon Welles, Aug. 12, 1862, *ORN* 23:292; Andrew H. Foote to Gustavus V. Fox, Jan. 11, 1862, *ORN* 22:494; Milligan, *Gunboats down the Mississippi,* 25–26; Merrill, "Cairo, Illinois," 247, 251; Hirsch, "Gunboat Personnel," 81; Riggs, "Sailors of the U.S.S. *Cairo,*" 267; Smith, *Timberclads,* 76–78.

3. Henry W. Halleck to Samuel Curtis, Dec. 17, 1861, Pension Application of Richard H. Cutter, I 44,405, RG 15, NARA, typescript; Andrew H. Foote to Gustavus V. Fox, Jan. 11, 1862, *ORN* 22:494; Grant to J. C. Kelton, Jan. 6, 1862, *ORA* 7:534 (first quotation); Grant to J. C. Kelton, Jan. 25, 1862, ibid., 565 (second quotation); Andrew H. Foote to Gustavus Fox, Jan. 27, 1862, in Thompson and Wainwright, *Confidential Correspondence of Gustavus Vasa Fox,* 34 (third quotation); Bennett, *Union Jacks,* 80–81.

4. Morrison Diary, Feb. 15, Feb. 17, 1862 (quotations); Court-Martial of Eugene Daily, case 3204, vol. 95, RG 125, NARA, available at Fold3.com.

5. Frederic R. Davis to Father, Apr. 15, 1862 (first quotation), Davis Papers; Frederic Davis to Father, n.d. [probably Apr. 22, 1862] (remaining quotations), ibid.

6. Andrew H. Foote to Gideon Welles, Feb. 24, 1862, *ORN* 22:632 (first and second quotations); Andrew H. Foote to Gideon Welles, Feb. 25, 1862, ibid. (third quotation); Andrew H. Foote to Montgomery C. Meigs, Feb. 26, 1862, Pension Application of Richard H. Cutter, I 44,405, RG 15, NARA, typescript; Enlisted Men Transferred from the U.S. Army to the Mississippi Flotilla, RG 94, NARA, available at Fold3.com.

7. Avery, *Fourth Illinois Cavalry,* 52 (quotation); Still, "Common Sailor," 27; Bennett, *Union Jacks,* 80–81. Approximately 1,400 men served in the fleet prior to June 31, 1862. Gudmestad Sailor Dataset; see Appendix 1 for a description of this source.

8. Coffinberry Diary, Aug. 1, 1863 (quotations); Muster Roll of the USS *Mound City,* Sept. 1861, box 2, Western Gunboat Flotilla: General Muster Books and Pay & Receipts, ca. 1862–ca. 1862, RG 217, NARA. The one-third figure is based on information from known transfers in Gudmestad Sailor Dataset.

9. Bennett, *Union Jacks,* 5–12; "Men Transferred from the Frigate USS *Roanoke* to the Western Flotilla," n.d., box 2, Western Gunboat Flotilla: General Muster Books and Pay & Receipts, ca. 1862–ca. 1862, RG 217, NARA; "Men Transferred from the Frigate USS *Sabine* to the Western Flotilla," n.d., ibid.; Gudmestad Sailor Dataset, N=89 (state of residence), N=111 (employment).

10. Merrill, "Cairo, Illinois," 251; Muster Roll of the USS *Great Western,* Dec. 31, 1862, RG 24–MRS, NARA.

11. Gudmestad Sailor Dataset, N=1,248 (first phase age), N=4,696 (second and third phases age).

12. Henneberry Journal, Oct. 26, 1863 (first quotation); William Bock to Father, Sept. 20, 1864, Bock Papers (second quotation); Kidder R. Breese to David D. Porter, May 3, 1864, *ORN* 26:102; Marvel, *Lincoln's Mercenaries,* 8, 99–102. The last known complaint from a commander of the flotilla about the poor quality of recruits was in May 1863. David D. Porter to Andrew H. Foote, May 16, 1863, *ORN* 24:678.

13. Some historians have pointed to the mutiny of men from the 58th Ohio Regiment on the USS *Benton* in February 1863 as evidence of recalcitrant sailors. See Merrill, "Cairo, Illinois," 251; and Bennett, *Union Jacks,* 124. These men were never sailors. Seven of the regiment's ten companies were temporarily "detached to service" on five ironclads. They were akin to sharpshooters or marines while on the boats and rejoined their regiment in July 1863. E. P. Jackson to Adjutant-General of the Army, May 22, 1863, *ORN* 24:629–30 (quotation); Byron Wilson to David D. Porter, Aug. 4, 1863, ibid., 340; Muster Roll of the USS *Mound City,* June 30, 1863, RG 24–MRS, NARA.

14. All percentages in the chapter are from Gudmestad Sailor Dataset, N=14,442.

15. Gudmestad Sailor Dataset, N=4,271.

16. Muster Roll of the USS *Tyler,* Dec. 31, 1862, RG 24–MRS, NARA (first quotation); Foos, *Short, Offhand Killing Affair,* 108–9 (second quotation); Guardino, "Gender, Soldiering, and Citizenship in the Mexican-American War," 23–46; Gudmestad Sailor Dataset, N=4,701.

17. Foner, *Fiery Trial,* 175, 215–16, 252; Reidy, "Black Men in Navy Blue during the Civil War," 156–57; Ramold, *Slaves, Sailors, Citizens,* 38–49; Brewer, "African American Sailors and the Unvexing of the Mississippi," 279; Bennett, *Union Jacks,* 157; Gudmestad Sailor Dataset, N=392 (Free Black), N=1,235 (Second Phase). I included the thirty-two Black men born outside of the United States in the cohort of free Black sailors.

18. Gudmestad Sailor Dataset, N=2,404.

19. Pension application of Walter Perry, WC 12,967, RG 15, NARA (quotations); Gudmestad Sailor Dataset, N=2,404. The states that contributed to the domestic slave trade were Delaware, the District of Columbia, Florida, Georgia, Maryland, North Carolina, South Carolina, and Virginia.

20. Seventy-eight, or 0.07 percent, of enslaved men indicated a state along the Atlantic Seaboard as their place of residence. Gudmestad Sailor Dataset, N=1,068.

21. Gudmestad Sailor Dataset, N=6,171 (state of residence for free men), N=11,707 (enlistment location for free men). The states in the Mississippi River valley are Alabama, Arkansas, Iowa, Illinois, Indiana, Kentucky, Louisiana, Michigan, Minnesota, Missouri, Ohio, Tennessee, Texas, and Wisconsin. The Eastern Seaboard states and district are Connecticut, the District of Columbia, Delaware, Florida, Georgia, Maine, Massachusetts, Maryland, New Hampshire, New Jersey, New York, North Carolina, Pennsylvania, Rhode Island, South Carolina, Virginia, Vermont, and West Virginia. The states and territories in the Far West are California, Colorado, Kansas, and Nebraska.

22. Gudmestad Sailor Dataset, N=11,143. Michael J. Bennett argues that one-third of the men who joined the Union navy were unemployed. In his examination of the rendezvous reports, he explains that a blank entry for occupation was the same as being unemployed prior to enlistment. See Bennett, *Union Jacks,* 7, 215n41. Muster rolls were different because blank entries in a variety of fields

were relatively common. For those entries with a blank entry in the occupation field, I examined a subsequent or previous muster roll, if one existed. I found over 100 instances of an occupation listed in another muster roll, including dozens of entries that went from blank to "None."

23. Michael J. Bennett places the percentage of captured Confederates who enlisted through a western rendezvous at 11.5 percent. Bennett, *Union Jacks,* 80, 250n19. It is difficult to use the muster rolls to determine how many Confederate prisoners of war served in the brown-water navy. There are no prison camps listed, so the prisoners of war who enlisted were almost certainly transported to a city like Cairo and officially enlisted there.

24. Gudmestad Sailor Dataset, N=14,559 (age); N=12,739 (adult height); "Who Fought?," in "Civil War Facts," American Battlefield Trust, Jan. 5, 2009, updated Nov. 20, 2023; Wilson and Pope, "Height of Union Army Recruits," 120; Clarke and Plant, *Of Age,* 5, 299. The average age for Union soldiers was 25.8 years old. I calculated the age of each sailor based on his date of enlistment.

25. Gudmestad Sailor Dataset; Bennett, *Union Jacks,* 5–9. Bennett's figures primarily reflect a profile of blue-water sailors because those men were about 86 percent of the Union navy. The rendezvous reports do not include onboard enlistments. For the Western Gunboat Flotilla, around 2 percent of native-born white Americans, immigrants, and free Black men enlisted onboard while nearly all escaped slaves did so.

26. Bennett, *Union Jacks,* 8–17; Henry O'Mahoney Memoir, Kerby A. Miller, Ph.D., private collection, 3; Affidavit of Clara P. Young in Pension Application of James C. Howe, MC 10,750 RG 15, NARA (quotation); Muster Roll of the USS *Oriole,* Mar. 30, 1865, RG 24–MRS, ibid.; Marvel, *Lincoln's Mercenaries,* 12–16. Frederic Davis, who was an army transfer, was one of the few enlisted men whose patriotism was evident in his writing. See Frederic E. Davis to Mother, Jan. 19, 1863, Davis Papers. Officers were more ideologically motivated than enlisted men. See Henry Browne to Symmes Browne, Dec. 25, 1861, *FTFWN,* 13; Symmes Browne to Fannie, May 25, 1862, ibid., 82; Clapp Diary, Feb. 2, 1863; and Scott Jordan to Brother, May 28, 1863, Jordan Letters. For a summary of what motivated Civil War soldiers, see Carmichael, *War for the Common Soldier,* 326–27n21.

27. John Swift to Rosie Whiteside, July 2, 1863, in Swift, "Letters from a Sailor on a Tinclad," 49 (quotations); Meacham, "Military and Naval Operations on the Mississippi," 392; William Van Cleaf to Mother, Feb. 16, 1862, Van Cleaf Papers.

28. Everson, "Service Afield and Afloat," 44; Pension Application of Walter Standish, WC 16,806, RG 15, NARA.

29. Daniel Francis Kemp to Parents, Oct. 2, 1862, Kemp Letters (first quotation); Dickinson Diary, May 17, 1863 (remaining quotations); Greenberg, *Manifest Manhood,* 10–14.

30. Kemp Reminiscences (first quotation); Dickinson Diary, May 16, 18, 1863; Bennett, *Union Jacks,* 28–29.

31. Kemp Reminiscences.

32. Scott Jordan to Judith Jordan, Apr. 5, 1863, Jordan Letters; Scott Jordan to Frank Jordan, Apr. 7, 1863, ibid.; Morrison Diary, Feb. 21, 1862 (quotation). For similar descriptions of Cairo, see Frederic R. Davis to Parents, May 6, 1862, Davis Papers; William Van Cleaf to Mother, Mar. 19, 1862, Van Cleaf Papers; and Daniel Francis Kemp to Father and Mother, Oct. 13, 1862, Kemp Letters.

33. Jeffrey, *Two Civil Wars,* 66–67n6 (quotation); Morrison Diary, Mar. 2, 1862; Galligan Diary, Oct. 1, 1863; Ringle, *Life in Mr. Lincoln's Navy,* 29–31; Canney, *Lincoln's Navy,* 101.

34. Frederic Davis to Father, Apr. 22, 1862, Davis Papers (first quotation); William Park Diary, Oct. 1, 1861, in Jeffrey, *Two Civil Wars,* 65 (second quotation, emphasis in original); Kemp Reminiscences, 3 (remaining quotations). The receiving boats were the USS *Great Western,* USS *New National,* USS *Clara Dolsen,* and USS *Maria Denning.*

35. Muster Roll of the USS *Lexington,* Dec. 31, 1862, RG 24–MRS, NARA; Pension Application of Joseph Cohen, IC 20,2027, RG 15, NARA; Williams, "Uncle Sam's Webfeet," 1–2; Ringle, *Life in Mr. Lincoln's Navy,* 40–41; Bennett, *Union Jacks,* 34–35. I could not locate the identifier that boys wore on their sleeve. The biographical information and ratings for the sailors in this and the following paragraphs are from Muster Rolls of the *Lexington,* 1863–65, RG 24–MRS, NARA.

36. Daniel Francis Kemp to Sister, Nov. 23, 1862, Kemp Letters; Canney, *Lincoln's Navy,* 129; Ringle, *Life in Mr. Lincoln's Navy,* 47.

37. Muster Roll of the USS *Lexington,* June 30, 1864, RG 24–MRS, NARA; O'Mahoney Memoir, 4 (first quotation); Kemp Reminiscences, 8; Pension Application of Isaac Simms, WC 4,139, RG 15, NARA (remaining quotations); Gudmestad Sailor Dataset, N=407; Canney, *Lincoln's Navy,* 129; Ringle, *Life in Mr. Lincoln's Navy,* 47. Hardin's rating was initially landsman but subsequently was coal heaver.

38. Canney, *Lincoln's Navy,* 102, 128. Masters-at-arms were older at enlistment (28.6 years old) and taller (five feet, eight inches) than most of the other men. Gudmestad Sailor Dataset, N=81.

39. Canney, *Lincoln's Navy,* 145–52; Smith, *Ironclad Captains,* 198–99.

40. Court-Martial of William D. Porter, case 776, vol. 40, RG 125, NARA, available at Fold3.com (first quotation); Phelps to Foote, July 6, 1862, quoted in Slagle, *Ironclad Captain,* 252 (remaining quotations). See the appropriate biographies in Smith, *Ironclad Captains.*

41. Clapp Diary, Feb. 11, 1863 (first quotation, emphasis in original); Scott Jordan to Judith Jordan, Aug. 8, 1863, Jordan Letters (second quotation).

42. Ezra Green to Mother, Apr. 21, 1862, Ezra Green Letters, FHS (first quotation); O'Mahoney Memoir, 4 (second quotation). Skouse varied but was usually potatoes and hardtack cooked in butter or lard. For a sailor who praised the navy's food, see Everson, "Service Afield and Afloat," 47–49.

43. Symmes Browne to Fannie, Jan. 20, 1862, *FTFWN,* 20 (quotation, emphasis in original); Scott Jordan to Judith Jordan, Apr. 12, Aug. 12, 1863, Sept. 18, 1864, Jordan Letters; Clapp Diary, Apr. 11, 1863; Slagle, *Ironclad Captain,* 323.

44. Gudmestad, *Steamboats and the Rise of the Cotton Kingdom,* 33–35; Milligan, *Gunboats down the Mississippi,* 9–10.

3. BECOMING MEN OF WAR

1. Foote, *Gentlemen and the Roughs,* 10 (first quotation); Henneberry Journal, Sept. 27, 1861 (second quotation); Frederic Davis to Father, n.d. [ca. Apr. 22, 1862]; William Van Cleaf to Brother, May 4, 1862, Van Cleaf Papers.

2. Greenberg, *Manifest Manhood,* 10–14; Foote, *Gentlemen and the Roughs,* 43–57.

3. Frederic Davis to Parents, May 29, 1862 (quotation), Davis Papers; Davis to Mother, Aug. 3, 1862, ibid.; Davis to Parents, Oct. 23, 1862, ibid.

4. Beilein, *A Man by Any Other Name,* xiii (quotation); Greenberg, *Manifest Manhood,* 10–14; Bennett, *Union Jacks,* 20, 53, 198–99; Foote, *Gentlemen and the Roughs,* 67–79.

5. John Swift to Harold Whiteside, n.d., in Swift, "Letters from a Sailor on a Tinclad," 57 (quotation); Galligan Diary, Apr. 6 (second quotation), 8, May 16, 20, 24, 26, Aug. 7, 1862; Bennett, *Union Jacks,* 81; Beilein, *A Man by Any Other Name,* 160; Ramold, *Baring the Iron Hand,* 4–6.

6. Bever, *At War with King Alcohol,* 14 (quotation); Dickinson Diary, Sept. 12, 1863; Thompson, *Friendly Enemies,* 31–33; Joseph M. Beilein Jr., "Whiskey, Wild Men, and Missouri's Guerrilla War," in McKnight and Myers, *Guerrilla Hunters,* 239; Bennett, *Union Jacks,* 105–6.

7. Ezra Green to Dear Friend, Feb. 22, 1862, Ezra Green Letters, FHS (first quotation); Galligan Diary, Sept. 9, 1862 (second quotation); Bennett, *Union Jacks,* 103–4, 109–11; Ramold, *Baring the Iron Hand,* 124–27. The tradition of serving grog was a holdover from the Royal Navy, although the British typically used rum instead of whiskey.

8. Herbert Saunders to Father, Mar. 25, 1864, in Huch, "Civil War Letters of Herbert Saunders," 21 (first and second quotation); Morrison Diary, May 24, 1862 (final quotation); Frederic Davis to Mother, Aug. 3, 1862, Davis Letters.

9. Dickinson Diary, Dec. 10, 14, 1863; Muster Roll of the USS *Tawah,* Sept. 30, 1863, RG 24–MRS, NARA; Miller Diary, Apr. 30, 1863 (quotation). The *Tawah*'s muster roll has fifty-three enlisted men.

10. Dickinson Diary, Dec. 10, 14 (first and second quotations), 1863; Henry O'Mahoney Memoir, Kerby A. Miller, Ph.D., private collection, 4 (remaining quotations); Daniel Francis Kemp to Parents, Apr. 25, 1863, Kemp Letters; Miller Diary, Mar. 17, 1864; Henry R. Holdrege Diary, Jan. 1, 1865, Hill Memorial Library, Louisiana State University; Henneberry Journal, Mar. 8, 1863; Deck Log of the USS *Champion,* June 10, 1864, RG 24–LB, NARA.

11. Herbert Saunders to Brother, May 3, 1864, in Huch, "Civil War Letters of Herbert Saunders," 26 (quotation); Dickinson Diary, Feb. 16, 1864.

12. Galligan Diary, Dec. 16, 1862; Pension Application of George Washington, C 2,581,691, RG 15, NARA (quotations); Park Journal, Aug. 6, 1862, in Jeffrey, *Two Civil Wars,* 95–96; Deck Log of the USS *Champion,* June 10, 1864, RG 24–LB, NARA; Greenberg, *Manifest Manhood,* 140–41.

13. Park Journal, Aug. 9, 1862, in Jeffrey, *Two Civil Wars,* 95–96, esp. 96n62; Henneberry Journal, Aug. 9, 1862.

14. Lyons Journal, Jan. 30, 1863 (first and second quotations); Deck Log of the USS *Osage,* Oct. 8, 1863, RG 24–LB, NARA (remaining quotations); Court-Martial of Edward McClain, case 3777, vol. 125, RG 125, ibid., available at Fold3.com. John G. Morrison did not mention the incident in his diary.

15. Lyons Journal, Mar. 11, 1863 (quotation); Thompson, *Friendly Enemies,* 21–22; Ramold, *Baring the Iron Hand,* 208–13. For other incidents of contempt, disrespect, or failure to follow orders, see Deck Log of the USS *Cricket,* Mar. 13, 1864, RG 24–LB, NARA; Deck Log of the USS *Osage,* Oct. 6, 1863, ibid.; Deck Log of the USS *Tyler,* Apr. 10, 1863, ibid.; Deck Log of the USS *Benton,* Apr. 2, 1863, ibid.; Deck Log of the USS *Champion,* May 12, July 26, 1864, ibid.; Deck Log of the USS *Mound City,* Nov. 1, 1863, ibid.; Deck Log of the USS *Louisville,* July 23, 1863, ibid.; Coffinberry Diary, July 23, 1863; Clapp Diary, Jan. 24, 1863; and Yost Diary, Oct. 8, 1863.

16. Thompson, *Friendly Enemies,* 21–22; John Swift to Harold Whiteside, n.d., in Swift, "Letters from a Sailor on a Tinclad," 58 (first and second quotations); Clapp Diary, Jan. 12, 1863 (final quotation); Ramold, *Baring the Iron Hand,* 208–13. See also note 15 above.

17. Statistics compiled from Deck Logs of the USS *Rattler,* 1863–64, RG 24–LB, NARA; and Muster Rolls of the USS *Rattler,* 1863–64, RG 24–MRS, ibid.

18. Yost Diary, Sept. 12, 1862.

19. Scott Jordan to Judith Jordan, Sept. 18, 1864 (quotations, emphasis in original); Thomas E. Smith to Wife, Oct. 12, 1863, Thomas E. Smith Letters, FHS; Henneberry Journal, Nov. 23, 1862; Daniel Francis Kemp to Father and Mother, Jan. 16, 1863, Kemp Letters; Bennett, *Union Jacks,* 126–28.

20. John Swift to Harold Whiteside, May 1864, in Swift, "Letters from a Sailor," 51 (quotations); Yost Diary, Oct. 13, 1862; True, "Life aboard a Gunboat," 37–39; Bennett, *Union Jacks,* 45; Slagle, *Ironclad Captain,* 127–29.

21. Dickinson Diary, Dec. 25, 1863, Jan. 1, 2, 5, 1864 (quotations); Critchell, *Recollections of a Fire Insurance Man,* 26–27.

22. True, "Life aboard a Gunboat," 37 (quotations); Ramold, *Baring the Iron Hand,* 4–6.

23. True, "Life aboard a Gunboat," 37 (first quotation); Morrison Diary, June 11, 1862 (second and third quotations); Still, *What Finer Tradition,* 82–82; Kemp Reminiscences, 9; Ringle, *Life in Mr. Lincoln's Navy,* 45; Bennett, *Union Jacks,* ix, 45. Officers made sailors holystone so much that they weakened the decks by scraping away layers of wood. See Samuel P. Lee to J. W. Livingston, Feb. 28, 1865, Mound City, IL Naval Station: Letters Received, July 29, 1864–Aug. 30, 1869, Squadron Letters, NARA.

24. Dickinson Diary, June 12, 1863 (quotation); Ezra Green to Mother, Apr. 12, 1862, Green Letters, FHS; Bennett, *Union Jacks,* 46–47; Hirsch, "Gunboat Personnel," 77.

25. Andrew H. Foote to Gideon Welles, Feb. 25, 1862, *ORN* 22:637.

26. Henneberry Journal, Sept. 4, 1863 (quotation); Bennett, *Union Jacks,* 115–16; Thompson, "Escaping the Mechanism," 352.

27. Ezra Green to Dear Friend, Feb. 22, 1862, Green Letters, FHS (quotation); Kemp Reminiscences, 41–42; "Exercise for 24 lb Howitzer," n.d., Laning Papers; True, "Life aboard a Gunboat," 39, 43; Clapp Diary, Feb. 8, 1863; Brewer, "African American Sailors and the Unvexing of the Mississippi," 282.

28. Bennett, *Union Jacks,* 49–51; "Exercise for 24 lb Howitzer."

29. Gudmestad Sailor Dataset, N=1,275 (phase 1), N=9.756 (phases 2–4); Walke, "Gun-Boats at Belmont and Fort Henry," 363 (quotations); Muster Roll of the USS *New Era,* Apr. 1, 1863, RG 24–MRS, NARA; Muster Roll of the USS *Mound City,* Jan 1. 1863, ibid.; Court-Martial of Joseph Johns, case 3426, vol. 108, RG 125, ibid., available at Fold3.com.

30. Galligan Diary, Dec. 21, 1861, Feb. 23, 1863 (quotations); Yost Diary, Oct. 9, 1862; Lyons Journal, Mar. 27, 1863. At the time of the competition, the USS *Baron de Kalb* was still named the *St. Louis.* Galligan sustained a grievous injury when a botched blast blew out his left eardrum, knocked out some of his teeth, and left him bleeding from the ears and mouth.

31. Gunner's Crew of the USS *Essex,* P0232–2304, Missouri History Museum, St. Louis.

32. Galligan Diary, Apr. 8, 1862; Mar. 29, Apr. 21, May 3, Aug. 3, 22, Dec. 3, 1862 (activities); and May 21 (quotation), 24–26 (punishments), 1862; Ramold, *Baring the Iron Hand,* 313.

33. Ramold, *Baring the Iron Hand,* 302–5; Bennett, "'Frictions,'" 119; Foote, *Gentlemen and the Roughs,* 120; Lyons Journal, June 3, 1863; William Van Cleaf to Mother, Sept. 5, 1862, Van Cleaf Papers; Dickinson Diary, June 8, 9, 1863; John Swift to Harold Whiteside, n.d., in Swift, "Letters from a Sailor on a Tinclad," 58; Miller Diary, Oct. 4, 1863; Morrison Diary, Jan. 10, 1863; Deck Log of the USS *Pittsburg,* Aug. 9, 1863, RG 24–LB, NARA.

34. Information drawn from RG 125, NARA, available at Fold3.com. I was unable to locate court-martial records for the Mississippi Squadron prior to 1863. Somewhat surprisingly, the navy brought charges against twenty-five brown-water officers in 1863.

35. Ramold, *Baring the Iron Hand,* 313. Statistics compiled from Deck Logs of the USS *Rattler,* 1863–64, RG 24–LB, NARA.

36. Holdrege Diary, Mar. 11–21, 1865 (first four quotations); Dickinson Diary, Feb. 17,1864 (remaining quotations).

37. Galligan Diary, May 20, July 22, 1862; Lyons Journal, Jan. 30, 1863; "Congressional Medal of Honor Winner John Gordon Morrison," accessed June 22, 2022.

4. EARLY COMBINED OPERATIONS

1. Symonds, introduction to *Union Combined Operations,* 2, 6–7; Symonds, "Navy's Evolutionary War," 26–34. Today, we use "joint operations" to describe military efforts that involve more than one branch of service and "combined operations" to describe those that involve more than one country. I am using "combined operations" because contemporaries used the phrase.

2. Hess, *Civil War in the West,* 9–10; Miller, *Vicksburg,* 35; Engle, *Struggle for the Heartland,* 3–9; Pratt, *Civil War on Western Waters,* 30.

3. Hughes, *Battle of Belmont,* 36–44; Joiner, *Mr. Lincoln's Brown Water Navy,* 35–36; Milligan, *Gunboats down the Mississippi,* 31–34; Smith, *Timberclads,* 144. The Confederate position on Iron Banks Bluff was sometimes called Fort DeRussey.

4. Andrew H. Foote to Gideon Welles, Nov. 9, 1861, *ORN* 22:399 (quotation), Hughes, *Battle of Belmont,* 45–59.

5. Hughes, *Battle of Belmont,* 60–61, 171 (quotation); Slagle, *Ironclad Captain,* 141; Walke, "Gun-Boats at Belmont and Fort Henry," 361; Chernow, *Grant,* 159; Milligan, *Gunboats down the Mississippi,* 34–36; Smith, *Timberclads,* 153–55.

6. Smith, *Grant Invades Tennessee,* 49–53; Milligan, *Gunboats down the Mississippi,* 36–37.

7. Seth L. Phelps to Andrew H. Foote, Dec. 10, 1861, *ORN* 22:457. The name and fate of the enslaved man is unknown.

8. Foner, *Fiery Trial,* 175; Martinez, *Confederate Slave Impressment in the Upper South;* Rodrigue, *Freedom's Crescent,* 54–55.

9. Report of Rear Admiral Foote, Nov. 13, 1862, *ORN* 22:314; Henry Halleck to Ulysses S. Grant, Jan. 30, 1862, *ORA* 7:121 (quotations); Joiner, *Mr. Lincoln's Brown Water Navy,* 39; Smith, *Grant Invades Tennessee,* 64–65. Sources are silent as to why Foote favored attacking Henry over Donelson.

10. Smith, *Grant Invades Tennessee,* 66–67; Tucker, *Andrew Foote,* 137.

11. Milligan, *Gunboats down the Mississippi,* 38.

12. Smith, *Grant Invades Tennessee,* 72.

13. Special Orders No. 1, Feb. 2, 1862, *ORN* 22:535–36 (quotations); Special Orders No. 2, Feb. 2, 1862, ibid., 536; Special Orders No. 3, Feb. 2, 1862, ibid., 537; "Autobiography," n.d., Laning Papers.

14. Walke, "Gun-Boats at Belmont and Fort Henry," 362; Joiner, *Mr. Lincoln's Brown Water Navy,* 40.

15. Park Journal, Feb. 6, 1862, in Jeffrey, *Two Civil Wars,* 75 (quotation); Henneberry Journal, Feb. 6, 1862.

16. Silverstone, *Warships of the Civil War Navies,* 151, 155.

17. Walke, *Naval Scenes and Reminiscences,* 61 (first quotation); "Autobiography," n.d., Laning Papers (remaining quotations); Walke, "Gun-Boats at Belmont and Fort Henry," 363–65; Henneberry Journal, Feb. 6, 1862; Galligan Diary, Feb. 6, 1862; Slagle, *Ironclad Captain,* 160; Smith, *Grant Invades Tennessee,* 118–19. The *Essex* used $560 worth of ammunition, while the *St. Louis* expended $296 in ordnance.

18. Walke, "Gun-Boats at Belmont and Fort Henry," 363 (first quotation); Galligan Diary, Feb. 6, 1862 (remaining quotations); Walke, "Naval Scenes," 63–64; "Autobiography," n.d., Laning Papers.

19. Park Journal, Feb. 6, 1862, in Jeffrey, *Two Civil Wars,* 76 (first quotation); Symmes Browne to Fannie, Feb. 9, 1862, *FTFWN,* 27; Report of Roger H. Stembel, Feb. 6, 1862, *ORN* 22:539; Report of Robert K. Riley, Feb. 6, 1862, ibid., 540.

20. Report of Andrew H. Foote, Feb. 7, 1862, *ORN* 22:539; Walke, "Gun-Boats at Belmont and Fort Henry," 365; Milligan, *Gunboats down the Mississippi,* 41; Smith, *Grant Invades Tennessee,* 113; Foote quoted in Slagle, *Ironclad Captain,* 161.

21. Seth L. Phelps to Andrew H. Foote, Feb. 10, 1862, *ORN* 22:571–75; Slagle, *Ironclad Captain,* 162–73.

22. Andrew H. Foote to Gideon Welles, Feb. 11, 1862, *ORN* 22:550; Henneberry Journal, Feb. 7, 1862; Milligan, *Gunboats down the Mississippi,* 45; Smith, *Grant Invades Tennessee,* 159–60.

23. Walke, "Western Flotilla at Fort Donelson, Island Number Ten, Fort Pillow, and Memphis," 431–33. The *Carondelet*'s efforts cost $1,112 in ordnance (for those keeping score).

24. Egbert Thompson to Andrew H. Foote, Feb. 17, 1862, *ORN* 22:592 (quotation); Miller, *Vicksburg,* 46; Smith, *Grant Invades Tennessee,* 216–17.

25. Milligan, *Gunboats down the Mississippi,* 46.

26. Walke, "Western Flotilla at Fort Donelson, Island Number Ten, Fort Pillow, and Memphis," 433; Report of Egbert Thompson, Feb. 13, 1862, *ORN* 22:592.

27. Walke, "Western Flotilla at Fort Donelson, Island Number Ten, Fort Pillow, and Memphis," 433 (first quotation); Park Journal, Feb. 14, 1862, in Jeffrey, *Two Civil Wars,* 78 (second quotation); Bowman and Scroggs, "Diary of a Confederate Soldier," 27 (third quotation).

28. Report of Egbert Thompson, Feb. 14, 1862, *ORN* 22:593; Park Journal, Feb. 14, 1862, in Jeffrey, *Two Civil Wars,* 78–79; Report of Henry Walke, Feb. 15, 1862, *ORN* 22:59; Walke, "Western Flotilla at Fort Donelson, Island Number Ten, Fort Pillow, and Memphis," 433 (quotation).

29. "Confederate Private at Fort Donelson," 478.

30. Tucker, *Andrew Foote,* 156; Andrew H. Foote to Gideon Welles, Feb. 15, 1862, *ORN* 22:585–86.

31. Andrew H. Foote to Gideon Welles, Feb. 15, 1862, *ORN* 22:585; Report of Egbert Thompson, Feb. 14, 1862, ibid., 593; Park Journal, Feb. 14, 1862, in Jeffrey, *Two Civil Wars,* 78–79 (first quotation); Walke, "Western Flotilla at Fort Donelson, Island Number Ten, Fort Pillow, and Memphis," 433–36 (second quotation, 436); Smith, *Grant Invades Tennessee,* 252–53; Milligan, *Gunboats down the Mississippi,* 47.

32. Andrew H. Foote to Gideon Welles, Feb. 15, 1862, *ORN* 22:585.

33. Miller, *Vicksburg,* 47–48; Tomblin, *Civil War on the Mississippi,* 57.

34. Tucker, *Andrew Foote,* 157–59.

35. Hess, *Civil War in the West,* 44 (quotation); Smith, *Grant Invades Tennessee,* 393–94.

36. "*Chicago Post* Narrative," Mar. 3, 1862, in Moore, *Rebellion Record,* 4:222 (second quotation);

James W. Shirk to Andrew H. Foote, Mar. 1, 1862, *ORN* 22:645; Smith, *Grant Invades Tennessee,* 393–94.

37. Biel, "Battle of Shiloh," 265–66; Smith, "'Gallant and Invaluable Service,'" 46–50.

38. Hoppin, *Life of Andrew Hull Foote,* 259; Tucker, *Andrew Foote,* 168–70; Daniel and Bock, *Island No. 10,* 27–35.

39. Andrew H. Foote to Caroline Foote, Feb. 23, 1862, *ORN* 22:626 (first and second quotations); Henry Halleck to G. W. Cullum and Andrew H. Foote, Mar. 4, 1862, *ORA* 8:588 (remaining quotations); Tucker, *Andrew Foote,* 164–66.

40. Tucker, *Andrew Foote,* 175–77; Daniel and Bock, *Island No. 10,* 4–6. Foote intended to bring the *Louisville,* but leaky boilers forced it to return to Cairo.

41. Daniel and Bock, *Island No. 10,* 27–35, 80–82; Symmes Browne to Fannie, Mar. 19, 1863, *FTFWN,* 43; Charles G. Henderson Diary, Mar. 17, 1862, Tennessee State Library and Archives; Morrison Diary, Mar. 17, 1862; Andrew H. Foote to Gideon Welles, Mar. 17, 1862, *ORN* 22:693; Deck Log of the USS *Benton,* Mar. 17, 1862, RG 24–LB, NARA; William Van Cleaf to Mother, Mar. 27, 1862, Van Cleaf Papers; Walke, "Western Flotilla at Fort Donelson, Island Number Ten, Fort Pillow, and Memphis," 439.

42. Andrew H. Foote to Gideon Welles, Mar. 20, 1862, *ORN* 22:697 (quotations); Daniel and Bock, *Island No. 10,* 84–86.

43. Daniel and Bock, *Island No. 10,* 91, 101–10.

44. John Pope to Henry Halleck, Mar. 27, 1862, *ORN* 22:703 (quotation); Deck Log of the USS *Benton,* Apr. 2, 1862, RG 24–LB, NARA; Tucker, *Andrew Foote,* 184–85.

45. Walke, "Western Flotilla at Fort Donelson, Island Number Ten, Fort Pillow, and Memphis," 442–43; Andrew H. Foote to Henry Walke, Mar. 30, 1862, *ORN* 22:705.

46. Morrison Diary, Apr. 4, 1862 (first and second quotations); W. H. Michael, "Mississippi Flotilla," *National Tribune,* June 14, 1888 (third quotation).

47. Walke, "Western Flotilla at Fort Donelson, Island Number Ten, Fort Pillow, and Memphis," 445 (quotation); Symmes Browne to Fannie, Apr. 11, 1862, *FTFWN,* 59; Daniel and Bock, *Island No. 10,* 124.

48. Park Journal, Apr. 6, 1862, in Jeffrey, *Two Civil Wars,* 81.

49. Stanley, *Personal Memoirs,* 90.

50. Stanley, *Personal Memoirs,* 90 (quotations); Daniel and Bock, *Island No. 10,* 129–30; Tomblin, *Civil War on the Mississippi,* 78.

51. John Pope to Henry Halleck, Apr. 9, 1862, *ORN* 22:724–25; Daniel and Bock, *Island No. 10,* 137.

52. Pratt, *Civil War on Western Waters,* 61.

5. DESTROYING THE CONFEDERATE FLEET

1. Andrew H. Foote to Gideon Welles, Apr. 12, 1862, *ORN* 23:3–4; Andrew H. Foote to Gideon Welles, Apr. 14, 1862, ibid., 4–5.

2. Yost Diary, Apr. 14, 1862.

3. Chatelain, *Defending the Arteries of Rebellion,* 80–88; Campbell, *Confederate Naval Forces on Western Waters,* 85–88.

4. Case, "Strategy and Tactics of Civil War Rams," 2–4.

5. Morrison Diary, Apr. 16, 1862 (first quotation), Apr. 18, 1863 (final quotation); Letter of Symmes Browne, Apr. 17, 1862, *FTFWN,* 63 (second quotation); Walke, "Western Flotilla at Fort Donelson, Island Number Ten, Fort Pillow, and Memphis," 447.

6. John Ludlow, J. S. McNeeley, and George E. Jones to Andrew H. Foote, Apr. 15, 1862, *ORN* 23:63 (first and second quotations); Symonds, *Lincoln and His Admirals,* 134 (final quotation); Tucker, *Andrew Foote,* 192.

7. Morrison Diary, May 9, 1862 (quotation); Deck Log of the USS *Benton,* May 9, 1862, RG 24–LB, NARA.

8. Milligan, *Gunboats down the Mississippi,* 63–64.

9. M. Jeff Thompson to P. G. T. Beauregard, May 10, 1862, *ORN* 23:54; Campbell, *Confederate Naval Forces on Western Waters,* 87–88; Chatelaine, *Defending the Arteries of Rebellion,* 123–26.

10. T. B. Gregory to Henry E. Maynadier, May 10, 1862, *ORN* 23:15–16.

11. Callender, "What a Boy Saw on the Mississippi," 61–62.

12. Callender, "What a Boy Saw on the Mississippi," 63–64 (quotations); "Account by a Participant," in Moore, *Rebellion Record,* 5:125.

13. Yost Diary, May 10, 1862; Deck Log of the USS *Benton,* May 10, 1862, RG 24–LB, NARA; Symmes Browne to Fannie, May 12, 1862 (first quotation), *FTFWN,* 76; unsigned letter to Parents, May 15, 1862 (second quotation), ibid., 78.

14. William Van Cleaf to Mother, May 10, 1862, Van Cleaf Papers (first quotation); Yost Diary, May 10, 1862 (second quotation); Morrison Diary, May 10, 1862 (remaining quotations); Walke, "Western Flotilla at Fort Donelson, Island Number Ten, Fort Pillow, and Memphis," 448; Milligan, *Gunboats down the Mississippi,* 66–67.

15. Seth Phelps to Andrew H. Foote, May 11, 1862, *ORN* 23:19 (first quotation); William Van Cleaf to Brother, May 28, 1862, Van Cleaf Papers (second quotation); Case, "Strategy and Tactics of Civil War Rams," 45–48; Joiner, *Mr. Lincoln's Brown Water Navy,* 67.

16. Morrison Diary, June 4, 1862 (quotation); Milligan, *Gunboats down the Mississippi,* 73.

17. Edwin M. Stanton to Charles Ellet Jr., Mar. 27, 1862, *ORN* 22:672 (quotation); Milligan, *Gunboats down the Mississippi,* 68–70; Joiner, *Mr. Lincoln's Brown Water Navy,* 67; Hearn, *Ellet's Brigade,* 7–9.

18. Milligan, *Gunboats down the Mississippi,* 71–72; Hearn, *Ellet's Brigade,* 17–19.

19. Hearn, *Ellet's Brigade,* 14–15; Milligan, *Gunboats down the Mississippi,* 71–72.

20. Report of James E. Montgomery, July 1, 1862, *ORA,* 52(1):39–40. Montgomery said that he purchased 20,000 barrels of coal to be delivered to Fort Pillow, but Major General Mansfield Lovell refused to pay for it.

21. Walke, "Ellet and His Steam-Rams at Memphis," 456.

22. Morrison Diary, June 6, 1862 (quotation); Yost Diary, June 6, 1862.

23. Walke, "Ellet and His Steam-Rams at Memphis," 456 (quotations); Henry Walke to Charles H. Davis, *ORN* 23:122; Hearn, *Ellet's Brigade,* 29–33.

24. Charles Ellet Jr. to Edwin Stanton, June 11, 1862, *ORN* 23:133; Hearn, *Ellet's Brigade,* 33–35.

25. Walke, "Ellet and His Steam-Rams at Memphis," 457; Hearn, *Ellet's Brigade,* 35.

26. Moore, *Rebellion Record,* 5:181 (first quotation); William Van Cleaf to Mother, June 6, 1862, Van Cleaf Papers (second quotation); Ezra Green to Mother, June 12, 1862, Ezra Green Letters, FHS; Charles H. Davis to Gideon Welles, June 6, 1862, *ORN* 23:120.

27. Ezra Green to Mother, June 12, 1862, Green Letters, FHS (first quotation); Morrison Diary, June 6, 1862 (second quotation).

28. Joiner, *Mr. Lincoln's Brown Water Navy,* 80–82; David G. Farragut to Charles H. Davis, June 28, 1862, *ORN* 23:231–32; Charles H. Davis to Gideon Welles, June 29, 1862, ibid., 232; Miller, *Vicksburg,* 149.

29. Gift, "Story of the *Arkansas,*" 49 (quotation); Bisbee, *Engines of Rebellion,* 67–70; Campbell, *Confederate Naval Forces on Western Waters,* 103; Flynt, "Run the Fleet," 113; Smith, *CSS* Arkansas, 43–45, 107–11; Brown, "Confederate Gun-Boat 'Arkansas,'" 572.

30. Read, "Reminiscences of the Confederate States Navy," 353; Brown, "Confederate Gun-Boat 'Arkansas,'" 572–73; Gift, "Story of the Arkansas," 49; Smith, *CSS* Arkansas, 80–81, 142–46; Flynt, "Run the Fleet," 115; Campbell, *Confederate Naval Forces on Western Waters,* 105–8.

31. Smith, *CSS* Arkansas, 133–35; Flynt, "Run the Fleet," 113; Henneberry Journal, July 16, 1862.

32. Coleman, "July Morning with the Rebel Ram 'Arkansas,'" 4 (quotation); Gift, "Story of the Arkansas," 50; Abstract Log of the *Tyler, ORN* 19:39; Smith, *CSS* Arkansas, 155–56; Hearn, *Ellet's Brigade,* 49–50.

33. Gift, "Story of the Arkansas," 52 (first quotation); Pension Application of William Story, IC 18,229, RG 15, NARA (second quotation); William Gwin to Charles H. Davis, July 16, 1863, *ORN* 19:39 (third quotation); Hearn, *Ellet's Brigade,* 50.

34. Morrison Diary, July 15, 1862 (first and second quotations); Gift, "Story of the Arkansas," 52 (third quotation); Read, "Reminiscences of the Confederate States Navy," 354 (final quotation); Deck Log of the USS *Carondelet,* July 15, 1862, RG 24–LB, NARA; Smith, *CSS* Arkansas, 164–65.

35. "Congressional Medal of Honor Winner John Gordon Morrison," accessed June 22, 2022 (first, second, and fourth quotation); Morrison Diary, July 15, 1862 (third quotation); Coleman, "July Morning with the Rebel Ram 'Arkansas,'" 5; Smith, *CSS* Arkansas, 166–67, 173; "John G Morrison," Congressional Medal of Honor Society, www.cmohs.org/recipients/john-g-morrison.

36. Smith, *CSS* Arkansas, 175–78.

37. William Van Cleaf to Mother, July 20, 1862, Van Cleaf Papers; James Laning to William Bock, June 24, 1891, Bock Papers (quotation).

38. Abstract Log of the Ram *Lancaster,* July 15, 1862, *ORN* 23:244.

39. Henneberry Journal, July 16, 1862 (first quotation); Brown, "Confederate Gun-Boat 'Arkansas,'" 576 (second quotation); Park Journal, July 16, 1862, in Jeffrey, *Two Civil Wars,* 89 (third quotation); William Van Cleaf to Mother, July 20, 1862, Van Cleaf Papers (fourth quotation); Smith, *CSS* Arkansas, 187–88.

40. Seth L. Phelps quoted in Slagle, *Ironclad Captain,* 269 (first quotation); William Van Cleaf to Brother, July 14, 1862, Van Cleaf Papers (second quotation); Report of Charles Davis, July 16, 1862, *ORN* 19:6 (third quotation); Deck Log of the USS *Benton,* July 15, 1862, RG 24–LB, NARA.

41. Gift, "Story of the *Arkansas,*" 119.

42. Charles H. Davis to Gideon Welles, July 16, 1862, *ORN* 19:6 (first quotation); David G. Farragut to Gideon Welles, July 17, 1862, ibid., 4 (second quotation); Gideon Welles to David G. Farragut, Aug. 2, 1862, ibid., 5–6; Gideon Welles to Charles H. Davis, Aug. 2, ibid., 7.

43. David G. Farragut to Charles H. Davis, July 16, 1862, *ORN* 23:236 (first quotation); Charles H. Davis to David G. Farragut, July 17, 1862, ibid., 237 (second quotation); Davis as quoted in McPherson, *War on the Waters,* 93 (third quotation); Smith, *CSS* Arkansas, 222–23, 230.

44. Smith, *CSS* Arkansas, 243; Hearn, *Ellet's Brigade,* 54–55.

45. Galligan Diary, July 21, 1862 (quotation); Henneberry Journal, July 22, 1862; Smith, *CSS* Arkansas, 245.

46. Smith, CSS *Arkansas,* 249.

47. Galligan Diary, July 22, 1862 (quotations); Henneberry Journal, July 22, 1862; Smith, *CSS* Arkansas, 249–54; Park Journal, July 22, 1862, in Jeffrey, *Two Civil Wars,* 91.

48. Smith, *CSS* Arkansas, 258–60; Hearn, *Ellet's Brigade,* 56–57.

49. Milligan, *Gunboats down the Mississippi,* 90.

50. Laas, "'Sleepless Sentinels,'" 26; Bennett, *Union Jacks,* 5; Chatelaine, *Defending the Arteries of Rebellion,* 302. Figures for number and types of boats in the Mississippi Squadron compiled from information in Silverstone, *Warships of the Civil War Navies,* and *ORN.*

51. Chatelaine, *Defending the Arteries of Rebellion,* 302–4; Case, "Strategy and Tactics of Civil War Rams," 7; Merrill, *Battle Flags South,* 73–78.

6. THE SOUTHERN AMBUSH STRATEGY

1. Marszalek, *Commander of All Lincoln's Armies,* 126–27; Ambrose, *Halleck,* 56–57; Hess, *Civil War in the West,* 50–51, 60–61, 92–93.

2. Miller, *Vicksburg,* 92–93.

3. Sharpe, "Art of Supplying Armies in the Field," 63; Galuszka, "Logistics in Warfare," 24; Hess, *Civil War Logistics,* 73, 137; Mountcastle, *Punitive War,* 56–57; Hess, *Civil War in the West,* 34–51; Woodworth, *Nothing but Victory,* 261.

4. As explained in Appendix 2, I used the *ORN* to compile this database. The documents it contains certainly understate the number of attacks.

5. Henry W. Halleck to Ulysses S. Grant, Mar. 18, 1862, *ORA* 10(2):46 (quotation); Don Carlos Buell to Henry W. Halleck, Mar. 19, 1862, ibid., 48; Alexander M. Pennock to Charles H. Davis, June 10, 1862, *ORN* 23:147; Andrew H. Foote to Gideon Welles, June 13, 1862, ibid., 155; Hess, *Civil War Supply and Strategy,* 31.

6. William L. Shea, "1862: A Continual Thunder," in *Rugged and Sublime: The Civil War in Arkansas,* ed. Mark K. Christ (Fayetteville: University of Arkansas Press, 1994), 38–42; McPherson, *Battle Cry of Freedom,* 404–5.

7. Bearss, "White River Expedition," 306. Col. Charles Ellet of the Ram Fleet refused to send any boats with the expedition. See Charles Ellet Jr. to Ewin M. Stanton, June 15, 1862, *ORN* 23:209.

8. Baron Proctor to Sister, June 28, 1862, Baron Proctor Letters, Rauner Special Collections Library, Dartmouth College.

9. Wilson McGunnegle to Charles H. Davis, June 18, 1862, *ORN* 23:166; George Fitch to Isaac Quinby, June 17, 1862, *ORA* 13:103; Symmes Browne to Cornelia C. Gunn, Aug. 9, 1862, *FTFWN,* 95; Bearss, "White River Expedition," 315–18.

10. Symmes Browne to Fannie, June 18, 1862, *FTFWN,* 93; Symmes Browne to Cornelia C. Gunn, Aug. 9, 1862, ibid., 96 (first quotation); Pension Application of Peter Dugan, IC 3,378, RG 15, NARA (second quotation); "Account by a Participant," in Moore, *Rebellion Record,* 5:225 (third quotation); Wilson McGunnegle to Charles H. Davis, June 18, 1862, *ORN* 23:166; John W. Dunnington to Stephen Mallory, June 21, 1862, ibid., 200; Bearss, "White River Expedition," 323.

11. *Cincinnati Daily Commercial,* June 20, 1862, quoted in Slagle, *Ironclad Captain,* 246 (first and second quotations); "Account by a Participant," 5:225 (third quotation); Jonathan Duble to Charles H. Davis, June 18, 1862, *ORN* 23:168–69 (final quotation); Symmes Browne to Cornelia C. Gunn, Aug. 9, 1862, *FTFWN,* 97.

12. Symmes Browne to Fannie, June 18, 1862, *FTFWN,* 93; Symmes Browne to Cecilia C. Gunn, Aug. 9, 1862, ibid., 98 (quotation); Memorandum of Jonathan Duble, June 18, 1862, *ORN* 23:169; Bringhurst and Swigart, *Forty-Sixth Regiment Indiana Volunteer Infantry,* 35.

13. Bearss, "White River Expedition," 330.

14. Bearss, "White River Expedition," 335.

15. General Orders No. 17 (Confederate), June 17, 1862, *ORN* 23:186–87 (quotation); Neal and Kremm, *Lion of the South,* 127–29; Hess, *Civil War in the West,* 66–67; Sutherland, *Savage Conflict,* 66–67.

16. Frederic Davis to Parents, July 8, 1862, Davis Papers; Frederic Davis to Father, July 16, 1862, ibid. (quotations); James W. Shirk to Charles H. Davis, July 9, 1862, *ORN* 23:193; Bearss, "White River Expedition," 344–58.

17. Sutherland, *Savage Conflict,* ix–xi; Mackey, *Uncivil War,* 19–20; Mountcastle, *Punitive War,* 22–23.

18. Sutherland, *Savage Conflict,* 127; Mackey, *Uncivil War,* 6; Sheehan-Dean, *Calculus of Violence,* 73–75. Outside of Arkansas, it seems that the brown-water navy normally fought Confederate ambush squads and civilian guerrilla bands.

19. Gudmestad Irregular Combat Dataset; see Appendix 2 for a description of this source. In this chapter and for the rest of the book, these figures exclude the expeditions into the White River, Steele's Bayou, the Yazoo Delta, and the Red River as well as attacks against Confederate installations. I excluded this combat because I wanted a reasonably effective measure of attacks against the Union supply system.

20. David D. Porter to Gideon Welles, Feb. 23, 1863, *ORN* 24:42–43 (quotations); Hess, *Civil War in the West,* 178–83.

21. Samuel Cooper to [Maj.] Gen. Richard Taylor, July 30, 1862, *OR* 15:791 (first quotation); Ritter, "Third Battery of Maryland Artillery," 396–97 (second quotation); Ballard, *Vicksburg,* 69; Sutherland, *Savage Conflict,* 66–67; Mackey, *Uncivil War,* 31–33; Barton A. Myers, "Partisan Ranger Petitions and the Confederacy's Authorized *Petite Guerre* Service," in McKnight and Myers, *Guerrilla Hunters,* 26. Few Partisan Rangers carried out attacks on riverine supply lines.

22. Ritter, "Third Battery of Maryland Artillery," 393 (quotation), 398.

23. Ritter, "Third Battery of Maryland Artillery," 398 (quotation); Deck Log of USS *Tyler,* Sept. 5, 1862, RG 24–LB, NARA: Deck Log of the USS *Benton,* Aug. 23, 1862, ibid.; Egbert Thompson to Charles H. Davis, Oct. 3, 1862, *ORN* 23:391; Everson, "Service Afield and Afloat," 52; LeRoy Fitch to A. M. Pennock, Oct. 22, 1862, *ORN* 22:437; Scott Jordan to Judith Jordan, July 4, 1864, Jordan Letters; Colton Greene to Maj. H. Ewing, May 26, 1864, *ORA* 34(1):948–50.

24. Colton Greene to Maj. H. Ewing, June 8, 1864, *ORA* 1:950–51.

25. Worthington Diary, Dec. 6, 1862, May 2, 3, 6, Sept. 16, 1863, in Woods, *Delta Diary,* 47, 54, 59, 67; Sillers, "Incidents of the War in Bolivar County," 149–51; Anderson, *Campaigning with Parsons' Texas Cavalry Brigade,* 94, 107.

26. Ritter, "Third Battery of Maryland Artillery," 398 (first quotation); Henry Orr to Father, Apr. 4, 1863, in Anderson, *Campaigning with Parsons' Texas Cavalry Brigade,* 94 (second quotation); J. M. Wainwright to G. V. Fox, July 29, 1862, in Thompson and Wainwright, *Confidential Correspondence of Gustavus Vasa Fox,* 339 (third quotation); Le Roy Fitch to David D. Porter, Oct. 21, 1862, *ORN* 23:436 (final quotation); Deck Log of the USS *Curlew,* Oct. 6, 1864, RG 24–LB, NARA.

27. Ritter, "Third Battery of Maryland Artillery," 397 (quotations); Thomas O. Selfridge to David D. Porter, May 6, 1863, *ORN* 24:637–38.

28. Ritter, "Third Battery of Maryland Artillery," 398 (first three quotations); Thomas O. Selfridge to K. R. Breese, May 8, 1863, *ORN* 24:639 (final quotation).

29. Ritter, "Third Battery of Maryland Artillery," 397–98 (first quotation); Amanda Worthington Diary, Dec. 6, 1862, May 2, 3, 6, Sept. 16 (second quotation), 1863, in Woods, *Delta Diary,* 47, 54, 55, 67.

30. Ritter, "Third Battery of Maryland Artillery," 399.

31. Ritter, "Third Battery of Maryland Artillery," 400 (quotation); Thomas E. Smith to David D. Porter, Mar. 18, 1863, *ORN* 25:4; Aaron Brown to N. B. Baker, July 6, 1863, *ORA* 24(2):290.

32. Ritter, "Third Battery of Maryland Artillery," 400 (quotation); Thomas E. Smith to David D. Porter, Mar. 18, 1863, *ORN* 25:4.

33. Ritter, "Third Battery of Maryland Artillery," 400 (first and second quotations); J. G. Lauman to Henry Binmore, May 19, 1863, *ORA* 24(2):144 (final quotation).

34. Ezra Green to Mother, Oct. 19, 1862, Ezra Green Letters, FHS; Browning and Silver, *Environmental History of the Civil War,* 27–29; Bell, *Mosquito Soldiers,* 10–11.

35. Yost Diary, May 13, 1862 (first quotation); Frederic Davis to Brother, June 21, 1862, Davis Letters (second quotation). See also Symmes Browne to Fannie, May 29, 1862, *FTFWN,* 82; John Swift to Rosie Whiteside, June 8, 1863, in Swift, "Letter from a Sailor on a Tinclad," 56; Clapp Diary, Apr. 21, 1863; Lyons Journal, May 21, 1863; and Bell, *Mosquito Soldiers,* 32–33.

36. Frederic Davis to Father, n.d. [probably Apr. 22, 1862], Davis Letters (first quotation); Dickinson Diary, June 20, 1863 (second quotation); Pension Application of Francis James, WC 7,159, RG 15, NARA (final quotation); Symmes Browne to Fannie, May 31, 1863, *FTFWN,* 183; Daniel Kemp to Father and Mother, Feb. 21, 1863, Kemp Letters.

37. Browning and Silver, *Environmental History of the Civil War,* 18–19; Humphreys, *Marrow of Tragedy,* 98; Seth L. Phelps to Alexander Pennock, Aug. 5, 1862, *ORN* 23:285; Edward W. Goble to Joe Boyd, July 1, 1863, Joseph B. Boyd Papers, Cincinnati Museum Center; Clapp Diary, Jan. 6, 1863; Thomas Gibson to David D. Porter, Sept. 13, 1864, *ORN* 26:559; Kemp Reminiscences, 49, Kemp Letters.

38. Morrison Diary, Mar. 19, 20, 23 (first quotation), 1862; True, "Life aboard a Gunboat," 38 (second quotation); Browning and Silver, *Environmental History of the Civil War,* 29–30; Bell, *Mosquito Soldiers,* 6, 19.

39. Frederic R. Davis to Parents, May 6, 1862, Davis Letters (first quotation); Morrison Diary, July 16, 1862 (second quotation); Pension Application of Peter Dugan, IC 3,378, RG 15, NARA; A. M. Pennock to Gideon Welles, July 30, 1862, *ORN* 23:270; Charles H. Davis to David G. Farragut, July 20, 1862, ibid., 237; C. H. Beauchamp to Charles H. Davis, July 25, 1862, ibid., 240–41; Extract from Diary of Flag Officer Davis, U.S. Navy, July 31, 1862, ibid., 271; Bell, *Mosquito Soldiers,* 59–61, 65.

40. Pension Application of Ann Bradford Stokes, IC 17,834, RG 15, NARA; Pension Application of Gilbert Stokes, I 5,547, ibid.; Roca, "Presence and Precedents," 91–110; Moore, "Unique Journal of the USS Red Rover." Albert Cashier was a transgender person who served as a male Union soldier and earned a pension.

41. Gudmestad Sailor Dataset; Alexander M. Pennock to Gideon Welles, July 30, 1862, *ORN* 23:270. The numbers of new enlistees were 298 in February, 22 in May, and 33 in June.

42. Extract from Diary of Flag Officer Davis, U.S. Navy, July 31, 1862, *ORN* 23:270–72 (quotation); Bell, *Mosquito Soldiers,* 59–61, 65; Joiner, *Mr. Lincoln's Brown Water Navy,* 82; Miller, *Vicksburg,* 93–94, 164–65. Miller argues that the failure to take Vicksburg cost Davis his command.

7. THE MISSISSIPPI SQUADRON'S WAR OF EXHAUSTION

1. Seth L. Phelps to Andrew H. Foote, Nov. 19, 1861, *ORN* 22:435 (quotation); William Gwin to Andrew H. Foote, Feb. 23, 1862, ibid., 634. The monthly average of the brown-water navy's attacks against insurgents or suspected insurgents were: first phase, 1.5; second phase, 6.3; third phase, 7.9; and fourth phase, 5.3. Figures from Gudmestad Irregular Combat Dataset.

2. Gudmestad Irregular Combat Dataset. As with the Confederate attacks, these figures exclude the expeditions into the White River, Steele's Bayou, the Yazoo Delta, and the Red River as well as attacks against Confederate installations. The percentage of onshore raids in this phase was 49 percent.

3. Deck Log of the USS *Rattler,* May 8, 1863, RG 24–LB, NARA (quotation); Report of Joshua Bishop, May 10, 1863, *ORN* 24:640–41; J. N. Gilham and William Ferguson to Joshua Bishop, May 8, 1863, ibid., 641–2. Union records also refer to "Blandonia."

4. J. N. Gilham and William Ferguson to Joshua Bishop, May 8, 1863, *ORN* 24:641–2 (first quotation); Report of Joshua Bishop, May 10, 1863, ibid., 640–41 (second quotation).

5. Yost Diary, Aug. 30, 1862 (quotation); Park Journal, Aug. 23, 24, 1862, in Jeffrey, *Two Civil Wars,* 97–99. For more such incidents, see Park Journal, Aug. 10, 28, Sept. 2, 1862, ibid., 96, 99, 100; and Galligan Diary, Sept. 3, 1862.

6. Sillers, "Incidents of the War in Bolivar County," 150 (first quotation); Henry Orr to Pa and Ma, June 19, 1863, in Anderson, *Campaigning with Parsons' Texas Cavalry Brigade,* 109 (second quotation). Gunboats that walked their salvoes fired one broadside close to the river, fired their next round a bit farther inland, fired their third salvo still farther, and so forth.

7. George D. Wise to Andrew H. Foote, June 12, 1862, *ORN* 23:154.

8. Myron J. Smith puts the number of tinclads at seventy-two. It is unclear how he counts the large tinclads *Black Hawk* and *Ouachita* as well as the tinclads in the West Gulf Blockading Squadron (*Carrabassett, Elk, Glide II, Meteor, Rodolph,* and *Wave*). See Smith, *Tinclads,* 39, 341–44.

9. David D. Porter to Andrew H. Foote, Nov. 6, 1862, *ORN* 23:466 (quotation); General Order No. 65 of David D. Porter, June 19, 1863, *ORN* 25:187; Huling, *Reminiscences of Gunboat Life,* 6; Smith, *Tinclads,* 39–40.

10. Charles H. Davis to Gideon Welles, June 28, 1862, *ORN* 23:245–46. Average crew size is drawn from Gudmestad Sailor Dataset.

11. Information compiled from Silverstone, *Warships of the Civil War Navies.* The USS *Neosho* and USS *Osage* had two guns in a revolving turret in the bow, while the USS *Chickasaw,* USS *Kickapoo,* USS *Milwaukee,* and USS *Winnebago* had revolving turrets in the bow and stern (four guns

total). The *Ozark* had two guns in a revolving turret and four guns in the casemate. The other boats added in the second phase included a cottonclad, a ram, and three ironclads.

12. Symonds, *Lincoln and His Admirals,* 189 (first quotation); David D. Porter to Gustavus Vasa Fox, July 26, 1862, in Thompson and Wainwright, *Confidential Correspondence of Gustavus Vasa Fox,* 125 (second quotation); Glatthaar, "Lord High Admiral of the U.S. Navy," 8–9.

13. Memorandum regarding the operations of the Mississippi Squadron, n.d., *ORN* 23:396 (first quotation); David D. Porter, General Order No. 4, Oct. 18, 1862, ibid., 421 (remaining quotations).

14. David D. Porter to Thomas O. Selfridge, Jan. 17, 1863, *ORN* 24:173–74 (quotation); Foote, "Rethinking the Confederate Home Front," 446–65; Lang, *In the Wake of War,* 28; Grimsley, *Hard Hand of War,* 3, 162–70; Ash, *When the Yankees Came,* 76–107; Sheehan-Dean, *Calculus of Violence,* 240–56.

15. Sutherland, "Guerrillas," 147–48; William T. Sherman to Charles C. Walcutt, Sept. 24, 1862, *ORA* 17(2):235 (first quotation); David D. Porter to William T. Sherman, Nov. 24, 1862, *ORN* 23:500–502 (remaining quotations); Foster, *Sherman's Mississippi Campaign,* 6; Glatthaar, "Lord High Admiral of the U.S. Navy," 10–15.

16. True, "Life aboard a Gunboat," 37 (quotations); Kemp, "Civil War Reminiscences," 24; Yost Diary, Oct. 14–15, 1862; Scott Jordan to Judith Jordan, Sept. 12, 1864, Jordan Letters.

17. David D. Porter to Gideon Welles, Oct. 21, 1862, *ORN* 23:428 (first and second quotations); Mackey, *Uncivil War,* 55 (remaining quotations); Hearn, *Ellet's Brigade,* 144–47.

18. David D. Porter to Gideon Welles, Oct. 21, 1862, *ORN* 23:428; Hearn, *Ellet's Brigade,* 73–77, 148–49, 189; Joiner, *Mr. Lincoln's Brown Water Navy,* 95–96; McPherson, *War on the Waters,* 188.

19. Clarke, *Warfare along the Mississippi,* 60 (quotations); Hearn, *Ellet's Brigade,* 144–47; Mackey, *Uncivil War,* 57.

20. Clarke, *Warfare along the Mississippi,* 59; Hearn, *Ellet's Brigade,* 144–45. The new fighting vessels were the USS *Autocrat,* USS *B. J. Adams,* USS *Baltic,* USS *Diana,* and USS *John Raine.* The Mississippi Marine Brigade also had the *E. H. Fairchild,* a supply boat, and the *Woodford,* a hospital boat. I did not include any of the brigade's vessels or men in my calculations of fleet size or sailor demographics.

21. Hearn, *Ellet's Brigade,* 147–48, 184; Mackey, *Uncivil War,* 57.

22. David D. Porter to James Prichett, Jan. 26, 1863, *ORN* 24:198 (first quotation); Thomas Selfridge to Joshua Bishop, Mar. 12, 1863, ibid., 468 (second quotation); Thomas O. Selfridge to David D. Porter, Mar. 14, 1863, ibid., 472 (third quotation). Selfridge's order to Bishop is misdated as 1862. Greenville and Bolivar are about twenty-five miles apart.

23. Brady, *War upon the Land,* 10, 97–98. An agroecosystem is the new ecological system that humans create when they "draw sustenance or profit from nature through agriculture and animal husbandry." Ibid., 10.

24. "Map Showing the New Cut-Off Made by Lt. Com. T. O. Selfridge, U.S.N., 1863," *ORN* 24:551 (first quotation); David D. Porter to Gideon Welles, Apr. 16, 1863, ibid., 458–59 (second quotation); Still, *What Finer Tradition,* 77–79. The Mississippi's new course eventually washed Napoleon into the river.

25. David D. Porter, General Order No. 21, Dec. 2, 1862, *ORN* 23:528; David D. Porter to James M. Prichett, Feb. 10, 1863, *ORN* 24:339; David D. Porter to C. L. Stevenson, Mar. 2, 1863, ibid., 366 (first and second quotations); Notice of David D. Porter, Feb. 24, 1863, ibid., 365 (remaining quotations).

26. Gudmestad Sailor Dataset, N=1,375 (first phase overall), N=2,612 (second phase overall), N=1,314 (first phase Cincinnati), N=2,441 (second phase Cincinnati); David D. Porter to Gideon Welles, Mar. 14, 1863, *ORN* 24:472.

27. David D. Porter to Andrew H. Foote, Jan. 3, 1863, *ORN* 23:603 (quotation); David D. Porter to Andrew H. Foote, May 16, 1863, *ORN* 24:678; Elias Smith to Gideon Welles, Aug. 24, 1863, Box 459, Squadron Letters, NARA; Gudmestad Sailor Dataset; Foner, *Fiery Trial,* 175, 215–16, 252; Reidy, "Black Men in Navy Blue during the Civil War," 156–57; Ramold, *Slaves, Sailors, Citizens,* 38–49; Brewer, "African American Sailors and the Unvexing of the Mississippi," 279; Rodrigue, *Freedom's Crescent,* 77–79.

28. Muster Rolls of the USS *Carondelet* and USS *Great Western,* Dec. 31, 1862, RG 24–MRS, NARA; Taylor, *Embattled Freedom;* Manning, *Troubled Refuge.*

8. BLACK SAILORS

1. Brewer, "African American Sailors and the Unvexing of the Mississippi," 279–86; Bennett, *Union Jacks,* 155–81; Ramold, *Slaves, Sailors, Citizens;* Reidy, "Black Men in Navy Blue during the Civil War," 154–67; Bellamy, "Becoming Men"; Bruns, *Black Sailors in the Civil War.*

2. Gudmestad Sailor Dataset, N=2,905. Joseph P. Reidy estimates that 20 percent of sailors in the entire navy were Black men; Michael J. Bennett puts the number for the entire navy at 18,000 men, or 15 percent; and Charles Brewer writes that 19 percent of the Mississippi Squadron's sailors were Black men but has no citation for the figure. See Reidy, "Black Men in Blue," 156–58; Bennett, *Union Jacks,* 169; and Brewer, "African American Sailors and the Unvexing of the Mississippi," 284.

3. Gudmestad Sailor Dataset, N=154 (includes Black men who indicated residence in a slave state as well as those born in a slave state but who did not indicate a state of residence); Kaye, *Joining Places,* 4–5 (first quotation); Pension Application of John Washington, WC 16,672, RG 15, NARA (second quotation); Brewer, "African American Sailors and the Unvexing of the Mississippi," 284; Kynoch, "Terrible Dilemmas," 104–27. For a discussion of how enslaved people strategized their movement, see Cooper, "'Lord, Until I Reach My Home,'" 81–88.

4. Pension Application of George Washington, C 2,581,691, RG 15, NARA; Muster Roll of the USS *Myrtle,* Mar. 31, 1865, RG 24–MRS, ibid. The muster roll lists Washington's enlistment date as August 8, 1862, while the pension application puts it as one week later.

5. Affidavit of William Keys, n.d., Pension Application of Allen Turner, W 3,315, RG 15, NARA (quotation). According to another witness testimony included with Turner's pension application, two other enslaved men (Henry Robinson and William Jones) left the plantation at the same time. The statement implies that the men intended to enlist in the navy, but I could not find them in Gudmestad Sailor Dataset.

6. Reidy, "Black Men in Navy Blue during the Civil War," 162; Kynoch, "Terrible Dilemmas," 116–21; Lande, "Emancipating Masculinity," 551; Taylor, *Embattled Freedom,* 28. A handful of formerly enslaved men were able to satisfy these contradictory objectives by finding work for their wives aboard gunboats.

7. Pension Application of George Washington, XC 2,581,691 (first and second quotations), RG 15, NARA; Affidavit of John McCoy, n.d., Pension Application of Walter Perry, WC 12,967 (third

quotation), ibid.; Lyons Journal, May 17, 1863 (final quotation); Amanda Worthington Diary, Apr. 23, 1863, in Woods, *Delta Diary,* 50; Pension Application of Green Benton, I 30,796, RG 15, NARA; Taylor, *Embattled Freedom,* 53; Eggleston, *President Lincoln's Recruiter,* 38–39. For an overview of the army's recruiting efforts, see Rodrigue, *Freedom's Crescent,* 177–78.

8. Pension Application of Charles Olden, WC 10,121, RG 15, NARA; Muster Roll of the USS *Marmora,* Aug. 31, 1863, RG 24–MRS, ibid.

9. Henneberry Journal, Jan. 1, 1863 (first quotation); Elias Smith to Gideon Welles, Aug. 24, 1863, Box 459, Squadron Letters, NARA (second quotation); Bennett, *Union Jacks,* 170–73. Bennett is correct when he argues that there was a "social war" on board Civil War vessels between Black and white sailors. By contrast, Steven J. Ramold asserts that there is "very little evidence of widespread racism by white sailors" and a minimum amount of discrimination, while Micah Paul Bellamy writes that Black sailors experienced a level of equality because they had "mutual respect" with white sailors. See Bennett, *Union Jacks,* 155 (quotation), 160–74; Ramold, *Slaves, Sailors, Citizens,* 111–12; and Bellamy, "Becoming Men," 117, 139 (quotation).

10. True, "Life aboard a Gunboat," 38 (first three quotations); Coffinberry Diary, May 1, 1863, (fourth quotation); Roca, "Presence and Precedents," 108 (fifth quotation); Muster Roll of the USS *Conestoga,* Dec. 31, 1862, RG 24–MRS, NARA (final quotation); Elias Smith to Gideon Welles, Aug. 24, 1863, Box 459, Squadron Letters, ibid.; William Van Cleaf to Mother, Apr. 9, 1862, Van Cleaf Papers; Morrison Diary, June 5, 1862; Lyons Journal, May 4, 1863; Daniel Kemp to Sister, Mar. 16, 1863, Kemp Letters; Porter, *Incidents and Anecdotes,* 89; Critchell, *Recollections of a Fire Insurance Man,* 26.

11. General Order No. 76 of David D. Porter, July 26, 1863, *ORN* 25:327–28.

12. Daniel Francis Kemp to Sister, Mar. 16, 1863, Kemp Letters (first and second quotations); Coffinberry Diary, July 29, 1863 (final quotation); Muster Roll of the USS *Louisville,* Sept. 30, 1863, RG 24–MRS, NARA; Bennett, *Union Jacks,* 170–73.

13. Park Journal, Sept. 6, 1862, in Jeffrey, *Two Civil Wars,* 101–2 (first quotation); Galligan Diary, Sept. 6, 1862 (remaining quotations). Black's son may have enlisted. Hershel Black was a twelve-year-old first-class boy who enlisted at Baton Rouge on January 17, 1863. Muster Roll of the USS *Essex,* July 20, 1863, RG 24–MRS, NARA.

14. Gideon Welles to Charles H. Davis, Apr. 30, 1862, *ORN* 23:81 (first quotation); Charles H. Davis to Gideon Welles, Aug. 12, 1862, ibid., 29; General Order of Charles H. Davis, Sept. 23, 1862, ibid., 375 (second quotation).

15. Gudmestad Sailor Dataset, N=2,957 (ratings); Muster Roll of the USS *Black Hawk,* Dec. 31, 1864, RG 24–MRS, NARA; Gideon Welles to Charles H. Davis, Apr. 30, 1862, *ORN* 23:81; General Order No. 76 of David D. Porter, July 26, 1863, *ORN* 25:327–28; Dickinson Diary, Oct.1, 1863 (quotation); Tow, "Personification and Masculation of Samuel Henry Dalton," 46. The word "boy" encoded a racial caste system in the United States. Whites in the antebellum South forced enslaved people to address them as "mister" or "miss" while whites routinely used "boy," "uncle," or "aunt" when addressing Black people.

16. Pension Application of Nelson Bailey, IC 20,131, RG 15, NARA; Deck Log of the USS *Carondelet,* May 9, 1864, RG 24–LB, ibid.; Muster Roll of the USS *Carondelet,* Dec. 31, 1862, RG 24–MRS, ibid.; Reidy, *Illusions of Emancipation,* 210.

17. Pension Application of Charles Olden, WC 10,121, RG 15, NARA (quotations). For Black

men who reported a rupture or hernia, see Pension Applications of William Smith, WC 15,035; Jerry Perry, IC 21,937; Alfred Bell, IC 19,339; George Lindsay, IC 12,851; Julius Baker, I 43,257; and William Baker, IC 13,716, ibid.

18. Gudmestad Sailor Dataset, N=851; Foner, *Fiery Trial,* 253.

19. Pension Application of Robert White, WC 13,255, RG 15, NARA. In a heavily embroidered memoir penned after the war, Porter wrote that he encountered White on the Red River. He said White was holding a horse for a woman, and Porter told the man that he was a bigger coward than the horse. White supposedly said he was not frightened and that he had moral courage. White's muster roll from the USS *Black Hawk* tells a different story. He enlisted at Cairo, Illinois, on November 17, 1862, long before the Red River Expedition. After he mustered out of the navy, White worked for Porter for several years. See Porter, *Incidents and Anecdotes,* 243–44; and Muster Roll of the USS *Black Hawk,* Dec. 31, 1863, RG 24–MRS, NARA.

20. Scott Jordan to Brother, Aug. 12, 1863, Jordan Letters (first quotation); Scott Jordan to Judith Jordan, Dec. 6, 1863, ibid. (second quotation); Muster Roll of the USS *Carondelet,* Dec. 31, 1863, RG 24–MRS, NARA; William Bock to George Bock, Feb. 17, 1864, Bock Papers (remaining quotations).

21. "Walker, Robert, 'Our Bob,'" photograph, WICR 32071-L, Wilson's Creek National Battlefield, Republic, MO; Muster Roll of the USS *Pittsburg,* Jan. 1, 1864, RG 24–MRS, NARA. See also Seth Phelps's description of "my boy," who was a contraband from the Vicksburg area. Slagle, *Ironclad Captain,* 323.

22. William Bock to Mother, Mar. 5, 1864, Bock Papers (quotation); Pension Application of Ann Stokes, IC 17,834, RG 15, NARA; Muster Roll of the USS *Red Rover,* Oct. 1, 1863, RG 24–MRS, ibid.; Moore, "Unique Journal of the USS Red Rover"; Reidy, *Illusions of Emancipation,* 276. The *Red Rover* had a few other women on board: Mary Dalton was a laundress, Betsey Young was a nurse, and Sister Adela and Sister Veronica were each identified as a "Sister of Charity." I could not identify the husband of the chambermaid on the *Lexington.* There were two carpenter's mates on its muster rolls, and both were identified as white men. See also the testimony of Nancy Clay, who said that she was employed as a chambermaid on the *Conestoga* and then the *Black Hawk.* Pension Application of Fleming Randolph, WC 6,919, RG 15, NARA. She might have been married to Henry Clay, a sailor on the *Black Hawk.* Muster Roll of USS *Black Hawk,* Dec. 31, 1864, RG 24–MRS, ibid.

23. *Rules and Regulations for Vessels of the Light Draft Flotillas in the Mississippi Squadron* (n.p., n.d.), Robert Wilkinson Papers, Special Collections and University Libraries, Rutgers University, 5–6 (first quotation); General Order No. 76 of David D. Porter, July 26, 1863, *ORN* 25:327–28; Deck Log of the USS *Carondelet,* Mar. 17, 1864, RG 24–LB, NARA; Coffinberry Diary, May 1, 1863 (second and third quotations); True, "Life aboard a Gunboat," 38 (remaining quotations); Bennett, *Union Jacks,* 164–67. Steven J. Ramold argues that messes in the Mississippi Squadron were not segregated and that the navy was fluid with regards to race relations. Ramold, *Slaves, Sailors, Citizens,* 112–13.

24. Deck Log of the USS *Carondelet,* June 23, 25, 1863, RG 24–LB, NARA.

25. Muster Roll of the USS *New Era,* Apr. 1, 1863, RG 24–MRS, NARA; Lyons Journal, June 7, 1863 (quotation); Deck Log of the USS *Carondelet,* June 28, 1863, RG 24–LB, NARA.

26. Meacham, "Military and Naval Operations on the Mississippi," 394.

27. Reidy, *Illusions of Emancipation,* 213; William Bock to brother, Feb. 17, 1864, Bock Papers, (first and second quotations, emphasis in original); Dickinson Diary, June 10–11, 1863 (third, fourth, and fifth quotations); Clapp Diary, Mar. 11, 1863 (final quotation, emphasis in original); Bennett, *Union Jacks,* 162–63, 170–76; Reidy, "Black Men in Navy Blue during the Civil War," 159. In Dickinson's case the punishment of the white sailors who attacked the Black men was light. The captain put some of them in irons, but "the Admiral"—probably Porter—intervened, and the men were released the next day. A marlinspike was a straight metal tool, typically a foot long, that looked something like a large needle. Sailors used it to tie marine ropework.

28. General Order No. 76 of David D. Porter, July 26, 1863, *ORN* 25:327–28.

29. Pension Application of William Johnson, WC 14,611, RG 15, NARA; Park Journal, Aug. 5, 1862, in Jeffrey, *Two Civil Wars,* 93; Deck Log of the USS *Pittsburg,* July 10 (quotation), 31, 1863, RG 24–LB, NARA. See also Pension Application of Walter Perry, WC 12,967, RG 15, ibid: Pension Application of James Powell, WC 14,982, ibid.

30. Muster Roll of the USS *Cincinnati,* Dec. 31, 1862, RG 24–MRS, NARA; Muster Roll of the USS *Pittsburg,* Apr. 1, 1865, ibid. A Black man named Butler was a coxswain on the USS *Judge Torrence.* Pension Application of George Washington, C 2,581,691, RG 15, ibid.

31. Court-Martial of Richard H. Smith, case 3322, vol. 102, RG 125, NARA, available at Fold3.com; Court-Martial of Richard Cornelius, case 3320 (quotations), ibid.; Ramold, *Slaves, Sailors, Citizens,* 151–54. The navy probably did not execute Cornelius. Thirteen months after his conviction, he was still confined on the USS *Great Western.* Alexander M. Pennock to Gideon Welles, Oct. 30, 1864, Squadron Letters, NARA, available at Fold3.com.

32. Clegg and Weaver, "Counterfactual Reparations," 12; Carpenter, "Naval Service as Opportunity"; James Speed to Edwin Stanton, Apr. 12, 1865, RG 60, General Records of the Department of Justice, Entry 2—Opinions on Legal Questions, vol. 15, National Archives at College Park, MD; Axtell, "American Steamboat Gothic," 393.

9. THE YAZOO PASS AND STEELE'S BAYOU EXPEDITIONS

1. Grabau, *Ninety-Eight Days,* 21–22. Loess soil is powdery, rich in nutrients, and erodes easily.

2. Miller, *Vicksburg,* 214–20; Joiner, *Mr. Lincoln's Brown Water Navy,* 96–97.

3. Smith, *Early Struggles for Vicksburg,* 92–95; Glatthaar, "Lord High Admiral of the U.S. Navy," 6; Glatthaar, *Partners in Command,* 163–65.

4. David D. Porter to Henry Walke, Nov. 21, 1862, *ORN* 23:495–96.

5. Report of Henry Walke, Dec. 13, 1862, *ORN* 23:546 (quotation); Smith, *Fight for the Yazoo,* 49.

6. Perry, *Infernal Machines,* 33; Campbell, *Confederate Naval Forces on Western Waters,* 170–72; Bearss, *Hardluck Ironclad,* 96.

7. Smith, *Fight for the Yazoo,* 60–77.

8. Alford, "Destruction of the Cairo," 253 (quotation); Bearss, *Hardluck Ironclad,* 95–96; Smith, *Fight for the Yazoo,* 77.

9. Report of Henry Walke, Dec. 13, 1862, *ORN* 23:546–47 (quotations); Smith, *Fight for the Yazoo,* 77–78.

10. Alford, "Destruction of the Cairo," 253.

11. Smith, *Fight for the Yazoo,* 80–81. While the USS *Cincinnati* was sunk at the Battle of Plum Point earlier that year, Union engineers raised the vessel, and it later returned to service.

12. Brown, "Service in the Mississippi Squadron," 302 (quotation); Smith, *Early Struggles for Vicksburg,* 188–90.

13. Yost Diary, Dec. 12, 1862; Walter Fentress to Henry Walke, Dec. 13, 1863, *ORN* 23:548; Thomas O. Selfridge to Henry Walke, Dec. 13, 1862, ibid., 549; Bearss, *Hardluck Ironclad,* 99; Smith, *Fight for the Yazoo,* 81–83.

14. Yost Diary, Dec. 12, 1862.

15. Yost Diary, Dec. 12, 1862 (quotations); Walter Fentress to Henry Walke, Dec. 13, 1863, *ORN* 23:548; Thomas O. Selfridge to Henry Walke, Dec. 13, 1862, ibid., 549; William R. Hoel to Henry Walke, Dec. 13, 1862, ibid., 550–51; Robert Getty to Henry Walke, Dec. 13, 1862, ibid., 552–53; Bearss, *Hardluck Ironclad,* 99; Smith, *Fight for the Yazoo,* 81–83.

16. Smith, *Fight for the Yazoo,* 84–85; Tomblin, *Civil War on the Mississippi,* 185–86.

17. Miller, *Vicksburg,* 236 (quotation), 237–38; Orders of William T. Sherman, Dec. 20, 1862, *ORN* 23:559–61.

18. Joiner, *Mr. Lincoln's Brown Water Navy,* 99; Smith, *Early Struggles for Vicksburg,* 246–61.

19. Smith, *Early Struggles for Vicksburg,* 425; Miller, *Vicksburg,* 257–58, 263–66.

20. Porter, *Incidents and Anecdotes,* 129 (quotation); Joiner, *Mr. Lincoln's Brown Water Navy,* 104; Glatthaar, *Partners in Command,* 169–70; Sesser, "Fort Hindman," last updated June 15, 2023.

21. Hess, *German in the Yankee Fatherland,* 54 (first and second quotations); Kemp to Father and Mother, Jan. 16, 1863, Kemp Letters (third quotation); Detailed Report of Acting Rear Admiral Porter, Jan. 11, 1863, *ORN* 24:107.

22. Daniel Kemp to Grandson, n.d., Kemp Letters; W. H. Michael, "Mississippi Flotilla," *National Tribune,* June 21, 1888 (quotation).

23. Miller, *Vicksburg,* 275.

24. Joiner, *Mr. Lincoln's Brown Water Navy,* 123–25; Miller, *Vicksburg,* 275.

25. Joiner, *Mr. Lincoln's Brown Water Navy,* 125; Smith, *Fight for the Yazoo,* 222.

26. Morrison Diary, Jan. 10, 1863 (quotation); Smith, *Joseph Brown and His Civil War Ironclads,* 71–78.

27. Report of George W. Brown, Feb. 4, 1863, *ORN* 24:249 (first and second quotations); James H. Wilson to John A. Rawlins, *ORA* 24(1):373 (remaining quotations); Yost Diary, Feb. 3, 1863; Smith, *Fight for the Yazoo,* 149–50; Ballard, *Vicksburg,* 175–76.

28. Byers, *With Fire and Sword,* 50–51 (first quotation); Clapp Diary, Feb. 22, 1863 (second quotation); Ballard, *Vicksburg,* 176.

29. Clapp Diary, Feb. 25, 1863 (quotations, emphases in original); Miller, *Vicksburg,* 284; Smith, *Fight for the Yazoo,* 183. A davit is a crane used to raise and lower smaller boats from or into the water.

30. Frederic Davis to Parents, Mar. 2, 1863, Davis Letters.

31. Yost Diary, Mar. 9, 1863 (first quotation); Frederic R. Davis to Parents, Mar. 12, 1863, Davis Letters (second quotation); Deck Log of the USS *Chillicothe,* Feb. 28, 1863, RG 24–LB, NARA; Deck Log of USS *Rattler,* Mar. 5, 1863, ibid.; Smith, *Fight for the Yazoo,* 193.

32. Yost Diary, Mar. 11, 1863.

33. Ballard, *Vicksburg,* 177–79; Miller, *Vicksburg,* 285–86; Smith, *Bayou Battles for Vicksburg,* 182–84.

34. Deck Log of the USS *Chillicothe,* Mar. 11, 1863, RG 24–LB, NARA (first quotation); Wat-

son Smith to David D. Porter, Mar. 11, 1863, *ORN* 24:268–70 (second quotation); James H. Wilson to John Rawlins, Mar. 15, 1863, *ORA* 24(1):380 (third quotation); Frederic Davis to Parents, Mar. 12, 1863, Davis Letters; Report of James P. Foster, Mar. 12, 1862, *ORN* 24:270–73; Ballard, *Vicksburg,* 182; West, "Gunboats in the Swamps," 162–63.

35. James P. Foster to David D. Porter, Apr. 13, 1863, *ORN* 24:273 (first quotation); James H. Wilson to John Rawlins, Mar. 16, 1863, *ORA* 24(1):383 (second quotation); Smith, *Fight for the Yazoo,* 217; Smith, *Joseph Brown and His Civil War Ironclads,* 71–78.

36. William Loring quoted in Smith, *Fight for the Yazoo,* 209 (quotation); Pension Application of James Duke, IC 22,520, RG 15, NARA; James P. Foster to Watson Smith, Mar. 14, 1863, *ORN* 24:275–76; John G. Walker to David D. Porter, Mar. 13, 1863, ibid., 275; Watson Smith to David D. Porter, Mar. 13, 1863, ibid., 273–74; Miller Diary, Mar. 13, 1863; Hess, *German in the Yankee Fatherland,* 78; Deck Log of the USS *Chillicothe,* Mar. 13, 1863, RG 24–LB, NARA.

37. J. H. Wilson to John A. Rawlins, Mar. 15, 1863, *ORA* 24(1):380 (quotations); West, "Gunboats in the Swamp," 161.

38. Watson D. Smith to David D. Porter, Mar. 17, *ORN* 24:280–81; Elias Smith to Gideon Welles, Aug. 24, 1863, Box 459, Squadron Letters, NARA (first quotation); Morrison Diary, Mar. 27, 1863 (second quotation).

39. Smith, *Fight for the Yazoo,* 240–41; Miller, *Vicksburg,* 288–91.

40. *New York Times,* Apr. 4, 1863 (first quotation); *National Tribune,* June 18, 1888 (second quotation); Daniel Francis Kemp to Sister, Mar. 16, 1863, Kemp Letters (final quotation); Smith, *Fight for the Yazoo,* 243–44.

41. David D. Porter to Gideon Welles, Mar. 26, 1863, *ORN* 24:474 (first quotation); Porter, *Incidents and Anecdotes,* 157 (remaining quotations); *National Tribune,* June 18, 1888.

42. *National Tribune,* June 18, 1888 (quotations); Porter, *Incidents and Anecdotes,* 148; Smith, *Fight for the Yazoo,* 255–56; Miller, *Vicksburg,* 293.

43. *National Tribune,* June 18, 1888.

44. Porter, *Incidents and Anecdotes,* 152 (quotation); *National Tribune,* June 18, 1888.

45. David D. Porter to William T. Sherman, Mar. 19, 1863, *ORN* 24:486 (first quotation); William T. Sherman to David D. Porter, Mar. 20, 1863, ibid., 487–88 (remaining quotations).

46. *National Tribune,* June 18, 1888 (first quotation); Report of David D. Porter, Mar. 26, 1863, *ORN* 24:476 (final quotation); Porter, *Incidents and Anecdotes,* 159.

47. Daniel Francis Kemp to Sister, Mar. 24, 1863, Kemp Letters (quotation); *National Tribune,* June 18, 1888; Report of Samuel W. Ferguson, Mar. 30, 1863, *ORA* 24(1):466; Miller, *Vicksburg,* 294–95; Smith, *Bayou Battles for Vicksburg,* 245–47.

48. Porter, *Incidents and Anecdotes,* 161 (quotation); Report of Col. Giles A. Smith, Mar. 28, 1863, *ORA* 24(1):439; Smith, *Fight for the Yazoo,* 267.

49. Daniel Francis Kemp to Sister, Mar. 24, 1863, Kemp Letters (quotation); *New York Times,* Apr. 4, 1863; Porter, *Incidents and Anecdotes,* 167.

50. Smith, *Fight for the Yazoo,* 268.

51. General Order, Mar. 21, 1863, *ORN* 24:488–89.

52. Detailed Report of Acting Rear Admiral David D. Porter, Mar. 26, 1863, *ORN* 24:477.

53. Report of Col. Giles A. Smith, Mar. 28, 1863, *ORA* 24(1):440 (first quotation); Detailed Report of Acting Rear Admiral David D. Porter, Mar. 26, 1863, *ORN* 24:477 (second quotation).

54. *National Tribune,* June 28, 1888 (quotation); Miller, *Vicksburg,* 297; Glatthaar, *Partners in Command,* 171–73.

55. Detailed Report of Acting Rear Admiral David D. Porter, Mar. 26, 1863, *ORN* 24:478 (quotation); Daniel Frances Kemp to Sister, Mar. 16, 1863, Kemp Letters; Morrison Diary, Mar. 27, 1863.

10. CAPTURING VICKSBURG

1. Porter to Welles, Feb. 2, 1863, *ORN* 24:218.

2. Miller, *Vicksburg,* 302.

3. Porter to Welles, Feb. 2, 1863, *ORN* 24:217 (quotation); Charles Rivers Ellet to David Porter, Feb. 2, 1863, ibid., 219–20.

4. David D. Porter to Charles Rivers Ellet, Feb. 2, 1863, *ORN* 24:218 (first quotation); Report of Acting Rear Admiral David D. Porter, Feb. 15, 1863, ibid., 222 (second quotation); Charles Rivers Ellet to David D. Porter, Feb. 5, 1863, ibid., 224; Charles Rivers Ellet to David D. Porter, Feb. 21, 1863, ibid., 384–85; David D. Porter to Gideon Welles, Feb. 22, 1863, ibid., 382; Miller, *Vicksburg,* 302–3.

5. George Brown to David Porter, Feb. 18, 1863, *ORN* 24:377–78.

6. J. L. Brent to E. Surget, Feb. 25, 1863, *ORN* 24:404 (quotation); George Brown to Gideon Welles, May 28, 1863, ibid., 380–81.

7. Gideon Welles to David D. Porter, Mar. 2, 1863, *ORN* 24:388.

8. Porter, *Incidents and Anecdotes,* 134 (quotation); Miller, *Vicksburg,* 304–5.

9. Miller, *Vicksburg,* 305.

10. Miller, *Vicksburg,* 306.

11. Henry Walke to Alfred W. Ellet, Mar. 24, 1863, *ORN* 20:16.

12. Charles Rivers Ellet to Alfred W. Ellet, Mar. 25, 1863, *ORN* 20:19–20 (quotations); Lyons Journal, Mar. 25, 1863.

13. Alfred W. Ellet to Charles R. Ellet, Mar. 25, 1863, *ORN* 20:20–22.

14. David Farragut to David D. Porter, Mar. 25, 1863, *ORN* 20:23–25.

15. David D. Porter to David G. Farragut, Mar. 26, 1863, *ORN* 20:11 (quotation); Miller, *Vicksburg,* 307.

16. David D. Porter to Gideon Welles, Mar. 26, 1863, *ORN* 24:479 (quotation); Miller, *Vicksburg,* 328.

17. Ulysses S. Grant to David D. Porter, Mar. 29, 1863, *ORN* 24:517 (quotations); Glatthaar, *Partners in Command,* 173–74.

18. David D. Porter to Ulysses S. Grant, Mar. 29, 1863, *ORN* 24:518; Glatthaar, "Lord High Admiral of the U.S. Navy," 14.

19. Smith, *Fight for the Yazoo,* 299.

20. Morrison Diary, Apr. 13–14, 1863 (quotations); Deck Log of the USS *Pittsburg,* Apr. 15, 1863, RG 24–LB, NARA; Lyons Journal, Apr. 16, 1863; *New York Times,* May 17, 1863.

21. James W. Shirk to David D. Porter, Apr. 17, 1863, *ORN* 24:563 (quotation); General Order of Acting Rear Admiral David D. Porter, Apr. 10, 1863, ibid., 554–55.

22. Joseph P. Boyd to Joe Boyd, Apr. 19. 1863, Joseph B. Boyd Papers (quotations), Cincinnati Museum Center; Miller, *Vicksburg,* 346.

23. Deck Log of the USS *Mound City,* Apr. 16, 1863, RG 24–LB, NARA (first quotation); Coffinberry Diary, Apr. 16, 1863 (second quotation); *New York Times,* May 17, 1863 (third quotation); Deck Log of the USS *Benton,* Apr. 16, 1863, RG 24–LB, NARA (final quotation).

24. Coffinberry Diary, Apr. 16, 1863 (first and second quotations); Braudaway, "Texan Records the Civil War Siege of Vicksburg, Mississippi," 100 (third quotation); Byron Wilson to David D. Porter, Apr. 17, 1863, *ORN* 24:559–60 (final quotation); Report of David D. Porter, Oct. 1862–May 1863, *ORN* 23:409.

25. Deck Log of the USS *Benton,* Apr. 16, 1863, RG 24–LB, NARA (first quotation); James Greer to David D. Porter, Apr. 17, 1863, *ORN* 24:555–56 (second quotation); Newton Bates to James A. Greer, Apr. 17, 1863, ibid., 556 (third quotation). Wright wrote of the run past Vicksburg on April 16, even though it stretched into a new day. It is possible that the current carried the *Benton* toward the eastern shore, and the pilot had no choice but to follow the main channel.

26. Lyons Journal, Apr. 16, 1863 (first and second quotations); *New York Times,* May 17, 1863 (final quotation).

27. Coffinberry Diary, Apr. 16, 1863 (first quotation); John McLeod Murphy to David D. Porter, Apr. 17, 1863, *ORN* 24:561 (second quotation); Selim E. Woodworth to David D. Porter, Apr. 17, 1863, ibid., 559 (remaining quotations); Henry A. Walke to David D. Porter, Apr. 17, 1863, ibid., 577.

28. Coffinberry Diary, Apr. 16, 1863 (quotations); Hamper, "War on the River," 25; E. K. Owen to David D. Porter, Apr. 17, 1863, *ORN* 24:559.

29. Morrison Diary, Apr. 17, 1863 (first three quotations); Deck Log of the USS *Mound City,* Apr. 16, 1863, RG 24–LB, NARA (final quotation); Byron Wilson to David D. Porter, Apr. 17, 1863, *ORN* 24:559–60; William R. Hoel to David D. Porter, Apr. 17, 1863, ibid., 560.

30. Porter, *Incidents and Anecdotes,* 176 (first quotation); James Shirk to David D. Porter, Apr. 17, 1863, *ORN* 24:562–63 (remaining quotations).

31. Porter, *Incidents and Anecdotes,* 177.

32. *New York Times,* May 17, 1863 (first quotation); Coffinberry Diary, Apr. 16, 1863 (second quotation); Deck Logs of the USS *Lafayette* and USS *Louisville,* Apr. 17, 1863, RG 24–LB, NARA; Miller, *Vicksburg,* 149–50.

33. Porter, *Incidents and Anecdotes,* 178.

34. Clapp Diary, May 5, 1863; Milligan, *Gunboats down the Mississippi,* 152; Miller, *Vicksburg,* 361.

35. Morrison Diary, Apr. 24, 1863 (quotation); Miller, *Vicksburg,* 362.

36. Clapp Diary, transcribed letter of Dan Kennedy, May 1, 1863 (first quotation); Scott Jordan to Judith Jordan, May 10, 1863, Jordan Letters (second quotation); Byron Wilson to David D. Porter, Apr. 30, 1863, *ORN* 24:618; E. K. Owen to David D. Porter, Apr. 30, 1863, ibid., 618–19; John McLeod Murphy to David D. Porter, May 2, 1863, ibid., 625–26.

37. Detailed Report of David D. Porter, Apr. 29, 1863, *ORN* 24:610–12 (first quotation); Morrison Diary, Apr. 29, 1863 (second quotation); Deck Log of the USS *Benton,* Apr. 29, 1863, RG 24–LB, NARA; James Greer to David D. Porter, Apr. 30, 1863, *ORN* 24:613.

38. Detailed Report of David D. Porter, Apr. 29, 1863, *ORN* 24:610–12 (first quotation); Deck Log of the USS *Tuscumbia,* Apr. 29, 1863, RG 24–LB, NARA (second quotation); James Shirk to David D. Porter, Apr. 30, 1863, *ORN* 24:620 (final quotation).

39. Morrison Diary, Apr. 29, 1863 (first quotation); Clapp Diary, Apr. 27, 1863 (second quotation).

40. Morrison Diary, Apr. 29, 1863 (first quotation); Bevier, *First and Second Missouri Confederate Brigades,* 412 (second quotation).

41. Fred Grant quoted in Ballard, *Vicksburg,* 219. Porter did not mention the wound in his official report or in his memoirs.

42. James Greet to David D. Porter, Apr. 30, 1863, *ORN* 24:615; Miller, *Vicksburg,* 363–64.

43. Lyons Journal, Apr. 30, 1863 (first quotation); Coffinberry Diary, Apr. 30, 1863 (second quotation); Miller, *Vicksburg,* 364–65.

44. Morrison Diary, May 3, 1863.

45. Kidder R. Breese to David D. Porter, May 2, 1863, *ORN* 24:589–91.

46. James M. Pritchett to Kidder R. Breese, May 2, 1863, *ORN* 24:592 (first quotation); Braudaway, "Texan Records the Civil War Siege of Vicksburg," 102 (remaining quotations); Frank M. Ramsay to Kidder R. Breese, May 3, 1863, *ORN* 24:593.

47. Clapp Diary, May 7, 1863 (first quotation); David D. Porter to Kidder R. Breese, May 14, 1863, *ORN* 24:596 (remaining quotations).

48. John C. Pemberton to James Chalmers, Apr. 18, 1863, *ORN* 24:716 (first quotation); James A. Greer to David D. Porter, July 28, 1863, *ORN* 25:33 (second quotation).

49. Scott Jordan to Brother, May 28, 1863, Jordan Letters (quotation); Deck Logs of USS *Louisville* and USS *Mound City,* May 22, 1863, RG 24–LB, NARA; Pension Application of John West, IC 7,422, RG 15, ibid.

50. Kemp Reminiscences (quotations); George M. Bache to David D. Porter, May 27, 1863, *ORN* 25:38–39; Bache to Porter, May 29, 1863, ibid., 42–43; Smith, *Siege of Vicksburg,* 93–94.

51. George M. Bache to David D. Porter, May 27, 1863, *ORN* 25:38–39; Bache to Porter, May 29, 1863, ibid., 42–43; Kemp Reminiscences; "Frank Bois," Congressional Medal of Honor Society, https://www.cmohs.org/recipients/frank-bois. Union engineers raised the *Cincinnati* in August 1863, and the navy put it back into service.

52. George M. Bache to David D. Porter, May 27, 1863, *ORN* 25:38–39; Bache to Porter, May 29, 1863, ibid., 42–43; Beyer and Keydel, *Deeds of Valor,* 2:46–49; "Thomas E Corcoran," Congressional Medal of Honor Society, https://www.cmohs.org/recipients/thomas-e-corcoran; "Henry Dow," ibid., https://www.cmohs.org/recipients/henry-dow; "Thomas Jenkins," ibid., https://www.cmohs.org/recipients/thomas-jenkins; "Martin McHugh," ibid., https://www.cmohs.org/recipients/martin-mchugh; "Thomas Hamilton," ibid., https://www.cmohs.org/recipients/thomas-w-hamilton.

53. Porter, *Incidents and Anecdotes,* 201 (quotation); Milligan, *Gunboats down the Mississippi,* 175–76; Miller, *Vicksburg,* 476–78.

54. Smith, *Siege of Vicksburg,* 533–34.

55. Grant, *Personal Memoirs,* 574 (quotation); Milligan, *Gunboats down the Mississippi,* 179–80.

56. Abraham Lincoln to James C. Conkling, Aug. 26, 1863, in Roe, *Speeches and Letters of Abraham Lincoln,* 210.

11. THE PATROL SYSTEM

1. Thomas O. Selfridge to Kidder R. Breese, May 8, 1863, *ORN* 24:639.

2. LeRoy Fitch to David D. Porter, Mar. 17, 1863, *ORN* 24:56–58 (quotation); Fitch to Porter, Mar. 18, 1863, ibid., 61; Hess, *Civil War in the West,* 178–80.

3. General Order No. 57, May 20, 1863, *ORN* 25:124; General Order No. 80, Aug. 19, ibid., 378–79; General Order No. 84, Aug. 20, 1863, ibid., 377; General Order No. 141, Dec. 19, 1863, ibid., 642–43; General Order No. 195, May 20, 1864, *ORN* 26:317–18; General Order No. 199, May 27, 1864; ibid., 329–30; Joiner, *Mr. Lincoln's Brown Water Navy,* 171–73; McPherson, *War on the Waters,* 187; Smith, *After Vicksburg,* 130.

4. General Order No. 84, Aug. 20, 1863, *ORN* 25:377 (quotation); David D. Porter to Joshua Bishop, Dec. 19, 1863, ibid., 640; David D Porter to Gideon Welles, Dec. 26, 1863, ibid., 661; John Swift to Rosie Whiteside, May [?], 1864, in Swift, "Letters from a Sailor on a Tinclad," 54; Patrick, "Fighting Sailor on the Western Rivers," 274; Huling, *Reminiscences of Gunboat Life,* 9.

5. David D Porter to Gideon Welles, Dec. 26, 1863, *ORN* 25:661. Porter's critics have complained that the surge in construction was "the most costly luxury the Government had ever been compelled to indulge in." Adams, *High Old Salts,* 177. Figures based on an examination of Silverstone, *Warships of the Civil War Navies.*

6. David D. Porter to Andrew H. Foote, May 16, 1863, *ORN* 24:678; Gudmestad Sailor Dataset, N=2,612 (second phase), N=4,197 (third phase); Muster Roll of the USS *Conestoga,* Dec. 31, 1863, RG 24–MRS, NARA; Marvel, *Lincoln's Mercenaries,* 179–81, 195, 208–13.

7. Gudmestad Irregular Combat Dataset.

8. David D. Porter to Thomas H. Yeatman, Dec. 3, 1862, *ORN* 23:528 (first quotation); David D. Porter to James M. Prichett, Feb. 10, 1863, *ORN* 24:339 (second quotation); Yost Diary, Feb. 16, 1863 (third quotation).

9. Gudmestad Irregular Combat Dataset. If attacks described in sailors' letters and diaries are included, there were at least twenty-four *more* incidents of food confiscation in phase three.

10. John A. Ellet to Alfred W. Ellet, May 20, 1863, *ORN* 20:41; Miller Diary, Jan. 20, 1864; Symmes Browne to Fannie, Sept. 1, 1863, *FTFWN,* 215 (quotation).

11. David D. Porter, General Order No. 21, Dec. 2, 1862, *ORN* 23:528 (quotations); David D. Porter to Joshua Bishop, Dec. 3, 1862, ibid., 528; David D. Porter to Thomas H. Yeatman, Dec. 3, 1862, ibid.; Order of David D. Porter, Dec. 10, 1862, ibid., 620; General Order No. 109, Oct. 14, 1863, *ORN* 25:501–2; Surdam, "Traders or Traitors," 305; O'Connor, "Lincoln and the Cotton Trade," 26–27.

12. William C. Hanford to Alexander M. Pennock, Feb. 18, 1863, *ORN* 24:336 (first quotation); A. F. O'Neil Diary, Oct. 8, 11, 1863, Charles O'Neil Papers, Library of Congress (remaining quotations).

13. David D. Porter to Gideon Welles, Nov. 12, 1863, *ORN* 25:536 (first quotation); David D. Porter to Gideon Welles, Oct. 27, 1862, *ORN* 23:452; David D. Porter to Edward Canby, June 9, 1864, *ORN* 26:377; John G. Mitchell to Frank Sherman, Nov. 17, 1864, ibid., 732; David D. Porter to William T. Sherman, Oct. 29, 1863, *ORN* 25:521; William Bock to Father, Apr. 19, 1864, Bock Papers (second quotation).

14. Smith, *After Vicksburg,* 132–34; Doyle, "Civil War in Greenville Bends," 146–47.

15. *Chicago Daily Tribune,* Nov. 4, 1863, quoted in Smith, *After Vicksburg,* 137; Symonds, *Civil War at Sea,* 75–76.

16. *Memphis Daily Appeal,* Nov. 17, 1863, 2 (first quotation); *New York Daily Tribune,* Dec. 26, 1864, 5 (remaining quotations); Smith, *After Vicksburg,* 138.

17. Smith, *After Vicksburg,* 69–72.

18. Dickinson Diary, Feb. 19–Mar. 30, 1864.

19. Mackey, *Uncivil War,* 134–35, 153–54; Smith, *After Vicksburg,* 56–60.

20. George Vance to [unreadable], Mar. 28, 1864, Samuel C. Vance Papers, Indiana Historical Society (quotations); Deck Log of the USS *Peosta,* Mar. 25, 1864, RG 24–LB, NARA; James W. Shirk to David D. Porter, Mar. 28, 1864, *ORN* 26:198; McPherson, *War on the Waters,* 190.

21. Daniel Francis Kemp to Sister, Mar. 16, 1863, Kemp Letters (first quotation); Frances Murdoch Journal, May 19, 1863, Special Collections, Virginia Tech University (second quotation); Sillers, "Incidents of the War in Bolivar County," 148; Lisa Tendrich Frank, "The Union War on Women," in McKnight and Myers, *Guerrilla Hunters,* 174–77. Frank has argued that Sherman's men stole or destroyed elite women's personal possessions because they recognized that such women were "ardent and active Confederates." See also Frank, *Civilian War,* 17. I group pillaging and plundering together and define them as the destruction or confiscation of civilian property that has no clear military purpose or use.

22. Park Journal, Aug. 23–24, 1862, in Jeffrey, *Two Civil Wars,* 97–98 (first quotation); Scott Jordan to Judith Jordan, Sept. 6, 1864, Jordan Letters (remaining quotations, emphasis in original).

23. Symmes Browne to Fannie, Feb. 1, 1863, *FTFWN,* 140 (first quotation); Morrison Diary, May 3, 1863 (second quotation); Thompson, "Escaping the Mechanism," 362–63.

24. Symmes Browne to Fannie, Feb. 16, 1863, *FTFWN,* 145 (quotation); Anderson, *Campaigning with Parsons' Texas Cavalry Brigade,* 54; Sillers, "Incidents of the War in Bolivar County," 151–52. See also LeRoy Fitch to David D. Porter, Apr. 2, 1863, *ORN* 24:64; Deck Log of the USS *Curlew,* Apr. 26, 1863, RG 24–LB, NARA; and Deck Log of the USS *Mound City,* May 10, 1864, ibid.

25. Thomas E. Smith to Wife, Dec. 2, 1863, Thomas E. Smith Letters, FHS (first quotation); Kemp Reminiscences, 52 (second quotation). See also Deck Log of the USS *Mound City,* May 10, 1864, RG 24–LB, NARA; LeRoy Fitch to David D. Porter, Apr. 2, 1863, *ORN* 24:64; and Scott Jordan to Judith Jordan, Sept. 18, 1864, Jordan Letters.

26. Muster Roll of the USS *Romeo,* Mar. 15, 1863, RG 24–MRS, NARA; Amanda Worthington Diary, July 25, Sept. 16 (quotations), 1863, in Woods, *Delta Diary,* 65, 67.

27. Porter to Major General Stevenson, Mar. 2, 1863, *ORN* 24:366; Nelson, *Ruin Nation,* 78 (quotation).

28. General Order No. 44, Apr. 10, 1863, *ORN* 24:539.

29. C. J. Field to David D. Porter, Dec. 26, 1863, *ORN* 25:698; John Routh to David D. Porter, Aug. 7, 1863, ibid., 696; A. T. Bowie to Thomas E. G. Ransom, Aug. 4, 1863, *ORA* 30(3):25 (quotation); Hearn, *Ellet's Brigade,* 179–256; Mountcastle, *Punitive War,* 79–83.

30. Gideon Welles to David D. Porter, Jan. 11, 1864, *ORN* 25:682 (first three quotations); Porter to Welles, Jan. 17, 1864, ibid., 693 (fourth quotation); Porter to Welles, May 11, 1864, *ORN* 26:293 (final quotation).

31. Sheehan-Dean, *Calculus of Violence,* 6–8.

32. Dickinson Diary, Dec. 28, 1863 (first quotation), Jan. 8 (second quotation), Mar. 8, 1864; Sheehan-Dean, *Calculus of Violence,* 81 (third quotation), 180–86; Herbert Saunders to Mother, Jan. 20, 1864, in Huch, "Civil War Letters of Herbert Saunders," 18; James P. Foster to David D. Porter, June 8, 1864, *ORN* 26:374; John Swift to Rosie Swift, n.d. [summer of 1863], in Swift, "Letters from a Sailor on a Tinclad," 49.

33. Court-Martial of B. J. Donahoe, case 3437, vol. 108, RG 125, NARA, available at Fold3.com; Court-Martial of Thomas D. Rice, case 3438, ibid.; Court-Marital of Edward Merriman, case 3439,

ibid.; Court-Martial of S. B. Coleman, case 3440, ibid.; Court-Martial of F. T. Coleman, case 3441, ibid.

34. Court-Martial of S. B. Coleman, case 3440, vol. 108, RG 125, NARA, available at Fold3.com (quotations); Court-Martial of F. T. Coleman, case 3441, ibid.

35. General Order No. 158, Jan. 18, 1864, *ORN* 25:701–2 (quotations); Report of Acting Rear Admiral S. P. Lee, Dec. 3, 1864, *ORN* 26:749; Report of Acting Rear Admiral S. P. Lee, Aug. 12, 1865, *ORN* 27:340.

36. Deck Log of the USS *Rattler,* Sept. 13, 1864, RG 24–LB, NARA; James A. Greer to David D. Porter, Sept. 14, 1863, *ORN* 25:405–9; Championhilz, "Well Do I Remember That Exciting Day," accessed Nov. 20, 2022 (quotation).

37. Gudmestad Irregular Combat Dataset. For a summary of the different perspectives on the efficacy of the patrol system, see Smith, *After Vicksburg,* 47.

12. MILITARY EMANCIPATION

1. The army's role in military emancipation in the lower Mississippi Valley is well documented, but historians have not studied the Mississippi Squadron's actions. See Manning, *Troubled Refuge;* Reidy, *Illusions of Emancipation;* Rodrigue, *Freedom's Crescent;* Taylor, *Embattled Freedom;* and Teters, *Practical Liberators.*

2. Gudmestad, *Steamboats and the Rise of the Cotton Kingdom,* 30–31, 38–39, 49; Coffin, *Reminiscences,* 147–50; Salafia, *Slavery's Borderland,* 168–70; Miles, "Of Waterways and Runaways"; Cecelski, *Waterman's Song.* My thanks to Joe Beilein for the insights in this paragraph.

3. Manning, *Troubled Refuge,* 99; Charles H. Davis to N. C. Bryant, July 13, 1862, *ORN* 23:257 (first and second quotations); Galligan Diary, July 25 (final quotation), Sept. 2, 1862; Muster Roll of the USS *Essex,* July 20, 1863, RG 24–MRS, NARA.

4. James Shirk to David D. Porter, Nov. 27, 1862, *ORN* 23:509 (quotation); Clapp Diary, Dec. 30, 1862; Yost Diary, Nov. 13, 1862; Henneberry Journal, Nov. 23, 1862.

5. David D. Porter to Gideon Welles, Jan. 16, 1863, *ORN* 24:172 (quotation); Rodrigue, *Freedom's Crescent,* 109–11.

6. Extracts from a Private Journal, Mar. 24, 1863, *ORN* 24:495 (first quotation); Daniel Kemp to Sister, Mar. 24, 1863, Kemp Letters (second quotation); Miller Diary, Mar. 27, 28 (final quotation), 1863; Reidy, *Illusions of Emancipation,* 13.

7. Wilkie, *Pen and Powder,* 308–9 (quotations); Miller, *Vicksburg,* 298–99.

8. Detailed Report of Acting Rear Admiral David D. Porter, Mar. 26, 1863, *ORN* 24:478 (first quotation); Reidy, *Illusions of Emancipation,* 73, 382n62.

9. Sheehan-Dean, *Calculus of Violence,* 133–36; Robinson, *Bitter Fruits of Bondage,* 179.

10. Horne, "Negotiating Freedom," 3.

11. Deck Log of the USS *Lafayette,* May 17, 18, 26 (first quotation), 31, 1863, RG 24–LB, NARA; Miller Diary, May 27 (second quotation), 29, June 7, 8, 1863; Cocanower and Gudmestad, "Self-Emancipation along the Lower Mississippi River in 1863," 22–25.

12. Lyons Journal, June 7 (first quotation), 8 (second and third quotation), 1863; Elias Smith to Gideon Welles, Aug. 24, 1863; Deck Log of the USS *Lafayette,* June 10, 1863, RG 24–LB, NARA; Deck Log of the USS *Pittsburg,* June 8, 1863, ibid.; Menn, *Large Slaveholders of Louisiana,* 226; Reidy,

Illusions of Emancipation, 219. Although Walke wrote a memoir after the war, he did not mention his conversation with Acklen nor did he discuss the *Lafayette*'s role in sheltering enslaved people.

13. Lyons Journal, June 10, 1863 (first quotation); Deck Log of the USS *Lafayette,* June 10, 1863, RG 24–LB, NARA (second quotation). The log refers to William Brandon as "General Brennan." Brandon owned Arcole plantation in Wilkinson County, Mississippi, and had his leg amputated at Malvern Hill in July 1862. Losson, "William Lindsay Brandon," accessed Dec. 21, 2021.

14. Lyons Journal, June 11, 1863 (quotations); Deck Logs of the USS *Lafayette* and USS *Pittsburg,* June 11, 1863, RG 24–LB, NARA. Lyons estimated the crowd to be 600 people, a number that does not square with the information that Smith recorded in the *Lafayette*'s log. It is possible, although unlikely, that the crew left 400 people on shore.

15. For a dataset containing the enslaved peoples' information, see Cocanower and Gudmestad, "Self-Emancipation along the Lower Mississippi River in 1863."

16. Gudmestad Sailor Dataset, N=613; Teters, *Practical Liberators,* 2–3 (quotation); Rothman, *Ledger and the Chain,* 303–4. Acklen had married Adelicia Franklin, whose previous husband was Isaac Franklin. After the war Angola became the site of convict leasing and later a Louisiana state prison.

17. Deck Log of the USS *Lafayette,* June 10–July 8, 1863 (quotation, June 15), RG 24–LB, NARA.

18. Miller Diary, June 11, 1863; Lyons Diary, June 11, 1863; Deck Log of the USS *Lafayette,* June 11, 1863, RG 24–LB, NARA.

19. Lyons Journal, June 17 (first quotation), 25 (second quotation), 1863; Cooper, "'Lord, Until I Reach My Home,'" 205–11.

20. Lyons Journal, June 17, 1863. The military did prosecute cases of sexual assault against Black women. See Taylor, *Embattled Freedom,* 84–86.

21. Lyons Diary, June 11, 1863 (quotation); Miller Diary, June 18–19, 1863; Deck Log of the USS *Lafayette,* June 11, 29, 1863, RG 24–LB, NARA; Deck Log of the USS *Pittsburg,* May 31, June 29, 1863, ibid.; Deck Log of the USS *Estrella,* June 12, 1863, ibid. All river distances are based on calculations from Bragg, *Historic Names and Places on the Lower Mississippi River.*

22. Galligan Diary, Aug. 24, 1862.

23. Deck Logs of the USS *Lafayette* (first quotation) and USS *Pittsburg* (second quotation), June 29, 1863, RG 24–LB, NARA; Robinson, *Bitter Fruits of Bondage,* 142; Sheehan-Dean, *Calculus of Violence,* 136–38.

24. Deck Log of the USS *Lafayette,* June 29, 1863, RG 24–LB, NARA; Menn, *Large Slaveholders of Louisiana,* 226.

25. Deck Log of the USS *Lafayette,* June 29, 1863, RG 24–LB, NARA; Muster Roll of the USS *Pittsburg,* Jan. 1, 1864, RG 24–MRS, ibid.; Pension Application of George Davey, I 8,406, RG 15, NARA; Pension Application of Joseph Adams, WC 11,418, ibid.; Jordan, *Tumult and Silence at Second Creek,* 113–14. The other men who enlisted were Joseph Adams (aka Madison Hughes), Solomon Dowdy, Wesley Dowdy, Charles Paine, and James West.

26. Deck Log of the USS *Lafayette,* July 2–3, 1863, RG 24–LB, NARA.

27. Reidy, *Illusions of Emancipation,* 13 (first quotation); Extract Journal of the USS *Richmond,* June 4, 1863, *ORN* 20:798 (second quotation); Glymph, *Women's Fight,* 97.

28. Scott Jordan to Judith Jordan, May 10, 1863, Jordan Letters; Deck Log of the USS *Carondelet,* May 10, 1863, RG 24–LB, NARA; Deck Log of the USS *Louisville,* July 4, 1863, ibid.; Coffinberry Di-

ary, June 13, 1863 (first quotation); E. K. Owen to David D. Porter, June 18, 1863, *ORN* 25:75–76 (second quotation); Daniel Kemp to Father and Mother, Aug. 7, 1863, Kemp Letters (third quotation); Daniel Kemp to Parents, Aug. 20, 1863, ibid. (final quotation); Glymph, *Women's Fight,* 223, 247.

29. Asboth to Major General Schofield, June 20, 1863, *ORN* 25:189; Manning, *Troubled Refuge,* 135; Taylor, *Embattled Freedom,* 60–68, 84–92; Glymph, *Women's Fight,* 224 (quotation). Such camps might have been marginally safer than riverside sites, but their establishment tore apart families and isolated those people forced to move to them.

30. Taylor, *Embattled Freedom,* 113–19; Rodrigue, *Freedom's Crescent,* 171–73; Manning, *Troubled Refuge,* 140; *Glymph, Women's Fight,* 238; Berlin et al., *Freedom* 631–34.

31. Taylor, *Embattled Freedom,* 211; Rodrigue, *Freedom's Crescent,* 349–53; Manning, *Troubled Refuge,* 144; Hermann, *Pursuit of a Dream,* 42–60; Reidy, *Illusions of Emancipation,* 179–81. By war's end, Davis Bend contained 10,000 people.

32. Deck Log of the USS *Curlew,* Mar. 20, May 5, 1863, RG 24–LB, NARA; Bock Diary, June 25, 1864 (first quotation); Deck Log of the USS *Rattler,* June 25, 1864, RG 24–LB, NARA (second quotation). For other instances of transportation, see David D. Porter to Alexander M. Pennock, Jan. 18, 1863, *ORN* 24:179; and Deck Log of the USS *Osage,* Aug. 25, 26, 1863, RG 24–LB, NARA.

33. Taylor, *Embattled Freedom,* 119–20; Rodrigue, *Freedom's Crescent,* 134; Miller, *Vicksburg,* 452–53.

34. Alfred W. Ellet to David D. Porter, July 3, 1863, *ORN* 25:215 (first quotation); David D. Porter to Gideon Welles, July 2, 1863, ibid., 213 (second quotation); Deck Log of the USS *Romeo,* June 29, 1863, RG 24–LB, NARA; Glymph, *Women's Fight,* 242–43.

35. S. S. Anderson to Theophilus H. Holmes, June 4, 1863, *ORA* 22(1):856–57; David D. Porter to Gideon Welles, July 2, 1863, *ORN* 25:212–14; J. G. Walker to E. Surget, July 10, 1863, *ORA* 24(2):466 (first quotation); Alfred W. Ellet to David D. Porter, *ORN* 25:215–16 (second quotation); *St. Louis Missouri Democrat,* n.d., reprinted in *ORA* 24(3):589–90; Hearn, *Ellet's Brigade,* 174–76; Reidy, *Illusions of Emancipation,* 113. The government plantations near Goodrich's Landing lasted until at least January 1864. Cooper, "Interactive Map of Contraband Camps," accessed Feb. 17, 2023.

36. Miller, *Vicksburg,* 454–55, Deck Logs of the USS *Choctaw* and USS *Lexington,* June 7, 1863, RG 24–LB, NARA.

37. Taylor, *Embattled Freedom,* 129.

38. E. W. Sutherland to David Porter, Feb. 16, 1863, *ORN* 24:361 (first quotation); Park Journal, Jan. 1, 1863, in Jeffrey, *Two Civil Wars,* 123 (next three quotations); Clapp Diary, June 21, 1863 (final quotation).

39. Taylor, *Embattled Freedom,* 132, Hess, *Civil War in the West,* 244; Frank M. Ramsay to David D. Porter, Dec. 7, 1863, *ORN* 25:620 (first quotation); Huling, *Reminiscences of Gunboat Life,* 79 (second quotation); Reidy, *Illusions of Emancipation,* 281.

40. Hahn, *Political Worlds of Slavery and Freedom,* 55–114.

13. THE RED RIVER EXPEDITION

1. Joiner, *Through the Howling Wilderness,* 1–2, 10–11; Parrish, "Red River Campaign," 506–9.

2. Joiner, *Mr. Lincoln's Brown Water Navy,* 144.

3. Parrish, "Red River Campaign," 509; Joiner, *Through the Howling Wilderness,* 52. Even though Banks was the de facto commanding officer, Grant did not officially designate him as commander of the campaign.

4. David D. Porter to Ulysses S. Grant, Feb. 14, 1863, *ORN* 24:342 (quotation); Joiner, *Mr. Lincoln's Brown Water Navy,* 144–45; Bennett, *Union Jacks,* 94–97; Slagle, *Ironclad Captain,* 402.

5. Report of Rear Admiral Porter, Mar. 15, 1864, *ORN* 26:24–26; Scott Jordan to Judith Jordan, Mar. 20, 1864, Jordan Letters (first quotation); Journal of Frank Church, Mar. 16, 1864, in Jones and Keuchel, *Civil War Marine,* 39 (second quotation); Joiner, *Mr. Lincoln's Brown Water Navy,* 149; Joiner, *Through the Howling Wilderness,* 29–31, 61.

6. Porter, *Incidents and Anecdotes,* 229–30.

7. Miller Diary, Mar. 18, 1864 (first quotation); Scott Jordan to Judith Jordan, Mar. 20, 1864, Jordan Letters (second quotation, emphasis in original); Gibson and Gibson, *Assault and Logistics,* 362–63.

8. James A. Greer to David D. Porter, Mar. 26, 1864, *ORN* 26:38; James A. Greer to David D. Porter, Mar. 30, 1864, ibid., 40–41 (quotations); James A. Greer to David D. Porter, May 17, 1864, ibid., 306–7; Henneberry Journal, Mar. 22, 1864; Park Journal, Mar. 24, 1864, in Jeffrey, *Two Civil Wars,* 180 (estimate); Deck Log of the USS *Benton,* Mar. 16, 27–30, 1864, RG 24–LB, NARA.

9. Deck Log of the USS *Osage,* Apr. 5, 1864, RG 24–LB, NARA (first quotation); Testimony of J. G. Wilson, in U.S. Congress, *Report of the Joint Committee on the Conduct of the War,* 81–82 (second quotation).

10. Everson, "Service Afield and Afloat," 53.

11. Deck Log of the USS *Black Hawk,* Mar. 31, 1864, RG 24–LB, NARA (first quotation); Deck Log of the USS *Essex,* Apr. 2, 1864, ibid. (second quotation); Pension Application of Nelson Bailey, IC 20,131, RG 15, ibid.

12. Joiner, *Mr. Lincoln's Brown Water Navy,* 149–50.

13. Joiner, *Through the Howling Wilderness,* 67–68; Noe, *Howling Storm,* 381–83; Parrish, "Red River Campaign," 510.

14. Selfridge, "Navy in the Red River," 363 (first quotation); Scott Jordan to Judith Jordan, Mar. 30, 1864, Jordan Letters (second quotation); Joiner, *Mr. Lincoln's Brown Water Navy,* 150.

15. Joiner, *Mr. Lincoln's Brown Water Navy,* 151–52.

16. Testimony of Nathaniel P. Banks, in U.S. Congress, *Report of the Joint Committee on the Conduct of the War,* 8 (first and second quotations); Testimony of David D. Porter, ibid., 275 (third quotation).

17. Scott Jordan to Judith Jordan, Apr. 7, 1864, Jordan Letters (first quotation); Henneberry Journal, Mar. 13, 1864 (remaining quotations); Joiner, *Mr. Lincoln's Brown Water Navy,* 152–53.

18. David D. Porter to William T. Sherman, Apr. 16, 1864, *ORA* 34(3):172; Joiner, *Mr. Lincoln's Brown Water Navy,* 149.

19. David D. Porter to William T. Sherman, Apr. 16, 1864, *ORA* 34(3):172.

20. Journal of Frank Church, Apr. 10–11, 1864, in Jones and Keuchel, *Civil War Marine,* 46.

21. Selfridge, "Navy in the Red River," 363 (first quotation); David D. Porter to Gideon Welles, Apr. 14, 1864, *ORN* 26:52 (remaining quotations); Thomas O. Selfridge to David D. Porter, Apr. 16, 1864, ibid., 49; Deck Log of the USS *Lexington,* Apr. 12, 1864, RG 24–LB, NARA; Joiner, *Mr. Lincoln's Brown Water Navy,* 156–57.

22. Journal of Frank Church, Apr. 13, 1864, in Jones and Keuchel, *Civil War Marine,* 47–48 (quotations); Deck Log of the USS *Chillicothe,* Apr. 13, 1864, RG 24–LB, NARA.

23. Porter, *Incidents and Anecdotes,* 235–36.

24. David D. Porter to Gideon Welles, Apr. 28, 1864, *ORN* 26:74 (first and second quotations); Porter, *Incidents and Anecdotes,* 239 (third quotation); Slagle, *Ironclad Captain,* 324, 371–71; Joiner, *Mr. Lincoln's Brown Water Navy,* 159.

25. David D. Porter to Gideon Welles, Apr. 28, 1864, *ORN* 26:74–76 (first and second quotations); Pension Application of Robert White, WC 13,255, RG 15, NARA; Testimony of Thomas Kilby Smith, in U.S. Congress, *Report of the Joint Committee on the Conduct of the War,* 207 (remaining quotations).

26. Seth L. Phelps to David D. Porter, Apr. 28, 1864, *ORN* 26:81 (quotation); David D. Porter to Gideon Welles, Apr. 28, 1864, ibid., 76–76; William Maitland to David D. Porter, June 26, 1864, ibid., 87.

27. J. S. Watson to David D. Porter, May 1, 1864, *ORN* 26:83; David D. Porter to Gideon Welles, Apr. 28, 1864, ibid., 76–76.

28. Seth L. Phelps quoted in Slagle, *Ironclad Captain,* 375; Abstract Log of USS *Fort Hindman, ORN* 26:786–87; David D. Porter to Gideon Welles, Apr. 28, 1864, *ORN* ibid., 76–77.

29. Seth L. Phelps to David D. Porter, Apr. 28, 1864, *ORN* 26:81–82; J. S. Watson to David D. Porter, May 1, 1864, ibid., 84; William Maitland to David D. Porter, June 26, 1864, ibid., 87.

30. Albert B. Paine, "An Exploit of the War," *St. Paul (MN) Pioneer Press,* May 20, 1895; David D. Porter to Gideon Welles, Apr. 28, 1864, *ORN* 26:92; George Wythe Baylor to Captain Ogden, Apr. 18, 1864, *ORA* 34(1):621; Order of K. R. Breese, May 4, 1864, *ORN* 26:107. The boats at Alexandria were the ironclads *Mound City, Louisville, Pittsburg, Carondelet,* and *Chillicothe;* monitors *Osage, Neosho,* and *Choctaw;* timberclad *Lexington;* and tinclads *Cricket, Fort Hindman,* and *Juliet.*

31. George Wythe Baylor to Captain Ogden, Apr. 18, 1864, *ORA* 34(1):622 (first quotation); Symmes Browne to Fannie, May 6, 1984, *FTFWN,* 275 (second quotation); George P. Lord to David D. Porter, May 8, 1864, *ORN* 26:112–14; Joiner, *Mr. Lincoln's Brown Water Navy,* 161.

32. George Wythe Baylor to Captain Ogden, Apr. 18, 1864, *ORA* 34(1):622 (first quotation); George P. Lord to David D. Porter, May 8, 1864, *ORN* 26:112–14; Perry Wilkes to Frank McCloskey, May 8, 1864, ibid., 114–15; Edward Morgan to David D. Porter, Feb. 27, 1865, ibid., 117–19 (second quotation); Journal of Frank Church, May 6–7, 1864, in Jones and Keuchel, *Civil War Marine,* 54.

33. David D. Porter to Gideon Welles, May 16, 1864, *ORN* 26:130 (quotation); Cron, "Colonel Bailey's Red River Dams," 421; Joiner, *Mr. Lincoln's Brown Water Navy,* 163–64.

34. Paine, "Exploit of the War," *St. Paul (MN) Pioneer Press,* May 20, 1895; Deck Log of the USS *Pittsburg,* May 4–6, 1864, RG 24–LB, NARA; George D. Robinson to D. C. Houston, June 13, 1864, *ORA* 34(1):251; Uri B. Pearsall to George B. Drake, Aug. 1, 1864, ibid., 253–54; Cron, "Colonel Bailey's Red River Dams," 422–23; Parrish, "Red River Campaign," 515.

35. David D. Porter to Gideon Welles, May 16, 1864, *ORN* 26:132.

36. Deck Logs of the USS *Pittsburg,* USS *Chillicothe,* and USS *Mound City,* May 8, 1864, RG 24–LB, NARA; Deck Log of the USS *Louisville,* May 9, 1864, ibid.; David D. Porter to Gideon Welles, May 16, 1864, *ORN* 26:131. There is disagreement in the sources about when these boats passed over the falls. I used information from the vessels' logs, which were immediate and most likely to have the correct dates.

37. David D. Porter to Gideon Welles, May 16, 1864, *ORN* 26:131 (quotations); Paine, "Exploit of the War," *St. Paul (MN) Pioneer Press,* May 20, 1895; Cron, "Colonel Bailey's Red River Dams," 424.

38. Paine, "Exploit of the War," *St. Paul (MN) Pioneer Press,* May 20, 1895.

39. Uri B. Pearsall to George B. Drake, Aug. 1, 1864, *ORA* 34(1):253–54 (quotation); Paine, "Exploit of the War," *St. Paul (MN) Pioneer Press,* May 20, 1895.

40. Deck Log of the USS *Carondelet,* May 9, 1864, RG 24–LB, NARA (first quotation); Deck Log of the USS *Mound City,* May 10, 1864, ibid. (second quotation); David D. Porter to Gideon Welles, May 19, 1864, *ORN* 26:156.

41. David D. Porter to Gideon Welles, May 19, 1864, *ORN* 26:156. With the heavy fighting along the Mississippi now done, the boats never restored their armor.

42. Deck Log of the USS *Chillicothe,* May 10, 1864, RG 24–LB, NARA (first quotation); Deck Log of the USS *Mound City,* May 11, 1864, ibid. (remaining quotations); Deck Log of the USS *Carondelet,* May 9–10, 1864, ibid.; Deck Log of the USS *Mound City,* May 10, 1864, ibid.; Uri B. Pearsall to George B. Drake, Aug. 1, 1864, *ORA* 34(1):253–54; Cron, "Colonel Bailey's Red River Dams," 424.

43. Paine, "Exploit of the War," *St. Paul (MN) Pioneer Press,* May 20, 1895.

44. Deck Log of the USS *Carondelet,* May 11, 1864, RG 24–LB, NARA (first quotation); Deck Log of the USS *Mound City,* May 11, 1864, ibid. (remaining quotations).

45. Deck Logs of the USS *Chillicothe,* USS *Carondelet,* USS *Mound City,* and USS *Pittsburg,* May 12, 1864, RG 24–LB, NARA; Cron, "Colonel Bailey's Red River Dams," 424; Paine, "Exploit of the War," *St. Paul (MN) Pioneer Press,* May 20, 1895; Journal of Frank Church, May, 13, 1864, in Jones and Keuchel, *Civil War Marine,* 56.

46. Scott Jordan to Judith Jordan, May 18, 1864, Jordan Letters (first quotation); Symmes Brown to Fannie, May 13, 1864, *FTFWN,* 277; Journal of Frank Church, May 20, 1864, in Jones and Keuchel, *Civil War Marine,* 59.

47. Joiner, *Through the Howling Wilderness,* xix.

48. Parrish, "Red River Campaign," 517.

49. RG 217, Certificates of Settlement of Prize Claims, 1863–84, NARA; MeasuringWorth.com, accessed Nov. 29, 2022; Everson, "Service Afield and Afloat," 53 (quotation). Martin's $100-plus share was equivalent to about $1,800 in 2022. In 1863 a first-class fireman earned $30 per month. Brewer, "African American Sailors and the Unvexing of the Mississippi," 280.

14. CONFEDERATE RESURGENCE

1. Hess, *Civil War in the West,* 211–14; Hess, *Civil War Supply and Strategy,* 139–49; Gibson and Gibson, *Assault and Logistics;* Glenny, "Devil's Navy," 25.

2. LeRoy Fitch to David D. Porter, June 26, 1864, *ORN* 26:441 (first quotation); James W. Shirk to David D. Porter, Aug. 12, 1864, ibid., 508 (second quotation); Hess, *Civil War Supply and Strategy,* 155–65; Hess, *Civil War in the West,* 244.

3. James Marshall to John G. Mitchell, June 1, 1864, *ORN* 26:353 (quotation); Scott Jordan to Judith Jordan, Oct. 31, Nov. 12, 1864, Jordan Letters.

4. John S. Marmaduke to Captain Thomas, June 11, 1864, *ORA* 34(1):947 (first quotation); DeWitt C. Morse to Archibald Beal, May 30, 1864, in Patrick, "Fighting Sailor on the Western Rivers,"

269–71 (remaining quotations); Smith, *Tinclads,* 231–38; Doyle, "Civil War in Greenville Bends," 158–59; Deck Log of the USS *Curlew,* May 24–26, 1864, RG 24–LB, NARA; Report of Acting Ensign H. B. O'Neill, May 24, 1864, *ORN* 26:324; E. K. Owen to David D. Porter, May 26, 1864, ibid., 327; Report of Colton Greene, June 8, 1864, ibid., 805–7; Colton Greene to Maj. H. Ewing, June 8, 1864, *ORA* 34(1):950–53.

5. Laas, "'Sleepless Sentinels,'" 26; Bennett, *Union Jacks,* 5. Figures for number and types of boats in the Mississippi Squadron compiled from Silverstone, *Warships of the Civil War Navies, and ORN.* The North Atlantic Blockading Squadron fluctuated between 84 and 119 vessels, about 9 of which were auxiliary ships. There were four blue-water squadrons: the North Atlantic Blockading Squadron, South Atlantic Blockading Squadron, East Gulf Coast Blockading Squadron, and West Gulf Coast Blockading Squadron. Tucker, *Blue & Gray Navies,* 102. Lass does not provide an estimate of the number of sailors in the North Atlantic Blockading Squadron.

6. Gudmestad Sailor Dataset, N=6,255 (last phase), N=1,703 (August 1864), N=1,511 (September 1864), N=14,420 (entire war).

7. Gudmestad Sailor Dataset; Marvel, *Lincoln's Mercenaries,* 8, 214–16; Axtell, "American Steamboat Gothic," 387.

8. William Bock to Father, Nov. 10, 1864, Bock Papers (quotation; emphasis in original); Muster Rolls of the USS *Oriole,* USS *Gamage,* and USS *Collier,* Apr. 1, 1865, RG 24–MRS, NARA; Marvel, *Lincoln's Mercenaries,* 219. The navy rejected some sailors who enlisted for a bounty as being unfit for service. See H. Brown to J. W. Livingston, May 3, 1865, Mound City, IL Naval Station: Letters Received, July 29, 1864–Aug. 30, 1869, Squadron Letters, NARA.

9. Frederic Davis to Father, n.d. [ca. Apr. 22, 1862] (first quotation); William Van Cleaf to Brother, May 4, 1862, Van Cleaf Papers; Clapp Diary, July 2, 1863 (second quotation). Clapp was quoting the Irish sailor. See also Ezra Green to Mother, July 13, 1862, Ezra Green Letters, FHS; Baron Proctor to John, Aug. 10, 1862, Baron Proctor Letters, Rauner Special Collections Library, Dartmouth College; Scott Jordan to Brother, May 28, 1863, Jordan Letters; and Scott Jordan to Judith Jordan, June 25, 28, 1864, ibid. One of the few enlisted sailors to write something positive about life in the Mississippi Squadron was James Henneberry. Despite penning a screed about the Emancipation Proclamation, Henneberry told his diary on January 1, 1863, that as he looked back over the previous year, he had "but little to complain of." Henneberry Journal, Jan. 1, 1863.

10. Morrison Diary, May 31, 1863.

11. Gudmestad Sailor Dataset, N=5,413; Murray and Hsieh, *Savage War,* 357. I could find no meaningful patterns in the sailors who persisted. Native-born white Americans, immigrants, and Black men continued in percentages that correlated to their ratio in the fleet. William Marvel disputes the 60-percent figure and cites a 20-percent reenlistment rate for the Union army. See Marvel, *Lincoln's Mercenaries,* 204, 274n31.

12. The boats were USS *Naumkeag* (15 percent), USS *Kenwood* (16 percent), USS *Benton* (18 percent), USS *Fairplay* (21 percent), USS *Alfred Robb* (22 percent), USS *Exchange* (23 percent), USS *Fawn* (24 percent), USS *Champion* (27 percent), and USS *Hastings* (47 percent). For this small study, I randomly selected vessels that had a complete run of muster rolls between September 30, 1863, and March 31, 1865. Student workers compiled the data. I determined the turnover rate by calculating the average number of sailors in two consecutive muster rolls as well as the number of bluejackets who

did not appear on the second roll; I then divided the latter by the former. The brown-water navy was probably different than the blue-water navy with regard to turnover rates. As Michael J. Bennett points out, blockade sailors normally served anywhere from six to eighteen months without leaving their ships. Bennett, *Union Jacks,* 66.

13. Herbert Saunders to Brother, Aug. 2, 1864, in Huch, "Civil War Letters of Herbert Saunders," 27; Herbert Saunders to Mother, Sept. 14, 1864, ibid., 27–28 (first and second quotations); Dickinson Diary, Feb. 14, 1864 (final quotation); Muster Roll of the USS *Tawah,* Oct. 1, 1864, RG 24–MRS, NARA.

14. Court-Martial of James Walker (quotation), case 3369, vol. 105, RG 125, NARA, available at Fold3.com; Court-Martial of Eugene Daily, case 3204, vol. 95, ibid.; Morrison Diary, Apr. 2, 1863.

15. David D. Porter to A. S. Bowen, Aug. 19, 1863, *ORN* 25:374 (quotation); Muster Rolls of the USS *Naumkeag,* Apr. 1, July 31, 1864, Jan. 1, 1865, RG 24–MRS, NARA.

16. Statistics compiled from the Deck Logs of the USS *Rattler,* 1863–64, RG 24–LB, NARA; and Muster Rolls of the USS *Rattler,* 1863–64, RG 24–MRS, ibid.; Bennett, *Union Jacks,* 102–3. For the *Rattler,* five deserters were listed only on the muster rolls, nine were listed only in the deck logs, and the rest were listed on both. More case studies for individual boats are needed.

17. Miller Diary, Aug. 19, 22–24, 26, 1864; Muster Roll of the USS *Lafayette,* Dec. 31, 1864, RG 24–MRS, NARA; Gudmestad Sailor Dataset, N=709 (prior to Jan. 1, 1863), N=3,969 (prior to May 1, 1864), N=10,266 (final phase).

18. Smith, *Civil War Biographies from the Western Waters,* 139.

19. Scott Jordan to Father, June 6, 1864, Jordan Letters (quotation); "Report of Captain Pennock," Oct. 15, 1864, *ORN* 26:692–93; Smith, *Civil War Biographies from the Western Waters,* passim. I cross-referenced the report with Smith's biographies as well as other references in the *ORN.* I found command dates or prior command experience for sixty officers.

20. Gudmestad Irregular Combat Dataset; James P. Foster to David D. Porter, July 13, 1864, *ORN* 26:474 (quotation).

21. Gudmestad Irregular Combat Dataset.

22. John Swift to Rosie Whiteside, June 8, 1864, in Swift, "Letters from a Sailor on a Tinclad," 55 (first and second quotations); Daniel Ullman to George B. Drake, Nov. 27, 1864, *ORN* 26:745 (third quotation); James P. Foster to David D. Porter, June 8, 1864, ibid., 374 (final quotation); Gudmestad Irregular Combat Dataset.

23. Park Journal, Mar. 24, 1864, in Jeffrey, *Two Civil Wars,* 180 (quotation); Sutherland, *Savage Conflict,* 51–52.

24. Le Roy Fitch to David D. Porter, June 9, 1864, *ORN* 26:384.

25. Henry Howland to J. L. Donaldson, Oct. 31, 1864, *ORN* 26:604; Smith, *Tinclads,* 276; Williams, "Johnsonville Raid," 235.

26. Evidence of Acting Master J. L. Bryant, n.d., *ORN* 26:602–3; Smith, *Tinclads,* 279.

27. Smith, *Tinclads,* 279.

28. Evidence of Acting Master J. L. Bryant, n.d., *ORN* 26:602–3; Smith, *Tinclads,* 279.

29. Muster Roll of the USS *Undine,* June 30, 1864, RG 24–MRS, NARA.

30. James W. Shirk to Samuel P. Lee, Nov. 5, 1864, *ORN* 26:610; Smith, *Tinclads,* 283–84.

31. General Order No. 199, *ORN* 26:329–30; Edward M. King to James W. Shirk, Nov. 4, 1864,

ibid., 610–11 (quotations); Williams, "Johnsonville Raid," 243; True, "Life aboard a Gunboat," 39; James W. Shirk to S. P. Lee, Nov. 5, 1864, *ORN* 26:610–13; Gibson and Gibson, *Assault and Logistics*, 386–90.

32. Nathan Bedford Forrest to E. Surget, Jan. 12, 1865, *ORN* 26:683 (quotation); Smith, *Tinclads*, 291.

33. Muster Roll of the USS *Elfin*, July 1, 1864, RG 24–MRS, NARA; Muster Roll of the USS *Key West*, Sept. 30, 1864, ibid.; Muster Roll of the USS *Tawah*, Oct. 1, 1864, ibid. There were 212 sailors with enlistment dates: 71 in 1863 and 141 in 1864.

34. Letter of R. L May, Nov. 7, 1864, *ORN* 26:547. Another source put the amount at $250,000, which seems too high. See William Bock to Father, Nov. 10, 1864, Bock Papers.

35. William Bock to Father, Nov. 10, 1864, Bock Papers (quotations, emphasis in original); Deck Log of the USS *Rattler*, Sept. 4, 1864, RG 24–LB, NARA; Smith, *Tinclads*, 263–64.

36. William Bock to Father, Nov. 10, 1864, Bock Papers.

37. Deck Log of the USS *Rattler*, Sept. 4, 1864, RG 24–LB, NARA; "Account of the Treachery of Capt. Daniel Glenny of the 'Rattler,' Aug.–Sept. 1864," Bock Papers (first and second quotations); William Bock to Father, Nov. 10, 1864, ibid. (final quotation).

38. "Account of the Treachery of Capt. Daniel Glenny of the 'Rattler,' Aug.–Sept. 1864," Bock Papers (quotations, emphasis in original); Deck Log of the USS *Rattler*, Sept. 4, 1864, RG 24–LB, NARA.

39. Deck Log of the USS *Rattler*, Sept. 11, 19, 1864, RG 24–LB, NARA.

40. Daniel Glenny to "Brother Officers," Sept. 11, 1864, Bock Papers (first and second quotations, emphasis in original); Deck Log of the USS *Rattler*, Nov. 4, 1864, RG 24–LB, NARA; N. B. Willets to R. L. May, Nov. 4, 1864, *ORN* 26:545.

41. Gudmestad Sailor Dataset, N=579. Also, 43 percent of the veterans were immigrants who tended to have maritime experience.

42. Hess, *Civil War Logistics*, 232–34.

EPILOGUE

1. True, "Life aboard a Gunboat," 43 (quotations, emphasis in original); H. Brown to J. W. Livingston, May 3, 1865, Mound City, IL, Naval Station: Letters Received, July 29, 1864–Aug. 30, 1869, Squadron Letters, NARA; "The Great Steamboats Sale," *Chicago Tribune*, Aug. 21, 1863, 1; "Great Sale of Gunboats at Mound City," ibid., Nov. 30, 1863, 1; Smith, *After Vicksburg*, 229–51; Samuel P. Lee to Gideon Welles, June 27, 1865, *ORN* 27:281–83.

2. William Murphy to Robert Murphy, Nov. 8, 1865, typescript in possession of Kerby A. Miller, Ph.D., University of Missouri, Columbia (first quotation); Pension Application of William A. Palmer, MC 8,648, RG 15, NARA (second quotation); Pension Application of John Anderegg, IC 17,518, ibid. For works that speak more generally to Civil War soldiers' adjustment to civilian life, see Jordan, *Marching Home;* and Carroll, *Invisible Wounds*.

3. J. E. Robinson to William Bock, Dec. 30, 1895, Bock Papers; James Laning to William Bock, June 24, 1891 (quotations), ibid.; undated newspaper clipping, ibid.; "Autobiography," n.d. Laning Papers; "A History of the U.S. Gunboat, Essex," n.d., ibid.; undated newspaper clipping, ibid.; "In

Memoriam," unidentified newspaper clipping, Feb. 6, 1880 (quotations), ibid.; Pension Application of Thomas Riley, IC 1,167,423, RG 15, NARA; Pension Application of William Rose (aka James Funk), WC 812,489, ibid.; Pension Application of Alison Emerson, W 9,159, ibid.

4. David D. Porter to John H. Dorman, Jan. 27, 1888 (quotations), John H. Dorman Papers, Ohio History Center, Columbus; Henry Walke to John H. Dorman, Feb. 9, 1888, ibid.; Smith, *Bayou Battles for Vicksburg,* 393–94.

5. "Grizzled Tars of the Carondelet Meet in Annual Reunion and Talk over Stirring Experiences during War of Rebellion," *Cincinnati Enquirer,* Apr. 17, 1902, 12; "Anniversary of the Battle of Vicksburg Observed by Survivors of the Gunboat Carondelet," ibid., Apr. 19, 1903, 10 (quotation); "Naval Veterans Tell of the Run Past Guns at Vicksburg," *Cincinnati Post,* Apr. 18, 1904, 10; National Register of Historic Places Inventory—Nomination Form for Vicksburg National Military Park, 12–13; Bearss, *Hardluck Ironclad.*

APPENDIX 1

1. Reidy, "Black Jack," 213–20; Reidy, "African-American Sailors' Project," 31–33, 43.

2. There are rudimentary muster rolls from 1862 in the Western Gunboat Flotilla Collection, RG 217NARA. They contain minimal information, however, and were not useful in gathering demographic data.

BIBLIOGRAPHY

MANUSCRIPT COLLECTIONS

Abraham Lincoln Presidential Library, Springfield, Illinois
William N. Bock Papers
George Robert Yost Papers

Buffalo History Museum, Buffalo, New York
Daniel Francis Kemp Civil War Correspondence and Reminiscences
Daniel Francis Kemp Letters

Chicago History Museum, Chicago, Illinois
James E. Henneberry Journal (photostat)
James Laning Papers

Cincinnati Museum Center, Cincinnati, Ohio
Joseph B. Boyd Papers

Emory University, Atlanta, Georgia
Frederic E. Davis Papers

Filson Historical Society, Louisville, Kentucky
Ezra Green Letters
Thomas E. Smith Letters

Henry O'Mahoney Memoir, n.d. Kerby A. Miller, Ph.D., private collection, University of Missouri, Columbia

Hill Memorial Library, Louisiana State University, Baton Rouge
John C. Elder Diary
Henry R. Holdrege Diary
Alexander R. Miller Diary

Indiana Historical Society, Indianapolis
Samuel C. Vance Papers

John Hay Library, Brown University, Providence, Rhode Island
S. B. Brittan Letter

Library of Congress, Washington, DC
Silas Casey Papers
Thomas Lyons Journal
Charles O'Neil Papers
Ninian Pinkney Papers
Edward Paul Reichhelm Collection

Montana Historical Society, Helena
Edward M. Galligan Diary, 1861–1863

National Archives, Washington, DC
Record Group 15, Pension Records
Record Group 24, Log Books
Record Group 24, Muster Rolls of Ships
Record Group 45, Register of Prize Cases, 1862–1871
Record Group 45, Letters Received by the Secretary of the Navy from Commanding Officers of Squadrons, Mississippi Squadron
Record Group 94, Records of the Adjutant General's Office (available at Fold3.com)
Record Group 125, Records of the Office of the Judge Advocate General (Navy), Navy Courts Martial Records, 1799–1867 (available at Fold3.com)
Record Group 217, Certificates of Settlement of Prize Claims, 1863–1884
Record Group 217, Index to Civil War Prize Lists, 1863–1868
Record Group 217.9.5, Prize Lists, 1862–1865
Record Group 217, Western Gunboat Flotilla Collection

Newberry Library, Chicago, Illinois
W. L. Park Journal

New York State Military Museum and Veterans Research Center, Saratoga Springs
"The Civil War Diary of John G. Morrison, 1861–1865," https://museum.dmna.ny.gov/application/files/8615/5059/7442/30thInf_Diary_Morrison.pdf (typescript)

Office of the Illinois Secretary of State, Springfield

Illinois Civil War Muster and Descriptive Rolls, https://www.ilsos.gov/isaveterans/civil mustersrch.jsp

Ohio History Center, Columbus

John H. Dorman Papers

Rauner Special Collections Library, Dartmouth College, Hanover, New Hampshire

Baron Proctor Letters

Rutherford B. Hayes Presidential Library and Museum, Fremont, Ohio

James A. Dickinson Diary, http://www.rbhayes.org/hayes/mssfind/285/dickinsonjames.htm

South Caroliniana Library, University of South Carolina, Columbia

F. T. Chew to Richard Hays Bacot, June 2, 1862, http://digital.tcl.sc.edu/cdm/ref/collection/civilwar/id/2526 accessed January 27, 2016

Southern Historical Collection, The Wilson Library, University of North Carolina at Chapel Hill

"List of Negroes working on the fortifications at Fort Pemberton," John G. Devereaux Papers #2149, web.lib.unc.edu

Special Collections, Virginia Tech University, Blacksburg

Frances A. Murdoch Journal, https://digitalsc.lib.vt.edu/items/show/2673

Special Collections and University Libraries, Rutgers University, New Brunswick, New Jersey

John Beekman Papers

Stephen Duncan Papers

Joseph Fry Letter

William Van Cleaf Papers

Robert Wilkinson Papers

Special Collections Research Center, Morris Library, Southern Illinois University, Carbondale

Diary of John W. Bell, http://collections.carli.illinois.edu/cdm/ref/collection/sic_civilw/id/2881

State Historical Society of Missouri, Columbia
Fayette Clapp Diary

Tennessee State Library and Archives, Nashville
Bradford Family Papers
Charles G. Henderson Diary
Thomas Fletcher Ragland Papers
Alexander Simplot Civil War Drawings

Western Reserve Historical Society, Cleveland, Ohio
Diary of Henry D. Coffinberry

GOVERNMENT DOCUMENTS AND PUBLICATIONS

National Register of Historic Places Inventory—Nomination Form for Mosby-Bennett House. 1980. U.S. Department of the Interior. https://npgallery.nps.gov/NRHP/GetAsset/NRHP/80003868_text.

National Register of Historic Places Inventory—Nomination Form for Vicksburg National Military Park. 1976. U.S. Department of the Interior. http://npshistory.com/publications/vick/nr-vicksburg-nmp.pdf.

Official Records of the Union and Confederate Navies in the War of the Rebellion. 30 vols. Washington, DC: Government Printing Office, 1894–1922.

U.S. Congress. *Report of the Joint Committee on the Conduct of the War, at the Second Session Thirty-Eighth Congress. Red River Expedition. Fort Fisher Expedition. Heavy Ordnance.* 38th Cong., 2nd Sess., Washington, DC: Government Printing Office, 1865.

War of the Rebellion: A Compilation of Official Records of the Union and Confederate Armies. 128 vols. Washington, DC: Government Printing Office, 1880–1901.

PRIMARY SOURCES

Adams, F. Colburn. *High Old Salts: Stories Intended for the Marines, but Told before an Enlightened Committee of Congress.* Washington, DC, 1876.

Alford, E. "Destruction of the Cairo." In Moore, *Rebellion Record,* 6:253.

Anderson, John Q., ed. *Campaigning with Parsons' Texas Cavalry Brigade, CSA: The War Journals and Letters of Four Orr Brothers, 12th Texas Cavalry Regiment.* Hillsboro, TX: Hill Junior College Press, 1967.

Avery, P. O. *History of the Fourth Illinois Cavalry Regiment.* Humboldt, NE: Enterprise, 1903.

Banasik, Michael E., ed. *Missouri Brothers in Gray: The Reminiscences and Letters of William J. Bull and John P. Bull.* Iowa City, IA: Camp Pope Bookshop, 1998.

Bartlett, John Russell. "The 'Brooklyn' at the Passage of the Forts." In Johnson and Buel, *Battles and Leaders of the Civil War,* 2:56–69.

Barton, Thomas H. *Autobiography of Dr. Thomas H. Barton, the Self-Made Physician of Syracuse, Ohio.* Charleston, WV: West Virginia Printing, 1890.

Bergeron, Arthur W., ed. *The Civil War Reminiscences of Major Silas T. Grisamore, C.S.A.* Baton Rouge: Louisiana State University Press, 1993.

Berlin, Ira, Thavolia Glymph, Steven F. Miller, Joseph P. Reidy, Leslie S. Rowland, and Julie Saville, eds. *Freedom: A Documentary History of Emancipation, 1861–1867.* Ser. 1, vol. 3, *The Wartime Genesis of Free Labor: The Lower South.* New York: Cambridge University Press, 1990.

Bevier, R. S. *History of the First and Second Missouri Confederate Brigades, 1861–1865; and from Wakarusa to Appomattox, a Military Autograph.* St. Louis: Bryan, Brand, 1879.

Biel, John G., ed. "The Battle of Shiloh: From the Letters and Diary of Joseph Dimmit Thompson." *Tennessee Historical Quarterly* 27 (September 1958): 250–74.

Bissell, J. W. "Sawing out the Channel above Island Number Ten." In Johnson and Buel, *Battles and Leaders of the Civil War,* 1:460–62.

Bowman, Larry G., and Jack B. Scroggs, eds. "Diary of a Confederate Soldier." *Military Review* 62 (February 1982): 20–34.

Bragg, Marion. *Historic Names and Places on the Lower Mississippi River.* Vicksburg: Mississippi River Commission, 1977.

Braudaway, Douglas Lee, ed. "A Texan Records the Civil War Siege of Vicksburg, Mississippi: The Journal of Maj. Maurice Kavanaugh Simons, 1863." *Southwestern Historical Quarterly* 105 (July 2001): 92–131.

Bringhurst, Thomas H., and Frank Swigart. *History of the Forty-Sixth Regiment Indiana Volunteer Infantry, September 1861–September 1865.* Logansport, IN: Wilson, Humphreys, 1888.

Brown, George W. "Service in the Mississippi Squadron, and Its Connection with the Siege of and Capture of Vicksburg." In *Personal Recollections of the War of the Rebellion: Addresses Delivered before the New York Commandery of the Loyal Legion of the United States, 1883–1891,* edited by James Grant Wilson and Titus Munson Coan, 1:302–13. New York Commandery: New York, 1891.

Brown, Isaac N. "The Confederate Gun-Boat 'Arkansas.'" In Johnson and Buel, *Battles and Leaders of the Civil War,* 3:572–79.

Byers, S. H. M. *With Fire and Sword.* New York: Neale, 1911.

Callender, Eliot. "What a Boy Saw on the Mississippi." In *Military Essays and Recollections: Papers Read before the Commandery of the State of Illinois, Military Order of the Loyal Legion of the United States,* edited by Alfred T. Andreas, Charles W. Davis, and William Eliot Furness, 51–67. Chicago: A. C. McClurg, 1891.

Christ, Mark K., ed. "'Them Dam'd Gunboats': A Union Sailor's Letters from the Arkansas Post Expedition." *Arkansas Historical Quarterly* 66 (Winter 2007): 452–67.

Clarke, Norman E., ed. *Warfare along the Mississippi: The Letters of Lieutenant Colonel George E. Currie.* Ann Arbor, MI: Edwards Brothers, 1961.

Coffin, Levi. *Reminiscences of Levi Coffin, the Reputed President of the Underground Railroad.* Cincinnati: Western Tract Society, 1876.

Coleman, S. B. "A July Morning with the Rebel Ram 'Arkansas.'" In *War Papers Read before the Commandery of the State of Michigan Military Order of the Loyal Legion of the United States,* 1:3–13. Detroit: Winn and Hammond, 1893.

"A Confederate Private at Fort Donelson, 1862." *American Historical Review* 31 (April 1926): 477–84.

Cooling, B. Franklin, ed. "A Virginian at Fort Donelson: Excerpts from the Prison Journal of John Henry Guy." *Tennessee Historical Quarterly* 27 (Summer 1968): 176–90.

Critchell, Robert S. *Recollections of a Fire Insurance Man, including His Experience in U.S. Navy (Mississippi Squadron) during the Civil War.* Chicago: By the author, 1909.

Cron, Frederick. "Colonel Bailey's Red River Dams." *Military Engineer* 29 (November–December 1937): 421–24.

Davis, Charles H. *The Life of Charles Henry Davis, Rear Admiral, 1807–1877.* Boston: Houghton Mifflin, 1899.

Eads, James B. "Recollections of Foote and the Gun-Boats." In Johnson and Buel, *Battles and Leaders of the Civil War,* 1:338–46.

Ellet, Alfred W. "Ellet and His Steam-Rams at Memphis." In Johnson and Buel, *Battles and Leaders of the Civil War,* 1:453–59.

Everson, Guy R., ed. "Service Afield and Afloat: A Reminiscence of the Civil War." *Indiana Magazine of History* 84 (March 1993): 35–56.

Flanders, Alan B., and Capt. Neale O. Westfall, USCG (Ret). *Memoirs of E. A. Jack: Steam Engineer, CSS* Virginia. White Stone, VA: Brandylane, 1998.

Foote, John A. "Notes on the Life of Admiral Foote." In Johnson and Buel, *Battles and Leaders of the Civil War,* 1:347.

Gift, George W. "The Story of the *Arkansas.*" In *Southern Historical Society Papers,* edited by Reverend J. William Jones, 12:163–70. Richmond: William Ellis Jones, 1884.

Grant, Ulysses S. *Personal Memoirs of U. S. Grant.* Vol. 1. New York: Charles L. Webster, 1885.

Grimsley, Mark, and Todd D. Miller, eds. *The Union Must Stand: The Civil War Diary of John Quincy Adams Campbell, Fifth Iowa Volunteer Infantry.* Knoxville: University of Tennessee Press, 2000.

Hamper, Stan, ed. "War on the River: A River Pilot's Mail." *Civil War Times Illustrated* 21 (October 1982): 24–31.

Hess, Earl J., ed. *A German in the Yankee Fatherland: The Civil War Letters of Henry A. Kircher.* Kent, OH: Kent State University Press, 1983.

Hoppin, James Mason. *Life of Andrew Hull Foote, Rear-Admiral United States Navy.* New York: Harper and Brothers, 1874.

Huch, Ronald K., ed. "The Civil War Letters of Herbert Saunders," *Register of the Kentucky Historical Society* 69 (1971): 17–29.

Huling, E. J. *Reminiscences of Gunboat Life in the Mississippi Squadron.* Saratoga Springs, NY: Sentinel Print, 1881.

Jeffrey, Katherine Bentley, ed. *Two Civil Wars: The Curious Shared Journal of a Baton Rouge Schoolgirl and a Union Sailor on the USS Essex.* Baton Rouge: Louisiana State University Press, 2016.

Johnson, Robert Underwood, and Clarence Clough Buel, eds. *Battles and Leaders of the Civil War,* 4 vols. New York: Century, 1884–87.

Joiner, Gary D., ed. *Little to Eat and Thin Mud to Drink: Letters, Diaries, and Memoirs from the Red River Campaigns, 1863–1864.* Knoxville: University of Tennessee Press, 2007.

Jones, James P., and Edward F. Keuchel, eds. *Civil War Marine: A Diary of the Red River Expedition, 1864.* Washington, DC: History and Museums Division, Headquarters, U.S. Marine Corps, 1975.

Mason, George. "Shiloh." In *Military Essays and Recollections: Papers Read before the Commandery of the State of Illinois, Military Order of the Loyal Legion,* 1:93–104. Chicago: A. C. McClurg, 1891.

McHatton-Ripley, Eliza. *From Flag to Flag: A Woman's Adventures and Experiences in the South during the War, in Mexico, and in Cuba.* New York: D. Appleton, 1889.

McHenry, Estill, comp. and ed. *Addresses and Papers of James B. Eads.* St. Louis: Slawson, 1884.

Meacham, Justin W. "Military and Naval Operations on the Mississippi." In *War Papers read before the Commandery of the State of Wisconsin, Military Order of the Loyal Legion of the United States,* edited by Amos P. Foster, 4:387–96. Milwaukee: Burdick & Allen, 1914.

Milligan, John D., ed. *From the Fresh-Water Navy, 1861–64: The Letters of Acting Master's Mate Henry R. Browne and Acting Ensign Symmes E. Brown.* Annapolis, MD: Naval Institute Press, 1970.

Milligan, John, ed. "Navy Life on the Mississippi River: An Excerpt from Union Sailor Daniel F. Kemp's Civil War Reminiscences." *Civil War Times Illustrated* 33 (May–June 1994): 16, 66–73.

Moore, Frank, ed. *The Rebellion Record: A Diary of American Events with Documents, Narratives, Illustrative Incidents, Poetry Etc.* 11 vols.. New York: G. P. Putnam, 1861–68.

Parsons, Lewis B. *Reports to the War Department by Brev. Maj. Gen. Lewis B. Parsons, Chief of Rail and River Transportation.* St. Louis: George Knapp, 1867.

Patrick, Jeffrey L., ed. "A Fighting Sailor on the Western Rivers: The Civil War Letters of 'Gunboat.'" *Journal of Mississippi History* 58 (Fall 1996): 255–83.

Porter, David Dixon. *Incidents and Anecdotes of the Civil War.* New York: D. Appleton, 1885.

———. *The Naval History of the Civil War.* New York: Sherman, 1886.

———. "The Opening of the Lower Mississippi." In Johnson and Buel, *Battles and Leaders of the Civil War,* 2:22–55.

Read, C. W. "Reminiscences of the Confederate States Navy." In *Southern Historical Society Papers,* edited by Reverend J. William Jones, 2:331–62. Richmond: William Ellis Jones, 1876.

Roca, Steven Louis. "Presence and Precedents: The *USS Red Rover* during the American Civil War, 1861–1865." *Civil War History* 44 (June 1998): 91–110.

Roe, Merwin, ed. *Speeches and Letters of Abraham Lincoln, 1832–1865.* London: J. M. Dent and Sons, 1912. Reprint, New York: E. P. Dutton, 1907.

Ritter, Capt. W. L. "Sketch of the Third Battery of Maryland Artillery." In *Southern Historical Society Papers, edited by Reverend J. William Jones, 10:392–401. Richmond: William Ellis Jones, 1882.*

Sears, Stephen W., ed. *The Selected Papers of George B. McClellan: Selected Correspondence, 1860–1865.* New York: Ticknor & Fields, 1989.

Selfridge, Thomas O. "The Navy in the Red River." In Johnson and Buel, *Battles and Leaders of the Civil War,* 4:362–65.

Sharpe, Henry G. "The Art of Supplying Armies in the Field as Exemplified during the Civil War." *Journal of the Military Service Institution of the United States* 18 (January 1896): 45–95.

Sillers, Walter. "Incidents of the War in Bolivar County, as Experienced by a Ten-Year-Old Boy, and as Given by Him." In *History of Bolivar County, Mississippi,* compiled by Florence Warfield Sillers and edited by Wirt A. Williams, 148–53. Jackson, MS: Hederman Brothers, 1948.

Simms, L. Moody, Jr., ed. "A Union Volunteer with the Mississippi Ram Fleet." *Lincoln Herald* 70 (Winter 1968): 189–92.

Simons, Don. *In Their Words: A Chronology of the Civil War in Chicot County, Arkansas, and Adjacent Waters of the Mississippi River.* Sulphur, LA: Wise, 1999.

Simpson, Brooks D., and Jean V. Berlin, eds. *Sherman's Civil War: Selected Correspondence of William T. Sherman, 1860–1865.* Chapel Hill: University of North Carolina Press, 1999.

Soley, James Russell. "The Union and Confederate Navies." In Johnson and Buel, *Battles and Leaders of the Civil War,* 1:611–31.

Stanley, D. S. *Personal Memoirs of Major-General D. S. Stanley, U.S.A.* Cambridge, MA: Harvard University Press, 1917.

Still, William N., Jr., ed. *What Finer Tradition: The Memoirs of Thomas O. Selfridge, Jr., Rear-Admiral, U.S.N.* Columbia: University of South Carolina Press, 1987.

Swift, Lester, ed. "Letters from a Sailor on a Tinclad." *Civil War History* 7 (March 1961): 48–62.

Taylor, Jesse. "The Defense of Fort Henry." In Johnson and Buel, *Battles and Leaders of the Civil War,* 1:368–72.

Thompson, Robert Means, and Richard Wainwright, eds. *Confidential Correspondence of Gustavus Vasa Fox Assistant Secretary of the Navy 1861–1865.* Vol. 2. New York: De Vinne, 1919.

True, Rowland Stafford. "Life aboard a Gunboat: A First Person Account." *Civil War Times Illustrated* 9 (February 1971): 37–43.

Walke, Henry. "Ellet and His Steam-Rams at Memphis." In Johnson and Buel, *Battles and Leaders of the Civil War,* 1:453–59.

———. "The Gun-Boats at Belmont and Fort Henry." In Johnson and Buel, *Battles and Leaders of the Civil War,* 1:358–67.

———. *Naval Scenes and Reminiscences of the United States, on the Southern and Western Waters.* New York: F. R. Reed, 1877.

———. "The Western Flotilla at Fort Donelson, Island Number Ten, Fort Pillow, and Memphis." In Johnson and Buel, *Battles and Leaders of the Civil War,* 1:43–52.

West, Eleanor Jordan, [ed.] *Dear Judith!: Letters Home from a Civil War Gun Boat to Family in Maine.* N.p.: self-published, 2007.

Wilkie, Franc B. *Pen and Powder.* Boston: Ticknor, 1888.

Woods, Woody, [ed.]. *A Delta Diary: Amanda Worthington's Civil War Diary.* N.p.: Olivewoods, 2016.

SECONDARY SOURCES

Allard, Dean C. "Naval Technology during the American Civil War." *American Neptune* 49 (Spring 1989): 114–22.

Ambrose, Stephen A. *Halleck: Lincoln's Chief of Staff.* Baton Rouge: Louisiana State University Press, 1962.

Arnold, James R. "Rough Work on the Mississippi." *Naval History* 13 (September–October 1999): 38–43.

Ash, Stephen V. *When the Yankees Came: Conflict and Chaos in the Occupied South, 1861–1865.* Chapel Hill: University of North Carolina Press, 1995.

Axtell, Matthew Adams. "American Steamboat Gothic: Disruptive Commerce and Slavery's Liquidation, 1832–1865." Ph.D. dissertation, Princeton University, 2016.

Bailey, Anne J. "The Mississippi Marine Brigade: Fighting Rebel Guerrillas on Western Waters." *Military History of the Southwest* 22 (Spring 1992): 31–42.

Ballard, Michael B. *Vicksburg: The Campaign That Opened the Mississippi.* Chapel Hill: University of North Carolina Press, 2004.

Baxter, James Phinney. *The Introduction of the Ironclad Warship.* 1933. Reprint, New York: Archon Books, 1968.

Bearss, Edwin C. *Hardluck Ironclad: The Sinking and Salvage of the* Cairo. Baton Rouge: Louisiana State University Press, 1966.

———. "The White River Expedition, June 10–July 15, 1862." *Arkansas Historical Quarterly* 21 (Winter 1962): 305–62.

Beilein, Joseph M., Jr. *Bushwhackers: Guerrilla Warfare, Manhood, and the Household in Civil War Missouri.* Kent, OH: Kent State University Press, 2016.

———. *A Man by Any Other Name: William Clarke Quantrill and the Search for American Manhood.* Athens: University of Georgia Press, 2023.

Beilein, Joseph M., Jr., and Matthew C. Hulbert, eds. *The Civil War Guerrilla: Unfolding the Black Flag in History, Memory, and Myth.* Lexington: University Press of Kentucky, 2015.

Bell, Andrew McIlwaine. *Mosquito Soldiers: Malaria, Yellow Fever, and the Course of the American Civil War.* Baton Rouge: Louisiana State University Press, 2010.

Bellamy, Micah Paul. "Becoming Men, Consequently: From 'Contraband' to Men through Naval Service in the American Civil War." Ph.D. dissertation. Liberty University, 2022.

Bennett, Michael J. "'Frictions': Shipboard Relations between White and Contraband Sailors." *Civil War History* 47 (June 2001): 118–45.

———. *Union Jacks: Yankee Sailors in the Civil War.* Chapel Hill: University of North Carolina Press, 2004.

Bever, Megan L. *At War with King Alcohol: Debating Drinking and Masculinity in the Civil War.* New York: University of North Carolina Press, 2022.

Beyer, W. F., and O. F. Keydel, eds. *Deeds of Valor from the Archives of the United States Government: How American Heroes Won the Medal of Honor.* 2 vols. Detroit: Perrien-Keydel, 1907.

Bisbee, Saxon T. *Engines of Rebellion: Confederate Ironclads and Steam Engineering in the American Civil War.* Tuscaloosa: University of Alabama Press, 2018.

Brady, Lisa M. *War upon the Land: Military Strategy and the Transformation of Southern Landscapes during the American Civil War.* Athens: University of Georgia Press, 2012.

———. "War upon the Land: Nature and Warfare in the American Civil War." Ph.D. dissertation, University of Kansas, 2003.

———. "The Wilderness of War: Nature and Strategy." *Environmental History* 10 (July 2005): 421–47.

Bragg, Marion. *Historic Names and Places on the Lower Mississippi River.* Vicksburg: Mississippi River Commission, 1977.

Brewer, Charles. "African American Sailors and the Unvexing of the Mississippi River." *Prologue* 4 (Winter 1998): 279–86.

Browning, Judkin, and Timothy Silver. *An Environmental History of the Civil War.* Chapel Hill: University of North Carolina Press, 2020.

Bruns, James H. *Black Sailors in the Civil War: A History of Fugitives, Freemen, and Freedmen aboard Union Vessels.* Jefferson, NC: McFarland, 2023.

Campbell, R. Thomas. *Confederate Naval Forces on Western Waters.* Jefferson, NC: McFarland, 2005.

Canney, Donald L. *Lincoln's Navy: The Ships, Men, and Organization, 1861–65.* Annapolis, MD: Naval Institute Press, 1998.

———. *The Old Steam Navy.* Vol. 2, *The Ironclads, 1842–1885.* Annapolis, MD: Naval Institute Press, 1993.

Carmichael, Peter S. *The War for the Common Soldier: How Men Thought, Fought, and Survived in Civil War Armies.* Chapel Hill: University of North Carolina Press, 2018.

Carpenter, Jackson Tucker. "Naval Service as Opportunity: A Comparison of Post-War Lives of White, Immigrant, and Black Sailors." Paper presented at Civil War Bluejackets Conference, Annapolis, MD, February 1, 2025.

Carroll, Dylan J. *Invisible Wounds: Mental Illness and Civil War Soldiers.* Baton Rouge: Louisiana State University Press, 2021.

Case, Ryan. "Strategy and Tactics of Civil War Rams on the Mississippi River." M.A. thesis, University of Arkansas, 2008.

Cecelski, David S. *The Waterman's Song: Slavery and Freedom in Maritime North Carolina.* Chapel Hill: University of North Carolina Press, 2001.

Chatelain, Neil P. *Defending the Arteries of Rebellion: Confederate Naval Operations in the Mississippi River Valley, 1861–1865.* New York: Savas Beattie, 2020.

Chernow, Ron. *Grant.* New York: Penguin, 2017.

Clarke, Frances M., and Rebecca Jo Plant. *Of Age: Boy Soldiers and Military Power in the Civil War Era.* New York: Oxford University Press, 2023.

Clegg, John, and Michael Weaver. "Counterfactual Reparations: The Effects of Federal Wealth Transfers to Black Sailors during the Reconstruction Era." Working paper, Price School, April 30, 2023. https://priceschool.usc.edu/wp-content/uploads/2024/10/weaver_apsa_2023.pdf.

Cocanower, Evan, and Robert Gudmestad. "Self-Emancipation along the Lower Mississippi River in 1863." *Journal of Slavery and Data Preservation* 5, no. 1 (2024): 22–27. https://doi.org/10.25971/2ac1-6c95.

Cooling, Benjamin Franklin. *Fort Donelson's Legacy: War and Society in Kentucky and Tennessee, 1862–1863.* Knoxville: University of Tennessee Press, 1997.

———. "A People's War: Partisan Conflict in Tennessee and Kentucky." In Sutherland, *Guerrillas, Unionists, and Violence,* 113–32.

Cooper, Abigail. "'Lord, Until I Reach My Home': Inside the Refugee Camps of the American Civil War." Ph.D. dissertation, University of Pennsylvania, 2015.

Daniel, Larry J., and Lynn N. Bock. *Island No. 10: Struggle for the Mississippi Valley.* Tuscaloosa: University of Alabama Press, 1996.

Denny, Norman R. "The Devil's Navy." *Civil War Times Illustrated* 35 (August 1996): 24–30.

Dilbeck, D. H. *A More Just War: How the Union Waged a Just War.* Chapel Hill: University of North Carolina Press, 2016.

Doyle, Daniel R. "The Civil War in the Greenville Bends." *Arkansas Historical Quarterly* 70 (Summer 2011): 131–61.

Drake, Brian Allen, ed. *The Blue, the Gray, and the Green: Toward an Environmental History of the Civil War.* Athens: University of Georgia Press, 2015.

Eggleston, Michael A. *President Lincoln's Recruiter: General Lorenzo Thomas and the United States Colored Troops in the Civil War.* Jefferson, NC: McFarland, 2013.

Engle, Stephen D. *The Civil War: The War in the West, 1861–July 1863.* Chicago: Fitzroy Dearborn, 2001.

———. *Struggle for the Heartland: The Campaigns from Fort Henry to Corinth.* Lincoln: University of Nebraska Press, 2001.

Fiege, Mark. "Gettysburg and the Organic Nature of the Civil War." In *Natural Enemy, Natural Ally: Toward an Environmental History of Warfare,* edited by Richard P. Tucker and Edmund Russell, 93–109. Corvallis: Oregon State University Press, 2004.

Flynt, David. "Run the Fleet: The Career of the C.S. Ram *Arkansas.*" *Journal of Mississippi History* 51 (May 1989): 107–32.

Foner, Eric. *The Fiery Trial: Abraham Lincoln and American Slavery.* New York: W. W. Norton, 2010.

Foos, Paul. *A Short, Offhand, Killing Affair: Soldiers and Social Conflict during the Mexican-American War.* Chapel Hill: University of North Carolina Press, 2002.

Foote, Lorien. *The Gentlemen and the Roughs: Manhood, Honor, and Violence in the Union Army.* New York: New York University Press, 2010.

———. "Rethinking the Confederate Home Front." *Journal of the Civil War Era* 7 (September 2017): 446–65.

Foster, Buck T. *Sherman's Mississippi Campaign.* Tuscaloosa: University of Alabama Press, 2006.

Frank, Lisa Tendrich. *The Civilian War: Confederate Women and Union Soldiers during Sherman's March.* Baton Rouge: Louisiana State University Press, 2015.

Galuszka, Douglas H. "Logistics in Warfare: The Significance of Logistics in the Army of the Cumberland during the Tullahoma and Chickamauga Campaigns." M.A. thesis, U.S. Army Command and General Staff College, 2005.

Gates, Paul W. *Agriculture and the Civil War.* New York: Alfred A. Knopf, 1965.

Gillespie, Michael. "The Great Gunboat Chase." *Civil War Times Illustrated* 33 (July–August 1994): 30–36.

Gibson, Charles Dana, and E. Kay Gibson. *Assault and Logistics: Union Army Coastal and River Operations, 1861–1866.* Camden, ME: Ensign, 1995.

Glatthaar, Joseph T. "Lord High Admiral of the U.S. Navy." *Military History Quarterly* 6 (Summer 1994): 6–26.

———. *Partners in Command: The Relationship between Leaders in the Civil War.* New York: Free Press, 1994.

Glenny, Norman R. "The Devil's Navy." *Civil War Times Illustrated* 35 (August 1996): 24–30.

Gordon, Leslie J. *A Broken Regiment: The 16th Connecticut's Civil War.* Baton Rouge: Louisiana State University Press, 2014.

Grabau, Warren E. *Ninety-Eight Days: A Geographer's View of the Vicksburg Campaign.* Knoxville: University of Tennessee Press, 2000.

Greenberg, Amy S. *Manifest Manhood and the Antebellum American Empire.* New York: Cambridge University Press, 2005.

Grimsley, Mark. *The Hard Hand of War: Union Military Policy toward Southern Civilians, 1861–1865.* New York: Cambridge University Press, 1995.

Guardino, Peter. "Gender, Soldiering, and Citizenship in the Mexican-American War of 1846–1848." *American Historical Review* 119 (February 2014): 23–46.

Gudmestad, Robert. "Elusive Victory: The Union Navy's War along the Western Waters." *Civil War History* 67 (June 2021): 79–109.

———. *Steamboats and the Rise of the Cotton Kingdom.* Baton Rouge: Louisiana State University Press, 2011.

Hackemer, Kurt. *The U.S. Navy and the Origins of the Military-Industrial Complex, 1847–1883.* Annapolis, MD: Naval Institute Press, 2001.

Hahn, Steven. *The Political Worlds of Slavery and Freedom.* Cambridge, MA: Harvard University Press, 2009.

Hearn, Chester G. *Admiral David Dixon Porter: The Civil War Years.* Annapolis, MD: Naval Institute Press, 1996.

———. *Ellet's Brigade: The Strangest Outfit of All.* Baton Rouge: Louisiana State University Press, 2000.

Hermann, Janet Sharp. *The Pursuit of a Dream.* New York: Oxford University Press, 1981.

Hess, Earl J. *The Civil War in the West: Victory and Defeat from the Appalachians to the Mississippi.* Chapel Hill: University of North Carolina Press, 2012.

———. *Civil War Logistics: A Study of Military Transportation.* Baton Rouge: Louisiana State University Press, 2017.

———. *Civil War Supply and Strategy: Feeding Men and Moving Armies.* Baton Rouge: Louisiana State University Press, 2020.

———. "Northern Response to the Ironclad: A Prospect for the Study of Military Technology." *Civil War History* 31 (June 1985): 126–43.

Hirsch, Charles B. "Gunboat Personnel on the Western Waters." *Mid-America* 34 (April 1952): 73–86.

Horne, William Iverson. "Negotiating Freedom: Reactions to Emancipation in West Feliciana Parish, Louisiana." Ph.D. dissertation, Loyola University, 2013.

Hughes, Nathaniel Cheairs, Jr. *The Battle of Belmont: Grant Strikes South.* Chapel Hill: University of North Carolina Press, 1991.

Humphreys, Margaret. *Marrow of Tragedy: The Health Crisis of the American Civil War.* Baltimore: Johns Hopkins University Press, 2013.

Huston, James A. "Logistical Support of Federal Armies in the Field." *Civil War History* 7 (March 1961): 36–47.

Johnson, Ludwell H. "Northern Profit and Profiteers: The Cotton Rings of 1864–1865." *Civil War History* 12 (June 1966): 101–15.

Joiner, Gary D. *Little to Eat and Thin Mud to Drink: Letters, Diaries, and Memoirs from the Red River Campaigns, 1863–1864.* Knoxville: University of Tennessee Press, 2015.

———. *Mr. Lincoln's Brown Water Navy: The Mississippi Squadron.* Lanham, MD: Rowman & Littlefield, 2007.

———. *Through the Howling Wilderness: The 1864 Red River Campaign and Union Failure in the West.* Knoxville: University of Tennessee Press, 2006.

Jordan, Brian Matthew. *Marching Home: Union Veterans and their Unending Civil War.* New York: Liveright, 2014.

———. *A Thousand May Fall: Life, Death, and Survival in the Union Army.* New York: Liveright, 2021.

Jordan, Winthrop D. *Tumult and Silence at Second Creek: An Inquiry into a Civil War Slave Conspiracy.* Baton Rouge: Louisiana State University Press, 1993.

Junger, Sebastian. *War.* New York: Twelve, 2011.

Kaye, Anthony E. *Joining Places: Slave Neighborhoods in the Old South.* Chapel Hill: University of North Carolina Press, 2009.

Kretz, Dale. *Administering Freedom: The State of Emancipation after the Freedmen's Bureau.* Chapel Hill: University of North Carolina Press, 2022.

Kynoch, Gary. "Terrible Dilemmas: Black Enlistment in the Union Army during the American Civil War." *Slavery & Abolition* 18 (August 1997): 104–27.

Laas, Virginia Jean. "'Sleepless Sentinels': The North Atlantic Blockading Squadron, 1862–1864." *Civil War History* 31 (March 1985): 24–38.

Lande, Jonathan. "Emancipating Masculinity: Black Union Deserters and Their Families in the Civil War South." *Journal of American History* 109 (December 2022): 548–70.

Lang, Andrew F. *In the Wake of War: Military Occupation, Emancipation, and Civil War America.* Baton Rouge: Louisiana State University Press, 2017.

Legan, Marshall Scott. "The Confederate Career of a Union Ram." *Louisiana History* 41 (Summer 2000): 277–300.

Lonn, Ella. *Foreigners in the Union Army and Navy.* 1952. Reprint, New York: Greenwood, 1969.

Luraghi, Raimondo. *A History of the Confederate Navy.* Translated by Paolo E. Coletta. Annapolis, MD: Naval Institute Press, 1996.

Mackey, Robert R. "Bushwhackers, Provosts, and Tories: The Guerrilla War in Arkansas." In Sutherland, *Guerrillas, Unionists, and Violence,* 171–85.

———. *The Uncivil War: Irregular Warfare in the Upper South, 1861–1865.* Norman: University of Oklahoma Press, 2004.

Manning, Chandra. *Troubled Refuge: Struggling for Freedom in the Civil War.* New York: Knopf, 2016.

Marszalek, John F. *Commander of All Lincoln's Armies: A Life of General Henry W. Halleck* (Cambridge, MA: Belknap, 2004).

Martinez, Jaime Amanda. *Confederate Slave Impressment in the Upper South.* Chapel Hill: University of North Carolina Press, 2013.

Marvel, William. *Lincoln's Mercenaries: Economic Motivation among Union Soldiers during the Civil War.* Baton Rouge: Louisiana State University Press, 2018.

McBride, William M. *Technological Change and the United States Navy, 1865–1945.* Baltimore: Johns Hopkins University Press, 2000.

McConnell, Stuart. *Glorious Contentment: The Grand Army of the Republic, 1865–1900.* Chapel Hill: University of North Carolina Press, 1992.

McKnight, Brian D., and Barton A. Myers, eds. *The Guerrilla Hunters: Irregular Conflicts during the Civil War.* Baton Rouge: Louisiana State University Press, 2017.

McPherson, James M. *Battle Cry of Freedom: The Civil War Era.* New York: Oxford University Press, 1988.

———. *War on the Waters: The Union and Confederate Navies, 1861–1865.* Chapel Hill: University of North Carolina Press, 2012.

Menn, Karl Joseph. *The Large Slaveholders of Louisiana, 1860.* New Orleans: Pelican, 1964.

Merrill, James M. *Battle Flags South: The Story of the Civil War Navies on Western Waters.* Rutherford, NJ: Fairleigh Dickinson University Press, 1970.

———. "Cairo, Illinois: Strategic Civil War River Port." *Journal of the Illinois State Historical Society* 76 (December 1983): 242–56.

Miller, Donald L. *Vicksburg: Grant's Campaign That Broke the Confederacy.* New York: Simon & Schuster, 2019.

Milligan, John D. "From Theory to Application: The Emergence of the American Ironclad War Vessel." *Military Affairs* 48 (July 1984): 126–32.

———. *Gunboats down the Mississippi.* Annapolis, MD: U.S. Naval Institute, 1965.

Miles, Tiya. "Of Waterways and Runaways: Reflections on the Great Lakes in Underground Railroad History." *Michigan Quarterly Review* 50, no. 3 (Summer 2011). http://hdl.handle.net/2027/spo.act2080.0050.320.

Mindell, David A. *Iron Coffin: War, Technology, and Experience aboard the USS Monitor.* Baltimore: Johns Hopkins University Press, 2012.

Moore, Emily. "The Unique Journal of the USS Red Rover." *Hektoen International: A Journal of Medical Humanities* (Spring 2015). https://hekint.org/2017/02/22/the-unique-journal-of-the-uss-red-rover/.

Mountcastle, Clay. *Punitive War: Confederate Guerrillas and Union Reprisals.* Lawrence: University Press of Kansas, 2009.

Murray, Williamson, and Wayne Wei-Siang Hsieh. *A Savage War: A Military History of the Civil War.* Princeton, NJ: Princeton University Press, 2016.

Neal, Diane, and Thomas W. Kremm. *Lion of the South: General Thomas C. Hindman.* Macon, GA: Mercer University Press, 1993.

Nelson, Megan Kate. *Ruin Nation: Destruction and the American Civil War.* Athens: University of Georgia Press, 2012.

Noe, Kenneth W. *The Howling Storm: Weather, Climate, and the American Civil War.* Baton Rouge: Louisiana State University Press, 2020.

O'Connor, Thomas H. "Lincoln and the Cotton Trade." *Civil War History* 7 (March 1961): 20–35.

Olmstead, Edwin, Wayne E. Stark, and Spencer C. Tucker. *The Big Guns: Civil War Siege, Seacoast, and Naval Cannon.* Alexandria Bay, NY: Museum Restoration Service, 1997.

Parrish, T. Michael. "The Red River Campaign, 1864: Profits, Politics, and Grand Strategy." In *The Oxford Handbook of the American Civil War,* edited by Lorien Foote and Earl J. Hess, 505–19. New York: Oxford University Press, 2021.

Perry, Milton F. *Infernal Machines: The Story of Confederate Submarine and Mine Warfare.* Baton Rouge: Louisiana State University Press, 1965.

Polser, Aubrey Henry. "The Administration of the United States Navy, 1861–1865." Ph.D. dissertation, University of Nebraska, 1975.

Pratt, Fletcher. *Civil War on Western Waters.* New York: Henry Holt, 1956.

Ramold, Steven J. *Baring the Iron Hand: Discipline in the Union Army.* DeKalb: Northern Illinois University Press, 2010.

———. *Slaves, Sailors, Citizens: African Americans in the Union Navy.* DeKalb: Northern Illinois University Press, 2002.

Reidy, Joseph P. "The African-American Sailors' Project: The Hidden History of the Civil War." *CRM: Cultural Resource Management* 20, no. 2 (1997): 31–33, 43.

———. "Black Jack: African American Sailors in the Civil War Navy." In *New Interpretations in Naval History: Selected Papers from the Twelfth Naval History Symposium Held at the United States Naval Academy, 26–27 October 1995,* edited by William D. Cogar, 213–20. Annapolis, MD: Naval Institute Press, 1997.

———. "Black Men in Navy Blue during the Civil War." *Prologue* 33 (Fall 2001): 154–67.

———. *Illusions of Emancipation: The Pursuit of Freedom and Equality in the Twilight of Slavery.* Chapel Hill: University of North Carolina Press, 2019.

Riggs, David F. "Sailors of the U.S.S. *Cairo*: Anatomy of a Gunboat Crew." *Civil War History* 28 (September 1982): 266–73.

Ringle, Dennis J. *Life in Mr. Lincoln's Navy.* Annapolis, MD: Naval Institute Press, 1998.

Ripley, Warren. *Artillery and Ammunition of the Civil War.* New York: Van Nostrand Reinhold, 1970.

Roberts, William H. *Civil War Ironclads: The U.S. Navy and Industrial Mobilization.* Baltimore: Johns Hopkins University Press, 2002.

Robinson, Armstead L. *Bitter Fruits of Bondage: The Demise of Slavery and the Collapse of the Confederacy, 1861–1865.* Charlottesville: University of Virginia Press, 2005.

Rodrigue, John C. *Freedom's Crescent: The Civil War and the Destruction of Slavery in the Lower Mississippi Valley.* New York: Cambridge University Press, 2023.

Rothman, Joshua D. *The Ledger and the Chain: How Domestic Slave Traders Shaped America.* New York: Basic Books, 2021.

Rowland, Alex. *Underwater Warfare in the Age of Sail.* Bloomington: Indiana University Press, 1978.

Ruminsky, Jarrett. "'Tradyville': The Contraband Trade and the Problem of Loyalty in Civil War Mississippi." *Journal of the Civil War Era* 2 (December 2012): 511–37.

Salafia, Matthew. *Slavery's Borderland: Freedom and Bondage along the Ohio River.* Philadelphia: University of Pennsylvania Press, 2013.

Shaffer, Donald R. *After the Glory: The Struggles of Black Civil War Veterans.* Lawrence: University Press of Kansas, 2004.

Sheehan-Dean, Aaron. *The Calculus of Violence: How Americans Fought the Civil War.* Cambridge, MA: Harvard University Press, 2018.

Silverstone, Paul H. *Warships of the Civil War Navies.* Annapolis, MD: Naval Institute Press, 1989.

Simons, Don R. *In Their Own Words: A Chronology of the Civil War in Chicot County, Arkansas, and Adjacent Waters of the Mississippi River.* Sulphur, LA: Wise, 1999.

Slagle, Jay. *Ironclad Captain: Seth Ledyard Phelps and the U.S. Navy, 1841–1864.* Kent, OH: Kent State University Press, 1996.

Smith, Merritt Roe, ed. *Military Enterprise and Technological Change: Perspectives on the American Experience.* Cambridge, MA: MIT Press, 1985.

Smith, Myron J., Jr. *After Vicksburg: The Civil War on Western Waters, 1863–1865.* Jefferson, NC: McFarland, 2021.

———. *Civil War Biographies from the Western Waters.* Jefferson, NC: McFarland, 2015.

———. *The CSS* Arkansas: *A Confederate Ironclad on Western Waters.* Jefferson, NC: McFarland, 2011.

———. *The Fight for the Yazoo, August 1862–July 1864: Swamps, Forts, and Fleets on Vicksburg's Northern Flank.* Jefferson, NC: McFarland, 2012.

———. *Ironclad Captains of the Civil War.* Jefferson, NC: McFarland, 2018.

———. *Joseph Brown and His Civil War Ironclads: The USS* Chillicothe, Indianola, *and* Tuscumbia. Jefferson, NC: McFarland, 2017.

———. *The Old War Horse: The USS* Benton *on Western Waters, 1853–1865.* Jefferson, NC: McFarland, 2024.

———. *The Timberclads in the Civil War: The* Lexington, Conestoga, *and* Tyler *on the Western Waters.* Jefferson, NC: McFarland, 2008.

———. *Tinclads in the Civil War: Union Light-Draught Gunboat Operations on Western Waters, 1862–1865.* Jefferson, NC: McFarland, 2010.

———. *The USS* Carondelet: *A Civil War Ironclad on Western Waters.* Jefferson, NC: McFarland, 2010.

Smith, Timothy B. *Bayou Battles for Vicksburg: The Swamp and River Expeditions, January 1–April 30, 1863.* Lawrence: University Press of Kansas, 2023.

———. *Early Struggles for Vicksburg: The Mississippi Central Campaign and Chickasaw Bayou, October 25–December 31, 1862.* Lawrence: University Press of Kansas, 2022.

———. "'Gallant and Invaluable Service': The United States Navy at the Battle of Shiloh." *West Tennessee Historical Society Papers* 58 (2008): 33–54.

———. *Grant Invades Tennessee: The 1862 Battles for Forts Henry and Donelson.* Lawrence: University Press of Kansas, 2016.

———. *Shiloh: Conquer or Perish.* Lawrence: University Press of Kansas, 2014.

———. *The Siege of Vicksburg: Climax of the Campaign to Open the Mississippi River, May 23–July 4, 1863.* Lawrence: University Press of Kansas, 2021.

Still, William N., Jr. *Iron Afloat: The Story of the Confederate Armorclads.* Nashville: Vanderbilt University Press, 1971.

Still, William. "The Common Sailor, the Civil War's Uncommon Man. Part I: The Yankee Blue Jackets." *Civil War Times Illustrated* 23 (February 1985): 24–39.

Stith, Matthew M. "'The Deplorable Condition of the Country': Nature, Society, and War on the Trans-Mississippi Frontier." *Civil War History* 58 (September 2012): 322–47.

Surdam, David G. "Traders or Traitors: Northern Cotton Trading during the Civil War." *Business and Economic History* 28 (Winter 1999): 301–12.

Sutherland, Daniel E. "1864: A Strange, Wild Time." In *Rugged and Sublime: The Civil War in Arkansas,* edited by Mark K. Christ, 105–44. Fayetteville: University of Arkansas Press, 1994.

———. "Guerrillas: The Real War in Arkansas." In *Civil War Arkansas: Beyond Battles and Leaders,* edited by Anne J. Bailey and Daniel E. Sutherland, 133–54. Fayetteville: University of Arkansas Press, 2000.

———, ed. *Guerrillas, Unionists, and Violence on the Confederate Home Front.* Fayetteville: University of Arkansas Press, 1999.

———. *A Savage Conflict: The Decisive Role of Guerrillas in the American Civil War.* Chapel Hill: University of North Carolina Press, 2013.

Symonds, Craig L. *The Civil War at Sea.* New York: Oxford University Press, 2009.

———. *Lincoln and His Admirals: Abraham Lincoln, the U.S. Navy, and the Civil War.* New York: Oxford University Press, 2008.

———. "The Navy's Evolutionary War." *Naval History* 25, no. 2 (March 2011): 26–34. https://www.usni.org/magazines/naval-history-magazine/2011/march/navys-evolutionary-war.

———, ed. *Union Combined Operations in the Civil War.* New York: Fordham University Press, 2010.

Taylor, Amy Murrell. *Embattled Freedom: Journeys through the Civil War's Slave Refugee Camps.* Chapel Hill: University of North Carolina Press, 2018.

Teters, Kristopher A. *Practical Liberators: Union Officers in the Western Theater during the Civil War.* Chapel Hill: University of North Carolina Press, 2018.

Thompson, Lauren K. "Escaping the Mechanism: Soldier Fraternization during the Siege at Petersburg." *Civil War History* 63 (December 2017): 349–76.

———. *Friendly Enemies: Soldier Fraternization throughout the American Civil War.* Lincoln: University of Nebraska Press, 2020.

Thompson, Scott F. "'The Negro Had Been Run Over Long Enough by White Men, and It Was Time They Defend Themselves': African-American Mutinies and the Long Emancipation, 1861–1974." Ph.D. dissertation, West Virginia University, 2021.

Tomblin, Barbara Brooks. *The Civil War on the Mississippi: Union Sailors, Gunboat Captains, and the Campaign to Open the River.* Lexington: University Press of Kentucky, 2016.

———. "From Sail to Steam: The Development of Steam Technology in the United States Navy, 1838–1865." Ph.D. dissertation, Rutgers University, 1988.

Tow, Michael. "The Personification and Masculation of Samuel Henry Dalton." Ph.D. dissertation. Southern Illinois University, 2014.

Tucker, Spencer C. *Andrew Foote: Civil War Admiral on Western Waters.* Annapolis, MD: Naval Institute Press, 2000.

———. "Armaments and Innovations: The Union Navy's Stubby Gun." *Naval History Magazine* 28, no. 2 (March 2014). https://www.usni.org/magazines/naval-history-magazine/2014/march/armaments-and-innovations-union-navys-stubby-gun.

———. *Blue & Gray Navies: The Civil War Afloat.* Annapolis, MD: Naval Institute Press, 2006.

Ural, Susannah J. *Hood's Texas Brigade: The Soldiers and Families of the Confederacy's Most Celebrated Unit.* Baton Rouge: Louisiana State University Press, 2017.

Walker, Thomas E. "The Origins of the Mississippi Marine Brigade: The First Use of Brown Water Tactics by the United States in the Civil War." M.A. thesis, Texas Christian University, 2006.

Wegner, Dana M. "The Old Navy: Little Egypt's Naval Station." *Proceedings of the United States Naval Institute* 98 (March 1972): 74–76.

West, Richard S., Jr. "Gunboats in the Swamps: The Yazoo Pass Expedition." *Civil War History* 9 (June 1963): 157–66.

Whyte, William. "Full Speed Ahead: Yankee Ironclads Unleased into the Volunteer State." *Tennessee Historical Quarterly* 69 (Spring 2010): 18–39.

Williams, Edward F., III. "The Johnsonville Raid and Nathan Bedford Forrest State Park." *Tennessee Historical Quarterly* 28 (Fall 1969): 225–51.

Williams, Glenn. "Uncle Sam's Webfeet: The Union Navy in the Civil War." *International Journal of Naval History* 1 (April 2002): 1–10.

Wilson, Sven E., and Clayne L. Pope. "The Height of Union Army Recruits: Family and Community Influences." In *Health and Labor Force Participation over the Life Cycle: Evidence from the Past,* edited by Dora L. Costa, 113–45. New York: University of Chicago Press, 2003.

Wolters, Timothy S. "Electric Torpedoes in the Confederacy: Reconciling Conflicting Histories." *Journal of Military History* 72 (July 2008): 755–83.

Woods, Michael E. *Arguing until Doomsday: Stephen Douglas, Jefferson Davis, and the Struggle for American Democracy.* Chapel Hill: University of North Carolina Press, 2020.

Woodworth, Steven E. *Nothing but Victory: The Army of the Tennessee, 1861–1865.* New York: Vintage Books, 2005.

WEBSITES

Championhilz. "Well Do I Remember That Exciting Day: The Capture of the Crew of the USS Rattler." *Mississippians in the Confederate Army* (blog). August 10, 2014. https://mississippiconfederates.wordpress.com/2014/08/10/well-do-i-remember-that-exciting-day-the-capture-of-the-crew-of-the-u-s-s-rattler/.

"Civil War Facts." American Battlefield Trust. Last update August 24, 2021. https://www.battlefields.org/learn/articles/civil-war-facts#What was the average soldier's age.

"Congressional Medal of Honor Winner John Gordon Morrison (1842–1897)." Lansingburgh Historical Society. August 20, 2022. https://lansingburghhistoricalsocietyarchives.org/people/congressional-medal-of-honor-recipient-john-gordon-morrison-1842-1897/.

Cooper, Abigail. "Interactive Map of Contraband Camps." *History Digital Projects.* January 1, 2014. https://repository.upenn.edu/handle/20.500.14332/2723.

Hughes, Dwight. "Town between the Rivers: Cairo, Illinois." Emerging Civil War. January 22, 2021. https://emergingcivilwar.com/2021/01/22/town-between-the-rivers-cairo-illinois/.

Kirby, Jack Temple. "The Civil War: An Environmental View." The Use of the Land: Perspectives on Stewardship. National Humanities Center. Revised July 2001. http://nationalhumanitiescenter.org/tserve/nattrans/ntuseland/essays/amcwar.htm.

Losson, Christopher. "William Lindsay Brandon." *Mississippi Encyclopedia.* Last update April 13, 2018. https://mississippiencyclopedia.org/entries/william-lindsay-brandon/.

MeasuringWorth. https://measuringworth.com/index.php.

Sesser, David. "Fort Hindman," *Encyclopedia of Arkansas.* Last updated June 16, 2023. https://encyclopediaofarkansas.net/entries/fort-hindman-8640/.

INDEX

Page numbers in italics refer to figures.